THE DAILY STUDY BIBLE SERIES
REVISED EDITION

THE GOSPEL OF
MATTHEW

Volume 2

THE GOSPEL OF
MATTHEW

Volume 2
(Chapters 11 to 28)

REVISED EDITION

Translated
with an Introduction and Interpretation
by
WILLIAM BARCLAY

THE WESTMINSTER PRESS
PHILADELPHIA

Revised Edition
Copyright © 1975 William Barclay

First published by The Saint Andrew Press
Edinburgh, Scotland

First Edition, June, 1957

Second Edition, June, 1958

Published by The Westminster Press®
Philadelphia, Pennsylvania

PRINTED IN THE UNITED STATES OF AMERICA

11   12   13   14   15

Library of Congress Cataloging in Publication Data

Bible. N.T. Matthew. English. Barclay. 1975.
The Gospel of Matthew.

(The Daily study Bible series. — Rev. ed.)
1. Bible. N.T. Matthew — Commentaries. I. Barclay,
William, lecturer in the University of Glasgow, ed.
II. Title. III. Series.
BS2573 1975   226'.2'077   74-28251
ISBN 0-664-21301-4 (v. 2)
ISBN 0-664-24101-8 (v. 2) pbk.

GENERAL INTRODUCTION

The Daily Study Bible series has always had one aim—to convey the results of scholarship to the ordinary reader. A. S. Peake delighted in the saying that he was a " theological middleman ", and I would be happy if the same could be said of me in regard to these volumes. And yet the primary aim of the series has never been academic. It could be summed up in the famous words of Richard of Chichester's prayer—to enable men and women " to know Jesus Christ more clearly, to love him more dearly, and to follow him more nearly ".

It is all of twenty years since the first volume of *The Daily Study Bible* was published. The series was the brain-child of the late Rev. Andrew McCosh, M.A., S.T.M., the then Secretary and Manager of the Committee on Publications of the Church of Scotland, and of the late Rev. R. G. Macdonald, O.B.E., M.A., D.D., its Convener.

It is a great joy to me to know that all through the years *The Daily Study Bible* has been used at home and abroad, by minister, by missionary, by student and by layman, and that it has been translated into many different languages. Now, after so many printings, it has become necessary to renew the printer's type and the opportunity has been taken to restyle the books, to correct some errors in the text and to remove some references which have become outdated. At the same time, the Biblical quotations within the text have been changed to use the Revised Standard Version, but my own original translation of the New Testament passages has been retained at the beginning of each daily section.

There is one debt which I would be sadly lacking in courtesy if I did not acknowledge. The work of revision and correction has been done entirely by the Rev. James Martin, M.A., B.D., Minister of High Carntyne Church, Glasgow. Had it not been for him this task would never have been undertaken, and it is impossible for me to thank him enough for the selfless toil he has put into the revision of these books.

It is my prayer that God may continue to use *The Daily Study Bible* to enable men better to understand His word.

Glasgow   WILLIAM BARCLAY

CONTENTS

viii **CONTENTS**

CONTENTS

x CONTENTS

CONTENTS

THE SIX ACCENTS IN THE VOICE OF JESUS

Matthew 11 is a chapter in which Jesus is speaking all the time; and, as he speaks to different people and about different things, we hear the accent of his voice vary and change. It will be of the greatest interest to look one by one at the six accents in the voice of Jesus.

THE ACCENT OF CONFIDENCE

Matthew 11: 1–6

> And when Jesus had completed his instructions to the twelve disciples, he left there to go on teaching and to go on making his proclamation in their towns.
>
> When John had heard in prison about the things that the Anointed One of God was doing, he sent to him and asked him through his disciples: " Are you the One who is to come, or, must we go on expecting another? " " Go back," said Jesus, " and give John the report of what you are hearing and seeing. The blind are having their sight restored, and the lame are walking; the lepers are being cleansed, and the deaf are hearing; the dead are being raised up, and the poor are receiving the good news. And blessed is the man who does not take offence at me."

THE career of John had ended in disaster. It was not John's habit to soften the truth for any man; and he was incapable of seeing evil without rebuking it. He had spoken too fearlessly *and too definitely for his own safety.*

Herod Antipas of Galilee had paid a visit to his brother in Rome. During that visit he seduced his brother's wife. He came home again, dismissed his own wife, and married the sister-in-law whom he had lured away from her husband. Publicly and sternly John rebuked Herod. It was never safe to rebuke an eastern despot and Herod took his revenge; John was thrown into the dungeons of the fortress of Machaerus in the mountains near the Dead Sea.

For any man that would have been a terrible fate, but for John the Baptist it was worse than for most. He was a child of the desert; all his life he had lived in the wide open spaces, with the clean wind on his face and the spacious vault of the sky for his roof. And now he was confined within the four narrow walls of an underground dungeon. For a man like John, who had perhaps never lived in a house, this must have been agony.

In Carlisle Castle there is a little cell. Once long ago they put a border chieftain in that cell and left him for years. In that cell there is one little window, which is placed too high for a man to look out of when he is standing on the floor. On the ledge of the window there are two depressions worn away in the stone. They are the marks of the hands of that border chieftain, the places where, day after day, he lifted himself up by his hands to look out on the green dales across which he would never ride again.

John must have been like that; and there is nothing to wonder at, and still less to criticize, in the fact that questions began to form themselves in John's mind. He had been so sure that Jesus was the One who was to come. That was one of the commonest titles of the Messiah for whom the Jews waited with such eager expectation (*Mark* 11: 9; *Luke* 13: 35; 19: 38; *Hebrews* 10: 37; *Psalm* 118: 26). A dying man cannot afford to have doubts; he must be sure; and so John sent his disciples to Jesus with the question: " Are you he who is to come, or shall we look for another? " There are many possible things behind that question.

(i) Some people think that the question was asked, not for John's sake at all, but *for the sake of his disciples*. It may be that when John and his disciples talked in prison, the disciples questioned whether Jesus was really he who was to come, and John's answer was: " If you have any doubts, go and see what Jesus is doing and your doubts will be at an end." If that is the case, it was a good answer. If anyone begins to argue with us about Jesus, and to question his supremacy, the best of all answers is not to counter argument with argument, but to say, " Give your life to him; and see what he can do with it." The supreme argument for Christ is not intellectual debate, but experience of his changing power.

(ii) It may be that John's question was the question of *impatience*. His message had been a message of doom (*Matthew* 3: 7–12). The axe was at the root of the tree; the winnowing process had begun; the divine fire of cleansing judgment had begun to burn. It may be that John was thinking: " When is Jesus going to start on action? When is he going to blast his enemies? When is the day of God's holy destruction to begin? " It may well be that John was impatient with Jesus because he was not what he expected him to be. The man who waits for savage wrath will always be disappointed in Jesus, but the man who looks for love will never find his hopes defeated.

(iii) Some few have thought that this question was nothing less than the question of dawning *faith and hope*. He had seen Jesus at the Baptism; in prison he had thought more and more about him; and the more he thought the more certain he was that Jesus was he who was to come; and now he put all his hopes to the test in this one question. It may be that this is not the question of a despairing and an impatient man, but the question of one in whose eyes the light of hope shone, and who asked for nothing but confirmation of that hope.

Then came Jesus's answer; and in his answer we hear the *accent of confidence*. Jesus's answer to John's disciples was: " Go back, and don't tell John what I am saying; *tell him what I am doing*. Don't tell John what I am claiming; *tell him what is happening*." Jesus demanded that there should be applied to him the most acid of tests, that of deeds. Jesus was the only person who could ever demand without qualification to be judged, not by what he said, but by what he did. The challenge of Jesus is still the same. He does not so much say, " Listen to what I have to tell you," as, " Look what I can do for you; see what I have done for others."

The things that Jesus did in Galilee he still does. In him those who were blind to the truth about themselves, about their fellow-men and about God, have their eyes opened; in him those whose feet were never strong enough to remain in the right way are strengthened; in him those who were tainted with the disease of sin are cleansed; in him those who were deaf to the voice of conscience and of God begin to listen; in him those who were dead and powerless in sin are raised to newness and loveliness of life; in him the poorest man inherits the riches of the love of God.

Finally comes the warning, " Blessed is he who takes no offence at me." This was spoken to John; and it was spoken because John had only grasped half the truth. John preached the gospel of divine holiness with divine destruction; Jesus preached the gospel of divine holiness with divine love. So Jesus says to John, " Maybe I am not doing the things you expected me to do. But the powers of evil are being defeated not by irresistible power, but by unanswerable love." Sometimes a man can be offended at Jesus because Jesus cuts across *his* ideas of what religion should be.

THE ACCENT OF ADMIRATION

Matthew 11: 7–11

> When they were going away, Jesus began to speak to the crowds about John. " What did you go out to the desert to see? " he said. " Was it a reed shaken by the wind? If it was not that, what did you go out to see? Was it to see a man clothed in luxurious clothes? Look you, the people who wear luxurious clothes are in kings' houses. If it was not that, what did you go out to see? Was it to see a prophet? Indeed it was, I tell you, and something beyond a prophet. This is he of whom it stands written: ' Look you, I am sending before you my messenger, who will prepare your way before you.' This is the truth I tell you—amongst those born of women no greater figure than John the Baptizer has ever emerged in history. But the least in the Kingdom of Heaven is greater than he is."

THERE are few men to whom Jesus paid so tremendous a tribute as he did to John the Baptizer. He begins by asking the people what they went into the desert to see when they streamed out to John.

(i) Did they go out to see a reed shaken by the wind? That can mean one of two things. (*a*) Down by the banks of the Jordan the long cane grass grew; and the phrase *a shaken reed* was a kind of proverb for *the commonest of sights*. When the people flocked to see John, were they going out to see something as ordinary as the reeds swaying in the wind on Jordan's banks? (*b*) *A shaken reed* can mean *a weak vacillator*, one who could no more stand foursquare to the winds of danger than a reed by the river's bank could stand straight when the wind blew.

Whatever else the people flocked out to the desert to see, they certainly did not go to see an ordinary person. The very fact that they did go out in their crowds showed how extraordinary John was, for no one would cross the street, let alone tramp into the desert, to see a commonplace kind of person. Whatever else they went out to see, they did not go to see a weak vacillator. Mr. Pliables do not end in prison as martyrs for the truth. John was neither as ordinary as a shaken reed, nor as spineless as the reed which sways with every breeze.

(ii) Did they go out to see a man clothed in soft and luxurious garments? Such a man would be a courtier; and, whatever else John was, he was not a courtier. He knew nothing of the courtier's art of the flattery of kings; he followed the dangerous occupation of telling the truth to kings. John was the ambassador of God, not the courtier of Herod.

(iii) Did they go out to see a prophet? The prophet is the *forthteller* of the truth of God. The prophet is the man in the confidence of God. " Surely the Lord God does nothing, without revealing his secret to his servants the prophets " (*Amos* 3: 7). The prophet is two things—he is the man with a message from God, and he is the man with the courage to deliver that message. The prophet is the man with God's wisdom in his mind, God's truth on his lips, and God's courage in his heart. That most certainly John was.

(iv) But John was something more than a prophet. The Jews

had, and still have, one settled belief. They believed that before the Messiah came, Elijah would return to herald his coming. To this day, when the Jews celebrate the Passover Feast, a vacant chair is left for Elijah. " Behold I will send you Elijah the prophet, before the great and terrible day of the Lord comes " (*Malachi* 4: 5). Jesus declared that John was nothing less than the divine herald whose duty and privilege it was to announce the coming of the Messiah. John was nothing less than the herald of God, and no man could have a greater task than that.

(v) Such was the tremendous tribute of Jesus to John, spoken with the accent of admiration. There had never been a greater figure in all history; and then comes the startling sentence: " But he who is least in the Kingdom of Heaven is greater than he."

Here there is one quite general truth. With Jesus there came into the world something absolutely new. The prophets were great; their message was precious; but with Jesus there emerged something still greater, and a message still more wonderful. C. G. Montefiore, himself a Jew and not a Christian, writes: " Christianity does mark a new era in religious history and in human civilization. What the world owes to Jesus and to Paul is immense; things can never be, and men can never think, the same as things were, and as men thought, before these two great men lived." Even a non-Christian freely admits that things could never be the same now that Jesus had come.

But what was it that John lacked? What is it that the Christian has that John could never have? The answer is simple and fundamental. *John had never seen the Cross.* Therefore one thing John could never know—the full revelation of the love of God. The holiness of God he might know; the justice of God he might declare; but the love of God in all its fulness he could never know. We have only to listen to the message of John and the message of Jesus. No one could call John's message a *gospel*, good news; it was basically a threat of destruction. It took Jesus and his Cross to show to men the length, breadth, depth and height of the love of God. It is a most amazing thing that it is possible for the humblest Christian to know more about God than the greatest of the Old Testament prophets. The man who has seen the Cross has seen the heart of God in a way that no man who lived before the Cross could ever see it. Indeed the least in the Kingdom of Heaven is greater than any man who went before.

So John had the destiny which sometimes falls to men; he had the task of pointing men to a greatness into which he himself did not enter. It is given to some men to be the signposts of God. They point to a new ideal and a new greatness which others will enter into, but into which they will not come. It is very seldom that any great reformer is the first man to toil for the reform with which his name is connected. Many who went before him glimpsed the glory, often laboured for it, and sometimes died for it.

Someone tells how from the windows of his house every evening he used to watch the lamp-lighter go along the streets lighting the lamps—*and the lamp-lighter was himself a blind man.* He was bringing to others the light which he himself would never see. Let a man never be discouraged in the Church or in any other walk of life, if the dream he has dreamed and for which he has toiled is never worked out before the end of the day. God needed John; God needs his signposts who can point men on the way, although they themselves cannot ever reach the goal.

VIOLENCE AND THE KINGDOM

Matthew 11: 12–15

" From the days of John the Baptist until now, the Kingdom of Heaven is taken by storm, and the violent take it by force. For up to John all the prophets and the Law spoke with the voice of prophecy; and, if you are willing to accept the fact, this is Elijah who was destined to come. He who has ears to hear let him hear."

IN verse 12 there is a very difficult saying, " The kingdom of heaven has suffered violence, and men of violence take it by

force." *Luke* has this saying in another form (*Luke* 16: 16):
" Since then the good news of the Kingdom of God is preached,
and every one enters it violently." It is clear that at some time
Jesus said something in which *violence* and the *kingdom* were
connected, something which was a dark and a difficult saying,
which no one at the time fully understood. Certainly Luke and
Matthew understood it in different ways.

Luke says that every man storms his way into the Kingdom;
he means, as Denney said, that the " Kingdom of heaven is not
for the well-meaning but for the desperate," that no one drifts
into the Kingdom, that the Kingdom only opens its doors to
those who are prepared to make as great an effort to get into it
as men do when they storm a city.

Matthew says that from the time of John until now the
Kingdom of heaven suffers violence and the violent take it by
force. The very form of that expression seems to look back over
a considerable time. It indeed sounds much more like a
comment of Matthew than a saying of Jesus. It sounds as if
Matthew was saying: " From the days of John, who was
thrown into prison, right down to our own times the Kingdom
of heaven has suffered violence and persecution at the hands of
violent men."

It is likely that we will get the full meaning of this difficult
saying by putting together the recollection of Luke and
Matthew. What Jesus may well have said is: " Always my
Kingdom will suffer violence; always savage men will try to
break it up, and snatch it away and destroy it; and therefore
only the man who is desperately in earnest, only the man in
whom the violence of devotion matches and defeats the violence
of persecution will in the end enter into it." It may well be that
this saying of Jesus was originally at one and the same time a
warning of violence to come and a challenge to produce a
devotion which would be even stronger than the violence.

It seems strange to find in verse 13 that the Law is said to
speak with the voice of prophecy; but it was the Law itself
which confidently declared that the voice of prophecy would
not die. " The Lord your God will raise up for you a Prophet

like me from among you, from your brethren." " I will raise up
for them a prophet like you from among their brethren; and I
will put my words in his mouth " (*Deuteronomy* 18: 15, 18). It
was because he broke the Law, as they saw it, that the orthodox
Jews hated Jesus; but, if they had only had eyes to see it, both
the Law and the prophets pointed to him.

Once again Jesus tells the people that John is the herald and
the forerunner whom they have awaited so long—*if they are
willing to accept the fact.* There is all the tragedy of the human
situation in that last phrase. The old proverb has it that you can
take a horse to the water, but you cannot make him drink. God
can send his messenger but men can refuse to recognize him,
and God can send his truth but men can refuse to see it. God's
revelation is powerless without man's response. That is why
Jesus ends with the appeal that he who has ears should use them
to hear.

THE ACCENT OF SORROWFUL REBUKE

Matthew 11: 16–19

" To what will I compare this generation? It is like children in the
market-place, calling to their companions, and saying, ' We piped
to you and you did not dance; we wailed and you did not mourn.'
For John came neither eating nor drinking, and they say, ' The
man is mad.' The Son of Man came eating and drinking, and they
say, ' Look you, a gluttonous man and a wine-drinker, the friend
of tax-collectors and sinners.' But wisdom is shown to be right by
her deeds."

JESUS was saddened by the sheer perversity of human nature.
To him men seemed to be like children playing in the village
square. One group said to the other: " Come on and let's play at
weddings," and the others said, " We don't feel like being happy
today." Then the first group said, " All right; come on and let's
play at funerals," and the others said, " We don't feel like being
sad today." They were what the Scots call *contrary.* No matter

what was suggested, they did not want to do it; and no matter what was offered, they found a fault in it.

John came, living in the desert, fasting and despising food, isolated from the society of men; and they said of him, " The man is mad to cut himself off from human society and human pleasures like that." Jesus came, mixing with all kinds of people, sharing in their sorrows and their joys, companying with them in their times of joy; and they said of him, " He is a socialite; he is a party-goer; he is the friend of outsiders with whom no decent person would have anything to do." They called John's asceticism madness; and they called Jesus' sociability laxness of morals. They could find a ground of criticism either way.

The plain fact is that when people do not want to listen to the truth, they will easily enough find an excuse for not listening to it. They do not even try to be consistent in their criticisms; they will criticize the same person, and the same institution, from quite opposite grounds. If people are determined to make no response they will remain stubbornly unresponsive no matter what invitation is made to them. Grown men and women can be very like spoiled children who refuse to play no matter what the game is.

Then comes Jesus' final sentence in this section: " Wisdom is shown to be right by her deeds." The ultimate verdict lies not with the cantankerous and perverse critics but with events. The Jews might criticize John for his lonely isolation, but John had moved men's hearts to God as they had not been moved for centuries; the Jews might criticize Jesus for mixing too much in ordinary life and with ordinary people, but in him people were finding a new life and a new goodness and a new power to live as they ought and a new access to God.

It would be well if we were to stop judging people and churches by our own prejudices and perversities; and if we were to begin to give thanks for any person and any church who can bring people nearer to God, even if their methods are not the methods which suit us.

THE ACCENT OF HEARTBROKEN CONDEMNATION

Matthew 11: 20–24

Then he began to reproach the cities in which the most numerous of his deeds of power had been done, because they did not repent. " Alas for you Chorazin! Alas for you Bethsaida! For, if the deeds of power which happened in you had happened in Tyre and Sidon, they would have repented in sackcloth and ashes long ago. But I tell you, it will be easier for Tyre and Sidon in the day of judgment than for you! And you Capernaum, is it not true that you have been lifted up to heaven? You will go down to Hell, for, if the deeds of power which happened in you had happened amongst the men of Sodom, they would have survived to this day. But I tell you—it will be easier for the land of the men of Sodom in the day of judgment than for you."

WHEN John came to the end of his gospel, he wrote a sentence in which he indicated how impossible it was ever to write a complete account of the life of Jesus: " But there are also many other things which Jesus did; were every one of them to be written, I suppose that the world itself could not contain the books that would be written." (*John* 21: 25). This passage of *Matthew* is one of the proofs of that saying.

Chorazin was probably a town an hour's journey north of Capernaum; Bethsaida was a fishing village on the west bank of Jordan, just as the river entered the northern end of the lake. Clearly the most tremendous things happened in these towns, and yet we have no account of them whatever. There is no record in the gospels of the work that Jesus did, and of the wonders he performed in these places, and yet they must have been amongst his greatest. A passage like this shows us how little we know of Jesus; it shows us—and we must always remember it—that in the gospels we have only the barest selection of Jesus' works. The things we do not know about Jesus far outnumber the things we do know.

We must be careful to catch the accent in Jesus's voice as he

said this. The Revised Standard Version has it: " Woe to you,
Chorazin! Woe to you, Bethsaida! " The Greek word for *woe*
which we have translated *alas* is *ouai*; and *ouai* expresses
sorrowful pity at least as much as it does anger. This is not the
accent of one who is in a temper because his self-esteem has
been touched; it is not the accent of one who is blazingly angry
because he has been insulted. It is the accent of sorrow, the
accent of one who offered men the most precious thing in the
world and saw it disregarded. Jesus' condemnation of sin is
holy anger, but the anger comes, not from outraged pride, but
from a broken heart.

What then was the sin of Chorazin, of Bethsaida, of Capernaum, the sin which was worse than the sin of Tyre and Sidon,
and of Sodom and Gomorrah? It must have been very serious
for again and again Tyre and Sidon are denounced for their
wickedness (*Isaiah* 23; *Jeremiah* 25: 22; 47: 4; *Ezekiel* 26:
3–7; 28: 12–22), and Sodom and Gomorrah were and are a
byword for iniquity.

(i) It was the sin of the people who forgot the responsibilities
of privilege. To the cities of Galilee had been given a privilege
which had never come to Tyre and Sidon, or to Sodom and
Gomorrah, for the cities of Galilee had actually seen and heard
Jesus. We cannot condemn a man who never had the chance to
know any better; but if a man who has had every chance to know
the right does the wrong, then he does stand condemned. We do
not condemn a child for that for which we would condemn an
adult; we would not condemn a savage for conduct which we
would condemn in a civilized man; we do not expect the person
brought up in the handicaps of a city slum to live the life of a
person brought up in a good and comfortable home. The
greater our privileges have been, the greater is our condemnation if we fail to shoulder the responsibilities and accept the
obligations which these privileges bring with them.

(ii) It was the sin of indifference. These cities did not attack
Jesus Christ; they did not drive him from their gates; they did
not seek to crucify him; they simply disregarded him. Neglect
can kill as much as persecution can. An author writes a book; it

is sent out for review; some reviewers may praise it, others may damn it; it does not matter so long as it is noticed; the one thing which will kill a book stone dead is if it is never noticed at all for either praise or blame.

An artist drew a picture of Christ standing on one of London's famous bridges. He is holding out his hands in appeal to the crowds, and they are drifting past without a second look; only one girl, a nurse, gives him any response. Here we have the modern situation in so many countries today. There is no hostility to Christianity; there is no desire to destroy it; there is blank indifference. Christ is relegated to the ranks of those who do not matter. Indifference, too, is a sin, and the worst of all, for indifference kills.

It does not burn a religion to death; it freezes it to death. It does not behead it; it slowly suffocates the life out of it.

(iii) And so we are face to face with one great threatening truth—*it is also a sin to do nothing*. There are sins of action, sins of deed; but there is also a sin of inaction, and of absence of deeds. The sin of Chorazin, of Bethsaida, and of Capernaum was the sin of doing nothing. Many a man's defence is: " But I never did anything." That defence may be in fact his condemnation.

THE ACCENT OF AUTHORITY

Matthew 11: 25–27

> At that time Jesus said: " I thank you, Father, Lord of heaven and earth, that you have hidden these things from the wise and the clever, and have revealed them to babes. Even so, Father, for thus it was your will in your sight. All things have been delivered to me by my Father; and no one really knows the Son except the Father, and no one really knows the Father except the Son, and he to whom the Son wishes to reveal his knowledge."

HERE Jesus is speaking out of experience, the experience that the Rabbis and the wise men rejected him, and the simple people accepted him. The intellectuals had no use for him; but the humble welcomed him. We must be careful to see clearly what Jesus meant here. He is very far from condemning intellectual power; what he is condemning is *intellectual pride.* As Plummer has it, " The heart, not the head, is the home of the gospel." It is not cleverness which shuts out; it is pride. It is not stupidity which admits; it is humility. A man may be as wise as Solomon, but if he has not the simplicity, the trust, the innocence of the childlike heart, he shuts himself out.

The Rabbis themselves saw the danger of this intellectual pride; they recognized that often simple people were nearer God than the wisest Rabbi. They had a parable like this. Once Rabbi Berokah of Chuza was in the market of Lapet, and Elijah appeared to him. The Rabbi asked, " Is there among the people in this market-place anyone who is destined to share in the life of the world to come? " At first Elijah said there was none. Then he pointed at one man, and said that that man would share in the life of the world to come. Rabbi Berokah went to the man and asked him what he did. " I am a jailer," said the man, " and I keep men and women separate. At night I place my bed between the men and the women so that no wrong will be committed." Elijah pointed at two other men, and said that they too would share in the life to come. Rabbi Berokah asked them what they did. " We are merry-makers," they said. " When we see a man who is downcast, we cheer him up. Also when we see two people quarrelling with one another, we try to make peace between them." The men who did the simple things, the jailer who kept his charges in the right way, the men who brought a smile and peace, were in the kingdom.

Again, the Rabbis had a story like this: " An epidemic once broke out in Sura, but in the neighbourhood of Rab's residence (a famous Rabbi) it did not appear. The people thought that this was due to Rab's merits, but in a dream they were told . . . that it happened because of the merits of a man who willingly lent hoe and shovel to someone who wished to dig a grave. A fire once broke out in Drokeret, but the neighbourhood of Rabbi Huna was spared. The people thought it was due to the merits

of Rabbi Huna, ... but they were told in a dream that it was
due to the merits of a certain woman, who used to heat her oven
and place it at the disposal of her neighbours." The man who
lent his tools to someone in need, the woman who helped her
neighbours as she could had no intellectual standing, but their
simple deeds of human love had won them the approval of God.
Academic distinctions are not necessarily distinctions in the
sight of God.

> " Still to the lowly soul
> He doth himself impart,
> And for his dwelling and his throne
> Chooseth the pure in heart."

This passage closes with the greatest claim that Jesus ever
made, the claim which is the centre of the Christian faith, that
he alone can reveal God to men. Other men may be sons of
God; he is *The Son*. John put this in a different way, when he
tells us that Jesus said, " He who has seen me has seen the
Father " (*John* 14: 9). What Jesus says is this: " If you want to
see what God is like, if you want to see the mind of God, the
heart of God, the nature of God, if you want to see God's whole
attitude to men—look at me! " It is the Christian conviction
that in Jesus Christ alone we see what God is like; and it is also
the Christian conviction that Jesus can give that knowledge to
anyone who is humble enough and trustful enough to receive it.

THE ACCENT OF COMPASSION

Matthew 11: 28–30

> " Come to me, all you who are exhausted and weighted down
> beneath your burdens, and I will give you rest. Take my yoke
> upon you, and learn of me, for I am gentle and lowly in heart, and
> you will find rest for your souls; for my yoke is easy and my
> burden is light."

JESUS spoke to men desperately trying to find God and
desperately trying to be good, who were finding the tasks

impossible and who were driven to weariness and to despair.

He says, " Come unto me all you who are exhausted." His invitation is to those who are exhausted with the search for the truth. The Greeks had said, " It is very difficult to find God, and, when you have found him, it is impossible to tell anyone else about him." Zophar demanded of Job: " Can you find out the deep things of God? " (*Job* 11: 7). It is Jesus' claim that the weary search for God ends in himself. W. B. Yeats, the great Irish poet and mystic, wrote: " Can one reach God by toil? He gives himself to the pure in heart. He asks nothing but our attention." The way to know God is not by mental search, but by giving attention to Jesus Christ, for in him we see what God is like.

He says, " Come unto me all you who are weighted down beneath your burdens." For the orthodox Jew religion was a thing of burdens. Jesus said of the Scribes and Pharisees: " They bind heavy burdens, hard to bear, and lay them on men's shoulders " (*Matthew* 23: 4). To the Jew religion was a thing of endless rules. A man lived his life in a forest of regulations which dictated every action of his life. He must listen for ever to a voice which said, " Thou shalt not."

Even the Rabbis saw this. There is a kind of rueful parable put into the mouth of Korah, which shows just how binding and constricting and burdensome and impossible the demands of the Law could be. " There was a poor widow in my neighbourhood who had two daughters and a field. When she began to plough, Moses (i.e. the Law of Moses) said, ' You must not plough with an ox and an ass together.' When she began to sow, he said, ' You must not sow your field with mingled seed.' When she began to reap and to make stacks of corn, he said, ' When you reap your harvest in your field, and have forgotten a sheaf in the field, you shall not go back to get it ' (*Deuteronomy* 24: 19), and ' you shall not reap your field to its very border ' (*Leviticus* 19: 9). She began to thresh, and he said, ' Give me the heave-offering, and the first and second tithe.' She accepted the ordinance and gave them all to him. What did the poor woman then do? She sold her field, and bought two sheep, to clothe herself from their fleece, and to have profit from their young.

When they bore their young, Aaron (i.e. the demands of the priesthood) came and said, ' Give me the first-born.' So she accepted the decision, and gave them to him. When the shearing time came, and she sheared them, Aaron came and said, ' Give me the first of the fleece of the sheep ' (*Deuteronomy* 18: 4). Then she thought: ' I cannot stand up against this man. I will slaughter the sheep and eat them.' Then Aaron came and said, ' Give me the shoulder and the two cheeks and the stomach ' (*Deuteronomy* 18: 3). Then she said, ' Even when I have killed them I am not safe from you. Behold they shall be *devoted*.' Then Aaron said, ' In that case they belong entirely to me ' (*Numbers* 18: 14). He took them and went away and left her weeping with her two daughters." The story is a parable of the continuous demands that the Law made upon men in every action and activity of life. These demands were indeed a burden.

Jesus invites us to take his yoke upon our shoulders. The Jews used the phrase *the yoke* for *entering into submission to.* They spoke of the yoke of the Law, the yoke of the commandments, the yoke of the Kingdom, the yoke of God. But it may well be that Jesus took the words of his invitation from something much nearer home than that.

He says, " My yoke is *easy*." The word *easy* is in Greek *chrēstos*, which can mean *well-fitting*. In Palestine ox-yokes were made of wood; the ox was brought, and the measurements were taken. The yoke was then roughed out, and the ox was brought back to have the yoke tried on. The yoke was carefully adjusted, so that it would fit well, and not gall the neck of the patient beast. The yoke was tailor-made to fit the ox.

There is a legend that Jesus made the best ox-yokes in all Galilee, and that from all over the country men came to him to buy the best yokes that skill could make. In those days, as now, shops had their signs above the door; and it has been suggested that the sign above the door of the carpenter's shop in Nazareth may well have been: " My yokes fit well." It may well be that Jesus is here using a picture from the carpenter's shop in Nazareth where he had worked throughout the silent years.

Jesus says, " My yoke fits well." What he means is: " The life I give you is not a burden to gall you; your task is made to measure to fit you." Whatever God sends us is made to fit our needs and our abilities exactly.

Jesus says, " My burden is light." As a Rabbi had it: " My burden is become my song." It is not that the burden is easy to carry; but it is laid on us in love; it is meant to be carried in love; and love makes even the heaviest burden light. When we remember the love of God, when we know that our burden is to love God and to love men, then the burden becomes a song. There is an old story which tells how a man came upon a little boy carrying a still smaller boy, who was lame, upon his back. " That's a heavy burden for you to carry," said the man. " That's no' a burden," came the answer. " That's my wee brother." The burden which is given in love and carried in love is always light.

CRISIS

IN *Matthew* 12 we read the history of a series of crucial events in the life of Jesus. In every man's life there are decisive moments, times and events on which the whole of his life hinges. This chapter presents us with the story of such a period in the life of Jesus. In it we see the orthodox Jewish religious leaders of the day coming to their final decision regarding Jesus—and that was rejection. It was not only rejection in the sense that they would have nothing to do with him; it was rejection in the sense that they came to the conclusion that nothing less than his complete elimination would be enough.

Here in this chapter we see the first definite steps, the end of which could be nothing other than the Cross. The characters are painted clear before us. On the one hand there are the Scribes and the Pharisees, the representatives of orthodox religion. We can see four stages in their increasing attitude of malignant hostility to Jesus.

(i) In verses 1–8, the story of how the disciples plucked the ears of corn on the Sabbath day, we see growing *suspicion*. The Scribes and Pharisees regarded with growing suspicion a teacher who was prepared to allow his followers to disregard the minutiæ of the Sabbath Law. This was the kind of thing which could not be allowed to spread unchecked.

(ii) In verses 9–14, the story of the healing of the man with the paralysed hand on the Sabbath day, we see active and hostile *investigation*. It was not by chance that the Scribes and Pharisees were in the synagogue on that Sabbath. Luke says they were there to watch Jesus (*Luke* 6: 7). From that time on Jesus would have to work always under the malignant eye of the orthodox leaders. They would do his steps, like private detectives, seeking the evidence on which they could level a charge against him.

(iii) In verses 22–32, the story of how the orthodox leaders charged Jesus with healing by the power of the devil, and of how he spoke to them of the sin which has no forgiveness, we see the story of deliberate and prejudiced *blindness*. From that time on nothing Jesus could ever do would be right in the eyes of these men. They had so shut their eyes to God that they were completely incapable of ever seeing his beauty and his truth. Their prejudiced blindness had launched them on a path from which they were quite incapable of ever turning back.

(iv) In verse 14 we see evil *determination*. The orthodox were not now content to watch and criticize; they were preparing to *act*. They had gone into council to find a way to put an end to this disturbing Galilaean. Suspicion, investigation, blindness were on the way to open action.

In face of all this the answer of Jesus is clearly delineated. We can see five ways in which he met this growing opposition.

(i) He met it with courageous *defiance*. In the story of the healing of the man with the paralysed hand (verses 9–14) we see him deliberately defying the Scribes and Pharisees. This thing was not done in a corner; it was done in a crowded synagogue. It was not done in their absence; it was done when they were there with deliberate intent to formulate a charge against him.

So far from evading the challenge, Jesus is about to meet it head on.

(ii) He met it with *warning*. In verses 22–32 we see Jesus giving the most terrible of warnings. He is warning those men that, if they persist in shutting their eyes to the truth of God, they are on the way to a situation where, by their own act, they will have shut themselves out from the grace of God. Here Jesus is not so much on the defence as on the attack. He makes quite clear where their attitude is taking them.

(iii) He met it with a staggering series of *claims*. He is greater than the Temple (verse 6), and the Temple was the most sacred place in all the world. He is greater than Jonah, and no preacher ever produced repentance so amazingly as Jonah did (verse 41). He is greater than Solomon, and Solomon was the very acme of wisdom (verse 42). His claim is that there is nothing in spiritual history than which he is not greater. There are no apologies here; there is the statement of the claims of Christ at their highest.

(iv) He met it with the statement that his teaching is *essential*. The point of the strange parable of the Empty House (verses 43–45) is that the Law may negatively empty a man of evil, but only the gospel can fill him with good. The Law therefore simply leaves a man an empty invitation for all evil to take up its residence within his heart; the gospel so fills him with positive goodness that evil cannot enter in. Here is Jesus' claim that the gospel can do for men what the Law can never do.

(v) Finally, he met it with an *invitation*. Verses 46–50 are in essence an invitation to enter into kinship with him. These verses are not so much a disowning of Jesus' own kith and kin as an invitation to all men to enter into kinship with him, through the acceptance of the will of God, as that will has come to men in him. They are an invitation to abandon our own prejudices and self-will and to accept Jesus Christ as Master and Lord. If we refuse, we drift farther away from God; if we accept, we enter into the very family and heart of God.

BREAKING THE SABBATH LAW

Matthew 12: 1–8

At that time Jesus went through the cornfields on the Sabbath day. His disciples were hungry, and they began to pluck the ears of corn and to eat them. When the Pharisees saw this, they said to him, " Look you, your disciples are doing that which it is not permitted to do on the Sabbath day." He said to them, " Have you not read what David and his friends did, when he was hungry —how he went into the house of God and ate the shewbread, which it was not permissible for him, nor for his friends to eat, but which the priests alone may eat? Or, have you not read in the Law that the priests profane the Sabbath, and yet remain blameless? I tell you that something greater than the Temple is here. But, if you had known the meaning of the saying, ' It is mercy that I wish, and not sacrifice,' you would not have condemned those who are blameless. For the Son of Man is Lord of the Sabbath."

(The last phrase should perhaps be translated: " For man is master of the Sabbath.")

IN Palestine in the time of Jesus the cornfields and the cultivated lands were laid out in long narrow strips; and the ground between the strips was always a right of way. It was on one of these strips between the cornfields that the disciples and Jesus were walking when this incident happened.

There is no suggestion that the disciples were stealing. The Law expressly laid it down that the hungry traveller was entitled to do just what the disciples were doing, so long as he only used his hands to pluck the ears of corn, and did not use a sickle: " When you go into your neighbour's standing grain, you may pluck the ears with your hand, but you shall not put a sickle to your neighbour's standing grain " (*Deuteronomy* 23: 25). W. M. Thomson in *The Land and the Book* tells how, when he was travelling in Palestine, the same custom still existed. One of the favourite evening dishes for the traveller is parched corn. " When travelling in harvest time," Thomson writes, " my muleteers have very often prepared parched corn in the even-

ings after the tent has been pitched. Nor is the gathering of
these green ears for parching ever regarded as stealing.... So,
also, I have seen my muleteers, as we passed along the wheat
fields, pluck off the ears, rub them in their hands, and eat the
grains unroasted, just as the apostles are said to have done."

In the eyes of the Scribes and Pharisees, the fault of the
disciples was not that they had plucked and eaten the grains of
corn, but that they had done so *on the Sabbath*. The Sabbath
Law was very complicated and very detailed. The commandment forbids work on the Sabbath day; but the interpreters of
the Law were not satisfied with that simple prohibition. Work
had to be defined. So thirty-nine basic actions were laid down,
which were forbidden on the Sabbath, and amongst them were
reaping, winnowing and threshing, and preparing a meal. The
interpreters were not even prepared to leave the matter there.
Each item in the list of forbidden works had to be carefully
defined. For instance, it was forbidden to carry a *burden*. But
what is a burden? A burden is anything which weighs as much
as two dried figs. Even the suggestion of work was forbidden;
even anything which might symbolically be regarded as work
was prohibited. Later the great Jewish teacher, Maimonides,
was to say, " To pluck ears is a kind of reaping." By their
conduct the disciples were guilty of far more than one breach of
the Law. By plucking the corn they were guilty of *reaping*; by
rubbing it in their hands they were guilty of *threshing*; by
separating the grain and the chaff they were guilty of *winnowing*; and by the whole process they were guilty of *preparing a
meal* on the Sabbath day, for everything which was to be eaten
on the Sabbath had to be prepared the day before.

The orthodox Jews took this Sabbath Law with intense
seriousness. *The Book of Jubilee* has a chapter (chapter 50)
about the keeping of the Sabbath. Whoever lies with his wife, or
plans to do anything on the Sabbath, or plans to set out on a
journey (even the contemplation of work is forbidden), or plans
to buy or sell, or draws water, or lifts a burden is condemned.
Any man who does any work on the Sabbath (whether the work
is in his house or in any other place), or goes a journey, or tills a

farm, any man who lights a fire or rides any beast, or travels by ship at sea, any man who strikes or kills anything, any man who catches an animal, a bird, or a fish, any man who fasts or who makes war on a Sabbath—the man who does these things shall die. To keep these commandments was to keep the Law of God; to break them was to break the Law of God.

There is no doubt whatever that, from their own point of view, the Scribes and Pharisees were entirely justified in finding fault with the disciples for breaking the Law, and with Jesus for allowing them, if not encouraging them, to do so.

THE CLAIM OF HUMAN NEED

Matthew 12: 1–8 (*continued*)

To meet the criticism of the Scribes and Pharisees Jesus put forward three arguments.

(i) He quoted the action of David (1 *Samuel* 21: 1–6) on the occasion when David and his young men were so hungry that they went into the tabernacle—not the Temple, because this happened in the days before the Temple was built—and ate the shewbread, which only the priests could eat. The shewbread is described in *Leviticus* 24: 5–9. It consisted of twelve loaves of bread, which were placed every week in two rows of six in the Holy Place. No doubt they were a symbolic offering in which God was thanked for his gift of sustaining food. These loaves were changed every week, and the old loaves became the perquisite of the priests and could only be eaten by them. On this occasion, in their hunger, David and his young men took and ate those sacred loaves, and no blame attached to them. The claims of human need took precedence over any ritual custom.

(ii) He quoted the Sabbath work of the Temple. The Temple ritual always involved work—the kindling of fires, the slaughter and the preparation of animals, the lifting of them on to the altar, and a host of other things. This work was actually doubled on the Sabbath, for on the Sabbath the offerings were doubled (cp. e.g. *Numbers* 28: 9). Any one of these actions would have been illegal for any ordinary person to perform on the Sabbath day. To light a fire, to slaughter an animal, to lift it up on to the altar would have been to break the Law, and hence to profane the Sabbath. But for the priests it was perfectly legal to do these things, for the Temple worship must go on. That is to say, worship offered to God took precedence of all the Sabbath rules and regulations.

(iii) He quoted God's word to Hosea the prophet: " I desire steadfast love and not sacrifice " (*Hosea* 6: 6). What God desires far more than ritual sacrifice is kindness, the spirit which knows no law other than that it must answer the call of human need.

In this incident Jesus lays it down that the claim of human need must take precedence of all other claims. The claims of worship, the claims of ritual, the claims of liturgy are important but prior to any of them is the claim of human need.

One of the modern saints of God is Father George Potter who, out of the derelict Church of St. Chrysostom's in Peckham, made a shining light of Christian worship and Christian service. To further the work he founded the Brotherhood of the Order of the Holy Cross, whose badge was the towel which Jesus Christ wore when he washed his disciples' feet. There was no service too menial for the brothers to render; their work for the outcast and for homeless boys with a criminal record or criminal potentialities is beyond all praise. Father Potter held the highest possible ideas of worship; and yet when he is explaining the work of the Brotherhood he writes of anyone who wishes to enter into its triple vow of poverty, chastity and obedience: " He mustn't sulk if he cannot get to Vespers on the Feast of St. Thermogene. He may be sitting in a police court waiting for a ' client '. . . . He mustn't be the type who goes into the kitchen and sobs just because we run short of incense. . . . We put prayer and sacraments first. We know we cannot do our best otherwise, but the fact is that we have to spend more time at the bottom of the Mount of Transfiguration than at the top."

He tells about one candidate who arrived, when he was just about to give his boys a cup of cocoa and put them to bed. " So I said, Just clean round the bath will you while it's wet? ' He stood aghast and stuttered, I didn't expect to clean up after dirty boys! ' Well, well! His life of devoted service to the Blessed Master lasted about seven minutes. He did not unpack." Florence Allshorn, the great principal of a women's missionary college, tells of the problem of the candidate who always discovers that her time for quiet prayer has come just when there are greasy dishes to be washed in not very warm water.

Jesus insisted that the greatest ritual service is the service of human need. It is an odd thing to think that, with the possible exception of that day in the synagogue at Nazareth, we have no evidence that Jesus ever conducted a church service in all his life on earth, but we have abundant evidence that he fed the hungry and comforted the sad and cared for the sick. Christian service is not the service of any liturgy or ritual; it is the service of human need. Christian service is not monastic retiral; it is involvement in all the tragedies and problems and demands of the human situation. Whittier had it rightly:

> " O brother man, fold to thy heart thy brother!
>   Where pity dwells, the peace of God is there;
> To worship rightly is to love each other,
>   Each smile a hymn, each kindly deed a prayer.
>
> For he whom Jesus loved hath truly spoken;
>   The holier worship which he deigns to bless
> Restores the lost, and binds the spirit broken,
>   And feeds the widow and the fatherless.
>
> Follow with reverent steps the great example
>   Of Him whose holy work was doing good;
> So shall the wide earth seem our Father's temple,
>   Each loving life a psalm of gratitude."

That is what we mean—or ought to mean—when we say, " Let us worship God! "

MASTER OF THE SABBATH

Matthew 12: 1–8 (*continued*)

THERE remains in this passage one difficulty which it is not possible to solve with absolute certainty. The difficulty lies in the last phrase, " For the Son of man is lord of the sabbath." This phrase can have two meanings.

(i) It may mean that Jesus is claiming to be Lord of the Sabbath, in the sense that he is entitled to use the Sabbath as he thinks fit. We have seen that the sanctity of the work of the Temple surpassed and over-rode the Sabbath rules and regulations; Jesus has just claimed that something greater than the Temple is here in him; therefore he has the right to dispense with the Sabbath regulations and to do as he thinks best on the Sabbath day. That may be said to be the traditional interpretation of this sentence, but there are real difficulties in it.

(ii) On this occasion Jesus is not defending *himself* for anything that he did on the Sabbath; he is defending his *disciples*; and the authority which he is stressing here is not so much his own authority as the authority of human need. And it is to be noted that when Mark tells of this incident he introduces another saying of Jesus as part of the climax of it: " The Sabbath was made for man, not man for the Sabbath " (*Mark* 2: 27).

To this we must add the fact that in Hebrew and Aramaic the phrase *son of man* is not a title at all, but simply a way of saying *a man*. When the Rabbis began a parable, they often began it: " There was a son of man who ... "; when we would simply say, " There was a man who ... " The Psalmist writes, " What is *man* that thou art mindful of him? and the *son of man* that thou dost care for him? " (*Psalm* 8: 4). Again and again the *Ezekiel* God addresses Ezekiel as *son of man*. " And he said to me: ' Son of man, stand upon your feet and I will speak with you ' " (*Ezekiel* 2: 1; cp. 2: 6; 2: 8; 3: 1, 4, 17, 25). In all these cases *son of man*, spelled without the capital letters, simply means *man*.

In the (early and best) Greek manuscripts of the New Testament all the words were written completely in capital letters. In these manuscripts (called *uncials*) it would not be possible to tell where special capitals are necessary. Therefore, in *Matthew* 12: 8, it may well be that *son of man* should be written without capital letters, and that the phrase does not refer to Jesus but simply to *man*.

If we consider that what Jesus is pressing is the claims of human need; if we remember that it is not himself but his disciples that he is defending; if we remember that Mark tells us that he said that the Sabbath was made for man and not man for the Sabbath; then we may well conclude that what Jesus said here is: " Man is not the slave of the Sabbath; he is the master of it, to use it for his own good." Jesus may well be rebuking the Scribes and Pharisees for enslaving themselves and their fellow-men with a host of tyrannical regulations; and he may well be here laying down the great principle of Christian freedom, which applies to the Sabbath as it does to all other things in life.

LOVE AND LAW

Matthew 12: 9–14

He left there and went into their synagogue. And, look you, there was a man there with a withered hand. So they asked him, " Is it permitted to heal on the Sabbath? " They asked this question in order that they might find an accusation against him. " What man will there be of you," he said, " who will have a sheep, and, if the sheep falls into a pit on the Sabbath day, will not take a grip of it, and lift it out? How much more valuable is a man than a sheep? So, then, it is permitted to do a good thing on the Sabbath day." Then he said to the man, " Stretch forth your hand! " He stretched it out, and it was restored, sound as the other. So the Pharisees went away and conferred against him, to find a way to destroy him.

THIS incident is a crucial moment in the life of Jesus. He deliberately and publicly broke the Sabbath Law; and the result was a conference of the orthodox leaders to search out a way to eliminate him.

We will not understand the attitude of the orthodox unless we understand the amazing seriousness with which they took the Sabbath Law. That Law forbade all work on the Sabbath day, and so the orthodox Jews would literally die rather than break it.

In the time of the rising under Judas Maccabaeus certain Jews sought refuge in the caves in the wilderness. Antiochus sent a detachment of men to attack them; the attack was made on the Sabbath day; and these insurgent Jews died without even a gesture of defiance or defence, because to fight would have been to break the Sabbath. 1 *Maccabees* tells how the forces of Antiochus " gave them battle with all speed. Howbeit they answered them not, neither cast they a stone at them, nor stopped the places where they lay hid; but said: ' Let us die in our innocency: heaven and earth shall testify for us, that ye put us to death wrongfully.' So they rose up against them in battle on the Sabbath, and they slew them with their wives and children and cattle, to the number of a thousand people " (1 *Maccabees* 2: 31–38). Even in a national crisis, even to save their lives, even to protect their nearest and their dearest, the Jews would not fight on the Sabbath.

It was because the Jews insisted on keeping the Sabbath Law that Pompey was able to take Jerusalem. In ancient warfare it was the custom for the attacker to erect a huge mound which overlooked the battlements of the besieged city and from the height of the mound to bombard the defences. Pompey built his mound on the Sabbath days when the Jews simply looked on and refused to lift a hand to stop him. Josephus says, " And had it not been for the practice, from the days of our forefathers, to rest on the seventh day, this bank could never have been perfected, by reason of the opposition the Jews would have made; for though our Law gave us leave then to defend ourselves against those that begin to fight with us and assault us (this was a concession), yet it does not permit us to meddle with our enemies while they do anything else " (Josephus: *Antiquities*, 14. 4. 2.).

Josephus recalls the amazement of the Greek historian Agatharchides at the way in which Ptolemy Lagos was allowed to capture Jerusalem. Agatharchides wrote: " There are a people called Jews, who dwell in a city the strongest of all cities, which the inhabitants call Jerusalem, and are accustomed to rest on every seventh day; at which time they make no use of their arms, nor meddle with husbandry, nor take care of any of the affairs of life, but spread out their hands in their holy places, and pray till evening time. Now it came to pass that when Ptolemy the son of Lagos came into this city with his army, these men, in observing this mad custom of theirs, instead of guarding the city, suffered their country to submit itself to a bitter lord; and their Law was openly proved to have commanded a foolish practice. This accident taught all other men but the Jews to disregard such dreams as these were, and not to follow the like idle suggestions delivered as a Law, when in such uncertainty of human reasonings they are at a loss what they should do " (Josephus: *Against Apion*, 1: 22). The rigorous Jewish observance of the Sabbath seemed to other nations nothing short of insanity, since it could lead to such amazing national defeats and disasters.

It was that absolutely immovable frame of mind that Jesus was up against. The Law quite definitely forbade healing on the Sabbath. It was true that the Law clearly laid it down that " every case when life is in danger supersedes the Sabbath Law." This was particularly the case in diseases of the ear, the nose, the throat and the eyes. But even then it was equally clearly laid down that steps could be taken to keep a man from getting worse, but not to make him better. So a plain bandage might be put on a wound, but not a medicated bandage, and so on.

In this case there was no question of the paralysed man's life being in danger; as far as danger went, he would be in no worse condition the next day. Jesus knew the Law; he knew what he was doing; he knew that the Pharisees were waiting and watching; *and yet he healed the man.* Jesus would accept no law which insisted that a man should suffer, even without danger to life, one moment longer than necessary. His love for humanity far surpassed his respect for ritual Law.

THE CHALLENGE ACCEPTED

Matthew 12: 9–14 (*continued*)

JESUS went into the synagogue, and in it was a man with a paralysed hand. Our gospels tell us nothing more about this man, but the *Gospel according to the Hebrews*, which was one of the early gospels which did not succeed in gaining an entry to the New Testament, tells us that he came to Jesus with the appeal: " I was a stone mason, seeking my living with my hands. I pray you, Jesus, to give me back my health, so that I shall not need to beg for food in shame."

But the Scribes and Pharisees were there, too. They were not concerned with the man with the paralysed hand; they were concerned only with the minutiæ of their rules and regulations. So they asked Jesus: " Is it permitted to heal on the Sabbath day? " Jesus knew the answer to that question perfectly well; he knew that, as we have seen, unless there was actual danger to life, healing was forbidden, because it was regarded as an act of work.

But Jesus was wise. If they wished to argue about the Law, he had the skill to meet them on their own ground. " Tell me," he said, " suppose a man has a sheep, and that sheep falls into a pit on the Sabbath day, will he not go and haul the sheep out of the pit? " That was, in fact, a case for which the Law provided. If an animal fell into a pit on the Sabbath, then it was within the Law to carry food to it, which in any other case would have been a burden, and to render it all assistance. " So," said Jesus, " it is permitted to do a good thing on the Sabbath; and, if it is permitted to do a good thing to a sheep, how much more must it be lawful to do it for a man, who is of so much more value than any animal."

Jesus reversed the argument. " If," he argued, " it is right to do good on the Sabbath, then to refuse to do good is evil." It was Jesus' basic principle that there is no time so sacred that it cannot be used for helping a fellow-man who is in need. We will not be judged by the number of church services we have attended, or by the number of chapters of the Bible we have read, or even by the number of the hours we have spent in prayer, but by the number of people we have helped, when their need came crying to us. To this, at the moment, the Scribes and Pharisees had nothing to answer, for their argument had recoiled on their own head.

So Jesus healed this man, and in healing him gave him three things.

(i) He gave him back his *health*. Jesus is vitally interested in the bodies of men. Paul Tournier, in his book *A Doctor's Case Book*, has some great things to pass on about healing and God. Professor Courvoisier writes that the vocation of medicine is " a service to which those are called, who, through their studies and the natural gifts with which the Creator has endowed them ... are specially fitted to tend the sick and to heal them. Whether or not they are aware of it, whether or not they are believers, this is from the Christian point of view fundamental, that doctors are, by their profession, fellow-workers with God." " Sickness and healing," said Dr. Pouyanne, " are acts of grace." " The doctor is an instrument of God's patience," writes Pastor Alain Perrot. " Medicine is a dispensation of the grace of God, who in his goodness takes pity on men and provides remedies for the evil consequences of their sin." Calvin described medicine as a gift from God. He who heals men is helping God. The cure of men's bodies is just as much a God-given task as the cure of men's souls; and the doctor in his practice is just as much a servant of God as the minister in his parish.

(ii) Because Jesus gave this man back his health, he also gave him back his *work*. Without work to do a man is half a man; it is in his work that he finds himself and his satisfaction. Over the years idleness can be harder than pain to bear; and, if there is work to do, even sorrow loses at least something of its bitterness. One of the greatest things that any human being can do for any other is to give him work to do.

(iii) Because Jesus gave this man back his health and his work, he gave him back his *self-respect*. We might well add a new beatitude: Blessed are those who give us back our self respect. A man becomes a man again when, on his two feet and with his own two hands, he can face life and with independence provide for his own needs and for the needs of those dependent on him.

We have already said that this incident was crisis. At the end of it the Scribes and Pharisees began to plot the death of Jesus. In a sense the highest compliment you can pay a man is to persecute him. It shows that he is regarded not only as dangerous but as effective. The action of the Scribes and Pharisees is the measure of the power of Jesus Christ. True Christianity may be hated, but it can never be disregarded.

THE CHARACTERISTICS OF THE SERVANT OF THE LORD

Matthew 12: 15–21

Because Jesus knew this, he withdrew from there: and many followed him and he healed them all; and he strictly enjoined them not to surround him with publicity. All this happened that there might be fulfilled the word which came through Isaiah and which says: " Look you, my servant, whom I have chosen! My beloved one in whom my soul finds delight! I will put my Spirit upon him, and he will tell the nations what justice is. He will not strive, nor will he cry aloud, nor will anyone hear his voice in the streets. He will not break the crushed reed, and he will not quench the smoking wick, till he sends forth his conquering judgment, and in his name shall the Gentiles hope."

Two things here about Jesus show that he never confounded recklessness with courage. First, for the time being, he withdrew. The time for the head-on clash had not yet come. He had work to do before the Cross took him to its arms. Second, he forbade men to surround him with publicity. He knew only too well how many false Messiahs had arisen; he knew only too well how inflammable the people were. If the idea got around that someone with marvellous powers had emerged, then certainly a political rebellion would have arisen and lives would have been needlessly lost. He had to teach men that Messiahship meant not crushing power but sacrificial service, not a throne but a cross, before they could spread his story abroad.

The question which Matthew uses to sum up the work of Jesus is from *Isaiah* 42: 1–4. In a sense it is a curious quotation, because in the first instance it referred to Cyrus, the Persian king (cp. *Isaiah* 45: 1). The original point of the quotation was this. Cyrus was sweeping onwards in his conquests; and the prophet saw those conquests as within the deliberate and definite plan of God. Although he did not know it, Cyrus, the Persian, was the instrument of God. Further, the prophet saw Cyrus as the gentile conqueror, as indeed he was. But although the original words referred to Cyrus, the complete fulfilment of the prophecy undoubtedly came in Jesus Christ. In his day the Persian king mastered the eastern world, but the true Master of all the world is Jesus Christ. Let us then see how wonderfully Jesus satisfied this forecast of Isaiah.

(i) He will tell the nations what justice is. Jesus came to bring men *justice*. The Greeks defined *justice* as *giving to God and to men that which is their due.* Jesus showed men how to live in such a way that both God and men receive their proper place in our lives. He showed us how to behave both towards God and towards men.

(ii) He will not strive, nor cry aloud, nor will anyone hear his voice in the streets. The word that is used for to *cry aloud* is the word that is used for the barking of a dog, the croaking of a raven, the bawling of a drunken man, the uproar of a discontented audience in a theatre. It means that Jesus would not brawl with men. We know all about the quarrels of conflicting parties, in which each tries to shout the other down. The hatred of theologians, the *odium theoligicum* is one of the tragedies of the Christian Church. We know all about the oppositions of politicians and of ideologies. In Jesus there is the quiet, strong serenity of one who seeks to conquer by love, and not by strife of words.

(iii) He will not break the crushed reed nor quench the smoking wick. The reed may be bruised and hardly able to stand erect; the wick may be weak and the light may be but a flicker. A man's witness may be shaky and weak; the light of his life may be but a flicker and not a flame; but Jesus did not come to discourage, but to encourage. He did not come to treat the weak with contempt, but with understanding; he did not come to extinguish the weak flame, but to nurse it back to a clearer and a stronger light. The most precious thing about Jesus is the fact that he is not the great discourager, but the great encourager.

(iv) In him the Gentiles will hope. With Jesus there came into the world the invitation, not to a nation but to all men, to share in and to accept the love of God. In him God was reaching out to every one with the offer of his love.

SATAN'S DEFENCES ARE BREACHED

Matthew 12: 22–29

Then there was brought to him a man possessed by a devil, blind and dumb; and he cured him, so that the dumb man spoke and saw. The crowds were beside themselves with amazement. " Surely," they said, " this cannot be the Son of David? " But, when they heard it, the Pharisees said, " The only way in which this fellow casts out devils, is by the help of Beelzeboul, the prince of the devils." When he saw what they were thinking, Jesus said to them, " Every kingdom which has reached a state of division against itself is laid waste; and any city or region which has reached a state of division against itself will not stand. If Satan is casting out Satan, he is in a state of division against himself. How then shall his kingdom stand? Further, if I cast out devils by the power of Beelzeboul, by whose power do your sons cast them out? They do cast them out, and therefore they convict you of hypocrisy in the charge which you level against me. But, if I cast out devils by the Spirit of God, then the Kingdom of God has come upon you. Or, how can anyone enter into the house of a strong man, and seize his goods, unless he first bind the strong man? Then he will be able to seize his house."

IN the eastern world it was not only mental and psychological illness which was ascribed to the influence of demons and devils; all illness was ascribed to their malignant power. Exorcism was therefore very commonly practised; and was in fact frequently completely effective.

There is nothing in that to be surprised at. When people believe in demon-possession, it is easy to convince themselves that they are so possessed; when they come under that delusion, the symptoms of demon-possession immediately arise. Even amongst ourselves anyone can think himself into having a headache, or can convince himself that he has the symptoms of an illness. When a person under such a delusion was confronted with an exorcist in whom he had confidence, often the delusion was dispelled and a cure resulted. In such cases if a man was convinced he was cured, he was cured.

In this instance Jesus cured a man who was deaf and dumb and whose infirmity was attributed to demon-possession. The people were amazed. They began to wonder if this Jesus could be the Son of David, so long promised and so long expected, the great Saviour and Liberator. Their doubt was due to the fact that Jesus was so unlike the picture of the Son of David in which they had been brought up to believe. Here was no glorious prince with pomp and circumstance; here was no rattle of swords nor army with banners; here was no fiery cross calling men to war; here was a simple carpenter from Galilee, in whose words was wisdom gentle and serene, in whose eyes was compassion, and in whose hands was mysterious power.

All the time the Scribes and Pharisees were looking grimly

on. They had their own solution of the problem. Jesus was casting out devils because he was in league with the prince of devils. Jesus had three unanswerable replies to that charge.

(i) If he was casting out devils by the help of the prince of devils, it could only mean that in the demonic kingdom there was schism. If the prince of devils was actually lending his power to the destruction of his own demonic agents, then there was civil war in the kingdom of evil, and that kingdom was doomed. Neither a house nor a city nor a district can remain strong when it is divided against itself. Dissension within is the end of power. Even if the Scribes and Pharisees were right, Satan's days were numbered.

(ii) We take Jesus's third argument second, because there is so much to be said about the second that we wish to take it separately. Jesus said, " If I am casting out devils—and that you do not, and cannot, deny—it means that I have invaded the territory of Satan, and that I am actually like a burglar despoiling his house. Clearly no one can get into a strong man's house until the strong man is bound and rendered helpless. Therefore the very fact that I have been able so successfully to invade Satan's territory is proof that he is bound and powerless to resist." The picture of the binding of the strong man is taken from *Isaiah* 49: 24-26.

There is one question which this argument makes us wish to ask. When was the strong man bound? When was the prince of the devils fettered in such a way that Jesus could make this breach in his defences? Maybe there is no answer to that question; but if there is, it is that Satan was bound during Jesus' temptations in the wilderness.

It sometimes happens that, although an army is not completely put out of action, it suffers such a defeat that its fighting potential is never quite the same again. Its losses are so great, its confidence is so shaken, that it is never again the force it was. When Jesus faced the Tempter in the wilderness and conquered him, something happened. For the first time Satan found someone whom not all his wiles could seduce, and whom not all his attacks could conquer. From that time the power of

Satan has never been quite the same. He is no longer the all-conquering power of darkness; he is the defeated power of sin. The defences are breached; the enemy is not yet conquered; but his power can never be the same again and Jesus can help others win the victory he himself won.

THE JEWISH EXORCISTS

Matthew 12: 22–29 (*continued*)

(iii) Jesus' second argument, to which we now come, was that the Jews themselves practised exorcism; there were Jews who expelled demons and wrought cures. If he was practising exorcism by the power of the prince of devils, then they must be doing the same, for they were dealing with the same diseases and they had at least sometimes the same effect. Let us then look at the customs and the methods of the Jewish exorcists, for they were a remarkable contrast to the methods of Jesus.

Josephus, a perfectly reputable historian, says that the power to cast out demons was part of the wisdom of Solomon, and he describes a case which he himself saw (Josephus: *Antiquities* 8. 2. 5.): " God also enabled Solomon to learn that skill which expels demons, which is a science useful and health-bringing to men. He composed such incantations also, by which distempers are alleviated. And he left behind him also the manner of using exorcisms, by which they drive away demons so that they never return, and this method of cure is of great force unto this day; for I have seen a certain man of my own country, whose name was Eleazar, releasing people who were demoniacal in the presence of Vespasian, and his sons, and his captains, and the whole multitude of his soldiers. The manner of the cure was this. He put a ring that had a root which was one of those sorts mentioned by Solomon in the nostrils of the demoniac, after which he drew out the demon through his nostrils; and when the man fell down immediately, he adjured the demon to return into him no more, making still mention of Solomon, and reciting the incantations which he composed. And when Eleazar would persuade and demonstrate to the spectators that he had such a power, he set a little way off a cup or basin full of water, and commanded the demon, as he went out of the man, to overturn it, and thereby to let the spectators know that he had left the man; and when this was done, the skill and wisdom of Solomon was shown very manifestly." Here was the Jewish method; here was the whole paraphernalia of magic. How different the serene word of power which Jesus uttered!

Josephus has further information about how the Jewish exorcists worked. A certain root was much used in exorcism. Josephus tells about it: " In the valley of Macherus there is a certain root called by the same name. Its colour is like to that of flame, and towards evening it sends out a certain ray like lightning. It is not easily taken by such as would do so, but recedes from their hands, nor will it yield itself to be taken quietly until either the urine of a woman, or her menstrual blood, be poured upon it; nay, even then it is certain death to those who touch it, unless anyone take and hang the root itself down from his hand, and so carry it away. It may also be taken another way without danger, which is this: they dig a trench all round about it, till the hidden part of the root be very small; they then tie a dog to it, and when the dog tries hard to follow him that tied him, this root is easily plucked up, but the dog dies immediately, as if it were instead of the man that would take the plant away; nor after this need anyone be afraid of taking it into their hands. Yet after all these pains in getting it, it is only valuable on account of one virtue which it possesses, that if it be brought to sick persons, it drives away those called demons " (Josephus: *Wars of the Jews* 7. 6. 3.). What a difference between Jesus' word of power, and this witch-doctoring which the Jewish exorcist used!

We may add one more illustration of Jewish exorcism. It comes from the apocryphal book of *Tobit*. Tobit is told by the angel that he is to marry Sara, the daughter of Raguel. She is a beautiful maiden with a great dowry, and she herself is good. She has been in turn married to seven different men, all of

whom perished on their wedding night, because Sara was loved
by a wicked demon, who would allow none to approach her.
Tobit is afraid, but the angel tells him, " On the night when thou
shalt come into the marriage chamber, thou shalt take the ashes
of perfume, and shalt lay them upon some of the heart and liver of
the fish, and shalt make a smoke with it; and the devil shall smell
it and flee away, and never come again any more " (*Tobit* 6: 16).
So Tobit did and the devil was banished for ever (*Tobit* 8: 1–4).

These were the things the Jewish exorcists did, and, as so
often, they were a symbol. Men sought their deliverance from the
evils and the sorrows of humanity in their magic and their incantations. Maybe even these things for a little while, in the mercy
of God, brought some relief; but in Jesus there came the word of
God with its serene power to bring to men the perfect deliverance which they had wistfully and even desperately sought,
and which, until he came, they had never been able to find.

One of the most interesting things in the whole passage is
Jesus' saying, " If it is by the Spirit of God that I cast out
demons, then the Kingdom of God has come upon you " (verse
28). It is significant to note that the sign of the coming of the
Kingdom was not full churches and great revival meetings, but
the defeat of pain.

THE IMPOSSIBILITY OF NEUTRALITY

Matthew 12: 30

" He who is not with me is against me, and he who does not gather
with me scatters abroad."

THE picture of *gathering* and *scattering* may come from either
of two backgrounds. It may come from *harvesting*; he who is
not sharing in gathering the harvest is scattering the grain
abroad, and is therefore losing it to the wind. It may come from
shepherding; he who is not helping to keep the flock safe by
bringing it into the fold is driving it out to the dangers of the
hills.

In this one piercing sentence Jesus lays down the impossi-

bility of neutrality. W. C. Allen writes: " In this war against
Satan's strongholds there are only two sides, for Christ or
against him, gathering with him or scattering with Satan." We
may take a very simple analogy. We may apply this saying
to ourselves and to the Church. *If our presence does nót
strengthen the Church, then our absence is weakening it.* There
is no halfway house. In all things a man has to choose his side;
abstention from choice, suspended action, is no way out, because the refusal to give one side assistance is in fact the giving
of support to the other.

There are three things which make a man seek this impossible neutrality.

(i) There is the sheer *inertia of human nature.* It is true of so
many people that the only thing they desire is to be left alone.
They automatically shrink away from anything which is disturbing, and even choice is a disturbance.

(ii) There is the sheer *cowardice of human nature.* Many a
man refuses the way of Christ because he is afraid to take the
stand which Christianity demands. The basic thing that stops
him is the thought of what other people will say. The voice of
his neighbours is louder in his ears than the voice of God.

(iii) There is the sheer *flabbiness of human nature.* Most
people would rather have security than adventure, and the older
they grow the more that is so. A challenge always involves
adventure; Christ comes to us with a challenge, and often we
would rather have the comfort of selfish inaction than the
adventure of action for Christ.

The saying of Jesus—" He who is not with me is against
me "—presents us with a problem, for both Mark and Luke
have a saying which is the very reverse, " He that is not against
us is for us " (*Mark* 9: 40; *Luke* 9: 50). But they are not so
contradictory as they seem. It is to be noted that Jesus spoke
the second of them when his disciples came and told him that
they had sought to stop a man from casting out devils in his
name, because he was not one of their company. So a wise
suggestion has been made. " He that is not with me is against
me," is a test that we ought to apply to *ourselves.* Am I truly on

the Lord's side, or, am I trying to shuffle through life in a state of cowardly neutrality? " He that is not against us is for us," is a test that we ought to apply to *others*. Am I given to condemning everyone who does not speak with my theology and worship with my liturgy and share my ideas? Am I limiting the Kingdom of God to those who think as I do?

The saying in this present passage is a test to apply to ourselves; the saying in *Mark* and *Luke* is a test to apply to others; for we must ever judge ourselves with sternness and other people with tolerance.

THE SIN BEYOND FORGIVENESS

Matthew 12: 31–33

" That is why I tell you that every sin and every blasphemy will be forgiven to men; but blasphemy against the Holy Spirit will not be forgiven. If anyone speaks a word against the Son of Man, it will be forgiven him; but if anyone speaks a word against the Holy Spirit, it will not be forgiven him, either in this world or in the world to come. Either assume that the tree is good and the fruit is good, or assume that the tree is rotten and the fruit is rotten. For the tree is known by its fruits."

IT is startling to find words about an unforgivable sin on the lips of Jesus the Saviour of men. So startling is this that some wish to take away the sharp definiteness of the meaning. They argue that this is only another example of that vivid Eastern way of saying things, as, for example, when Jesus said that a man must *hate* father and mother truly to be his disciple, and that it is not to be understood in all its awful literalness, but simply means that the sin against the Holy Spirit is supremely terrible.

In support certain Old Testament passages are quoted. " But the person who does anything with a high hand, whether he is native or a sojourner, reviles the Lord, and that person shall be cut off from among his people. Because he has despised the word of the Lord, and has broken his commandment, that person shall be entirely cut off " (*Numbers* 15: 30, 31). " There-

fore I swear to the house of Eli that the iniquity of Eli's house
shall not be expiated by sacrifice or offering for ever " (1
Samuel 3: 14). " The Lord of hosts has revealed himself in my
ears. ' Surely this iniquity will not be forgiven you till you die,'
says the Lord God of hosts " (*Isaiah* 22: 14).

It is claimed that these texts say much the same as Jesus
said, and that they are only insisting on the grave nature of the
sin in question. We can only say that these Old Testament texts
do not have the same air nor do they produce the same
impression. There is something very much more alarming in
hearing words about a sin which has no forgiveness from the
lips of him who was the incarnate love of God.

There is one section in this saying which is undoubtedly
puzzling. In the Revised Standard Version Jesus is made to say
that a sin against the Son of man is forgivable, whereas a sin
against the Holy Spirit is not forgivable. If that is to be taken as
it stands, it is indeed a hard saying. Matthew has already said
that Jesus is the touchstone of all truth (*Matthew* 10: 32, 33);
and it is difficult to see what the difference between the two sins is.

But it may well be that at the back of this there is a
misunderstanding of what Jesus said. We have already seen (cp.
notes on *Matthew* 12: 1–8) that the Hebrew phrase *a son of
man* means simply *a man*, and that the Jews used this phrase
when they desired to speak of *any man*. When we would say,
" There was a man . . .," the Jewish Rabbi would say, " There
was a son of man. . . . " It may well be that what Jesus said was
this: " If any man speaks a word against *a man*, it will be
forgiven; but if any man speaks a word against the Holy Spirit
it will not be forgiven."

It is quite possible that we may misunderstand a merely
human messenger from God; but we cannot misunderstand—
except deliberately—when God speaks to us through his own
Holy Spirit. A human messenger is always open to miscon-
struction; but the divine messenger speaks so plainly that he
can only be wilfully misunderstood. It certainly makes this
passage easier to understand, if we regard the difference
between the two sins as a sin against God's human messenger,

which is serious, but not unforgivable, and a sin against God's divine messenger, which is completely wilful, and which, as we shall see, can end by becoming unforgivable.

THE LOST AWARENESS

Matthew 12: 31–33 (*continued*)

LET us then try to understand what Jesus meant by the sin against the Holy Spirit. One thing is necessary. We must grasp the fact that Jesus was not speaking about the Holy Spirit *in the full Christian sense of the term*. He could not have been, for Pentecost had to come before the Holy Spirit came upon men in all his power and light and fulness. This must be interpreted in light of the *Jewish* conception of the Holy Spirit.

According to Jewish teaching the Holy Spirit had two supreme functions. First, the Holy Spirit brought God's truth to men; second, the Holy Spirit enabled men to recognize and to understand that truth when they saw it. So then a man, as the Jews saw it, needed the Holy Spirit, both to receive and to recognise God's truth. We may express this in another way. *There is in man a Spirit-given faculty which enables him to recognize goodness and truth when he sees them.*

Now we must take the next step in our attempt to understand what Jesus meant. *A man can lose any faculty if he refuses to use it.* This is true in any sphere of life. It is true physically; if a man ceases to use certain muscles, they will atrophy. It is true mentally; many a man at school or in his youth has acquired some slight knowledge of, for example, French or Latin or music; but that knowledge is long since gone because he did not exercise it. It is true of all kinds of perception. A man may lose all appreciation of good music, if he listens to nothing but cheap music; he may lose the ability to read a great book, if he reads nothing but ephemeral productions; he may lose the faculty of enjoying clean and healthy pleasure, if he for long enough finds his pleasure in things which are degraded and soiled.

Therefore a man can lose the ability to recognize goodness and truth when he sees them. If he for long enough shuts his eyes and ears to God's way, if he for long enough turns his back upon the messages which God is sending him, if he for long enough prefers his own ideas to the ideas which God is seeking to put into his mind, in the end he comes to a stage when he cannot recognize God's truth and God's beauty and God's goodness when he sees them. He comes to a stage when his own evil seems to him good, and when God's good seems to him evil.

That is the stage to which these Scribes and Pharisees had come. They had so long been blind and deaf to the guidance of God's hand and the promptings of God's Spirit, they had insisted on their own way so long, that they had come to a stage when they could not recognize God's truth and goodness when they saw them. They were able to look on incarnate goodness and call it incarnate evil; they were able to look on the Son of God and call him the ally of the devil. The sin against the Holy Spirit is the sin of so often and so consistently refusing God's will that in the end it cannot be recognized when it comes even full-displayed.

Why should that sin be *unforgivable*? What differentiates it so terribly from all other sins? The answer is simple. *When a man reaches that stage, repentance is impossible.* If a man cannot recognize the good when he sees it, he cannot desire it. If a man does not recognize evil as evil, he cannot be sorry for it, and wish to depart from it. And if he cannot, in spite of failures, love the good and hate the evil, then he cannot repent; and if he cannot repent, he cannot be forgiven, for repentance is the only condition of forgiveness. It would save much heartbreak if people would realize that the one man who cannot have committed the sin against the Holy Spirit is the man who fears he has, for the sin against the Holy Spirit can be truly described as the loss of all sense of sin.

It was to that stage the Scribes and Pharisees had come. They had so long been deliberately blind and deliberately deaf to God that they had lost the faculty of recognizing him when they were confronted with him. It was not God who had banished them beyond the pale of forgiveness; they had shut themselves out. Years of resistance to God had made them what they were.

There is a dreadful warning here. We must so heed God all our days that our sensitivity is never blunted, our awareness is never dimmed, our spiritual hearing never becomes spiritual deafness. It is a law of life that we will hear only what we are listening for and only what we have fitted ourselves to hear.

There is a story of a country man who was in the office of a city friend, with the roar of the traffic coming through the windows. Suddenly he said, " Listen! " " What is it? " asked the city man. " A grasshopper," said the country man. Years of listening to the country sounds had attuned his ears to the country sounds, sounds that a city man's ear could not hear at all. On the other hand, let a silver coin drop, and the chink of the silver would have immediately reached the ears of the money-maker, while the country man might never have heard it at all. Only the expert, the man who has made himself able to hear it, will pick out the note of each individual bird in the chorus of the birds. Only the expert, the man who has made himself able to hear it, will distinguish the different instruments in the orchestra and catch a lonely wrong note from the second violins.

It is the law of life that we hear what we have trained ourselves to hear; day by day we must listen to God, so that day by day God's voice may become, not fainter and fainter until we cannot hear it at all, but clearer and clearer until it becomes the one sound to which above all our ears are attuned.

So Jesus finishes with the challenge: " If I have done a good deed, you must admit that I am a good man; if I have done a bad deed, then you may think me a bad man. You can only tell a tree's quality by its fruits, and a man's character by his deeds." But what if a man has become so blind to God that he cannot recognize goodness when he sees it?

HEARTS AND WORDS

Matthew 12: 34–37

" You brood of vipers, how can you who are evil speak good things? For it is from the overflow of the heart that the mouth speaks. The good man brings out good things from his good treasure house; and the evil man brings out evil things out of his evil treasure house. I tell you that every idle word which men shall speak, of that word shall they render accounts in the day of judgment; for by your words you will be acquitted, and by your words you will be condemned."

IT is little wonder that Jesus chose to speak here about the awful responsibility of words. The Scribes and Pharisees had just spoken the most terrible words. They had looked on the Son of God and called him the ally of the devil. Such words were dreadful words indeed. So Jesus laid down two laws.

(i) The state of a man's heart can be seen through the words he speaks. Long ago Menander the Greek dramatist said: " A man's character can be known from his words." That which is in the heart can come to the surface only through the lips; a man can produce through his lips only what he has in his heart. There is nothing so revealing as words. We do not need to talk to a man long before we discover whether he has a mind that is wholesome or a mind that is dirty; we do not need to listen to him long before we discover whether he has a mind that is kind or a mind that is cruel; we do not need to listen for long to a man who is preaching or teaching or lecturing to find out whether his mind is clear or whether it is muddled. We are continually revealing what we are by what we say.

(ii) Jesus laid it down that a man would specially render account for his *idle* words. The word that it used for idle is *aergos*; *ergon* is the Greek for a *deed*; and the prefix *a*—means *without*; *aergos* described that which was *not meant to produce anything*. It is used, for instance of a barren tree, of fallow land, of the Sabbath day when no work could be done, of an idle man. Jesus was saying something which is profoundly true. There are in fact two great truths here.

(*a*) It is the words which a man speaks without thinking, the words which he utters when the conventional restraints are removed, which really show what he is like. As Plummer puts it, " The carefully spoken words may be a calculated hypocrisy." When a man is consciously on his guard, he will be careful what he says and how he says it; but when he is off his guard, his words reveal his character. It is quite possible for a man's public utterances to be fine and noble, and for his private conversation to be coarse and salacious. In public he carefully chooses what he says; in private he takes the sentinels away, and any word leaves the gateway of his lips. It is so with anger; a man will say in anger what he really thinks and what he has often wanted to say, but which the cool control of prudence has kept him from saying. Many a man is a model of charm and courtesy in public, when he knows he is being watched and is deliberately careful about his words; while in his own house he is a dreadful example of irritability, sarcasm, temper, criticism, querulous complaint because there is no one to hear and to see. It is a humbling thing—and a warning thing—to remember that the words which show what we are are the words we speak when our guard is down.

(*b*) It is often these words which cause the greatest damage. A man may say in anger things he would never have said if he was in control of himself. He may say afterwards that he never meant what he said; but that does not free him from the responsibility of having said it; and the fact that he has said it often leaves a wound that nothing will cure, and erects a barrier that nothing will take away. A man may say in his relaxed moment a coarse and questionable thing that he would never have said in public—and that very thing may lodge in some-one's memory and stay there unforgotten. Pythagoras, the Greek philosopher, said, " Choose rather to fling a chance stone than to speak a chance word." Once the hurting word or the soiling word is spoken nothing will bring it back; and it pursues a course of damage wherever it goes.

Let a man examine himself. Let him examine his words that he may discover the state of his heart. And let him remember that God does not judge him by the words he speaks with care and deliberation, but by the words he speaks when the conventional restraints are gone and the real feelings of his heart come bubbling to the surface.

THE ONLY SIGN

Matthew 12: 38–42

> Then the Scribes and Pharisees answered him: " Teacher," they
> said, " we wish to see a sign from you." He answered, " It is an
> evil and apostate generation which seeks a sign. No sign will be
> given to it, except the sign of Jonah the prophet. For, as Jonah
> was in the belly of the whale three days and three nights, so the
> Son of Man will be in the heart of the earth for three days and
> three nights. At the judgment the men of Nineveh will be witnesses
> against this generation, and they will condemn it, because they
> repented at the preaching of Jonah, and, look you, something
> more than Jonah is here. The Queen of the South will rise in
> judgment with this generation, and will condemn it, because she
> came from the ends of the earth to listen to the wisdom of
> Solomon and, look you, something more than Solomon is here! "

" THE Jews," said Paul, " demand signs " (1 *Corinthians* 1:
22). It was characteristic of the Jews that they asked signs and
wonders from those who claimed to be the messengers of God.
It was as if they said, " Prove your claims by doing something
extraordinary." Edersheim quotes a passage from the Rabbinic
stories to illustrate the kind of thing that popular opinion
expected from the Messiah: " When a certain Rabbi was asked
by his disciples about the time of the Messiah's coming, he said,
' I am afraid you will also ask me for a sign.' When they
promised that they would not do so, he told them that the gate
of Rome would fall and be rebuilt, and fall again, when there
would not be time to restore it before the Son of David came.
On this they pressed him in spite of his remonstrance for a sign.
A sign was given them, that the waters which issued from the
cave of Banias were turned into blood.

Again, when the teaching of Rabbi Eliezer was challenged,
he appealed to certain signs. First, a locust bean tree moved at
his bidding, one hundred, or according to some, four hundred
cubits. Next the channels of water were made to flow back-
wards. The walls of the academy leaned forward, and were only

arrested at the bidding of another Rabbi. Lastly Eliezer exclaimed: ' If the Law is as I teach, let it be proved from heaven.' A voice came from the sky saying, ' What have you to do with Rabbi Eliezer, for the instruction is as he teaches? ' "

That is the kind of sign that the Jews desired. They did so because they were guilty of one fundamental mistake. They desired to see God in the *abnormal*; they forgot that we are never nearer God, and God never shows himself to us so much and so continually as in the ordinary things of every day.

Jesus calls them an evil and *adulterous* generation. The word *adulterous* is not to be taken literally; it means *apostate*. Behind it there is a favourite Old Testament prophetic picture. The relationship between Israel and God was conceived of as a marriage bond with God the husband and Israel the bride. When therefore Israel was unfaithful and gave her love to other gods, the nation was said to be adulterous and to go a-whoring after strange gods. *Jeremiah* 3: 6–11 is a typical passage. There the nation is said to have gone up into every high mountain, and under every green tree, and to have played the harlot. Even when Israel had been put away for infidelity by God, Judah did not take the warning and still played the harlot. Her whoredoms defiled the land, and she committed adultery with stone and tree. The word describes something worse than physical adultery; it describes that infidelity to God from which all sin, physical and spiritual, springs.

Jesus says that the only sign which will be given to this nation is the sign of *Jonah the prophet*. Here we have a problem. Matthew says that the sign is that, as Jonah was in the belly of the whale three days and three nights, the Son of man will be in the heart of the earth for three days and three nights. It is to be noted that these are not the words of Jesus, but the explanation of Matthew. When Luke reports this incident (*Luke* 11: 29–32) he makes no mention at all of Jonah being in the belly of the whale. He simply says that Jesus said, " For as Jonah became a sign to the men of Nineveh, so will the Son of Man be to this generation " (*Luke* 11: 30).

The fact is that Matthew understood wrongly the point of

what Jesus said; and in so doing he made a strange mistake for Jesus was not in the heart of the earth for three nights, but only for two. He was laid in the earth on the night of the first Good Friday and rose on the morning of the first Easter Sunday. The point is that to the Ninevites *Jonah himself* was God's sign, and Jonah's words were God's message.

Jesus is saying, " You are asking for a sign—*I am God's sign.* You have failed to recognize me. The Ninevites recognized God's warning in Jonah; the Queen of Sheba recognized God's wisdom in Solomon. In me there has come to you a greater wisdom than Solomon ever had, and a greater message than Jonah ever brought—but you are so blind that you cannot see the truth and so deaf that you cannot hear the warning. And for that very reason the day will come when these people of old time who recognized God when they saw him will be witnesses against you, who had so much better a chance, and failed to recognize God because you refused to do so."

Here is a tremendous truth—*Jesus is God's sign*, just as Jonah was God's message to the Ninevites and Solomon God's wisdom to the Queen of Sheba. The one real question in life is: " What is our reaction when we are confronted with God in Jesus Christ? " Is that reaction bleak hostility, as it was in the case of the Scribes and Pharisees? Or, is it humble acceptance of God's warning and God's truth as it was in the case of the people of Nineveh, and of the Queen of Sheba? The all-important question is: " What do you think of the Christ? "

THE PERIL OF THE EMPTY HEART

Matthew 12: 43–45

" When an unclean spirit goes out of a man, it goes through waterless places, seeking for rest, and does not find it. Then it says, ' I will go back to my house, from which I came out,' and when it comes, it finds it empty, swept and in perfect order. Then it goes and brings with it seven other spirits more evil than itself, and they go in and take up their residence there. So the last state of that man becomes worse than the first; so it will be with this evil generation."

THERE is a whole world of the most practical truth in this compact and eerie little parable about the haunted house.

(i) The evil spirit is banished from the man, not destroyed. That is to say that, in this present age, evil can be conquered, driven away—but it cannot be destroyed. It is always looking for the opportunity to counter-attack and regain the ground that is lost. Evil is a force which may be at bay but is never eliminated.

(ii) That is bound to mean that a negative religion can never be enough. A religion which consists in *thou shalt nots* will end in failure. The trouble about such a religion is that it may be able to cleanse a man by prohibiting all his evil actions, but *it cannot keep him cleansed.*

Let us think of this in actual practice. A drunkard may be reformed; he may decide that he will no longer spend his time in the public house; but he must find something else to do; he must find something to fill up his now empty time, or he will simply slip back into his evil ways. A man whose constant pursuit has been pleasure, may decide that he must stop; but he must find something else to do to fill up his time, or he will simply, through the very emptiness of his life, drift back to his old pursuits. A man's life must not only be sterilized from evil; it must be fructified to good. It will always remain true that ' Satan finds some mischief still for idle hands to do." And if one kind of action is banished from life, another kind must be substituted for it, for life cannot remain empty.

(iii) It therefore follows that the only permanent cure for evil action is Christian action. Any teaching which stops at telling a man what he must not do is bound to be a failure; it must go on to tell him what he must do. The one fatal disease is idleness; even a sterilized idleness will soon be infected. The easiest way to conquer the weeds in a garden is to fill the garden with useful things. The easiest way to keep a life from sin is to fill it with healthy action.

To put it quite simply, the Church will most easily keep her converts when she gives them Christian work to do. Our aim is not the mere negative absence of evil action; it is the positive presence of work for Christ. If we are finding the temptations of evil very threatening, one of the best ways to conquer them is to plunge into activity for God and for our fellow-men.

TRUE KINSHIP

Matthew 12: 46–50

> While he was still speaking to the crowds, look you, his mother and his brothers stood outside, for they were seeking an opportunity to speak to him. Someone said to him: " Look you, your mother and your brothers are standing outside, seeking an opportunity to speak to you." He answered the man who had spoken to him: " Who is my mother? And who are my brothers? " And he stretched out his hand towards his disciples. " See," he said, " my mother and my brothers! Whoever does the will of my Father in heaven is my brother and sister and mother."

IT was one of the great human tragedies of Jesus's life that, during his lifetime, his nearest and dearest never understood him. " For even his brothers," says John, " did not believe in him " (*John* 7: 5). Mark tells us that when Jesus set out on his public mission, his friends tried to restrain him, for they said that he was mad (*Mark* 3: 21). He seemed to them to be busily engaged in throwing his life away in a kind of insanity.

It has often been the case that, when a man embarked on the way of Jesus Christ, his nearest and dearest could not understand him, and were even hostile to him. " A Christian's only relatives," said one of the early martyrs, " are the saints." Many of the early Quakers had this bitter experience. When Edward Burrough was moved to the new way, " his parents resenting his ' fanatical spirit ' drove him forth from his home." He pleaded humbly with his father: " Let me stay and be your servant. I will do the work of the hired lad for thee. Let me stay! " But, as his biographer says, " His father was adamant, and much as the boy loved his home and its familiar surroundings, he was to know it no more."

True friendship and true love are founded on certain things without which they cannot exist.

(i) Friendship is founded on a common ideal. People who are very different in their background, their mental equipment, and even their methods, can be firm friends, if they have a common ideal, for which they work, and towards which they press.

(ii) Friendship is founded on a common experience, and on the memories which come from it. It is when two people have together passed through some great experience and when they can together look back on it, that real friendship begins.

(iii) True love is founded on obedience. " You are my friends," said Jesus, " *if you do what I command you* " (*John* 15: 14). There is no way of showing the reality of love unless by the spirit of obedience.

For all these reasons true kinship is not always a matter of a flesh and blood relationship. It remains true that blood is a tie that nothing can break and that many a man finds his delight and his peace in the circle of his family. But it is also true that sometimes a man's nearest and dearest are the people who understand him least, and that he finds his true fellowship with those who work for a common ideal and who share a common experience. This certainly is true—even if a Christian finds that those who should be closest to him are those who are most out of sympathy with him, there remains for him the fellowship of Jesus Christ and the friendship of all who love the Lord.

MANY THINGS IN PARABLES

Matthew 13 is a very important chapter in the pattern of the gospel.

(i) It shows a definite turning-point in the ministry of Jesus. At the beginning of his ministry we find him teaching in the *synagogues*; but now we find him teaching on the *seashore*. The change is very significant. It was not that the door of the synagogue was as yet finally shut to him, but it was closing. Even yet in the synagogue he would find a welcome from the common people; but the official leaders of Jewish orthodoxy were now in open opposition to him. When he entered a synagogue now, it would not be to find only an eager crowd of listeners; it would be also to find a bleak-eyed company of Scribes and Pharisees and elders weighing and sifting every word to find a charge against him, and watching every action to turn it into an accusation.

It is one of the supreme tragedies that Jesus was banished from the Church of his day; but that could not stop him from bringing his invitation to men; for when the doors of the synagogue were closed against him, he took to the temple of the open air, and taught men in the village streets, and on the roads, and by the lake-side, and in their own homes. The man who has a real message to deliver, and a real desire to deliver it, will always find a way of giving it to men.

(ii) The great interest of this chapter is that here we see Jesus beginning to use to the full his characteristic method of teaching *in parables*. Even before this he had used a way of teaching which had the germ of the parable in it. The simile of the salt and the light (5: 13–16), the picture of the birds and the lilies (6: 26–30), the story of the wise and the foolish builder (7: 24–27), the illustration of the garments and the wine-skins (9: 16, 17), the picture of the children playing in the market-place (11: 16, 17) are all embryo parables. They are truth in pictures.

But it is in this chapter that we find Jesus's way of using parables fully developed and at its most vivid. As someone has said, " Whatever else is true of Jesus, it is certainly true that he was one of the world's supreme masters of the short story." Before we begin to study these parables in detail, let us ask why Jesus used this method and what are the great teaching advantages which it offers.

(*a*) The parable always *makes truth concrete*. There are very few people who can grasp and understand abstract ideas; most people think in pictures. We could for long enough try to put into words what *beauty* is, and at the end of it no one would be very much the wiser; but if we can point at someone and say, " That is a beautiful person," no more description is needed. We might try for long enough to define *goodness* and in the end leave no clear idea of goodness in people's minds; but everyone recognizes a good person and good deed when he sees them. In order to be understood, every great word must become flesh, every great idea must take form and shape in a person; and the first great quality of a parable is that it makes truth into a picture which all men can see and understand.

(*b*) It has been said that all great teaching *begins from the here and now in order to get to the there and then*. If a man wishes to teach people about things which they do not understand, he must begin from things which they do understand. The parable begins with material which every man understands because it is within his own experience, and from that it leads him on to things which he does not understand, and opens his eyes to things which he has failed to see. The parable opens a man's mind and eyes by beginning from where he is and leading him on to where he ought to be.

(*c*) The great teaching virtue of the parable is that it compels *interest*. The surest way to interest people is to tell them stories. The parable puts truth in the form of a story; the simplest definition of a parable is in fact that it is " an earthly story with a heavenly meaning." People will not listen, and their attention cannot be retained, unless they are interested; with simple people it is stories which awaken and maintain interest, and the parable is a story.

(*d*) The parable has the great virtue that it enables and compels a man *to discover truth for himself*. It does not do a man's thinking for him; it says, " Here is a story. What is the truth in it? What does it mean *for you*? Think it out for yourself."

There are some things which a man cannot be told; he must discover them for himself. Walter Pater once said that you cannot tell a man the truth; you can only put him into a position in which he can discover it for himself. Unless we discover truth for ourselves, it remains a second-hand and external thing; and further, unless we discover truth for ourselves, we will almost certainly forget it quickly. The parable, by compelling a man to draw his own conclusions and to do his own thinking, at one and the same time makes truth real to him and fixes it in his memory.

(e) The other side of that is that the parable *conceals truth from those who are either too lazy to think or too blinded by prejudice to see*. It puts the responsibility fairly and squarely on the individual. It *reveals* truth to him who desires truth; it *conceals* truth from him who does not wish to see the truth.

(f) One final thing must be remembered. The parable, as Jesus used it, was *spoken*; it was not read. Its impact had to be immediate, not the result of long study with commentaries and dictionaries. It made truth flash upon a man as the lightning suddenly illuminates a pitch-dark night. In our study of the parables that means two things for us.

First, it means that we must amass every possible detail about the background of life in Palestine, so that the parable will strike us as it did those who heard it for the first time. We must think and study and imagine ourselves back into the minds of those who were listening to Jesus.

Second, it means that generally speaking a parable *will have only one point*. A parable is not an allegory; an allegory is a story in which every possible detail has an inner meaning; but an allegory has to be *read and studied*; a parable is *heard*. We must be very careful not to make allegories of the parables and to remember that they were designed to make one stabbing truth flash out at a man the moment he heard it.

THE SOWER WENT OUT TO SOW

Matthew 13: 1–9, 18–23

On that day, when he had gone out from the house, Jesus sat on the seashore; and such great crowds gathered to hear him that he went into a boat, and sat there; and the whole crowd took their stand on the seashore; and he spoke many things in parables to them. " Look! " he said, " the sower went out to sow; and, as he sowed, some seed fell by the wayside: and the birds came and devoured it. But some seed fell upon stony ground, where it had not much earth; and, because it had no depth of earth, it sprang up immediately; but when the sun rose it was scorched, and it withered away because it had no root. Other seed fell upon thorns, and the thorns came up, and choked the life out of it. But others fell on good ground, and yielded fruit, some a hundredfold, some sixtyfold, some thirtyfold. Who has ears, let him hear."

. . . .

" Listen then to the meaning of the parable of the sower. When anyone hears the word of the kingdom, and does not understand it, the evil one comes, and snatches away that which was sown in his heart. This is represented by the picture of the seed which was sown by the wayside. The picture of the seed which was sown on the stony ground represents the man who hears the word, and immediately receives it with joy. But he has no root in himself, and is at the mercy of the moment, and so, when affliction and persecution come, because of the word, he at once stumbles. The picture of the seed which is sown among the thorns represents the man who hears the word, but the cares of this world and the seduction of riches choke the word, and it bears no crop. The picture of the seed which was sown on the good ground represents the man who hears the word and understands it. He indeed bears fruit and produces some a hundredfold, some sixtyfold, some thirtyfold."

HERE is a picture which anyone in Palestine would understand. Here we actually see Jesus using the here and now to get to the there and then. There is a point which the Revised Standard Version obscures. The Revised Standard Version has: " *A* sower went out to sow." The Greek is not *a* sower, but: " *The* sower went out to sow."

What in all likelihood happened was that, as Jesus was using the boat by the lakeside as a pulpit, in one of the fields near the shore a sower was actually sowing, and Jesus took the sower, whom they could all see, as a text, and began: " Look at the sower there sowing his seed in that field! " Jesus began from something which at the moment they could actually see to open their minds to truth which as yet they had never seen.

In Palestine there were two ways of sowing seed. It could be sown by the sower scattering it broadcast as he walked up and down the field. Of course, if the wind was blowing, in that case some of the seed would be caught by the wind and blown into all kinds of places, and sometimes out of the field altogether. The second way was a lazy way, but was not uncommonly used. It was to put a sack of seed on the back of an ass, to tear or cut a hole in the corner of the sack, and then to walk the animal up and down the field while the seed ran out. In such a case some of the seed might well dribble out while the animal was crossing the pathway and before it reached the field at all.

In Palestine the fields were in long narrow strips; and the ground between the strips was always a right of way. It was used as a common path; and therefore it was beaten as hard as a pavement by the feet of countless passers-by. That is what Jesus means by the wayside. If seed fell there, and some was bound to fall there in whatever way it was sown, there was no more chance of its penetrating into the earth than if it had fallen on the road.

The stony ground was not ground filled with stones; it was what was common in Palestine, a thin skin of earth on top of an underlying shelf of limestone rock. The earth might be only a very few inches deep before the rock was reached. On such ground the seed would certainly germinate; and it would germinate quickly, because the ground grew speedily warm with the heat of the sun. But there was no depth of earth and when it sent down its roots in search of nourishment and moisture, it would meet only the rock, and would be starved to death, and quite unable to withstand the heat of the sun.

The thorny ground was deceptive. When the sower was sowing, the ground would look clean enough. It is easy to make a garden look clean by simply turning it over; but in the ground still lay the fibrous roots of the couch grass and the bishop weed and all the perennial pests, ready to spring to life again. Every gardener knows that the weeds grow with a speed and a strength that few good seeds can equal. The result was that the good seed and the dormant weeds grew together; but the weeds were so strong that they throttled the life out of the seed.

The good ground was deep and clean and soft; the seed could gain an entry; it could find nourishment; it could grow unchecked; and in the good ground it brought forth an abundant harvest.

THE WORD AND THE HEARER

Matthew 13: 1–9, 18–23 (*continued*)

THIS parable is really aimed at two sets of people.

(*a*) It is aimed at the *hearers of the word*. It is fairly frequently held by scholars that the interpretation of the parable in verses 18–23 is not the interpretation of Jesus himself, but the interpretation of the preachers of the early Church, and that it is not in fact correct. It is said that it transgresses the law that a parable is not an allegory, and that it is too detailed to be grasped by listeners at first hearing. If Jesus was really pointing at an actual sower sowing seed, that does not seem a valid objection; and, in any event, the interpretation which identifies the different kinds of soil with different kinds of hearers has always held its place in the Church's thought, and must surely have come from some authoritative source. If so, why not from Jesus himself?

If we take the parable as a warning to hearers, it means that there are different ways of accepting the word of God, and the fruit which it produces depends on the heart of him who accepts it. The fate of any spoken word depends on the hearer. As it has been said, " A jest's prosperity lies not in the tongue of him who tells it, but in the ear of him who hears it." A jest will succeed when it is told to a man who has a sense of humour and is prepared to smile. A jest will fail when it is told to a humourless creature or to a man grimly determined not to be amused. Who then are the hearers described and warned in this parable?

(i) There is the hearer *with the shut mind*. There are people

into whose minds the word has no more chance of gaining entry
than the seed has of settling into the ground that has been
beaten hard by many feet. There are many things which can
shut a man's mind. Prejudice can make a man blind to
everything he does not wish to see. The unteachable spirit can
erect a barrier which cannot easily be broken down. The
unteachable spirit can result from one of two things. It can be
the result of pride which does not know that it needs to know;
and it can be the result of the fear of new truth and the refusal to
adventure on the ways of thought. Sometimes an immoral
character and a man's way of life can shut his mind. There may
be truth which condemns the things he loves and which accuses
the things he does; and many a man refuses to listen to or to
recognize the truth which condemns him, for there are none so
blind as those who deliberately will not see.

(ii) There is the hearer with the mind like the shallow ground.
He is the man who *fails to think things out and think them
through.*

Some people are at the mercy of every new craze. They take
a thing up quickly and just as quickly drop it. They must
always be in the fashion. They begin some new hobby or begin
to acquire some new accomplishment with enthusiasm, but the
thing becomes difficult and they abandon it, or the enthusiasm
wanes and they lay it aside. Some people's lives are littered with
things they began and never finished. A man can be like that
with the word. When he hears it he may be swept off his feet
with an emotional reaction; but no man can live on an emotion.
A man has a mind and it is a moral obligation to have an
intelligent faith. Christianity has its demands, and these
demands must be faced before it can be accepted. The Christian
offer is not only a privilege, it is also a responsibility. A sudden
enthusiasm can always so quickly become a dying fire.

(iii) There is the hearer who has *so many interests in life that
often the most important things, get crowded out.* It is characteristic of modern life that it becomes increasingly crowded and
increasingly fast. A man becomes too busy to pray; he becomes
so preoccupied with many things that he forgets to study the

word of God: he can become so involved in committees and good works and charitable services that he leaves himself no time for him from whom all love and service come. His business can take such a grip of him that he is too tired to think of anything else. It is not the things which are obviously bad which are dangerous. It is the things which are good, for the " second best is always the worst enemy of the best." It is not even that a man deliberately banishes prayer and the Bible and the Church from his life; it can be that he often thinks of them and intends to make time for them, but somehow in his crowded life never gets round to it. We must be careful to see that Christ is not shouldered out of the topmost niche in life.

(iv) There is the man who is like the good ground. In his reception of the word there are four stages. Like the good ground, *his mind is open.* He is at all times willing to learn. He is prepared *to hear.* He is never either too proud or too busy to listen. Many a man would have been saved all kinds of heartbreak, if he had simply stopped to listen to the voice of a wise friend, or to the voice of God. *He understands.* He has thought the thing out and knows what this means for him, and is prepared to accept it. *He translates his hearing into action.* He produces the good fruit of the good seed. The real hearer is the man who listens, who understands, and who obeys.

NO DESPAIR

Matthew 13: 1–9, 18–23 (*continued*)

(*b*) We said this parable had a double impact. We have looked at the impact it was designed to have on *those who hear the word.* But it was equally designed to have an impact on *those who preach the word.* Not only was it meant to say something to the listening growds; it was also meant to say something to the inner circle of the disciples.

It is not difficult to see that in the hearts of the disciples there must sometimes have been a certain discouragement. To them

Jesus was everything, the wisest and the most wonderful of all.
But, humanly speaking, he had very little success. The doors of
the synagogue were shutting against him. The leaders of
orthodox religion were his bitterest critics and were obviously
out to destroy him. True, the crowds came to hear him, but
there were so few who were really changed, and so many who
came to reap the benefit of his healing power, and, who, when
they had received it, went away and forgot. There were so many
who came to Jesus only for what they could get. The disciples
were faced with a situation in which Jesus seemed to rouse
nothing but hostility in the leaders of the Church, and nothing
but a very evanescent response in the crowd. It is nothing
surprising if in the hearts of the disciples there was sometimes
deep disappointment. What then does the parable say to the
preacher who is discouraged?

Its lesson is clear—*the harvest is sure*. For discouraged
preachers of the word the lesson is in the climax of the parable,
in the picture of the seed which brought forth abundant fruit.
Some seed may fall by the wayside and be snatched away by
the birds; some seed may fall on the shallow ground and never
come to maturity; some seed may fall among the thorns and be
choked to death; but in spite of all that *the harvest does come*.
No farmer expects every single seed he sows to germinate and
bring forth fruit. He knows quite well that some will be blown
away by the wind, and some will fall in places where it cannot
grow; but that does not stop him sowing. Nor does it make him
give up hope of the harvest. The farmer sows in the confidence
that, even if some of the seed is wasted, none the less the harvest
will certainly come.

So then this is a parable of encouragement to those who sow
the seed of the word.

(i) When a man sows the seed of the word, he does not know
what he is doing or what effect the seed is having. H. L. Gee
tells this story. In the church where he worshipped there was a
lonely old man, old Thomas. He had outlived all his friends and
hardly anyone knew him. When Thomas died, Gee had the
feeling that there would be no one to go to the funeral so he

decided to go, so that there might be someone to follow the old man to his last resting-place.

There was no one else and it was a wild, wet day. The funeral reached the cemetery; and at the gate there was a soldier waiting. He was an officer, but on his raincoat there were no rank badges. The soldier came to the graveside for the ceremony; when it was over he stepped forward and before the open grave swept his hand to a salute that might have been given to a king. H. L. Gee walked away with this soldier, and as they walked, the wind blew the soldier's raincoat open to reveal the shoulder badges of a brigadier.

The brigadier said to Gee: " You will perhaps be wondering what I am doing here. Years ago Thomas was my Sunday School teacher; I was a wild lad and a sore trial to him. He never knew what he did for me, but I owe everything I am or will be to old Thomas, and today I had to come to salute him at the end." Thomas did not know what he was doing. No preacher or teacher ever does. It is our task to sow the seed, and to leave the rest to God.

(ii) When a man sows the seed, he must not look for quick results. There is never any haste in nature's growth. It takes a long, long time before an acorn becomes an oak; and it may take a long, long time before the seed germinates in the heart of a man. But often a word dropped into a man's heart in his boyhood lies dormant until some day it awakens and saves him from some great temptation or even preserves his soul from death. We live in an age which looks for quick results, but in the sowing of the seed we must sow in patience and in hope, and sometimes must leave the harvest to the years.

THE TRUTH AND THE LISTENER

Matthew 13: 10–17, 34, 35

The disciples came and said to him: " Why do you speak to them in parables? " " To you," he answered them, " it has been given to know the secrets of the Kingdom, which only a disciple can

understand, but to them it has not been so given. For it will be
given to him who already has, and he will have an overflowing
knowledge. But what he has will be taken away from him who has
not. It is for that reason that I speak to them in parables, for
although they can see, they do not see; and although they can
hear, they do not hear or understand. There is being fulfilled in
them Isaiah's prophecy which says, ' You will certainly hear, but
you will not understand; and you will certainly look, but you will
not see; for the heart of this people has grown fat, and they hear
dully with their ears, and their eyes are smeared, lest at any time
they should see with their eyes, and hear with their ears, and
understand with their heart, and turn, and I will heal them. But
blessed are your eyes for they see, and your ears because they
hear.' This is the truth I tell you—many prophets and righteous
men longed to see things that you are seeing, and did not see them,
and to hear the things that you are hearing, and did not hear them.

. . . .

Jesus spake all these things to the crowds in parables, and it
was not his custom to speak to them without a parable. He did
this that that which was spoken through the prophet might be
fulfilled: " I will open my mouth in parables: I will utter things
which have been hidden since the foundation of the world."

THIS is a passage full of difficult things; and we must take time
to try to seek out its meaning. First of all there are two general
things at the beginning which, if we understand them, will go far
to light up the whole passage.

The Greek word in verse 11, which I have translated *secrets*
(as the Revised Standard Version also does), is *musteria*. This
means literally *mysteries* which is, in fact, how the Authorized
Version renders it. In New Testament times this word *mystery*
was used in a special and a technical way. To us a *mystery*
means simply something dark and difficult and impossible to
understand, something *mysterious*. But in New Testament times
it was the technical name for something which was unintel-
ligible to the outsider but crystal clear to the man who had been
initiated.

In the time of Jesus in both Greece and Rome the most
intense and real religion was found in what were known as the

Mystery Religions. These religions had all a common character. They were in essence passion plays in which was told in drama the story of some god or goddess who had lived and suffered and died and who had risen again to blessedness. The initiate was given a long course of instruction in which the inner meaning of the drama was explained to him; that course of instruction extended over months and even years. Before he was allowed finally to see the drama he had to undergo a period of fasting and abstinence. Everything was done to work him·up to a state of emotion and of expectation. He was then taken to see the play; the atmosphere was carefully constructed; there was cunning lighting; there were incenses and perfumes; there was sensuous music; there was in many cases a noble liturgy. The drama was then played out; and it was intended to produce in the worshipper a complete identification with the god whose story was told on the stage. The worshipper was intended literally to share in the divinity's life and sufferings and death and resurrection, and therefore shared in his immortality. The cry of the worshipper in the end was: " I am Thou, and Thou art I."

We take an actual example. One of the most famous of all the mysteries was the mystery of Isis. Osiris was a wise and good king. Seth, his wicked brother, hated him, and with seventy-two conspirators persuaded him to come to a banquet. There he persuaded him to enter a cunningly wrought coffin which exactly fitted him. When Osiris was in the coffin, the lid was snapped down and the coffin was flung into the Nile. After long and weary search, Isis, the faithful wife of Osiris, found the coffin and brought it home in mourning. But when she was absent from home, the wicked Seth came again, stole the body of Osiris, cut it into fourteen pieces, and scattered it throughout all Egypt. Once again Isis set out on her weary and sorrowful quest. After long search she found all the pieces; by a wondrous power the pieces were fitted together and Osiris rose from the dead; and he became for ever afterwards the immortal king of the living and the dead.

It is easy to see how moving a story that could be made to

one who had undergone a long instruction, to one who saw it in the most carefully calculated setting. There is the story of the good king; there is the attack of sin; there is the sorrowing search of love; there is the triumphant finding of love; there is the raising to a life which has conquered death. It was with that experience that the worshipper was meant to identify himself, and he was supposed to emerge from it, in the famous phrase of the Mystery Religions, " reborn for eternity ".

That is a mystery; something meaningless to the outsider, but supremely precious to the initiate. In point of fact the Lord's Supper is like that. To one who has never seen such a thing before, it will look like a company of men eating little pieces of bread and drinking little sips of wine, and it might even appear ridiculous. But to the man who knows what he is doing, to the man initiated into its meaning, it is the most precious and the most moving act of worship in the Church.

So Jesus says to his disciples: " Outsiders cannot understand what I say; but you know me; you are my disciples; you can understand." Christianity *can be understood only from the inside.* It is only after personal encounter with Jesus Christ that a man can understand. To criticize from outside is to criticize in ignorance. It is only the man who is prepared to become a disciple who can enter into the most precious things of the Christian faith.

LIFE'S STERN LAW

Matthew 13: 10–17, 34, 35 (*continued*)

THE second general thing is the saying in verse 12 that still more will be given to the man who has, and even what he has will be taken away from the man who has not. At first sight this seems nothing less than cruel; but so far from being cruel, it simply states a truth which is an inescapable law of life.

In every sphere of life more is given to the man who has, and what he has is taken away from the man who has not. In the world of scholarship the student who labours to amass knowledge is capable of acquiring more knowledge. It is to him that the research, the advanced courses, the deeper things are given; and that is so because by his diligence and fidelity he has made himself fit to receive them. On the other hand, the student who is lazy and refuses to work inevitably loses even the knowledge which he has.

Many a person in childhood and schooldays had a smattering of Latin or of French or of some other language, and in later life lost every word, because he never made any attempt to develop or use them. Many a person had some skill in a craft or game and lost it, because he neglected it. The diligent and hard-working person is in a position to be given more and more; the lazy person may well lose even what he has. Any gift can be developed; and, since nothing in life stands still, if a gift is not developed, it is lost.

It is so with goodness. Every temptation we conquer makes us more able to conquer the next and every temptation to which we fall makes us less able to withstand the next attack. Every good thing we do, every act of self-discipline and of service, makes us better able for the next; and every time we fail to use such an opportunity we make ourselves less able to seize the next when it comes.

Life is always a process of gaining more or losing more. Jesus laid down the truth that the nearer a man lives to him, the nearer to the Christian ideal he will grow. And the more a man drifts away from Christ, the less he is able to reach to goodness; for weakness, like strength, is an increasing thing.

MAN'S BLINDNESS AND GOD'S PURPOSE

Matthew 13: 10–17, 34, 35 (*continued*)

VERSES 13–17 of this passage are among the most difficult verses in the whole gospel narrative. And the fact that they appear differently in the different gospels shows how much that difficulty was felt in the early Church. Being the earliest gospel, we would expect *Mark* to be the nearest to the actual words of Jesus. It (4: 11, 12) has:

> To you has been given the secret of the kingdom of God, but for those outside everything is in parables; so that they may indeed see but not perceive, and may indeed hear but not understand; lest they should turn again, and be forgiven.

If these verses be taken at their superficial value with no attempt to understand their real meaning, they make the extraordinary statement that Jesus spoke to men in parables in order that they might not understand, and in order to prevent them turning to God and finding forgiveness.

Matthew is later than *Mark* and makes one significant change:

> This is why I speak to them in parables, because seeing they do not see, and hearing they do not here, nor do they understand.

As *Matthew* has it, Jesus spoke in parables because men were too blind and deaf to glimpse the truth in any other way.

It is to be noted that this saying of Jesus leads into a quotation from *Isaiah* 6: 9, 10. That was another passage which caused a great deal of heart-searching. In the Revised Standard Version, which is a literal translation of the Hebrew, it runs:

> Go, and say to this people: " Hear and hear, but do not understand; see and see, but do not perceive." Make the heart of this people fat, and their ears heavy, and shut their eyes; lest they see with their eyes, and hear with their ears, and understand with their hearts, and turn and be healed.

Again it sounds as if God had deliberately blinded the eyes and deafened the ears and hardened the hearts of the people, so that they would be unable to understand. The nation's lack of understanding is made to seem a deliberate act of God.

Just as *Matthew* toned down *Mark*, so the *Septuagint*, the Greek translation of the Hebrew scriptures, and the version which most Jews used in the time of Jesus, toned down the original Hebrew:

Go, say to this people: " Ye shall hear indeed, but ye shall not understand; and seeing ye shall see and not perceive." For the heart of this people has become gross, and with their ears they hear heavily, and their eyes they have closed, lest at any time they should see with their eyes, and hear with their ears, and understand with their heart, and should be converted, and I should heal them.

The *Septuagint*, so to speak, removes the responsibility from God and lays it fairly and squarely upon the people.

What is the explanation of all this? We may be certain of one thing—whatever else this passage means, it cannot mean that Jesus deliberately delivered his message in such a way that people would fail to understand it. Jesus did not come to hide the truth from men; he came to reveal it. And beyond a doubt there were times when men grasped that truth.

When the orthodox Jewish leaders heard the threat of the Parable of the Wicked Husbandmen, they understood all right, and recoiled in horror from its message to say: " God forbid! " (*Luke* 20: 16). And in verses 34 and 35 of this present passage Jesus quotes a saying of the Psalmist:

Give ear, O my people, to my teaching; incline your ears to the words of my mouth. I will open my mouth in a parable; I will utter dark sayings from of old, things that we have heard and known, that our fathers have told us.

That is a quotation from *Psalm* 78: 1–3, and in it the Psalmist knows that what he is saying will be understood, and that he is recalling men to truth that both they and their fathers have known.

The truth is that the words of Isaiah, and the use that Jesus made of them, must be read with insight and with an attempt to put ourselves in the position both of Isaiah and of Jesus. These words tell of three things.

(i) They tell of a prophet's *bewilderment*. The prophet brought a message to people which to him was crystal clear; and he was bewildered that they could not understand it. That is repeatedly the experience of both the preacher and the teacher. Often when we preach or teach or discuss things with people, we try to tell them something which to us is relevant, vivid, of absorbing interest and of paramount importance, and they hear it with a complete lack of interest, understanding, and urgency. And we are amazed and bewildered that what means so much to us apparently means nothing at all to them, that what kindles a fire in our bones leaves them stone cold, that what thrills and moves our hearts leaves them icily indifferent. That is the experience of every teacher and preacher and evangelist.

(ii) They tell of a prophet's *despair*. It was Isaiah's feeling that his preaching was actually doing more harm than good, that he might as well speak to a brick wall, that there was no way into the mind and the heart of this deaf and blind people, that, as far as any effects went, they seemed to be getting worse instead of better. Again that is the experience of every teacher and preacher. There are times when those whom we seek to win seem, in spite of all our efforts, to be getting further away from, instead of nearer to, the Christian way. Our words go whistling down the wind; our message meets the impenetrable barrier of men's indifference; the result of all our work seems less than nothing, for at the end of it men seem further away from God than they were at the beginning.

(iii) But these words tell of something more than a prophet's bewilderment and a prophet's despair; they also tell of a prophet's *ultimate faith*. Here we find ourselves face to face with a Jewish conviction apart from which much of what the prophet, and of what Jesus, and of what the early Church said is not fully intelligible.

To put it simply, it was a primary article of Jewish belief that *nothing in this world happens outside the will of God*; and when they said *nothing* they meant *literally nothing*. It was just as much God's will when men did not listen as when they did; it was just as much God's will when men refused to understand the truth as when they welcomed it. The Jew clung fast to the belief that everything had its place in the purpose of God and that somehow God was weaving together success and failure, good and evil in a web of his designing.

The ultimate purpose of everything was good. It is exactly

this thought that Paul plays on in *Romans* 9: 11. These are the chapters which tell how the Jews, the chosen people of God, actually refused God's truth and crucified God's son when he came to them. That sounds inexplicable. But what was the result of it? The gospel went out to the Gentiles; and the ultimate result is that the Gentiles will some day gather in the Jews. The apparent evil is gathered up in a larger good, for all is within the plan of God.

That is what Isaiah was feeling. At first he was bewildered and in despair; then the light came and in effect he said " I cannot understand the conduct of this people; but I know that all this failure is somehow in the ultimate purpose of God, and he will use it for his own ultimate glory and for the ultimate good of men." Jesus took these words of Isaiah and used them to encourage his disciples; he said in effect, " I know that this looks disappointing; I know how you are feeling when men's minds and hearts refuse to receive the truth and when their eyes refuse to recognize it; but in this, too, there is purpose—and some day you will see it."

Here is our own great encouragement. Sometimes we see our harvest and we are glad; sometimes there seems to be nothing but barren ground, nothing but total lack of response, nothing but failure. That may be so to human eyes and human minds, but at the back of it there is a God who is fitting even that failure into the divine plan of his omniscient mind and his omnipotent power. There are no failures and there are no loose ends in the ultimate plan of God.

THE ACT OF AN ENEMY

Matthew 13: 24–30, 36–43

Jesus put forward another parable. " The Kingdom of Heaven," he said to them, " is like what happened when a man sowed good seed in his field. When men slept, his enemy came and sowed darnel in the middle of the corn, and went away. When the green grain grew, and when it began to produce its crop, then the darnel

appeared. The servants of the master of the house came to him
and said, ' Sir, did we not sow good seed in your field? From
where, then, did it get the darnel? ' ' An enemy has done this,' he
said to them. The servants said to him, ' Do you wish us to go and
collect the darnel? ' But he said, ' No; for if you gather the darnel
the danger is that you may root up the corn at the same time. Let
them both grow together until the harvest time; and at the time of
the harvest I will say to the reapers, " First gather the darnel and
bind them into bundles for burning. But gather the corn into my
storehouse." ' "

.   .   .   .

When he had sent the crowds away, he went into the house. His
disciples came to him. " Explain to us," they said, " The parable
of the darnel in the field." He answered: " He who sows the good
seed is the Son of Man. The field is the world. The good seed
stands for the sons of the Kingdom; the darnel is the sons of the
evil one. The enemy who sowed it is the devil. The harvest is the
end of this age; the reapers are the angels. Just as the darnel is
gathered and burned with fire, so it will be at the end of this age.
The Son of Man will send his angels, and they will gather all the
stumbling-blocks, and all those who act lawlessly, out of the
Kingdom, and will cast them into the furnace of fire; and weeping
and gnashing of teeth will be there. Then the righteous will shine
as the sun in the Kingdom of their Father. Who has ears let him
hear."

THE pictures in this parable would be clear and familiar
to a Palestinian audience. Tares were one of the curses
against which a farmer had to labour. They were a weed
called bearded darnel (*lolium temulentum*). In their early
stages the tares so closely resembled the wheat that it was
impossible to distinguish the one from the other. When both
had headed out it was easy to distinguish them; but by that
time their roots were so intertwined that the tares could not be
weeded out without tearing the wheat out with them.

Thomson in *The Land and the Book* tells how he saw the
tares in the Wady Hamam: " The grain is just in the proper
stage of development to illustrate the parable. In those parts
where the grain has headed out, the tares have done the same,

and there a child cannot mistake them for wheat or barley; but when both are less developed, the closest scrutiny will often fail to detect them. I cannot do it at all with any confidence. Even the farmers, who in this country generally weed their fields, do not attempt to separate the one from the other. They would not only mistake good grain for them, but very commonly the roots of the two are so intertwined that it is impossible to separate them without plucking up both. Both, therefore, must be left to grow together until the time of harvest."

The tares and the wheat are so like each other that the Jews called the tares *bastard wheat*. The Hebrew for tares is *zunim*, whence comes the Greek *zizanion*; *zunim* is said to be connected with the word *zanah*, which means *to commit fornication*; and the popular story is that the tares took their origin in the time of wickedness which preceded the flood, for at that time the whole creation, men, animals and plants, all went astray, and committed fornication and brought forth contrary to nature. In their early stages the wheat and the tares so closely resembled each other that the popular idea was that the tares were a kind of wheat which had gone wrong.

The wheat and tares could not be safely separated when both were growing, but in the end they had to be separated, because the grain of the bearded darnel is slightly poisonous. It causes dizziness and sickness and is narcotic in its effects, and even a small amount has a bitter and unpleasant 'taste. In the end it was usually separated by hand. Levison describes the process: " Women have to be hired to pick the darnel grain out of the seed which is to be milled. . . . As a rule the separation of the darnel from the wheat is done after the threshing. By spreading the grain out on a large tray which is set before the women, they are able to pick out the darnel, which is a seed similar in shape and size to wheat, but slate-grey in colour."

So then the darnel in its early stages was indistinguishable from the wheat, but in the end it had to be laboriously separated from it, or the consequences were serious.

The picture of a man deliberately sowing darnel in someone else's field is by no means only imagination. That was actually sometimes done. To this day in India one of the direst threats which a man can make to his enemy is " I will sow bad seed in your field." And in codified Roman law this crime is forbidden and its punishment laid down.

The whole series of pictures within this parable was familiar to the people of Galilee who heard it for the first time.

THE TIME FOR JUDGMENT

Matthew 13: 24–30, 36–43 (*continued*)

IT may well be said that in its lessons this is one of the most practical parables Jesus ever told.

(i) It teaches us that there is always a hostile power in the world, seeking and waiting to destroy the good seed. Our experience is that both kinds of influence act upon our lives, the influence which helps the seed of the word to flourish and to grow, and the influence which seeks to destroy the good seed before it can produce fruit at all. The lesson is that we must be for ever on our guard.

(ii) It teaches us how hard it is to distinguish between those who are in the Kingdom and those who are not. A man may appear to be good and may in fact be bad; and a man may appear to be bad and may yet be good. We are much too quick to classify people and label them good or bad without knowing all the facts.

(iii) It teaches us not to be so quick with our judgments. If the reapers had had their way, they would have tried to tear out the darnel and they would have torn out the wheat as well. Judgment had to wait until the harvest came. A man in the end will be judged, not by any single act or stage in his life, but by his whole life. Judgment cannot come until the end. A man may make a great mistake, and then redeem himself and, by the grace of God, atone for it by making the rest of life a lovely thing. A man may live an honourable life and then in the end wreck it all by a sudden collapse into sin. No one who sees only part of a thing can judge the whole; and no one who knows only part of a man's life can judge the whole man.

(iv) It teaches us that judgment does come in the end. Judgment is not hasty, but judgment comes. It may be that, humanly speaking, in this life the sinner seems to escape the consequences, but there is a life to come. It may be that, humanly speaking, goodness never seems to enter into its reward, but there is a new world to redress the balance of the old.

(v) It teaches us that the only person with the right to judge is God. It is God alone who can discern the good and the bad; it is God alone who sees all of a man and all of his life. It is God alone who can judge.

So, then, ultimately this parable is two things—it is a warning not to judge people at all, and it is a warning that in the end there comes the judgment of God.

THE SMALL BEGINNING

Matthew 13: 31, 32

> Jesus put forward another parable to them: " The Kingdom of Heaven is like a grain of mustard seed, which a man took and sowed in his field. It is the smallest of all seeds, and, when it has grown, it is the greatest of herbs, and it becomes a tree, so that the birds of the air come and lodge in its branches."

THE mustard plant of Palestine was very different from the mustard plant which we know in this country. To be strictly accurate the mustard seed is not the smallest of seeds; the seed of the cypress tree, for instance, is still smaller; but in the east it was proverbial for smallness. For example, the Jews talked of a drop of blood as small as a mustard seed; or, if they were talking of some tiny breach of the ceremonial law, they would speak of a defilement as small as a mustard seed; and Jesus himself used the phrase in this way when he spoke of faith as a grain of mustard seed (*Matthew* 17: 20).

In Palestine this little grain of mustard seed did grow into something very like a tree. Thomson in *The Land and the Book* writes: " I have seen this plant on the rich plain of Akkar as tall as the horse and his rider." He says, " With the help of my guide, I uprooted a veritable mustard-tree which was more than twelve feet high." In this parable there is no exaggeration at all.

Further, it was a common sight to see such mustard bushes or trees surrounded with a cloud of birds, for the birds love the little black seeds of the tree, and settle on the tree to eat them.

Jesus said that his Kingdom was like the mustard seed and its growth into a tree. The point is crystal clear. The Kingdom of Heaven starts from the smallest beginnings, but no man knows where it will end. In eastern language and in the Old Testament itself one of the commonest pictures of a great empire is the picture of a great tree, with the subject nations depicted as birds finding rest and shelter within its branches (*Ezekiel* 31: 6). This parable tells us that the Kingdom of Heaven begins very small but that in the end many nations will be gathered within it.

It is the fact of history that the greatest things must always begin with the smallest beginnings.

(i) An idea which may well change civilization begins with one man. In the British Empire it was William Wilberforce who was responsible for the freeing of the slaves. The idea of that liberation came to him when he read an exposure of the slave trade by Thomas Clarkson. He was a close friend of Pitt, then Prime Minister, and one day he was sitting with him and George Grenville in Pitt's garden at Holwood. It was a scene of beauty, with the Vale of Keston opening out before them, but the thoughts of Wilberforce were not on that but on the blots of the world. Suddenly Pitt turned to him: " Wilberforce," he said, " why don't you give a notice of a motion on the slave-trade? " An idea was sown in the mind of one man, and that idea changed life for hundreds of thousands of people. An idea must find a man willing to be possessed by it; but when it finds such a man an unstoppable tide begins to flow.

(ii) A witness must begin with one man. Cecil Northcott tells

in one of his books that a group of young people from many
nations were discussing how the Christian gospel might be
spread. They talked of propaganda, of literature, of all the ways
of disseminating the gospel in the twentieth century. Then the
girl from Africa spoke. " When we want to take Christianity to
one of our villages," she said, " we don't send them books. We
take a Christian family and send them to live in the village and
they make the village Christian by living there." In a group or
society, or school or factory, or shop or office, again and again
it is the witness of one individual which brings in Christianity.
The one man or woman set on fire for Christ is the person who
kindles others.

(iii) A reformation begins with one person. One of the great
stories of the Christian Church is the story of Telemachus. He
was a hermit of the desert, but something told him—the call of
God—that he must go to Rome. He went. Rome was nominally
Christian, but even in Christian Rome the gladiatorial games
went on, in which men fought with each other, and crowds
roared with the lust for blood. Telemachus found his way to the
games. Eighty thousand people were there to spectate. He was
horrified. Were these men slaughtering each other not also
children of God? He leaped from his seat, right into the arena,
and stood between the gladiators. He was tossed aside. He
came back. The crowd were angry; they began to stone him.
Still he struggled back between the gladiators. The prefect's
command rang out; a sword flashed in the sunlight, and
Telemachus was dead. Suddenly there was a hush; suddenly the
crowd realized what had happened; a holy man lay dead.
Something happened that day to Rome, for there were never
again any gladiatorial games. By his death one man had let
loose something that cleansed an empire. Someone must begin a
reformation; he need not begin it in a nation; he may begin it in
his home or where he works. If he begins it no man knows
where it will end.

(iv) But this was one of the most personal parables Jesus ever
spoke. Sometimes his disciples must have despaired. Their little
band was so small and the world was so wide. How could they

ever win and change it. Yet with Jesus an invincible force entered the world. Hugh Martin quotes H. G. Wells as saying, " His is easily the dominant figure in history. ... A historian without any theological bias whatever should find that he simply cannot portray the progress of humanity honestly without giving a foremost place to a penniless teacher from Nazareth." In this parable Jesus is saying to his disciples, and to his followers today, that there must be no discouragement, that they must serve and witness each in his place, that each one must be the small beginning from which the Kingdom grows until the kingdoms of the earth finally become the Kingdom of God

> " Though few and small and weak your bands,
>   Strong in your Captain's strength,
>   Go to the conquest of all lands;
>   All must be His at length."

THE TRANSFORMING POWER OF CHRIST

Matthew 13: 33

> He spoke another parable to them: " The Kingdom of Heaven is like leaven, which a woman took and hid in three measures of meal, until the whole was leavened."

IN this chapter there is nothing more significant than the sources from which Jesus drew his parables. In every case he drew them from the scenes and activities of everyday life. He began with things which were entirely familiar to his hearers in order to lead them to things which had never yet entered their minds. He took the parable of the sower from the farmer's field and the parable of the mustard seed from the husbandman's garden; he took the parable of the wheat and the tares from the perennial problem which confronts the farmer in his struggle with the weeds, and the parable of the drag-net from the seashore of the Sea of Galilee. He took the parable of the hidden treasure from the everyday task of digging in a field, and the parable of the pearl of great price from the world of commerce and trade. But in this parable of the leaven Jesus came nearer home than in any other because he took it from the kitchen of an ordinary house.

In Palestine bread was baked at home; three measures of meal was, as Levinson points out, just the average amount which would be needed for a baking for a fairly large family, like the family at Nazareth. Jesus took his parable of the Kingdom from something that he had often seen his mother, Mary, do. Leaven was a little piece of dough kept over from a previous baking, which had fermented in the keeping.

In Jewish language and thought leaven is almost always connected with an *evil* influence; the Jews connected fermentation with putrefaction and leaven stood for that which is evil (cp. *Matthew* 16: 6; 1 *Corinthians* 5: 6–8; *Galatians* 5: 9). One of the ceremonies of preparation for the Passover Feast was that every scrap of leaven had to be sought out from the house and burned. It may well be that Jesus chose this illustration of the Kingdom deliberately. There would be a certain shock in hearing the Kingdom of God compared to leaven; and the shock would arouse interest and rivet attention, as an illustration from an unusual and unexpected source always does.

The whole point of the parable lies in one thing—*the transforming power of the leaven*. Leaven changed the character of a whole baking. Unleavened bread is like a water biscuit, hard, dry, unappetizing and uninteresting; bread baked with leaven is soft and porous and spongy, tasty and good to eat. The introduction of the leaven causes a transformation in the dough; and the coming of the Kingdom causes a transformation in life.

Let us gather together the characteristics of this transformation.

(i) Christianity transformed life for *the individual man*. In 1 *Corinthians* 6: 9, 10, Paul gathers together a list of the most terrible and disgusting kinds of sinners, and then, in the next verse, there comes the tremendous statement: " And such were some of you." As Denney had it, we must never forget that the function and the power of Christ is to make bad men good. The transformation of Christianity begins in the individual life, for through Christ the victim of temptation can become the victor over it.

(ii) There are four great social directions in which Christianity transformed life. Christianity transformed life for *women*. The Jew in his morning prayer thanked God that he had not made him a Gentile, a slave or a woman. In Greek civilization the woman lived a life of utter seclusion, with nothing to do beyond the household tasks. K. J. Freeman writes of the life of the Greek child or young man even in the great days of Athens, " When he came home, there was no home life. His father was hardly ever in the house. His mother was a nonentity, living in the women's apartments; he probably saw little of her." In the eastern lands it was often possible to see a family on a journey. The father would be mounted on an ass; the mother would be walking, and probably bent beneath a burden. One demonstrable historical truth is that Christianity transformed life for women.

(iii) Christianity transformed life for *the weak and the ill*. In heathen life the weak and the ill were considered a nuisance. In Sparta a child, when he was born, was submitted to the examiners; if he was fit, he was allowed to live; if he was weakly or deformed, he was exposed to death on the mountain side. Dr. A. Rendle Short points out that the first blind asylum was founded by Thalasius, a Christian monk; the first free dispensary was founded by Apollonius, a Christian merchant; the first hospital of which there is any record was founded by Fabiola, a Christian lady. Christianity was the first faith to be interested in the broken things of life.

(iv) Christianity transformed life for *the aged*. Like the weak, the aged were a nuisance. Cato, the Roman writer on agriculture, gives advice to anyone who is taking over a farm: " Look over the livestock and hold a sale. Sell your oil, if the price is satisfactory, and sell the surplus of your wine and grain. Sell worn-out oxen, blemished cattle, blemished sheep, wool, hides, an old wagon, old tools, *an old slave, a sickly slave*, and whatever else is superfluous." The old, whose day's work was done, were fit for nothing else than to be discarded on the rubbish heaps of life. Christianity was the first faith to regard men as persons and not instruments capable of doing so much work.

(v) Christianity transformed life for *the child*. In the immediate background of Christianity, the marriage relationship had broken down, and the home was in peril. Divorce was so common that it was neither unusual nor particularly blameworthy for a woman to have a new husband every year. In such circumstances children were a disaster; and the custom of simply exposing children to death was tragically common. There is a well-known letter from a man Hilarion, who was gone off to Alexandria, to his wife Alis, whom he has left at home. He writes to her: " If—good luck to you—you bear a child, if it is a boy, let it live; if it is a girl, throw it out." In modern civilization life is almost built round the child; in ancient civilization the child had a very good chance of dying before it had begun to live.

Anyone who asks the question: " What has Christianity done for the world? " has delivered himself into a Christian debator's hands. There is nothing in history so unanswerably demonstrable as the transforming power of Christianity and of Christ on the individual life and on the life of society.

THE WORKING OF THE LEAVEN

Matthew 13: 33 (*continued*)

THERE remains only one question in regard to this parable of the leaven. Almost all scholars would agree that it speaks of the transforming power of Christ and of his Kingdom in the life of the individual and of the world; but there is a difference of opinion as to how that transforming power works.

(i) It is sometimes said that the lesson of this parable is that the Kingdom works unseen. We cannot see the leaven working in the dough, any more than we can see a flower growing, but the work of the leaven is always going on. Just so, it is said, we cannot see the work of the Kingdom, but always the Kingdom is working and drawing men and the world ever nearer to God.

This, then, would be a message of encouragement. It would mean that at all times we must take the long view, that we must not compare things of the present day with last week, month, or even last year, but that we must look back down the centuries, and then we will see the steady progress of the Kingdom. As A. H. Clough had it:

> " Say not, ' The struggle nought availeth;
>   The labour and the wounds are vain;
> The enemy faints not nor faileth,
>   And as things have been they remain.'
>
> If hopes were dupes, fears may be liars;
>   It may be, in yon smoke concealed,
> Your comrades chase even now the fliers,
>   And, but for you, possess the field.
>
> For while the tired waves, vainly breaking,
>   Seem here no painful inch to gain,
> Far back, through creeks and inlets making,
>   Comes silent, flooding in, the main.
>
> And, not by eastern windows only,
>   When daylight comes, comes in the light;
> In front the sun climbs slow, how slowly!
>   But westward, look! the land is bright."

On this view the parable teaches that with Jesus Christ and his gospel a new force has been let loose in the world, and that, silently but inevitably, that force is working for righteousness in the world and God indeed is working his purpose out as year succeeds to year.

(ii) But it has sometimes been said, as for instance by C. H. Dodd, that the lesson of the parable is the very opposite of this, and that, so far from being unseen, the working of the Kingdom can be plainly seen. The working of the leaven is plain for all to see. Put the leaven into the dough, and the leaven changes the dough from a passive lump into a seething, bubbling, heaving mass. Just so the working of the Kingdom is a violent and disturbing force plain for all to see. When Christianity came to Thessalonica the cry was: " These men who have turned the world upside down have come here also " (*Acts* 17: 6). The action of Christianity is disruptive, disturbing, violent in its effect.

There is undeniable truth there. It is true that men crucified Jesus Christ because he disturbed all their orthodox habits and conventions; again and again it has been true that Christianity has been persecuted because it desired to take both men and society and remake them. It is abundantly true that there is nothing in this world so disturbing as Christianity; that is, in fact, the reason why so many people resent it and refuse it, and wish to eliminate it.

When we come to think of it, we do not need to choose between these two views of the parable, because they are both true. There is a sense in which the Kingdom, the power of Christ, the Spirit of God, is always working, whether or not we see that work; and there is a sense in which it is plain to see. Many an individual life is manifestly and violently changed by Christ; and at the same time there is the silent operation of the purposes of God in the long road of history.

We may put it in a picture like this. The Kingdom, the power of Christ, the Spirit of God, is like a great river, which for much of its course glides on beneath the ground unseen, but which ever and again comes to the surface in all its greatness, plain for all to see. This parable teaches both that the Kingdom is for ever working unseen, and that there are times in every individual life and in history when the work of the Kingdom is so obvious, and so manifestly powerful, that all can see it.

ALL IN THE DAY'S WORK

Matthew 13: 44

" The Kingdom of Heaven is like a treasure which lay hidden in a field. A man found it, and hid it; and, as a result of his joy, away he goes, and sells everything that he has, and buys the field."

ALTHOUGH this parable sounds strange to us, it would sound perfectly natural to people in Palestine in the days of Jesus, and even to this day it paints a picture which people in the East would know well.

In the ancient world there were banks, but not banks such as ordinary people could use. Ordinary people used the ground as the safest place to keep their most cherished belonging. In the parable of the talents the worthless servant hid his talent in the ground, lest he should lose it (*Matthew* 25: 25). There was a rabbinic saying that there was only one safe repository for money—the earth.

This was still more the case in a land where a man's garden might at any time become a battlefield. Palestine was probably the most fought over country in the world; and, when the tide of war threatened to flow over them, it was common practice for people to hide their valuables in the ground, before they took to flight, in the hope that the day would come when they could return and regain them. Josephus speaks of " the gold and the silver and the rest of that most precious furniture which the Jews had, and which the owners treasured up underground against the uncertain fortunes of war."

Thomson in *The Land and the Book*, which was first published in 1876, tells of a case of treasure discovery which he himself came upon in Sidon. There was in that city a famous avenue of acacia trees. Certain workmen, digging in a garden on that avenue, uncovered several copper pots full of gold coins. They had every intention of keeping the find to themselves; but there were so many of them, and they were so wild with excitement, that their treasure trove was discovered and claimed by the local government. The coins were all coins of Alexander the Great and his father Philip. Thomson suggests that, when Alexander unexpectedly died in Babylon, news came through to Sidon, and some Macedonian officer or government official buried these coins with the intention of appropriating them in the chaos which was bound to follow Alexander's death. Thomson goes on to tell how there are even people who make it their life's business to search for hidden treasure, and

that they get into such a state of excitement that they have been
known to faint at the discovery of one single coin. When Jesus
told this story, he told the kind of story that anyone would
recognize in Palestine and in the east generally.

It may be thought that in this parable Jesus glorifies a man
who was guilty of very sharp practice in that he hid the
treasure, and then took steps to possess himself of it. There are
two things to be said about that. First, although Palestine in the
time of Jesus was under the Romans and under Roman law, in
the ordinary, small, day to day things it was traditional Jewish
law which was used; and in regard to hidden treasure Jewish
Rabbinic law was quite clear: " What finds belong to the finder,
and what finds must one cause to be proclaimed? These finds
belong to the finder—if a man finds scattered fruit, scattered
money . . . these belong to the finder." In point of fact this man
had a prior right to what he had found.

Second, even apart from that, when we are dealing with any
parable, the details are never meant to be stressed; the parable
has one main point, and to that point everything else is
subservient. In this parable the great point is the joy of the
discovery that made the man willing to give up everything to
make the treasure indubitably his own. Nothing else in the
parable really matters.

(i) The lesson of this parable is, first, that the man found the
precious thing, not so much by chance, as *in his day's work*. It
is true to say that he stumbled all unexpectedly upon it, but he
did so *when he was going about his daily business*. And it is
legitimate to infer that he must have been going about his daily
business with diligence and efficiency, because he must have
been digging deep, and not merely scraping the surface, in order
to strike against the treasure. It would be a sad thing, if it were
only in churches, in so-called holy places, and on so-called
religious occasions that we found God, and felt close to him.

There is an unwritten saying of Jesus which never found its
way into any of the gospels, but which rings true: " Raise the
stone and thou shalt find me; cleave the wood and I am there."
When the mason is working on the stone, when the carpenter is

working with the wood, Jesus Christ is there. True happiness, true satisfaction, the sense of God, the presence of Christ are all to be found in the day's work, when that day's work is honestly and conscientiously done. Brother Lawrence, great saint and mystic, spent much of his working life in the monastery kitchen amidst the dirty dishes, and he could say, " I felt Jesus Christ as close to me in the kitchen as ever I did at the blessed sacrament."

(ii) The lesson of this parable is, second, that it is worth any sacrifice to enter the Kingdom. What does it mean to enter the Kingdom? When we were studying the Lord's Prayer (*Matthew* 6: 10), we found that we could say that the Kingdom of God is a state of society upon earth where God's will is as perfectly done as it is in heaven. Therefore to enter the Kingdom is to accept and to do God's will. So, then, it is worth anything to do God's will. Suddenly, as the man discovered the treasure, there may flash upon us, in some moment of illumination, the conviction of what God's will is for us. To accept it may be to give up certain aims and ambitions which are very dear, to abandon certain habits and ways of life which are very difficult to lay down, to take on a discipline and self-denial which are by no means easy, in a word, to take up our cross and follow after Jesus. But there is no other way to peace of mind and heart in this life and to glory in the life to come. It is indeed worth giving up everything to accept and to do the will of God.

THE PRECIOUS PEARL

Matthew 13: 45, 46

" Again, the Kingdom of Heaven is like a merchant who was seeking goodly pearls. When he had found a very valuable pearl, he went away and sold everything he had, and bought it."

IN the ancient world pearls had a very special place in men's hearts. People desired to possess a lovely pearl, not only for its money value, but for its beauty. They found a pleasure in simply handling it and contemplating it. They found an aesthetic joy simply in possessing and looking at a pearl. The main sources of pearls in those days were the shores of the Red Sea and far-off Britain itself; but a merchant would scour the markets of the world to find a pearl which was of surpassing beauty. There are certain most suggestive truths hidden in this parable.

(i) It is suggestive to find the Kingdom of Heaven compared to a pearl. To the ancient peoples, as we have just seen, a pearl was the loveliest of all possessions; that means that the Kingdom of Heaven is the loveliest thing in the world. Let us remember what the Kingdom is. To be in the Kingdom is to accept and to do the will of God. That is to say, to do the will of God is no grim, grey, agonizing thing; it is a lovely thing. Beyond the discipline, beyond the sacrifice, beyond the self-denial, beyond the cross, there lies the supreme loveliness which is nowhere else. There is only one way to bring peace to the heart, joy to the mind, beauty to the life, and that is to accept and to do the will of God.

(ii) It is suggestive to find that there are other pearls but only one pearl of great price. That is to say, there are many fine things in this world and many things in which a man can find loveliness. He can find loveliness in knowledge and in the reaches of the human mind, in art and music and literature and all the triumphs of the human spirit; he can find loveliness in serving his fellow-men, even if that service springs from humanitarian rather than from purely Christian motives; he can find loveliness in human relationships. These are all lovely, but they are all lesser loveliness. The supreme beauty lies in the acceptance of the will of God. This is not to belittle the other things; they too are pearls; but the supreme pearl is the willing obedience which makes us friends of God.

(iii) We find in this parable the same point as in the previous one but with a difference. The man who was digging the field was not searching for treasure; it came on him all unaware. The man who was searching for pearls was spending his life in the search.

But no matter whether the discovery was the result of a moment or the result of a life-time's search, the reaction was the same—everything had to be sold and sacrificed to gain the precious thing. Once again we are left with the same truth—that, however a man discovers the will of God for himself, whether it be in the lightning flash of a moment's illumination or at the end of a long and conscious search, it is worth anything unhesitatingly to accept it.

THE CATCH AND THE SEPARATION

Matthew 13: 47–50

" Again, the Kingdom of Heaven is like a net which was cast into the sea, and which gathered all kinds of things. When it was full, they hauled it up on to the shore, and sat down, and collected the good contents into containers, but threw the useless contents away. So it will be at the end of the age. The angels will come, and they will separate the evil from the righteous, and they will cast them into the furnace of fire. There will be weeping and gnashing of teeth there."

IT was the most natural thing in the world that Jesus should use illustrations from fishing when he was speaking to fishermen. It was as if he said to them: " Look how your daily work speaks to you of the things of heaven."

In Palestine there were two main ways of fishing. One was with the casting-net, the *amphiblēstron*. It was a hand-net which was cast from the shore. Thomson describes the process: " The net is in shape like the top of a bell-tent, with a long cord fastened to the apex. This is tied to the arm, and the net so folded that, when it is thrown, it expands to its utmost circumference, around which are strung beads of lead to make it drop suddenly to the bottom. Now, see the actor; half bent, and more than half naked, he keenly watches the playful surf, and there he spies his game tumbling in carelessly toward him. Forward he leaps to meet it. Away goes the net, expanding as it flies, and its leaded circumference strikes the bottom ere the silly fish is aware that its meshes have closed around him. By the aid of the cord the fishermen leisurely draws up the net and the fish with it. This requires a keen eye, an active frame, and great skill in throwing the net. He, too, must be patient, watchful, wide awake, and prompt to seize the exact moment to throw."

The second way of fishing was with the drag-net, the *sagēnē*, what we would call the seine net or the trawl. This is the way referred to in this parable. The seine net was a great square net with cords at each corner, and weighted so that, at rest, it hung, as it were, upright in the water. When the boat began to move, the net was drawn into the shape of a great cone and into the cone all kinds of fish were swept.

The net was then drawn to land, and the catch was separated. The useless material was flung away; the good was put into containers. It is interesting to note that sometimes the fish were put alive into containers filled with water. There was no other way to transport them in freshness over any time or any distance.

There are two great lessons in this parable.

(i) It is in the nature of the drag-net that it does not, and cannot, discriminate. It is bound to draw in all kinds of things in its course through the water. Its contents are bound to be a mixture. If we apply that to the Church, which is the instrument of God's Kingdom upon earth, it means that the Church cannot be discriminative but is bound to be a mixture of all kinds of people, good and bad, useless and useful.

There have always been two views of the Church—the exclusive and the inclusive. The exclusive view holds that the Church is for people who are good, people who are really and fully committed, people who are quite different from the world. There is an attraction in that view, but it is not the New Testament view, because, apart from anything else, *who is to do the judging*, when we are told that we must not judge? (*Matthew* 7: 1). It is not any man's place to say who is committed to Christ and who is not. The inclusive view feels instinctively that the Church must be open to all, and that, like the drag-net, so long as it is a human institution it is bound to be a mixture. That is exactly what this parable teaches.

(ii) But equally this parable teaches that the time of separation will come when the good and the bad are sent to their respective destinations. That separation, however, certain as it is, is not man's work but God's. Therefore it is our duty to gather in all who will come, and not to judge or separate, but to leave the final judgment to God.

OLD GIFTS USED IN A NEW WAY

Matthew 13: 51, 52

> Jesus said, " Have you understood all these things? " They said to him: " Yes." He said to them: " That is why every scribe, who has been instructed in the Kingdom of Heaven, is like a householder who brings out of his treasure-house things new and old."

WHEN Jesus had finished speaking about the Kingdom, he asked his disciples if they had understood. And they had understood, at least in part. Then Jesus goes on to speak about the scribe, instructed in the Kingdom of Heaven, bringing out of his treasure-house things old and new. What Jesus is in effect saying is this: " You are able to understand, because you came to me with a fine heritage. You came with all the teaching of the law and the prophets. A scribe comes to me with a lifetime of study of the law and of all its commandments. That background helps you to understand. But after you have been instructed by me, you have the knowledge, not only of the things you used to know, but of things you never knew before, and even the knowledge which you had before is illuminated by what I have told to you."

There is something very suggestive here. For it means that Jesus never desired or intended that any man should forget all he knew when he came to him; but that he should see his knowledge in a new light and use it in a new service. When he does that, what he knew before becomes a greater treasure than ever it was.

Every man comes to Jesus Christ with some gift and with some ability. Jesus does not ask that he should give up his gift. So many people think that when a man declares for Christ he must give things up and concentrate upon the so-called religious things. But a scholar does not give up his scholarship when he becomes a Christian; rather he uses it for Christ. A business man need not give up his business; rather he should run it as a Christian would. One who can sing, or dance, or act, or paint need not give up his art, but must use his art as a Christian would. The sportsman need not give up his sport, but must play as a Christian would. Jesus did not come to empty life but to fill it, not to impoverish life but to enrich it. Here we see Jesus telling men, not to abandon their gifts, but to use them even more wonderfully in the light of the knowledge which he has given them.

THE BARRIER OF UNBELIEF

Matthew 13: 53–58

When Jesus had concluded these parables, he left there. He went into his native place and he taught them in their synagogue. His teaching was such that they were astonished and said, " Where did this man get this wisdom and these powers? Is not this the son of the carpenter? Is not his mother called Mary? And are James and Joseph and Simon and Judas not his brothers? Where did he get all these things? " And they were offended at him. Jesus said to them, " A prophet is not without honour except in his own native place and in his own family." And he did not do many deeds of power there because of their unbelief.

IT was natural that at some time Jesus should pay a visit to Nazareth where he had been brought up. And yet it was a brave thing to do. The hardest place for a preacher to preach is the church where he was a boy; the hardest place for a doctor to practise is the place where people knew him when he was young.

But to Nazareth Jesus went. In the synagogue there was no definite person to give the address. Any distinguished stranger present might be asked by the ruler of the synagogue to speak, or anyone who had a message might venture to give it. There was no danger that Jesus would not be given the opportunity to speak. But when he did speak, all that he encountered was hostility and incredulity. They would not listen to him because they knew his father and his mother and his brothers and his sisters. They could not conceive that anyone who had lived among them had any right to speak as Jesus was speaking. The prophet, as so often happens, had no honour in his own country; and their attitude to him raised a barrier which made it impossible for Jesus to have any effect upon them.

There is a great lesson here. In any church service the congregation preaches more than half the sermon. The congregation brings an atmosphere with it. That atmosphere is either a barrier through which the preacher's word cannot penetrate; or else it is such an expectancy that even the poorest sermon becomes a living flame.

Again, we should not judge a man by his background and his family connections, but by what he is. Many a message has been killed stone dead, not because there was anything wrong with it; but because the minds of the hearers were so prejudiced against the messenger that it never had a chance.

When we meet together to listen to the word of God, we must come with eager expectancy, and must think, not of the man who speaks, but of the Spirit who speaks through him.

THE TRAGIC DRAMA OF JOHN THE BAPTIST

Matthew 14: 1–12

At that time Herod the tetrarch heard the report about Jesus, and said to his servants, " This is John the Baptizer. He has been raised from the dead, and because of this, these deeds of power

work in him." For Herod had seized John the Baptizer, and had
bound him and put him in prison, because of Herodias, his
brother Philip's wife, for John insisted to him: " It is not right for
you to have her." So he wished to kill him, but he was afraid of
the crowd, for they regarded him as a prophet. On the occasion of
Herod's birthday celebrations the daughter of Herodias danced in
public and delighted Herod. Hence he affirmed with an oath that
he would give her whatsoever she might ask. Urged on by her
mother, she said, " Give me here and now the head of John the
Baptizer on a dish." The king was distressed, but, because of his
oath, and because of those who sat at table with him, he ordered
the request to be granted. So he sent and had John beheaded in the
prison. And his head was brought on a dish and given to the
maiden; and she brought it to her mother. His disciples came and
took away the body and buried him. And they came and told
Jesus about it.

In this tragic drama of the death of John the Baptist, the
dramatis personae stand clearly delineated and vividly displayed.

(i) There is John himself. As far as Herod was concerned
John had two faults. (*a*) He was too popular with the people.
Josephus also tells the story of the death of John, and it is from
this point of view that he tells it. Josephus writes (*Antiquities of
the Jews*, 18. 5. 2): " Now when many others came in crowds
about him, for they were greatly moved by hearing his words,
Herod, who feared lest the great influence John had over the
people might put it into his power and inclination to raise a
rebellion (for they seemed ready to do anything he should
advise), thought it best, by putting him to death, to prevent any
mischief he might cause, and not bring himself into difficulties
by sparing a man who might make him repent of it when it was
too late. Accordingly he was sent a prisoner out of Herod's
suspicious temper to Machaerus ... and was there put to
death." As Josephus read the facts, it was Herod's suspicious
jealousy of John which made him kill John. Herod, like every
weak and suspicious and frightened tyrant, could think of no
way of dealing with a possible rival other than killing him.

(*b*) But the gospel writers see the story from a different point of view. As they see it, Herod killed John because he was a man who told the truth. It is always dangerous to rebuke a tyrant, and that is precisely what John did.

The facts were quite simple. Herod Antipas was married to a daughter of the king of the Nabatean Arabs. He had a brother in Rome also called Herod; the gospel writers call this Roman Herod, Philip; his full name may have been Herod Philip, or they may simply have got mixed up in the complicated marriage relationships of the Herods. This Herod who stayed in Rome was a wealthy private individual, who had no kingdom of his own. On a visit to Rome, Herod Antipas seduced his brother's wife, and persuaded her to leave his brother and to marry him. In order to do so he had to put away his own wife, with, as we shall see, disastrous consequences to himself. In doing this, apart altogether from the moral aspect of the question, Herod broke two laws. He divorced his own wife without cause, and he married his sister-in-law, which was a marriage, under Jewish law, within the prohibited relationships. Without hesitation John rebuked him.

It is always dangerous to rebuke an eastern despot, and by his rebuke John signed his own death warrant. He was a man who fearlessly rebuked evil wherever he saw it. When John Knox was standing for his principles against Queen Mary, she demanded whether he thought it right that the authority of rulers should be resisted. His answer was: " If princes exceed their bounds, madam, they may be resisted and even deposed." The world owes much to the great men who took their lives in their hands and had the courage to tell even kings and queens that there is a moral law which they break at their peril.

(ii) There is Herodias. As we shall see, she was the ruination of Herod in every possible sense, although she was a woman not without a sense of greatness. At the moment we simply note that she was stained by a triple guilt. She was a woman of loose morals and of infidelity. She was a vindictive woman, who nursed her wrath to keep it warm, and who was out for revenge, even when she was justly condemned. And—perhaps worst of all—she was a woman who did not hesitate to use even her own daughter to realize her own vindictive ends. It would have been bad enough if she herself had sought ways of taking vengeance on the man of God who confronted her with her shame. It was infinitely worse that she used her daughter for her nefarious purposes and made her as great a sinner as herself. There is little to be said for a parent who stains a child with guilt in order to achieve some evil personal purpose.

(iii) There is Herodias's daughter, Salome. Salome must have been young, perhaps sixteen or seventeen years of age. Whatever she may later have become, in this instance she is surely more sinned against than sinning. There must have been in her an element of shamelessness. Here was a royal princess who acted as a dancing-girl. The dances which these girls danced were suggestive and immoral. For a royal princess to dance in public at all was an amazing thing. Herodias thought nothing of outraging modesty and demeaning her daughter, if only she could gain her revenge on a man who had justly rebuked her.

THE FALL OF HEROD

Matthew 14: 1–12 (*continued*)

(iv) There is Herod himself. He is called the *tetrarch*. *Tetrarch* literally means *the ruler of a fourth part*; but it came to be used quite generally, as here, of any subordinate ruler of a section of a country. Herod the Great had many sons. When he died, he divided his territory into three, and, with the consent of the Romans, willed it to three of them. To Archelaus he left Judaea and Samaria; to Philip he left the northern territory of Trachonitis and Ituraea; to Herod Antipas—the Herod of this story—he left Galilee and Peraea. Herod Antipas was by no means an exceptionally bad king; but here he began on the road that led to his complete ruin. We may note three things about him.

(*a*) He was a man with a guilty conscience. When Jesus became prominent, Herod immediately leaped to the conclusion

that this was John come back to life again. Origen has a most
interesting suggestion about this. He points out that Mary, the
mother of Jesus, and Elisabeth, the mother of John, were closely
related (*Luke* 1: 36). That is to say, Jesus and John were blood
relations. And Origen speaks of a tradition which says that
Jesus and John closely resembled each other in appearance. If
that was the case, then Herod's guilty conscience might appear
to him to have even more grounds for its fears. He is the great
proof that no man can rid himself of a sin by ridding himself
of the man who confronts him with it. There is such a thing as
conscience, and, even if a man's human accuser is eliminated,
his divine accuser is still not silenced.

(*b*) Herod's action was typical of a weak man. He kept a
foolish oath and broke a great law. He had promised Salome to
give her anything she might ask, little thinking what she would
request. He knew well that to grant her request, so as to keep
his oath, was to break a far greater law; and yet he chose to do
it because he was too weak to admit his error. He was more
frightened of a woman's tantrums than of the moral law. He
was more frightened of the criticism, and perhaps the amuse-
ment, of his guests, than of the voice of conscience. Herod was
a man who could take a firm stand on the wrong things, even
when he knew what was right; and such a stand is the sign, not
of strength, but of weakness.

(*c*) We have already said that Herod's action in this case was
the beginning of his ruin, and so it was. The result of his
seduction of Herodias and his divorce of his own wife, was that
(very naturally) Aretas, the father of his wife, and the ruler of
the Nabateans, bitterly resented the insult perpetrated against
his daughter. He made war against Herod, and heavily defeated
him. The comment of Josephus is: " Some of the Jews thought
that the destruction of Herod's army came from God, and that
very justly, as a punishment for what he did against John, who
was called the Baptist " (*Antiquities of the Jews*, 18. 5. 2).
Herod was in fact only rescued by calling in the power of the
Romans to clear things up.

From the very beginning Herod's illegal and immoral

alliance with Herodias brought him nothing but trouble. But the influence of Herodias was not to stop there. The years went by and Caligula came to the Roman throne. The Philip who had been tetrarch of Trachonitis and Ituraea died, and Caligula gave the province to another of the Herod family named Agrippa; and with the province he gave him the title of king. The fact that Agrippa was called king moved Herodias to bitter envy. Josephus says, " She was not able to conceal how miserable she was, by reason of the envy she had towards him " (*Antiquities of the Jews*, 18. 7. 1). The consequence of her envy was that she incited Herod to go to Rome and to ask Caligula that he too should be granted the title of king, for Herodias was determined to be a queen. " Let us go to Rome," she said, " and let us spare no pains or expenses, either of silver or gold, since they cannot be kept for any better use than for the obtaining of a kingdom."

Herod was very unwilling to take action; he was naturally lazy, and he also foresaw serious trouble. But this persistent woman had her way. Herod prepared to set out to Rome; but Agrippa sent messengers to forestall him with accusations that Herod was preparing treacherously to rebel from Rome. The result was that Caligula believed Agrippa's accusations, took Herod's province from him, with all his money, and gave it to Agrippa, and banished Herod to far off Gaul to languish there in exile until he died.

So in the end it was through Herodias that Herod lost his fortune and his kingdom, and dragged out a weary existence in the far away places of Gaul. It is just here that Herodias showed her one flash of greatness and of magnanimity. She was in fact Agrippa's sister, and Caligula told her that he did not intend to take her private fortune from her and that for Agrippa's sake she need not accompany her husband into exile. Herodias answered, " Thou indeed, O Emperor, actest after a magnificent manner, and as becomes thyself, in what thou offerest me; but the love which I have for my husband hinders me from partaking of the favour of thy gift; for it is not just that I, who have been a partner in his prosperity, should forsake him in his misfortune " (*Antiquities of the Jews*, 18. 7. 2). And so Herodias accompanied Herod to his exile.

If ever there was proof that sin brings its own punishment, that proof lies in the story of Herod. It was an ill day when Herod first seduced Herodias. From that act of infidelity came the murder of John, and in the end disaster, in which he lost all, except the woman who loved him and ruined him.

COMPASSION AND POWER

Matthew 14: 13–21

> When Jesus heard the news (of the death of John), he withdrew from there in a boat, into a deserted place alone. When the crowds heard of it, they followed him on foot from the towns. When he had disembarked, he saw a great crowd, and he was moved with compassion for them to the depths of his being, and healed their sick. When it had become late, his disciples came to him: " The place is deserted," they said, " and the hour for the evening meal has already passed. Send the crowds away, in order that they may go into the villages, and buy themselves food." But Jesus said to them, " Give them food to eat yourselves." They said to him, " We have nothing except five loaves and two fishes." He said, " Bring them here to me." So he ordered the crowds to sit down on the green grass. He took the five loaves and the two fishes, and looked up to heaven, and said a blessing, and broke the loaves and gave them to the disciples, and the disciples gave them to the crowds; and they all ate and were satisfied. They took up what was left over, twelve baskets full of the fragments. The number of those who ate was about five thousand men, apart from women and children.

GALILEE must have been a place where it was very difficult to be alone. Galilee was a small country, only 50 miles from north to south and 25 miles from east to west, and Josephus tells us that in his time within that small area there were 204 towns and villages, none with a population of less than 15,000 people. In such a thickly populated area it was not easy to get away from

people for any length of time. But it was quiet on the other side
of the lake, and at its widest the lake was only 8 miles wide.
Jesus' friends were fisherfolk; and it was not difficult to
embark on one of their boats and seek retirement on the east
side of the lake. That is what Jesus did when he heard of the
death of John.

There were three perfectly simple and natural reasons why
Jesus should seek to be alone. He was human and he needed
rest. He never recklessly ran into danger, and it was well to
withdraw, lest too early he should share the fate of John. And,
most of all, with the Cross coming nearer and nearer, Jesus
knew that he must meet with God before he met with men. He
was seeking rest for his body and strength for his soul in the
lonely places.

But he was not to get it. It would be easy to see the boat set
sail and to deduce where it was going; and the crowds flocked
round the top of the lake and were waiting for him at the other
side when he arrived. So Jesus healed them and, when the
evening came, he fed them before they took the long road home.
Few of Jesus' miracles are so revealing as this.

(i) It tells us of the compassion of Jesus. When he saw the
crowds he was moved with compassion to the depths of his
being. That is a very wonderful thing. Jesus had come to find
peace and quiet and loneliness; instead he found a vast crowd
eagerly demanding what he could give. He might so easily have
resented them. What right had they to invade his privacy with
their continual demands? Was he to have no rest and quiet, no
time to himself at all?

But Jesus was not like that. So far from finding them a
nuisance, he was moved with compassion for them. Premanand, the great Christian who was once a wealthy high-caste
Indian, says in his autobiography: " As in the days of old, so
now our message to the non-Christian world has to be the same,
that *God cares.*" If that be so, we must never be too busy for
people, and we must never even seem to find them a trouble and
a nuisance. Premanand also says: " My own experience has
been that when I or any other missionary or Indian priest

showed signs of restlessness or impatience towards any
educated and thoughtful Christian or non-Christian visitors,
and gave them to understand that we were hard-pressed for
time, or that it was our lunch- or tea-time and that we could not
wait, then at once such enquirers were lost, and never returned
again." We must never deal with people with one eye on the
clock, and as if we were anxious to be rid of them as soon as we
decently can.

Premanand goes on to relate an incident which, it is not too
much to say, may have changed the whole course of the spread
of Christianity in Bengal. " There is an account somewhere of
how the first Metropolitan Bishop of India failed to meet the
late Pandit Iswar Chandar Vidyasagar of Bengal through
official formality. The Pandit had been sent as spokesman of
the Hindu community in Calcutta, to establish friendly relations with the Bishop and with the Church. Vidyasagar, who
was the founder of a Hindu College in Calcutta and a social
reformer, author and educationalist of repute, returned disappointed without an interview, and formed a strong party of
educated and wealthy citizens of Calcutta to oppose the Church
and the Bishop, and to guard against the spread of Christianity.
. . . The formality observed by one known to be an official of the
Christian Church turned a friend into a foe." What an opportunity for Christ was lost because someone's privacy could not
be invaded except through official channels. Jesus never found
any man a nuisance, even when his whole being was crying out
for rest and quiet—and neither must his followers.

(ii) In this story we see Jesus witnessing that all gifts are from
God. He took the food and he said a blessing. The Jewish grace
before meals was very simple: " Blessed art thou, Jehovah our
God, King of the universe, who bringest forth bread from the
earth." That would be the grace which Jesus said, for that was
the grace which every Jewish family used. Here we see Jesus
showing that it is God's gifts which he brings to men. The grace
of gratitude is rare enough towards men; it is rarer still towards
God.

THE PLACE OF THE DISCIPLE IN THE
WORK OF CHRIST

Matthew 14: 13–21 (*continued*)

(iii) This miracle informs us very clearly of the place of the disciple in the work of Christ. The story tells that Jesus gave to the disciples and the disciples gave to the crowd. Jesus worked through the hands of his disciples that day, and he still does.

Again and again we come face to face with this truth which is at the heart of the Church. It is true that the disciple is helpless without his Lord, but it is also true that the Lord is helpless without his disciple. If Jesus wants something done, if he wants a child taught or a person helped, he has to get a man to do it. He needs people through whom he can act, and through whom he can speak.

Very early in the days of his enquiring, Premanand came into contact with Bishop Whitley at Ranchi. He writes: " The Bishop read the Bible with me daily, and sometimes I read Bengali with him, and we talked together in Bengali. The longer I lived with the Bishop the closer I came to him, and found that his life revealed Christ to me, and his deeds and words made it easier for me to understand the mind and teaching of Christ about which I read daily in the Bible. I had a new vision of Christ, when I actually saw Christ's life of love, sacrifice and self-denial in the everyday life of the Bishop. He became actually the epistle of Christ to me."

Jesus Christ needs disciples through whom he can work and through whom his truth and his love can enter into the lives of others. He needs men to whom he can give, in order that they may give to others. Without such men he cannot get things done and it is our task to be such men for him.

It would be easy to be daunted and discouraged by a task of such magnitude. But there is another thing in this story that may lift up our hearts. When Jesus told the disciples to feed the crowd, they told him that all they had was five loaves and two fishes; and yet with what they brought to him, Jesus wrought his miracle. Jesus sets every one of us the tremendous task of communicating himself to men; but he does not demand from us splendours and magnificences that we do not possess. He says to us, " Come to me as you are, however ill-equipped; bring to me what you have, however little, and I will use it greatly in my service." Little is always much in the hands of Christ.

(iv) At the end of the miracle there is that strange little touch that the fragments were gathered up. Even when a miracle could feed men sumptuously there was no waste. There is something to note here. God gives to men with munificence, but a wasteful extravagance is never right. God's generous giving and our wise using must go hand in hand.

THE MAKING OF A MIRACLE

Matthew 14: 13–21 (*continued*)

THERE are some people who read the miracles of Jesus, and feel no need to understand. Let them remain for ever undisturbed in the sweet simplicity of their faith. There are others who read and their minds question and they feel they must understand. Let them take no shame of it, for God comes far more than half way to meet the questing mind. But in whatever way we approach the miracles of Jesus, one thing is certain. We must never be content to regard them as something which *happened*; we must always regard them as something which *happens*. They are not isolated events in history; they are demonstrations of the always and forever operative power of Jesus Christ. There are three ways in which we can look at this miracle.

(i) We may look at it as a simple multiplication of loaves and fishes. That would be very difficult to understand; and would be something which happened once and never repeated itself. If we regard it that way, let us be content; but let us not be critical and condemnatory of anyone who feels that he must find another way.

(ii) Many people see in this miracle a sacrament. They have felt that those who were present received only the smallest morsel of food, and yet with that were strengthened for their journey and were content. They have felt that this was not a meal where people glutted their physical appetite; but a meal where they ate the spiritual food of Christ. If that be so, this is a miracle which is re-enacted every time we sit at the table of our Lord; for there comes to us the spiritual food which sends us out to walk with firmer feet and greater strength the way of life which leads to God.

(iii) There are those who see in this miracle something which in a sense is perfectly natural, and yet which in another sense is a real miracle, and which in any sense is very precious. Picture the scene. There is the crowd; it is late; and they are hungry. But was it really likely that the vast majority of that crowd would set out around the lake without any food at all? Would they not take something with them, however little? Now it was evening and they were hungry. *But they were also selfish.* And no one would produce what he had, lest he have to share it and leave himself without enough. Then Jesus took the lead. Such as he and his disciples had, he began to share with a blessing and an invitation and a smile. And thereupon all began to share, and before they knew what was happening, there was enough and more than enough for all.

If this is what happened, it was not the miracle of the multiplication of loaves and fishes; it was the miracle of the changing of selfish people into generous people at the touch of Christ. It was the miracle of the birth of love in grudging hearts. It was the miracle of changed men and women with something of Christ in them to banish their selfishness. If that be so, then in the realest sense Christ fed them with himself and sent his Spirit to dwell within their hearts.

It does not matter how we understand this miracle. One thing is sure—when Christ is there, the weary find rest and the hungry soul is fed.

IN THE HOUR OF TROUBLE

Matthew 14: 22–27

> Immediately he compelled his disciples to embark in the boat and
> to go on ahead to the other side, until he should send away the
> crowds. When he had sent away the crowds, he went up into a
> mountain by himself to pray. When it was late, he was there alone.
> The boat was by this time in the middle of the sea, battered by the
> waves, for the wind was contrary. About three o'clock in the
> morning, he came to them walking on the sea. When the disciples
> saw him walking on the sea they were alarmed. " This is an
> apparition," they said, and they cried out from fear. Immediately
> Jesus spoke to them. " Courage! " he said. " It is I. Do not be
> afraid."

THE lesson of this passage is abundantly clear but what actually
happened is not. First of all, let us set the scene.

After the feeding of the multitude Jesus sent his disciples
away. Matthew says that he *compelled* them to embark on the
boat and go on ahead. At first sight the word *compelled* sounds
strange; but if we turn to John's account of the incident we will
most likely find the explanation. John tells us that after the
feeding of the multitude, the crowd wished to come and to make
him a king by force (*John* 6: 15). There was a surge of popular
acclamation, and in the excited state of Palestine a revolution
might well have there and then begun. It was a dangerous
situation, and the disciples might well have complicated it, for
they, too, were still thinking of Jesus in terms of earthly power.
Jesus sent away his disciples because a situation had arisen
with which he could best deal alone, and in which he did not
wish them to become involved.

When he was alone, he went up into a mountain to pray; and
by this time the night had come. The disciples had set out back
across the lake. One of the sudden storms, for which the lake
was notorious, had come down, and they were struggling
against the winds and the waves, and making little progress. As
the night wore on, Jesus began to walk round the head of the

lake to reach the other side. Matthew has already told us that, when Jesus fed the crowds, he made them sit down on *the green grass*. By that we know it must have been the springtime. Very likely it was near the Passover time, which was in the middle of April. If that is so, the moon would be full. In ancient times the night was divided into four *watches*—6 p.m. to 9 p.m., 9 p.m. to 12 midnight, 12 midnight to 3 a.m., and 3 a.m. to 6 a.m. So at three o'clock in the morning, Jesus, walking on the high ground at the north of the lake, clearly saw the boat fighting with the waves, and came down to the shore to help.

It is then that there is a real difficulty in knowing what happened. In verses 25 and 26 we read twice about Jesus walking *on the sea*, and the curious thing is that the two phrases in the Greek for *on the sea* are different. In verse 25 it is *epi tēn thalassan*, which can equally mean *over the sea*, and *towards* the sea. In verse 26 it is *epi tēs thalassēs*, which can mean *on the sea*, and which is actually the very same phrase which is used in *John 21: 1* for *at the sea*, that is by the sea-shore, of Tiberias. Still further, the word which is used for *walking* in both verses 25 and 26 is *peripatein*, which means *to walk about*.

The truth is that there are two perfectly possible interpretations of this passage, so far as the actual Greek goes. It may describe a miracle in which Jesus actually walked on the water. Or, it may equally mean that the disciples' boat was driven by the wind to the northern shore of the lake, that Jesus came down from the mountain to help them when he saw them struggling in the moonlight, and that he came walking through the surf and the waves towards the boat, and came so suddenly upon them that they were terrified when they saw him. Both of these interpretations are equally valid. Some will prefer one, and some the other.

But, whatever interpretation of the Greek we choose, the significance is perfectly clear. *In the hour of the disciples' need Jesus came to them.* When the wind was contrary and life was a struggle, Jesus was there to help. No sooner had a need arisen, than Jesus was there to help and to save.

In life the wind is often contrary. There are times when we are up against it and life is a desperate struggle with ourselves, with our circumstances, with our temptations, with our sorrows, with our decisions. At such a time no man need struggle alone, for Jesus comes to him across the storms of life, with hand stretched out to save, and with his calm clear voice bidding us take heart and have no fear.

It does not really matter how we take this incident; it is in any event far more than the story of what Jesus once did in a storm in far-off Palestine; it is the sign and the symbol of what he always does for his people, when the wind is contrary and we are in danger of being overwhelmed by the storms of life.

COLLAPSE AND RECOVERY

Matthew 14: 28–33

> Peter got down from the boat and walked on the water to come to Jesus. But, when he saw the wind, he was afraid; and, when he began to sink below the water, he cried out, " Lord, save me! " Immediately Jesus stretched out his hand and grasped him. " O man of little faith! " he said. " Why did you begin to have doubts? " And when they got into the boat, the wind sank. And those in the boat knelt in reverence before him, saying, " Truly you are the Son of God."

THERE is no passage in the New Testament in which Peter's character is more fully revealed than this. It tells us three things about him.

(i) Peter was given to acting upon impulse and without thinking of what he was doing. It was his mistake that again and again he acted without fully facing the situation and without counting the cost. He was to do exactly the same when he affirmed undying and unshakable loyalty to Jesus (*Matthew* 26: 33–35), and then denied his Lord's name. And yet there are worse sins than that, because Peter's whole trouble was that he was ruled by his heart; and, however he might sometimes fail, his heart was always in the right place and the instinct of his heart was always love.

(ii) Because Peter acted on impulse, he often failed and came to grief. It was always Jesus's insistence that a man should look at a situation in all its bleak grimness before he acted (*Luke* 9: 57, 58; *Matthew* 16: 24, 25). Jesus was completely honest with men; he always bade them see how difficult it was to follow him before they set out upon the Christian way. A great deal of Christian failure is due to acting upon an emotional moment without counting the cost.

(iii) But Peter never finally failed, for always in the moment of his failure he clutched at Christ. The wonderful thing about him is that every time he fell, he rose again; and that it must have been true that even his failures brought him closer and closer to Jesus Christ. As has been well said, a saint is not a man who never fails; a saint is a man who gets up and goes on again every time he falls. Peter's failures only made him love Jesus Christ the more.

These verses finish with another great and permanent truth. When Jesus got into the boat, the wind sank. The great truth is that, wherever Jesus Christ is, the wildest storm becomes a calm. Olive Wyon, in her book *Consider Him*, quotes a thing from the letters of St. Francis of Sales. St. Francis had noticed a custom of the country districts in which he lived. He had often noticed a farm servant going across a farmyard to draw water at the well; he also noticed that, before she lifted the brimming pail, the girl always put a piece of wood into it. One day he went out to the girl and asked her, " Why do you do that? " She looked surprised and answered, as if it were a matter of course, " Why? to keep the water from spilling ... to keep it steady! " Writing to a friend later on, the bishop told this story and added: " So when your heart is distressed and agitated, put the Cross into its centre to keep it steady! " In every time of storm and stress, the presence of Jesus and the love which flows from the Cross bring peace and serenity and calm.

THE MINISTRY OF CHRIST

Matthew 14: 34–36

> When they had crossed over, they came to land at Gennesaret.
> When the men of that place recognized him, they sent the news
> that he had come to the whole surrounding countryside, and they
> brought to him all those who were ill, and besought him to be
> allowed only to touch the fringe of his robe; and all who touched
> him were restored to health.

THIS is just one of Matthew's almost colourless little connecting
passages. It is a sentence or two of the gospel story that the eye
might easily pass over as quite unimportant; and yet it is very
revealing of Jesus.

(i) There is beauty in it. No sooner did Jesus appear
anywhere than men were crowding and clamouring for his help;
and he never refused it. He healed them all. There is no word
here that he preached or taught at any length; there is simply
the record that he healed. The most tremendous thing about
Jesus was that he taught men what God was like by *showing*
men what God was like. He did not *tell* men that God cared; he
showed men that God cared. There is little use preaching the
love of God in words without showing the love of God in
action.

(ii) But there is also pathos here. No one can read this
passage without seeing in it the grim fact that there were
hundreds and thousands of people who desired Jesus only for
what they could get out of him. Once they had received the
healing which they sought, they were not really prepared to go
any further. It has always been the case that people have
wanted the privilege of Christianity without its responsibilities.
It has always been the case that so many of us remember God
only when we need him. Ingratitude towards God and towards
Jesus Christ is the ugliest of all sins; and there is no sin of
which men are more often and more consistently guilty.

CLEAN AND UNCLEAN

Matthew 15: 1–9

> Then the Pharisees and Scribes from Jerusalem approached Jesus.
> " Why," they said, " do your disciples transgress the tradition of
> the elders? They do so transgress, because they do not wash their
> hands before they eat bread." Jesus answered them: " Why do
> you too transgress God's commandment, because of your tradi-
> tion? For God said, ' Honour your father and your mother,' and,
> ' He who curses his father and mother, let him die '; but, as for
> you, you say, ' Whoever says to his father or his mother: " That
> by which you might have been helped by me is a dedicated gift,"
> will certainly not honour his father and his mother, and is yet
> guiltless.' You have annulled the commandment of God through
> your tradition. Hypocrites, Isaiah in his prophecy described you
> well: ' This people honours me with their lips, but their heart is far
> from me. It is in vain that they reverence me; for it is man-made
> commandments that they teach as their teaching.' "

IT is not too much to say that, however difficult and obscure
this passage may seem to us, it is one of the most important
passages in the whole gospel story. It represents a head-on clash
between Jesus and the leaders of orthodox Jewish religion. Its
opening sentence makes it clear that the Scribes and Pharisees
had come all the way from Jerusalem to Galilee to put their
questions to Jesus. On this occasion it need not be thought
that the questions are malicious. The Scribes and Pharisees are
not ill-naturedly seeking to entangle Jesus. They are genuinely bewildered; and in a very short time they are going to be
genuinely outraged and shocked; for the basic importance of
this passage is that it is not so much a clash between Jesus and
the Pharisees in a personal way; it is something far more—it is
the collision of two views of religion and two views of the
demands of God.

Nor was there any possibility of a compromise, or even a
working agreement, between these two views of religion. Inevitably the one had to destroy the other. Here, then, embedded in

this passage, is one of the supreme religious contests in history. To understand it we must try to understand the background of Jewish Pharisaic and Scribal religion.

In this passage there meets us the whole conception of *clean* and *unclean*. We must be quite clear that this idea of cleanness and uncleanness has nothing to do with physical cleanness, or, except distantly, with hygiene. It is entirely a ceremonial matter. For a man to be clean was for him to be in a state where he might worship and approach God; for him to be unclean was for him to be in a state where such a worship and such an approach were impossible.

This uncleanness was contracted by contact with certain persons or things. For instance, a woman was unclean if she had a haemorrhage, even if that haemorrhage was her normal monthly period; she was unclean for a stated time after she had had a child; every dead body was unclean, and to touch it was to become unclean; every Gentile was unclean.

This uncleanness was transferable; it was, so to speak, infectious. For instance, if a mouse touched an earthenware vessel, that vessel was unclean and unless it was ritually washed and cleansed, everything put into it was unclean. The consequence was that anyone who touched that vessel, or who ate or drank from its contents became unclean; and in turn anyone who touched the person who had so become unclean also became unclean.

This is not only a Jewish idea; it occurs in other religions. To a high-caste Indian anyone not belonging to his own caste is unclean; if that person becomes a Christian, he is still more seriously unclean. Premanand tells us what happened to himself. He became a Christian; his family ejected him. Sometimes he used to come back to see his mother, who was broken-hearted at what she considered his apostasy, but still loved him dearly. Premanand says: " As soon as my father came to know that I was visiting my mother in the daytime while he was away at the office, he ordered the door-keeper, a stalwart up-country man, Ram Rup ... not to allow me to enter the house." Ram Rup was persuaded to slacken his vigilance. " At last my mother won over Ram Rup, the door-keeper, and I was allowed to enter her presence. The prejudice was so great that even the menial Hindu servants of the house would not wash the plates on which I was fed by my mother. Sometimes my aunt would purify the place and the seat on which I had sat by sprinkling Ganges water, or water mixed with cow dung." Premanand was unclean, and everything he touched became unclean.

We must note that there was nothing moral about this. The touching of certain things produced uncleanness; and this uncleanness debarred from the society of men and the presence of God. It was as if some special infection hung like an aura about certain persons and things. We may understand this a little better if we remember that even in western civilization this idea is not completely dead, although it works here mainly in reverse. There are still those who find in a four-leafed clover, or in some metal or wooden charm, or in a black cat, something which brings good fortune.

So, here is an idea which sees in religion something which consists in avoiding contact with certain things and people because they are unclean; and, then, if that contact should have been made, in taking the necessary ritual cleansing measures to rid oneself of the contracted uncleanness. But we must pursue this a little further.

THE FOODS WHICH ENTER INTO A MAN

Matthew 15: 1–9 (*continued*)

THE laws of cleanness and uncleanness had a further wide area of application. They laid down what a man might eat, and what he might not eat. Broadly speaking all fruit and vegetables were clean. But, in regard to living creatures, the laws were strict. These laws are in *Leviticus* 11.

We may briefly summarize them. Of beasts only those can be eaten who part the hoof and chew the cud. That is why no Jew can eat the flesh of the pig, the rabbit, or the hare. In no case may the flesh of an animal which has died a natural death be eaten (*Deuteronomy* 14: 21). In all cases the blood must be drained from the carcase; the orthodox Jew still buys his meat from a *kosher* butcher, who sells only meat so treated. Ordinary fat upon the flesh might be eaten, but the fat on the kidneys and on the entrails of the abdomen, which we call suet, might not be eaten. In regard to sea food, only sea creatures which have both fins and scales may be eaten. This means that shellfish, such as lobsters, are unclean. All insects are unclean, with one exception, locusts. In the case of animals and fish there is a standard test, as we have seen, of what might be eaten, and what might not be eaten. In the case of birds there is no such test; and the list of unclean and forbidden birds is in *Leviticus* 11: 13–21.

There were certain identifiable reasons for all this.

(i) The refusal to touch dead bodies, or to eat the flesh of an animal which had died from natural causes, may well have had something to do with the belief in evil spirits. It would be easy to think of a demon as taking up residence in such a body, and so gaining entry into the body of the eater.

(ii) Certain animals were sacred in other religions; for instance, the cat and the crocodile were sacred to the Egyptians; and it would be very natural for the Jews to regard as unclean any animal which another nation worshipped. The animal would then be reckoned a kind of idol and therefore dangerously unclean.

(iii) As Dr. Rendle Short points out in his most helpful book, *The Bible and Modern Medicine*, certain of the regulations were in fact wise from the point of view of health and hygiene. Dr. Short writes: " True, we eat the pig, the rabbit and the hare, but these animals are liable to parastic infections and are safe only if the food is well-cooked. The pig is an unclean feeder, and harbours two worms, trichina and a tape worm, which may be passed on to man. The danger is minimal under present conditions in this country, but it would have been far otherwise in Palestine of old, and such food was better avoided." The prohibition of eating anything with blood in it comes from the fact that the blood is the life in Jewish thought. This is a natural thought, for, as blood flows away, life ebbs away. And the life belongs to God, and to God alone. The same idea explains the prohibition of eating the fat. The fat is the richest part of the carcase, and the richest part must be given to God. In some cases, although they are few, there was sound sense behind the prohibitions and the food laws.

(iv) There remain a large number of cases in which things and beasts and animals were unclean for no reason at all except that they were. Taboos are always inexplicable; they are simply superstitions, by which certain living things came to be connected with good or with bad fortune, with cleanness or uncleanness.

These things would not in themselves matter very much, but the trouble and the tragedy were that they had become to the Scribes and Pharisees matters of life and death. To serve God, to be religious, was to observe these good laws. If we put it in the following way, we will see the result. To the Pharisaic mind the prohibition of eating rabbit's or pig's flesh was just as much a commandment of God as the prohibition of adultery; it was therefore just as much a sin to eat pork or rabbit as to seduce a woman and enjoy illegal sexual intercourse. Religion had got itself mixed up with all kinds of external rules and regulations; and, since it is much easier both to observe rules and regulations and to check up on those who do not, these rules and regulations had *become* religion to the orthodox Jews.

THE WAYS OF CLEANSING

Matthew 15: 1–9 (*continued*)

Now we come to the particular impact of this on the passage we are studying. It was clearly impossible to avoid all kinds of ceremonial uncleanness. A man might himself avoid unclean things, but how could he possibly know when on the street he had touched someone who was unclean? This was further complicated by the fact that there were Gentiles in Palestine, and the very dust touched by a Gentile foot became unclean.

To combat uncleanness an elaborate system of washings was worked out. These washings became ever more elaborate. At first there was a hand-washing on rising in the morning. Then there grew up an elaborate system of hand-washing whose use was at first confined to the priests in the Temple before they ate that part of the sacrifice which was their perquisite. Later these complicated washings came to be demanded by the strictest of the orthodox Jews for themselves and for all who claimed to be truly religious.

Edersheim in *The Life and Times of Jesus the Messiah* outlines the most elaborate of these washings. Water jars were kept ready to be used before a meal. The minimum amount of water to be used was a quarter of a log, which is defined as enough to fill one and a half egg-shells. The water was first poured on both hands, held with the fingers pointed upwards, and must run up the arm as far as the wrist. It must drop off from the wrist, for the water was now itself unclean, having touched the unclean hands, and, if it ran down the fingers again, it would again render them unclean. The process was repeated with the hands held in the opposite direction, with the fingers pointing down; and then finally each hand was cleansed by being rubbed with the fist of the other. A really strict Jew would do all this, not only before a meal, but also between each of the courses.

The question of the Jewish orthodox leaders to Jesus is: "Why do your disciples not observe the laws of washing which our tradition lays down?"

They speak of *the tradition of the elders*. To the Jew the Law had two sections. There was *the written Law* which was contained in scripture itself; and there was *the oral Law*, which consisted of the developments, such as those in hand-washing, which the Scribes and the experts had worked out through the generations; and all these developments were the tradition of the elders, and were regarded as just as much, if not more, binding than the written Law. Again we must stop to remember the salient point—to the orthodox Jew all this ritual ceremony *was* religion; this is what, as they believed, God demanded. To do these things was to please God, and to be a good man. To put it in another way, all this business of ritual washing was regarded as just as important and just as binding as the Ten Commandments themselves. Religion had become identified with a host of external regulations. It was as important to wash the hands in a certain way as to obey the commandment: " Thou shalt not covet."

BREAKING GOD'S LAW TO KEEP MAN'S LAW

Matthew 15: 1–9 *(continued)*

JESUS did not answer the question of the Pharisees directly. What he did was to take an example of the operation of the oral and ceremonial law to show how its observance so far from being obedience to the Law of God, could become actual contradiction of that Law.

Jesus says that the Law of God lays it down that a man shall honour his father and his mother; then he goes on to say that if a man says, " It is a gift," he is free from the duty of honouring his father and his mother. If we look at the parallel passage in *Mark*, we see that the phrase is: " It is *Korban*." What is the meaning of this obscure passage to us? In point of fact it can have two meanings, because *Korban* has two meanings.

(i) *Korban* can mean *that which is dedicated* to God. Now suppose that a man had a father or mother in poverty and in need; and suppose that his poor parent came to him with a request for help. There was a way in which the man could avoid giving any help. He could, as it were, *officially* dedicate all his money and all his property to God and to the Temple; his property would then be *Korban*, God-dedicated; then he could say to his father or mother: " I'm very sorry, I can give you nothing; all my belongings are dedicated to God." He could use a ritual practice to evade the basic duty of helping and honouring his father and mother. He could take a scribal regulation to wipe out one of the Ten Commandments.

(ii) But *Korban* has another meaning, and it may well be that it is this second meaning which is at issue here. *Korban* was used as an oath. A man might say to his father or mother: " *Korban*, if anything I have will ever be used to help you." Now suppose this man to have remorse of conscience; suppose him to have made the refusal in a moment of anger, or temper, or even of irritation; suppose him to have second and kinder and more filial thoughts, and to feel that after all there was a duty to help his parents. In such a case any reasonable person would say that that man had undergone a genuine repentance, and that his change of mind was a good thing; and that since he was now prepared to do the right thing and obey the Law of God he should be encouraged to follow that line.

The strict Scribe said, " No. Our Law says that no oath can ever be broken." He would quote *Numbers* 30: 2: " When a man vows a vow to the Lord, or swears an oath to bind himself by a pledge, he shall not break his word; he shall do according to all that proceeds out of his mouth." The Scribe would legalistically argue: " You took an oath; and for no reason can you ever break it." That is to say, the Scribe would hold a man to a reckless oath, taken in a moment of passion, an oath which actually compelled a man to break the higher law of humanity and of God.

That is what Jesus meant. He meant: " You are using your scribal interpretations, your traditions, to compel a man to dishonour his father and mother, even when he himself has repented and has seen the better way."

The strange and tragic thing was that the Scribes and Pharisees of the day were actually going against what the greatest Jewish teachers had said. Rabbi Eliezer said, " The door is opened for a man on account of his father and his mother," and he meant that, if any man had sworn an oath which dishonoured his father and his mother, and had then repented of it, the door was open to him to change his mind and to take a different way, even if an oath had been sworn. As so often, Jesus was not presenting men with unknown truth; he was reminding them of things that God had already told them, and that they had already known but had forgotten, because they had come to prefer their own man-made ingenuities to the great simplicities of the Law of God.

Here is the clash and the collision; here is the contest between two kinds of religion and two kinds of worship. To the Scribes and Pharisees religion was the observance of certain outward rules and regulations and rituals, such as the correct way to wash the hands before eating; it was the strict observance of a legalistic outlook on all life. To Jesus religion was a thing which had its seat in the heart; it was a thing which issued in compassion and kindness, which are above and beyond the law.

To the Scribes and Pharisees worship was ritual, ceremony law; to Jesus worship was the clean heart and the loving life. Here is the clash. And that clash still exists. What is worship? Even today there are many who would say that worship is not worship unless it is carried out by a priest ordained in a certain succession, in a building consecrated in a certain way, and from a liturgy laid down by a certain Church. And all these things are externals.

One of the greatest definitions of worship ever laid down was laid down by William Temple: " To worship is to quicken the conscience by the holiness of God, to feed the mind with the truth of God, to purge the imagination by the beauty of God, to open the heart to the love of God, to devote the will to the purpose of God." We must have a care lest we stand aghast at the apparent blindness of the Scribes and the Pharisees, lest we are shocked by their insistence on outward ceremonial, and at the same time be ourselves guilty of the same fault in our own way. Religion can never be founded on any ceremonies or ritual; religion must always be founded on personal relationships between man and God.

THE REAL GOODNESS AND THE REAL EVIL

Matthew 15: 10–20

Jesus called the crowd and said to them: " Listen and understand. It is not that which goes into the mouth which defiles a man; but what comes out of the mouth, *that* defiles a man." Then his disciples came to him and said, " Do you know that when the Pharisees heard your saying, they were shocked by it? " He answered: " Every plant which my heavenly Father did not plant will be rooted up. Let them be. They are blind guides. If the blind lead the blind, both of them will fall into the ditch." Peter said to him, " Tell us what this dark saying means." He said, " Are you even yet without understanding? Do you not know that everything which goes into a man's mouth goes down into the stomach, and is evacuated out into the drain? But that which comes out of the mouth comes from the heart, and it is these things which defile a man. For from the heart come pernicious thoughts, acts of murder, adultery, theft, false witness, slander. It is these things which defile a man. To eat with unwashed hands does not defile a man."

IT may well be held that for a Jew this was the most startling thing Jesus ever said. For in this saying he does not only condemn Scribal and Pharisaic ritual and ceremonial religion; he actually wipes out large sections of the book of *Leviticus*. This is not a contradiction of the tradition of the elders alone; this is a contradiction of scripture itself. This saying of Jesus cancels all the food laws of the Old Testament. Quite possibly these laws might still stand as matters of health and hygiene and common-sense and medical wisdom; but they could never again stand as matters of religion. Once and for all Jesus lays it down that what matters is not the state of a man's ritual observance, but the state of a man's heart.

No wonder the Scribes and Pharisees were shocked. The very ground of their religion was cut from beneath their feet. This statement was not simply alarming; it was revolutionary. If Jesus was right, their whole theory of religion was wrong. They identified religion and pleasing God with the observing of rules and regulations which had to do with cleanness and with uncleanness, with what a man ate and with how he washed his hands before he ate it; Jesus identified religion with the state of a man's heart, and said bluntly that these Pharisaic and Scribal regulations had nothing to do with religion. Jesus said that the Pharisees were blind guides who had no idea of the way to God, and that, if people followed them, all they could expect was to stray off the road and to fall into the ditch. And Jesus was profoundly right.

(i) If religion consists in external regulations and observances it is two things. It is far *too easy*. It is very much easier to abstain from certain foods and to wash the hands in a certain way than it is to love the unlovely and the unlovable, and to help the needy at the cost of one's own time and money and comfort and pleasure.

We have still not fully learned this lesson. To go to church regularly, to give liberally to the church, to be a member of a Bible reading circle are all external things. They are means towards religion; but they are not religion. We can never too often remind ourselves that religion consists in personal relationships and in an attitude to God and our fellow-men.

Further, if religion consists in external observances, it is quite *misleading*. Many a man has a faultless life in externals but has the bitterest and the most evil thoughts within his heart. The teaching of Jesus is that not all the outward observances in the world can atone for a heart where pride and bitterness and lust hold sway.

(ii) It is Jesus' teaching that the part of a man that matters is his heart. " Blessed are the pure in heart, for they shall see God " (*Matthew* 5: 8). As Burns had it in the *Epistle to Davie*:

> " The heart aye's the part aye
> That makes us right or wrang."

What matters to God is not so much *how* we act, but *why* we act; not so much what we *actually do*, but what we *wish in our heart of hearts to do*. " Man," as Aquinas had it, " sees the deed, but God sees the intention."

It is Jesus' teaching—and it is a teaching which condemns every one of us—that no man can call himself good because he observes external rules and regulations; he can call himself good only when his heart is pure. That very fact is the end of pride, and the reason why every one of us can say only, " God be merciful to me a sinner."

FAITH TESTED AND FAITH ANSWERED

Matthew 15: 21–28

And Jesus left there, and withdrew to the districts of Tyre and Sidon. And, look you, a Canaanite woman from these parts came and cried, " Have pity upon me, Sir, Son of David! My daughter is grievously afflicted by a demon." But he answered her not a word. His disciples came and asked him, " Send her away, for she is shrieking behind us." Jesus answered, " I was sent only to the lost sheep of Israel." She came and knelt in entreaty before him. " Lord," she said, " help me! " Jesus answered, " It is not right to take the children's bread, and to throw it to the pet dogs." She said, " True, Lord, but even the dogs eat of the pieces which fall from their master's table." Then Jesus answered her, " Woman, great is your faith! Let it be done for you as you wish." And her daughter was restored to health from that hour.

THERE are tremendous implications in this passage. Apart from anything else, it describes the only occasion on which Jesus was ever outside of Jewish territory. The supreme significance of the passage is that it fore-shadows the going out of the gospel to the whole world; it shows us the beginning of the end of all the barriers.

For Jesus this was a time of deliberate withdrawal. The end was coming near; and he wished some time of quiet when he could prepare for the end. It was not so much that he wished to prepare himself, although that purpose was also in his mind, but rather that he wished some time in which he could prepare his disciples against the day of the Cross. There were things which he must tell them, and which he must compel them to understand.

There was no place in Palestine where he could be sure of privacy; wherever he went, the crowds would find him. So he went right north through Galilee until he came to the land of Tyre and Sidon where the Phoenicians dwelt. There, at least for a time, he would be safe from the malignant hostility of the Scribes and Pharisees, and from the dangerous popularity of the people, for no Jew would be likely to follow him into Gentile territory.

This passage shows us Jesus seeking a time of quiet before the turmoil of the end. This is not in any sense a picture of him running away; it is a picture of him preparing himself and his disciples for the final and decisive battle which lay so close ahead.

But even in these foreign parts Jesus was not to be free from the clamant demand of human need. There was a woman who had a daughter who was grievously afflicted. She must have heard somehow of the wonderful things which Jesus could do; and she followed him and his disciples crying desperately for help. At first Jesus seemed to pay no attention to her. The disciples were embarrassed. " Give her what she wants," they said, " and be rid of her." The reaction of the disciples was not really compassion at all; it was the reverse; to them the woman was a nuisance, and all they wanted was to be rid of her as quickly as possible. To grant a request to get rid of a person who is, or may become, a nuisance is a common enough reaction; but it is very different from the response of Christian love and pity and compassion.

But to Jesus there was a problem here. That he was moved with compassion for this woman we cannot for a moment doubt. But she was a Gentile. Not only was she a Gentile; she belonged to the old Canaanite stock, and the Canaanites were the ancestral enemies of the Jews. Even at that very time, or not much later, Josephus could write: " Of the Phoenicians, the Tyrians have the most ill-feeling towards us." We have already seen that, if Jesus was to have any effect, he had to limit his objectives like a wise general. He had to begin with the Jews; and here was a Gentile crying for mercy. There was only one thing for him to do; he must awaken true faith in the heart of this woman.

So Jesus at last turned to her: " It is not right to take the children's bread and to throw it to the pet dogs." To call a person a dog was a deadly and a contemptuous insult. The Jew spoke with arrogant insolence about " Gentile dogs," " infidel dogs," and later " Christian dogs." In those days the dogs were the unclean scavengers of the street—lean, savage, often diseased. But there are two things to remember.

The tone and the look with which a thing is said make all the difference. A thing which seems hard can be said with a disarming smile. We can call a friend " an old villain ", or "a rascal ", with a smile and a tone which take all the sting out of it and fill it with affection. We can be quite sure that the smile on Jesus' face and the compassion in his eyes robbed the words of all insult and bitterness.

Second, it is the diminutive word for *dogs* (*kunaria*) which is used, and the *kunaria* were not the street dogs, but the little household pets, very different from the pariah dogs who roamed the streets and probed in the refuse heaps.

The woman was a Greek; she was quick to see, and she had all a Greek's ready wit. " True," she said, " but even the dogs get their share of the crumbs which fall from their master's table." And Jesus' eyes lit up with joy at such an indomitable faith; and he granted her the blessing and the healing which she so much desired.

THE FAITH WHICH WON THE BLESSING

Matthew 15: 21–28 (*continued*)

THERE are certain things about this woman which we must note.

(i) First and foremost, she had *love*. As Bengel said of her,

" She made the misery of her child her own." Heathen she might be, but in her heart there was that love for her child which is always the reflection of God's love for his children. It was love which made her approach this stranger; it was love which made her accept his silence and yet still appeal; it was love which made her suffer the apparent rebuffs; it was love which made her able to see the compassion beyond and behind the words of Jesus. The driving force of this woman's heart was love; and there is nothing stronger and nothing nearer God than that very thing.

(ii) This woman had *faith*. (*a*) It was a *faith which grew* in contact with Jesus. She began by calling him *Son of David*; that was a popular title, a political title. It was a title which looked on Jesus as a great and powerful wonder worker, but which looked on him in terms of *earthly* power and glory. She came asking a boon of one whom she took to be a great and powerful *man*. She came with a kind of superstition as she might have come to any magician. She ended by calling Jesus *Lord*.

Jesus, as it were, compelled her to look at himself, and in him she saw something that was not expressible in earthly terms at all, but was nothing less than divine. That is precisely what Jesus wanted to awaken in her before he granted her request. He wanted her to see that *a request to a great man* must be turned into *a prayer to the living God*. We can see this woman's faith growing as she is confronted with Christ, until she glimpsed him, however distantly, for what he was.

(*b*) It was a faith which *worshipped*. She began by following; she ended upon her knees, She began with a request; she ended in prayer. Whenever we come to Jesus, we must come first with adoration of his majesty, and only then with the statement of our own need.

(iii) This woman had *indomitable persistence*. She was undiscourageable. So many people, it has been said, pray really because they do not wish to miss a chance. They do not really believe in prayer; they have only the feeling that something might just possibly happen. This woman came because Jesus was not just a possible helper; he was her only hope. She came

with a passionate hope, a clamant sense of need, and a refusal
to be discouraged. She had the one supremely effective quality
in prayer—*she was in deadly earnest.* Prayer for her was no
ritual form; it was the outpouring of the passionate desire of her
soul, which somehow felt that she could not—and must
not—and need not—take no for an answer.

(iv) This woman had *the gift of cheerfulness.* She was in the
midst of trouble; she was passionately in earnest; and yet she
could smile. She had a certain sunny-heartedness about her. God
loves the cheerful faith, the faith in whose eyes there is always
the light of hope, the faith with a smile which can light the
gloom.

This woman brought to Christ a gallant and an audacious
love, a faith which grew until it worshipped at the feet of the
divine, an indomitable persistence springing from an uncon-
querable hope, a cheerfulness which would not be dismayed.
That is the approach which cannot help finding an answer to its
prayers.

THE BREAD OF LIFE

Matthew 15: 29–39

And Jesus left there, and went to the Sea of Galilee; and he went
up into a mountain, and he was sitting there; and great crowds
came to him, bringing with them people who were lame and blind
and deaf and maimed, and laid them at his feet, and he healed
them, so that the crowd were amazed when they saw the dumb
speaking, the maimed restored to soundness, and the lame walking, and the blind seeing; and they praised the God of Israel.

Jesus called his disciples to him. " My heart is sorry for the
crowd," he said, " because they have stayed with me now for
three days, and they have nothing to eat. I do not wish to send
them away hungry in case they collapse on the road." The
disciples said to him, " Where could we find enough loaves in a
desert place to satisfy such a crowd? " Jesus said to them, " How
many loaves have you? " They said, " Seven, and a few little
fishes." He gave orders to the crowd to sit down on the ground,

and he took the seven loaves and the fishes, and, when he had given thanks, he broke them and gave them to the disciples, and the disciples gave them to the crowds. And they gathered what remained of the fragments, seven hampers full. Those who ate were four thousand men, apart from women and children. When he had sent the crowds away, he embarked on the boat, and went to the district of Magadan.

WE have already seen that when Jesus set out on his journey to the districts of the Phoenicians, he was entering upon a period of deliberate withdrawal that he might prepare himself and his disciples for the last days which lay ahead. One of the difficulties about the gospels is that they do not give us any definite indication of times and dates; these we have to work out for ourselves, using such hints as the story may give us. When we do, we find that Jesus' period of retiral with his disciples was very much longer than we might think from a casual reading of the story.

When Jesus fed the five thousand (*Matthew* 14: 15–21; *Mark* 6: 31–44), it was the spring time, for at no other time would the grass be green in that hot land (*Matthew* 14: 19; *Mark* 6: 39). After his discussions with the Scribes and Pharisees he withdrew to the districts of Tyre and Sidon (*Mark* 7: 24; *Matthew* 15: 21). That in itself was no small journey on foot.

For the next note of time and place we go to *Mark* 7: 31 " Then he returned from the region of Tyre, and went through Sidon to the Sea of Galilee, through the region of the Deca-polis." That was a strange way of travelling. Sidon is *north* of Tyre; the Sea of Galilee is *south* of Tyre; and the Decapolis was a confederation of ten Greek cities on the *east* of the Sea of Galilee. That is to say Jesus went *north* in order to go *south*. It is as if to get from one end of the base of a triangle to the other he went right round by the apex. It is as if he went from Edinburgh to Glasgow by way of Perth, or from Bristol to London by way of Manchester. It is clear that Jesus deliberately lengthened out this journey to have as long as possible with his disciples before the last journey to Jerusalem.

Finally he came to the Decapolis, where, as we learn from Mark (*Mark* 7: 31), the incidents of our passage happened. Here we get our next hint. On this occasion when the crowd were bidden to sit down, they sat on the ground (*epi tēn gēn*), on the earth; it was by this time high summer and the grass was scorched, leaving only the bare earth.

That is to say, this northern journey took Jesus *almost six months*. We know nothing about what happened in the course of these six months; but we can be perfectly sure that they were the most important six months through which the disciples ever lived; for in them Jesus deliberately taught and instructed them, and opened their minds to the truth. It is a thing to remember that the disciples had six months apart with Jesus before the testing time came.

Many scholars think that the feeding of the five thousand and the feeding of the four thousand are different versions of the same incident; but that is not so. As we have seen, the date is different; the first took place in the spring, the second in the summer. The people and the place are different. The feeding of the four thousand took place in Decapolis. *Decapolis* literally means *ten cities*, and the Decapolis was a loose federation of ten free Greek cities. On this occasion there would be many Gentiles present, perhaps more Gentiles than Jews. It is that fact that explains the curious phrase in verse 31, " They glorified *the God of Israel.*" To the Gentile crowds this was a demonstration of the power of the God of Israel. There is another curious little hint of difference. In the feeding of the five thousand the baskets which were used to take up the fragments are called *kophinoi*; in the feeding of the four thousand they are called *sphurides*. The *kophinos* was a narrow-necked, flask-shaped basket which Jews often carried with them, for a Jew often carried his own food, lest he should be compelled to eat food which had been touched by Gentile hands and was therefore unclean. The *sphuris* was much more like a hamper; it could be big enough to carry a man, and it was a kind of basket that a Gentile would use.

The wonder of this story is that in these healings and in this feeding of the hungry, we see the mercy and the compassion of Jesus going out to the Gentiles. Here is a kind of symbol and foretaste that the bread of God was not to be confined to the Jews; that the Gentiles were also to have their share of him who is the living bread.

THE GRACIOUSNESS OF JESUS

Matthew 15: 29–39 (*continued*)

IN this passage we see fully displayed the graciousness and the sheer kindness of Jesus Christ. We see him relieving every kind of human need.

(i) We see him curing physical *disability*. The lame, the maimed, the blind and the dumb are laid at his feet and cured. Jesus is infinitely concerned with the bodily pain of the world; and those who bring men health and healing are still doing the work of Jesus Christ.

(ii) We see him concerned for the *tired*. The people are tired and he wants to strengthen their feet for a long, hard road. Jesus is infinitely concerned for the world's wayfarers, for the world's toilers, for those whose eyes are weary and whose hands are tired.

(iii) We see him feeding the *hungry*. We see him giving all he has to relieve physical hunger and physical need. Jesus is infinitely concerned for men's bodies, just as he is for their souls.

Here we see the power and the compassion of God going out to meet the many needs of the human situation.

In writing of this passage Edersheim has a lovely thought: he points out that in three successive stages of his ministry, Jesus ended each stage by setting a meal before his people. First, there was the feeding of the five thousand; that came at the end of his ministry in Galilee, for Jesus was never to teach and preach and heal in Galilee again. Second, there was this feeding of the four thousand. This came at the end of his brief ministry to the Gentiles, beyond the bounds of Palestine—first in the districts of Tyre and Sidon and then in the Decapolis. Third and last, there was the Last Supper in Jerusalem, when Jesus came to the final stage of the days of his flesh.

Here indeed is a lovely thought. Jesus always left men with strength for the way; always he gathered men to him to feed them with the living bread. Always he gave them himself before he moved on. And still he comes to us offering us also the bread which will satisfy the immortal hunger of the human soul, and in the strength of which we shall be able to go all the days of our life.

BLIND TO THE SIGNS

Matthew 16: 1–4

> The Pharisees and Sadducees came to him, trying to put him to the test, and asked him to show them a sign from Heaven. He answered them: " When evening comes, you say, ' It will be fine weather, because the sky is red.' And early in the morning you say, ' It will be stormy today, because the sky is red and threatening.' You know how to discern the face of the sky, but you cannot discern the signs of the times. An evil and apostate generation seeks for a sign. No sign will be given to it except the sign of Jonah." And he left them and went away.

HOSTILITY, like necessity, makes strange bedfellows. It is an extraordinary phenomenon to find a combination of the Pharisees and Sadducees. They stood for both beliefs and policies which were diametrically opposed. The Pharisees lived life according to the minutiae of the oral and the scribal law; the Sadducees rejected the oral and the scribal law completely, and accepted only the written words of the Bible as their law of life. The Pharisees believed in angels and in the resurrection of the body and the Sadducees did not, an opposition which Paul made use of when he was on trial before the Sanhedrin (*Acts* 23: 6–10). And—in this case most important of all—the Pharisees were not a political party and were prepared to live under any government which would allow them to observe their own religious principles; the Sadducees were the small, wealthy aristocracy, who were the collaborationist party and were quite prepared to serve and co-operate with the Roman government, in order to retain their wealth and their privileges. Further, the Pharisees looked for and longed for the Messiah; the Sadducees did not. It would have been well-nigh impossible to find two more different sects and parties; and yet they came together in their envenomed desire to eliminate Jesus. All error has this in common—that it is hostile to Christ.

The demand of the Pharisees and the Sadducees was for a sign. As we have already seen, the Jews had a way of wishing a prophet or a leader to authenticate his message by some abnormal and extraordinary sign (*Matthew* 12: 38–40). It is Jesus' reply that the sign was there, if they could only see it. They were weather-wise. They knew the same weather saying that we ourselves know:

" A red sky at night is the shepherd's delight;
A red sky in the morning is the shepherd's warning."

They knew very well that a red sky in the evening presaged fine weather; and that a red sky in the morning was the warning of a storm to come. But they were blind to the signs of the times.

Jesus told them that the only sign they would receive was *the sign of Jonah.* We have already seen what the sign of Jonah was (*Matthew* 12: 38–40). Jonah was the prophet who converted the people of Nineveh and turned them from their evil ways towards God. Now the sign which turned the people of Nineveh to God was not the fact that Jonah was swallowed by the great sea monster. Of that they knew nothing; and Jonah never used it as a means of appeal. The sign of Jonah was *Jonah himself and his message from God.* It was the emergence of the prophet and the message which he brought which changed life for the people of Nineveh.

So what Jesus is saying is that God's sign is *Jesus himself and his message.* It is as if he said to them: " In me you are confronted with God and with the truth of God. What more

could you possibly need? But you are so blind that you cannot
see it." There is truth and there is warning here. Jesus Christ is
God's last word. Beyond him the revelation of God cannot go.
Here is God plain for all to see. Here is God's message plain for
all to hear. Here is God's sign to man. It is the warning truth
that, if Jesus cannot appeal to men, nothing can. If Jesus cannot
convince men, no one can. If men cannot see God in Jesus, they
cannot see God in anything or anyone. When we are confronted
with Jesus Christ, we are confronted with God's final word and
God's ultimate appeal. If that is so, what can be left for the man
who throws away that last chance, who refuses to listen to that
last word, who rejects that last appeal?

THE DANGEROUS LEAVEN

Matthew 16: 5–12

> When the disciples came to the other side, they had forgotten to
> take loaves with them. Jesus said to them, " See that you beware
> of the leaven of the Pharisees and Sadducees." They argued
> amongst themselves: " He must be saying this because we did not
> bring loaves." Jesus knew what they were thinking. " Why," he
> said, " are you arguing among yourselves, you of little faith,
> because you have no loaves? Do you not yet understand, and do
> you not remember the five loaves of the five thousand, and how
> many baskets you took up? And do you not remember the seven
> loaves of the four thousand, and how many hampers you took up?
> How is it that you do not understand that it was not about loaves
> that I spoke to you? Beware of the leaven of the Pharisees and
> Sadducees! " Then they understood that he did not tell them to
> beware of the leaven that is in loaves, but of the teaching of the
> Pharisees and Sadducees.

WE are presented here with a passage of very great difficulty. In
fact, we can only guess at its meaning.

Jesus and his disciples had set out for the other side of the
lake and the disciples had forgotten to take any bread with
them. For some reason they were quite disproportionately

worried and disturbed by this omission. Jesus said to them: " See that you beware of the leaven of the Pharisees and Sadducees." Now the word *leaven* has two meanings. It has its physical and literal meaning, a little piece of fermented dough, without which bread cannot be baked. It was in that sense that the disciples understood Jesus to speak about leaven. With their minds fixed on the forgotten loaves, all that they could think of was that he was warning them against a certain kind of dangerous leaven. They had forgotten to bring bread which meant that, if they were to obtain any, they must buy it from the Gentiles on the other side of the lake. Now no Jew who was strictly orthodox could eat any bread which had been baked or handled by a Gentile. Therefore the problem of getting bread on the other side of the lake was insoluble. The disciples may well have thought that Jesus was saying, " You have forgotten the bread which is clean; take care when you get to the other side of the lake that you do not pollute yourselves by buying bread with defiling leaven in it."

The disciples' minds were running on nothing but bread. So Jesus asked them to remember. " Remember," he said, " the feeding of the five thousand and of the four thousand; and remember the plenty there was to eat, and the abundance which was left over. And when you remember these things, surely you will stop fussing about trifles. You have surely seen that in my presence these trifling problems have already been solved and can be solved again. Stop worrying and trust me."

That was put so bluntly and so clearly that the disciples were bound to understand. Then Jesus repeated his warning: " Beware of the leaven of the Pharisees and Sadducees! " *Leaven* has a second meaning which is metaphorical and not literal and physical. It was the Jewish metaphorical expression for an *evil influence*. To the Jewish mind leaven was always symbolic of evil. It is fermented dough; the Jew identified fermentation with putrefaction; leaven stood for all that was rotten and bad. Leaven has the power to permeate any mass of dough into which it is inserted. Therefore leaven stood for an evil influence liable to spread through life and to corrupt it.

Now the disciples understood. They knew that Jesus was not talking about bread at all; but he was warning them against the evil influence of the teaching and the beliefs of the Pharisees and Sadducees.

What would be in Jesus' mind when he warned against the evil influence of the teaching of the Pharisees and Sadducees? That is something which we can only surmise; but we do know the characteristics of the minds of the Pharisees and Sadducees.

(i) The Pharisees saw religion in terms of laws and commandments and rules and regulations. They saw religion in terms of outward ritual and outward purity. So Jesus is saying, " Take care lest you make your religion a series of ' thou shalt nots ' in the way the Pharisees do. Take care that you do not identify religion with a series of outward actions, and forget that what matters is the state of a man's heart." This is a warning against living in legalism and calling it religion; it is a warning against a religion which looks on a man's outward actions and forgets the inner state of his heart.

(ii) The Sadducees had two characteristics, which were closely connected. They were wealthy and aristocratic, and they were deeply involved in politics. So Jesus may well have been saying, " Take care that you never identify the kingdom of heaven with outward goods, and that you never pin your hopes of bringing it in to political action." This may well be a warning against giving material things too high a place in our scheme of values and against thinking that men can be reformed by political action. Jesus may well have been reminding men that material prosperity is far from being the highest good, and that political action is far from producing the most important results. The true blessings are the blessings of the heart; and the true change is not the change of outward circumstances but the change of the hearts of men.

THE SCENE OF THE GREAT DISCOVERY

Matthew 16: 13–16

When Jesus had come into the districts of Caesarea Philippi, he asked his disciples, " Who do men say that the Son of Man is? " They said, " Some say John the Baptist, others Elijah, others Jeremiah, or one of the prophets." He said to them, " And you—who do you say that I am? " Simon Peter answered, " You are the Anointed One, the Son of the living God."

HERE we have the story of another withdrawal which Jesus made. The end was coming very near and Jesus needed all the time alone with his disciples that he could gain. He had so much to say to them and so much to teach them, although there were many things which then they could not bear and could not understand.

To that end he withdrew to the districts of Caesarea Philippi. Caesarea Philippi lies about twenty-five miles north-east of the Sea of Galilee. It was outside the domain of Herod Antipas, who was the ruler of Galilee, and within the area of Philip the Tetrarch. The population was mainly non-Jewish, and there Jesus would have peace to teach the Twelve.

Confronting Jesus at this time was one clamant and demanding problem. His time was short; his days in the flesh were numbered. The problem was—was there anyone who understood him? Was there anyone who had recognized him for who and what he was? Were there any who, when he was gone from the flesh, would carry on his work, and labour for his kingdom? Obviously that was a crucial problem, for it involved the very survival of the Christian faith. If there were none who had grasped the truth, or even glimpsed it, then all his work was undone; if there were some few who realized the truth, his work was safe. So Jesus was determined to put all to the test and ask his followers who they believed him to be.

It is of the most dramatic interest to see *where* Jesus chose to ask this question. There can have been few districts with more religious associations than Caesarea Philippi.

(i) The area was scattered with temples of the ancient Syrian Baal worship. Thomson in *The Land and the Book* enumerates no fewer than fourteen such temples in the near neighbourhood. Here was an area where the breath of ancient religion was in the very atmosphere. Here was a place beneath the shadow of the ancient gods.

(ii) Not only the Syrian gods had their worship here. Hard by Caesarea Philippi there rose a great hill, in which was a deep cavern; and that cavern was said to be the birthplace of the great god Pan, the god of nature. So much was Caesarea Philippi identified with that god that its original name was Panias, and to this day the place is known as Banias. The legends of the gods of Greece gathered around Caesarea Philippi.

(iii) Further, that cave was said to be the place where the sources of the Jordan sprang to life. Josephus writes: " This is a very fine cave in a mountain, under which there is a great cavity in the earth; and the cavern is abrupt, and prodigiously deep, and full of still water. Over it hangs a vast mountain, and under the cavern arise the springs of the River Jordan." The very idea that this was the place where the River Jordan took its rise would make it redolent of all the memories of Jewish history. The ancient faith of Judaism would be in the air for anyone who was a devout and pious Jew.

(iv) But there was something more. In Caesarea Philippi there was a great temple of white marble built to the godhead of Caesar. It had been built by Herod the Great. Josephus says: " Herod adorned the place, which was already a very remarkable one, still further by the erection of this temple, which he dedicated to Caesar." In another place Josephus describes the cave and the temple: " And when Caesar had further bestowed on Herod another country, he built there also a temple of white marble, hard by the fountains of Jordan. The place is called Panium, where there is the top of a mountain which is raised to an immense height, and at its side, beneath, or at its bottom, a dark cave opens itself; within which there is a horrible precipice that descends abruptly to a vast depth. It contains a mighty quantity of water, which is immovable; and when anyone lets down anything to measure the depth of the earth beneath the water, no length of cord is sufficient to reach it." Later it was Philip, Herod's son, who further beautified and enriched the temple, changed the name of Panias to Caesarea—Caesar's town—and added his own name—*Philippi*, which means *of Philip*—to distinguish it from the Caesarea on the coasts of the Mediterranean. Still later, Herod Agrippa was to call the place Neroneas in honour of the Emperor Nero. No one could look at Caesarea Philippi, even from the distance, without seeing that pile of glistening marble, and thinking of the might and of the divinity of Rome.

Here indeed is a dramatic picture. Here is a homeless, penniless Galilaean carpenter, with twelve very ordinary men around him. At the moment the orthodox are actually plotting and planning to destroy him as a dangerous heretic. He stands in an area littered with the temples of the Syrian gods; in a place where the ancient Greek gods looked down; in a place where the history of Israel crowded in upon the minds of men; where the white marble splendour of the home of Caesar-worship dominated the landscape and compelled the eye. And there—of all places—this amazing carpenter stands and asks men who they believe him to be, and expects the answer, The Son of God. It is as if Jesus deliberately set himself against the background of the world's religions in all their history and their spendour, and demanded to be compared with them and to have the verdict given in his favour. There are few scenes where Jesus' consciousness of his own divinity shines out with a more dazzling light.

THE INADEQUACY OF HUMAN CATEGORIES

Matthew 16: 13–16 (*continued*)

So then at Caesarea Philippi Jesus determined to demand a verdict from his disciples. He must know before he set out from

Jerusalem and the Cross if anyone had even dimly grasped who and what he was. He did not ask the question directly; he led up to it. He began by asking what people were saying about him, and who they took him to be.

Some said that he was John the Baptist. Herod Antipas was not the only man who felt that John the Baptist was so great a figure that it might well be that he had come back from the dead.

Others said that he was Elijah. In doing so, they were saying two things about Jesus. They were saying that he was as great as the greatest of the prophets, for Elijah had always been looked on as the summit and the prince of the prophetic line. They were also saying that Jesus was the forerunner of the Messiah. As *Malachi* had it, the promise of God was: " Behold, I will send you Elijah the prophet before the great and terrible day of the Lord comes " (*Malachi* 4: 5). To this day the Jews expect the return of Elijah before the coming of the Messiah, and to this day they leave a chair vacant for Elijah when they celebrate the Passover, for when Elijah comes, the Messiah will not be far away. So the people looked on Jesus as the herald of the Messiah and the forerunner of the direct intervention of God.

Some said that Jesus was Jeremiah. Jeremiah had a curious place in the expectations of the people of Israel. It was believed that, before the people went into exile, Jeremiah had taken the ark and the altar of incense out of the Temple, and hidden them away in a lonely cave on Mount Nebo; and that, before the coming of the Messiah, he would return and produce them, and the glory of God would come to the people again (2 *Maccabees* 2: 1–12). In 2 *Esdras* 2: 18 the promise of God is: " For thy help I will send my servants Isaiah and Jeremiah."

There is a strange legend of the days of the Maccabaean wars. Before the battle with Nicanor, in which the Jewish commander was the great Judas Maccabaeus, Onias, the good man who had been high priest, had a vision. He prayed for victory in the battle. " This done, in like manner there appeared a man with grey hairs, and exceeding glorious, who was of a

wonderful and excellent majesty. Then Onias answered saying:
' This is a lover of the brethren, who prayeth much for the
people, and for the holy city, to wit, Jeremiah, the prophet of
God.' Whereupon Jeremiah, holding forth his right hand, gave
to Judas a sword of gold, and, in giving it to him, spake thus:
' Take this holy sword, a gift from God, with which thou shalt
wound the adversaries of my people Israel ' " (2 *Maccabees* 15:
1–14). Jeremiah also was to be the forerunner of the coming of
the Messiah, and his country's help in time of trouble.

When the people identified Jesus with Elijah and with
Jeremiah they were, according to their lights, paying him a
great compliment and setting him in a high place, for Jeremiah
and Elijah were none other than the expected forerunners of the
Anointed One of God. When they arrived, the Kingdom would
be very near indeed.

When Jesus had heard the verdicts of the crowd, he asked the
all-important question: " And *you*—who do you say I am? " At
that question there may well have been a moment's silence,
while into the minds of the disciples came thoughts which they
were almost afraid to express in words; and then Peter made his
great discovery and his great confession; and Jesus knew that
his work was safe because there was at least someone who
understood.

It is interesting to note that each of the three gospels has its
own version of the saying of Peter. *Matthew* has:
You are the Christ, the Son of the living God.
Mark is briefest of all (*Mark* 8: 29):
You are the Christ.
Luke is clearest of all (*Luke* 9: 20):
You are the Christ of God.
Jesus knew now that there was at least someone who had
recognized him for the Messiah, the Anointed One of God, the
Son of the living God. The word *Messiah* and the word *Christ*
are the same; the one is the Hebrew and the other is the Greek
for *The Anointed One*. Kings were ordained to office by
anointing, as they still are. The Messiah, the Christ, the
Anointed One is God's King over men.

Within this passage there are two great truths.

(i) Essentially Peter's discovery was that human categories, even the highest, are inadequate to describe Jesus Christ. When the people described Jesus as Elijah or Jeremiah or one of the prophets they thought they were setting Jesus in the highest category they could find. It was the belief of the Jews that for four hundred years the voice of prophecy had been silent; and they were saying that in Jesus men heard again the direct and authentic voice of God. These were great tributes; but they were not great enough; for there are no human categories which are adequate to describe Jesus Christ.

Once Napoleon gave his verdict on Jesus. " I know men," he said, " and Jesus Christ is more than a man." Doubtless Peter could not have given a theological account and a philosophic expression of what he meant when he said that Jesus was the Son of the living God; the one thing of which Peter was quite certain was that no merely human description was adequate to describe him.

(ii) This passage teaches that our discovery of Jesus Christ must be a *personal discovery*. Jesus' question is: " *You*—what do *you* think of me? " When Pilate asked him if he was the king of the Jews, his answer was: " Do you say this of your own accord, or did others say it to you about me? " (*John* 18: 33, 34).

Our knowledge of Jesus must never be at second hand. A man might know every verdict ever passed on Jesus; he might know every Christology that the mind of man had ever thought out; he might be able to give a competent summary of the teaching about Jesus of every great thinker and theologian— and still not be a Christian. Christianity never consists in *knowing about* Jesus; it always consists in *knowing Jesus*. Jesus Christ demands a personal verdict. He did not ask only Peter, he asks every man: " *You*—what do *you* think of me? "

THE GREAT PROMISE

Matthew 16: 17–19

> Jesus answered him, " Blessed are you, Simon son of Jonah,
> because flesh and blood has not revealed this unto you, but my
> Father who is in Heaven. And I tell you, that you are Peter, and
> on this rock I will build my Church, and the gates of Hades will
> not prevail against it. I will give you the keys of the Kingdom of
> Heaven; and whatever you bind on earth will remain bound in
> heaven; and whatever you loose on earth will remain loosed in
> heaven."

THIS passage is one of the storm-centres of New Testament
interpretation. It has always been difficult to approach it calmly
and without prejudice, for it is the Roman Catholic foundation
of the position of the Pope and of the Church. It is taken by the
Roman Catholic Church to mean that to Peter were given the
keys which admit or exclude a man from heaven, and that to
Peter was given the power to absolve or not to absolve a man
from his sins. It is further argued by the Roman Catholic
Church that Peter, with these tremendous rights, became the
bishop of Rome; and that this power descended to all the
bishops of Rome; and that it exists today in the Pope, who is
the head of the Church and the Bishop of Rome.

It is easy to see how impossible any such doctrine is for a
Protestant believer; and it is also easy to see how Protestant
and Roman Catholic alike may approach this passage, not with
the single-hearted desire to discover its meaning, but with the
determination to yield nothing of his own position, and, if
possible, to destroy the position of the other. Let us then try to
find its true meaning.

There is a play on words. In Greek *Peter* is *Petros* and a *rock*
is *petra*. Peter's Aramaic name was *Kephas*, and that also is the
Aramaic for a *rock*. In either language there is here a play upon
words. Immediately Peter had made his great discovery and
confession, Jesus said to him: " You are *petros*, and on this
petra I will build my Church."

Whatever else this is, it is a word of tremendous praise. It is a metaphor which is by no means strange or unusual to Jewish thought.

The Rabbis applied the word *rock* to Abraham. They had a saying: " When the Holy One saw Abraham who was going to arise, he said, ' Lo, I have discovered a rock (*petra*) to found the world upon.' Therefore he called Abraham *rock* (*sur*), as it is said: ' Look unto the rock whence ye are hewn.' " Abraham was the rock on which the nation and the purpose of God were founded.

Even more the word *rock* (*sur*) is again and again applied to God himself. " He is the Rock; his work is perfect " (*Deuteronomy* 32: 4). " For their rock is not as our Rock " (*Deuteronomy* 32: 31). " There is no rock like our God " (1 *Samuel* 2: 2). " The Lord is my rock, and my fortress, and my deliverer " (2 *Samuel* 22: 2). The same phrase occurs in *Psalm* 18: 2. " Who is a rock, except our God? " (*Psalm* 18: 31). The same phrase is in 2 *Samuel* 22: 32.

One thing is clear. To call anyone a *rock* was the greatest of compliments; and no Jew who knew his Old Testament could ever use the phrase without his thoughts turning to God, who alone was the true rock of his defence and salvation. What then did Jesus mean when in this passage he used the word *rock*? To that question at least four answers have been given.

(i) Augustine took the *rock* to mean *Jesus himself*. It is as if Jesus said: " You are Peter; and on myself as rock I will found my Church; and the day will come when, as the reward of your faith, you will be great in the Church."

(ii) The second explanation is that the rock is the truth that Jesus Christ is the Son of the living God. To Peter that great truth had been divinely revealed. The fact that Jesus Christ is the Son of God is indeed the foundation stone of the Church's faith and belief, but it hardly seems to bring out the play on words which is here.

(iii) The third explanation is that the rock is Peter's faith. On the faith of Peter the Church is founded. That faith was the spark which was to kindle the faith of the world-wide Church. It was the initial impetus which was one day to bring the universal Church into being.

(iv) The last interpretation is still the best. It is that Peter himself is the rock, but in a special sense. He is not the rock on which the Church is founded; that rock is God. He is the first stone of the whole Church. Peter was the first man on earth to discover who Jesus was; he was the first man to make the leap of faith and see in him the Son of the living God. In other words, Peter was the first member of the Church, and, in that sense, the whole Church is built on him. It is as if Jesus said to Peter: " Peter, you are the first man to grasp who I am; you are therefore the first stone, the foundation stone, the very beginning of the Church which I am founding." And in ages to come, everyone who makes the same discovery as Peter is another stone added into the edifice of the Church of Christ.

Two things help to make this clear.

(i) Often the Bible uses pictures for the sake of one definite point. The details of the picture are not to be stressed; it is one point which is being made. In connection with the Church the New Testament repeatedly uses the picture of *building*, but it uses that picture for many purposes and from many points of view. Here Peter is the foundation, in the sense that he is the one person on whom the whole Church is built, for he was the first man to discover who Jesus was. In *Ephesians* 2: 20 the prophets and the apostles are said to be the foundation of the Church. It is on their work and on their witness and on their fidelity that the Church on earth, humanly speaking, depends. In the same passage, Jesus Christ is the chief *corner-stone*; he is the force who holds the Church together. Without him the whole edifice would disintegrate and collapse. In 1 *Peter* 2: 4–8 all Christians are living stones who are to be built into the fabric of the Church. In 1 *Corinthians* 3: 11 Jesus is the only foundation, and no man can lay any other. It is clear to see that the New Testament writers took the picture of *building* and used it in many ways. But at the back of it all is always the idea that Jesus Christ is the real foundation of the Church, and the only power who holds the Church together. When Jesus said to

Peter that on him he would found his Church, he did not mean that the Church *depended* on Peter, as it depended on himself and on God the Rock. He did mean that the Church *began* with Peter; in that sense Peter is the foundation of the Church; and that is an honour that no man can take from him.

(ii) The second point is that the very word *Church* (*ekklēsia*) in this passage conveys something of a wrong impression. We are apt to think of the Church as an institution and an organization with buildings and offices, and services and meetings, and organizations and all kinds of activities. The word that Jesus almost certainly used was *quahal*, which is the word the Old Testament uses for *the congregation of Israel*, the gathering of the people of the Lord. What Jesus said to Peter was: " Peter, you are the beginning of the new Israel, the new people of the Lord, the new fellowship of those who believe in my name." Peter was the first of the fellowship of believers in Christ. It was not a Church in the human sense, still less a Church in a denominational sense, that began with Peter. What began with Peter was the fellowship of all believers in Jesus Christ, not identified with any Church and not limited to any Church, but embracing all who love the Lord.

So then we may say that the first part of this controversial passage means that Peter is the foundation stone of the Church in the sense that he was the first of that great fellowship who joyfully declare their own discovery that Jesus Christ is Lord; but that, in the ultimate sense, it is God himself who is the rock on which the Church is built.

THE GATES OF HELL

Matthew 16: 17–19 (*continued*)

JESUS goes on to say that the gates of Hades shall not prevail against his Church. What does that mean? The idea of *gates prevailing* is not by any means a natural or an easily understood picture. Again there is more than one explanation.

(i) It may be that the picture is the picture of a *fortress*. This suggestion may find support in the fact that on the top of the mountain overlooking Caesarea Philippi there stand today the ruins of a great castle which may well have stood there in all its glory in the time of Jesus. It may be that Jesus is thinking of his Church as a fortress, and the forces of evil as an opposing fortress; and is saying that the embattled might of evil will never prevail against the Church.

(ii) Richard Glover has an interesting explanation. In the ancient east the *Gate* was always the place, especially in the little towns and villages, where the elders and the rulers met and dispensed counsel and justice. For instance, the law is laid down that, if a man has a rebellious and disobedient son, he must bring him " to the elders of his city at the gate of the place where he lives " (*Deuteronomy* 21: 19), and there judgment will be given and justice done. In *Deuteronomy* 25: 7 the man with a certain problem is told to " go up to the gate to the elders." The gate was the scene of simple justice where the elders met. So *the gate* may have come to mean *the place of government*. For long, for instance, the government of Turkey was called the *Sublime Porte* (*porte* being the French for *gate*). So then the phrase would mean: The powers, the government of Hades will never prevail against the Church.

(iii) There is a third possibility. Suppose we go back to the idea that the rock on which the Church is founded is the conviction that Jesus is none other than the Son of the living God. Now Hades was not the place of punishment, but the place where, in primitive Jewish belief, all the dead went. Obviously, the function of gates is *to keep things in*, to confine them, shut them up, control them. There was one person whom the gates of Hades could not shut in; and that was Jesus Christ. He burst the bonds of death. As the writer of *Acts* has it, " It was not possible for him to be held by death. . . . Thou wilt not abandon my soul to Hades, nor let thy Holy One see corruption " (*Acts* 2: 24, 27). So then this may be a triumphant reference to nothing less than the coming Resurrection. Jesus may be saying: " You have discovered that I am the Son of the living God. The time will soon come when I will be crucified, and the gates of Hades will close behind me. But they are powerless to shut me in. The gates of Hades have no power against me the Son of the living God."

However we take it, this phrase triumphantly expresses the indestructibility of Christ and his Church.

THE PLACE OF PETER

Matthew 16: 17–19 (*continued*)

WE now come to two phrases in which Jesus describes certain privileges which were given to and certain duties which were laid on Peter.

(i) He says that he will give to Peter *the keys of the Kingdom.* This is an obviously difficult phrase; and we will do well to begin by setting down the things about it of which we can be sure.

(*a*) The phrase always signified some kind of very special power. For instance, the Rabbis had a saying: " The keys of birth, of the rain, and of the resurrection of the dead belong to God." That is to say, only God has the power to create life, to send the rain, and to raise the dead to life again. The phrase always indicates a special power.

(*b*) In the New Testament this phrase is regularly attached to Jesus. It is in his hands, and no one else's, that the keys are. In *Revelation* 1: 18 the risen Christ says: " I am the living one; I died, and behold I am alive for evermore, and I have the keys of Death and Hades." Again in *Revelation* 3: 7 the Risen Christ is described as, " The holy one, the true one, who has the key of David, who opens and no one shall shut, who shuts and no one opens." This phrase must be interpreted as indicating a certain divine right, and whatever the promise made to Peter, it cannot be taken as annulling, or infringing, a right which belongs alone to God and to the Son of God.

(*c*) All these New Testament pictures and usages go back to a picture in *Isaiah* (*Isaiah* 22: 22). Isaiah describes Eliakim, who will have the key of the house of David on his shoulder, and who alone will open and shut. Now the duty of Eliakim was to be *the faithful steward of the house.* It is the steward who carries the keys of the house, who in the morning opens the door, and in the evening shuts it, and through whom visitors gain access to the royal presence. So then what Jesus is saying to Peter is that in the days to come, he will be *the steward of the Kingdom.* And in the case of Peter the whole idea is that of *opening*, not shutting, the door of the Kingdom.

That came abundantly true. At Pentecost, Peter opened the door to three thousand souls (*Acts* 2: 41). He opened the door to the Gentile centurion Cornelius, so that it was swinging on its hinges to admit the great Gentile world (*Acts* 10). *Acts* 15 tells how the Council of Jerusalem opened wide the door for the Gentiles, and how it was Peter's witness which made that possible (*Acts* 15: 14; *Simeon* is *Peter*). The promise that Peter would have the keys to the Kingdom was the promise that Peter would be the means of opening the door to God for thousands upon thousands of people in the days to come. But it is not only Peter who has the keys of the Kingdom; every Christian has; for it is open to every one of us to open the door of the Kingdom to some other and so to enter into the great promise of Christ.

(ii) Jesus further promised Peter that what he *bound* would remain *bound*, and what he *loosed* would remain *loosed.* Richard Glover takes this to mean that Peter would lay men's sins, bind them, to men's consciences, and that he would then loose them from their sins by telling them of the love and the forgiveness of God. That is a lovely thought, and no doubt true, for such is the duty of every Christian preacher and teacher, but there is more to it than that.

To loose and *to bind* were very common Jewish phrases. They were used especially of the decisions of the great teachers and the great Rabbis. Their regular sense, which any Jew would recognize was *to allow* and *to forbid. To bind* something was *to declare it forbidden; to loose* was *to declare it allowed.* These were the regular phrases for taking decisions in regard to the law. That is in fact the only thing these phrases in such a context would mean. So what Jesus is saying to Peter is: " Peter, you are going to have grave and heavy responsibilities laid upon you. You are going to have to take decisions which will affect the welfare of the whole Church. You will be the guide and the director of the infant Church. And the decisions you give will be so important, that they will affect the souls of men in time and in eternity."

The privilege of the keys meant that Peter would be the steward of the household of God, opening the door for men to enter into the Kingdom. The duty of binding and loosing meant that Peter would have to take decisions about the Church's life and practice which would have the most far-reaching consequences. And indeed, when we read the early chapters of *Acts*, we see that in Jerusalem that is precisely what Peter did.

When we paraphrase this passage which has caused so much argument and controversy, we see that it deals, not with ecclesiastical forms but with the things of salvation. Jesus said to Peter: " Peter, your name means a rock, and your destiny is to be a rock. You are the first man to recognize me for what I am, and therefore you are the first stone in the edifice of the fellowship of those who are mine. Against that fellowship the embattled powers of evil will no more prevail than they will be able to hold me captive in death. And in the days to come, you must be the steward who will unlock the doors of the Kingdom that Jew and Gentile may come in; and you must be the wise administrator and guide who will solve the problems and direct the work of the infant and growing fellowship."

Peter had made the great discovery; and Peter was given the great privilege and the great responsibility. It is a discovery which everyone must make for himself; and, when he has made it, the same privilege and the same responsibility are laid upon him.

THE GREAT REBUKE

Matthew 16: 20–23

> He gave orders to his disciples to tell no one that he was God's Anointed One. From that time Jesus began to show his disciples that he must go to Jerusalem, and suffer many things from the elders and chief priests and scribes, and be killed and be raised on the third day. Peter caught hold of him, and began to urge upon him: " God forbid that this should happen to you! This must never come to you! " He turned and said to Peter, " Get behind me, Satan! You are putting a stumbling-block in my way. Your ideas are not God's but men's."

ALTHOUGH the disciples had grasped the fact that Jesus was God's Messiah, they still had not grasped what that great fact meant. To them it meant something totally different from what it meant to Jesus. They were still thinking in terms of a conquering Messiah, a warrior king, who would sweep the Romans from Palestine and lead Israel to power. That is why Jesus commanded them to silence. If they had gone out to the people and preached their own ideas, all they would have succeeded in doing would have been to raise a tragic, rebellion; they could have produced only another outbreak of violence doomed to disaster. Before they could preach that Jesus was the Messiah, they had to learn what that meant. In point of fact, Peter's reaction shows just how far the disciples were from realizing just what Jesus meant when he claimed to be the Messiah and the Son of God.

So Jesus began to seek to open their eyes to the fact that for him there was no way but the way of the Cross. He said that he must go to Jerusalem and suffer at the hands of the " elders and chief priests and scribes." These three groups of men were in fact the three groups of which the Sanhedrin was composed. The elders were the respected men of the people; the chief priests were predominantly Sadducees; and the scribes were Pharisees. In effect, Jesus is saying that he must suffer at the hands of the orthodox religious leaders of the country.

No sooner had Jesus said that than Peter reacted with
violence. Peter had been brought up on the idea of a Messiah of
power and glory and conquest. To him the idea of a suffering
Messiah, the connection of a cross with the work of the
Messiah, was incredible. He " caught hold " of Jesus. Almost
certainly the meaning is that he flung a protecting arm round
Jesus, as if to hold him back from a suicidal course. " This,"
said Peter, " must not and cannot happen to you." And then
came the great rebuke which makes us catch our breath—" Get
behind me, Satan! " There are certain things which we must
grasp in order to understand this tragic and dramatic scene.

We must try to catch the tone of voice in which Jesus spoke.
He certainly did not say it with a snarl of anger in his voice and
a blaze of indignant passion in his eyes. He said it like a man
wounded to the heart, with poignant grief and a kind of
shuddering horror. Why should he react like that?

He did so because in that moment there came back to him
with cruel force the temptations which he had faced in the
wilderness at the beginning of his ministry. There he had been
tempted to take the way of power. " Give them bread, give them
material things," said the tempter, " and they will follow you."
" Give them sensations," said the tempter, " give them wonders,
and they will follow you." " Compromise with the world," said
the tempter. " Reduce your standards, and they will follow
you." It was precisely the same temptations with which Peter
was confronting Jesus all over again.

Nor were these temptations ever wholly absent from the
mind of Jesus. Luke sees far into the heart of the Master. At the
end of the temptation story, Luke writes: " And when the devil
had ended every temptation, he departed from him until an
opportune time " (*Luke* 4: 13). Again and again the tempter
launched this attack. No one wants a cross; no one wants to die
in agony; even in the Garden that same temptation came to
Jesus, the temptation to take another way.

And here Peter is offering it to him now. The sharpness and
the poignancy of Jesus' answer are due to the fact that Peter
was urging upon him the very things which the tempter was

always whispering to him, the very things against which he had to steel himself. Peter was confronting Jesus with that way of escape from the Cross which to the end beckoned to him.

That is why Peter was *Satan*. *Satan* literally means *the Adversary*. That is why Peter's ideas were not God's but men's. Satan is any force which seeks to deflect us from the way of God; Satan is any influence which seeks to make us turn back from the hard way that God has set before us; Satan is any power which seeks to make human desires take the place of the divine imperative.

What made the temptation more acute was the fact that it came from one who loved him. Peter spoke as he did only because he loved Jesus so much that he could not bear to think of him treading that dreadful path and dying that awful death. The hardest temptation of all is the one which comes from protecting love. There are times when fond love seeks to deflect us from the perils of the path of God; but the real love is not the love which holds the knight at home, but the love which sends him out to obey the commandments of the chivalry which is given, not to make life easy, but to make life great. It is quite possible for love to be so protecting that it seeks to protect those it loves from the adventure of the warfare of the soldier of Christ, and from the strenuousness of the pathway of the pilgrim of God. What really wounded Jesus' heart and what really made him speak as he did, was that the tempter spoke to him that day through the fond but mistaken love of Peter's hot heart.

THE CHALLENGE BEHIND THE REBUKE

Matthew 16: 20–23 (*continued*)

BEFORE we leave this passage, it is interesting to look at two very early interpretations of the phrase: " Get behind me, Satan! " Origen suggested that, Jesus was saying to Peter: " Peter, your place is *behind* me, not *in front* of me. It is your place *to follow* me in the way I choose, not to try *to lead* me in the way you would like me to go." If the phrase can be interpreted in that way, something at least of its sting is removed, for it does not banish Peter from Christ's presence; rather it recalls him to his proper place, as a follower walking in the footsteps of Jesus. It is true for all of us that we must ever take the way of Christ and never seek to compel him to take our way.

A further development comes when we closely examine this saying of Jesus in the light of his saying to Satan at the end of the temptations as Matthew records it in *Matthew* 4: 10. Although in the English translations the two passages sound different they are almost, but not quite, the same. In *Matthew* 4: 10 the Revised Standard Version translates: " Begone, Satan! " and the Greek is: " *Hupage Satana.*" (The final *e* of *hupage* is pronounced as the *e* in *the*, and the *g* is hard as in *get*). In the Revised Standard Version translation of *Matthew* 16: 23, Jesus says to Peter: " Get behind me, Satan," and the Greek is: " *Hupage opiso mou, Satana.*"

The point is that Jesus' command to Satan is simply: " Begone! " while his command to Peter is: " Begone *behind me*! " that is to say, " Become my follower again." Satan is banished from the presence of Christ; Peter is recalled to be Christ's follower. The one thing that Satan could never become is a follower of Christ; in his diabolical pride he could never submit to that; that is why he is Satan. On the other hand, Peter might be mistaken and might fall and might sin, but for him there was always the challenge and the chance to become a follower again. It is as if Jesus said to Peter: " At the moment you have spoken as Satan would. But that is not the real Peter speaking. You can redeem yourself. Come behind me, and be my follower again, and even yet, all will be well." The basic difference between Peter and Satan is precisely the fact that Satan would never get behind Jesus. So long as a man is prepared to try to follow, even after he has fallen, there is still for him the hope of glory here and hereafter.

THE GREAT CHALLENGE

Matthew 16: 24–26

> Then Jesus said to his disciples: " If anyone wishes to come after me, let him deny himself, and take up his cross, and let him follow me. For whoever wishes to keep his life safe, will lose it; and whoever loses his life for my sake, will find it. For what shall a man be profited if he shall gain the whole world at the penalty of the price of his life? Or what will a man give in exchange for his life? "

HERE we have one of the dominant and ever-recurring themes of Jesus' teaching. These are things which Jesus said to men again and again (*Matthew* 10: 37–39; *Mark* 8: 34–37; *Luke* 9: 23–27; 14: 25–27; 17: 33; *John* 12: 25). Again and again he confronted them with the challenge of the Christian life. There are three things which a man must be prepared to do, if he is to live the Christian life.

(i) He must *deny himself.* Ordinarily we use the word *self-denial* in a restricted sense. We use it to mean giving up something. For instance, a week of self-denial may be a week when we do without certain pleasures or luxuries in order to contribute to some good cause. But that is only a very small part of what Jesus meant by self-denial. To deny oneself means in every moment of life to say no to self and yes to God. To deny oneself means once, finally and for all to dethrone self and to enthrone God. To deny oneself means to obliterate self as the dominant principle of life, and to make God the ruling principle, more, the ruling passion, of life. The life of constant self-denial is the life of constant assent to God.

(ii) He must *take up his cross.* That is to say, he must take up the burden of sacrifice. The Christian life is the life of sacrificial service. The Christian may have to abandon personal ambition to serve Christ; it may be that he will discover that the place where he can render the greatest service to Jesus Christ is somewhere where the reward will be small and the prestige non-existent. He will certainly have to sacrifice time and leisure and pleasure in order to serve God through the service of his fellow-men.

To put it quite simply, the comfort of the fireside, the pleasure of a visit to a place of entertainment, may well have to be sacrificed for the duties of the eldership, the calls of the youth club, the visit to the home of some sad or lonely soul. He may well have to sacrifice certain things he could well afford to possess in order to give more away. The Christian life is the sacrificial life.

Luke, with a flash of sheer insight, adds one word to this command of Jesus: " Let him take up his cross *daily*." The really important thing is not the great moments of sacrifice, but a life lived in the constant hourly awareness of the demands of God and the need of others. The Christian life is a life which is always concerned with others more than it is concerned with itself.

(iii) He must *follow Jesus Christ*. That is to say, he must render to Jesus Christ a perfect obedience. When we were young we used to play a game called " Follow my Leader." Everything the leader did, however difficult, and, in the case of the game, however ridiculous, we had to copy. The Christian life is a constant following of our leader, a constant obedience in thought and word and action to Jesus Christ. The Christian walks in the footsteps of Christ, wherever he may lead.

LOSING AND FINDING LIFE

Matthew 16: 24–26 (*continued*)

THERE is all the difference in the world between *existing* and *living*. To exist is simply to have the lungs breathing and the heart beating; to live is to be alive in a world where everything is worth while, where there is peace in the soul, joy in the heart, and a thrill in every moment. Jesus here gives us the recipe for *life* as distinct from *existence*.

(i) The man who plays for safety loses life. Matthew was

writing somewhere between A.D. 80 and 90. He was therefore writing in some of the bitterest days of persecution. He was saying: " The time may well come when you can save your life by abandoning your faith; but if you do, so far from saving life, in the real sense of the term you are losing life." The man who is faithful may die but he dies to live; the man who abandons his faith for safety may live, but he lives to die.

In our day and generation it is not likely to be a question of martyrdom, but it still remains a fact that, if we meet life in the constant search for safety, security, ease and comfort, if every decision is taken from worldly-wise and prudential motives, we are losing all that makes life worth while. Life becomes a soft and flabby thing, when it might have been an adventure. Life becomes a selfish thing, when it might have been radiant with service. Life becomes an earthbound thing when it might have been reaching for the stars. Someone once wrote a bitter epitaph on a man: " He was born a man and died a grocer." Any trade or profession might be substituted for the word grocer. The man who plays for safety ceases to be a man, for man is made in the image of God.

(ii) The man who risks all—and maybe looks as if he had lost all—for Christ finds life. It is the simple lesson of history that it has always been the adventurous souls, bidding farewell to security and safety, who wrote their names on history and greatly helped the world of men. Unless there had been those prepared to take risks, many a medical cure would not exist. Unless there had been those prepared to take risks, many of the machines which make life easier would never have been invented. Unless there were mothers prepared to take risks, no child would ever be born. It is the man who is prepared " to bet his life that there is a God " who in the end finds life.

(iii) Then Jesus speaks with warning: " Suppose a man plays for safety; suppose he gains the whole world; then suppose that he finds that life is not worth living, what can he give to get life back again? " And the grim truth is that he cannot get life back again. In every decision of life we are doing something to ourselves; we are making ourselves a certain kind of person; we are building up steadily and inevitably a certain kind of character; we are making ourselves able to do certain things and quite unable to do others. It is perfectly possible for a man to gain all the things he set his heart upon, and then to awaken one morning to find that he has missed the most important things of all.

The *world* stands for material things as opposed to God; and of all material things there are three things to be said. (*a*) No one can take them with him at the end; he can take only himself; and if he degraded himself in order to get them, his regret will be bitter. (*b*) They cannot help a man in the shattering days of life. Material things will never mend a broken heart or cheer a lonely soul. (*c*) If by any chance a man gained his material possessions in a way that is dishonourable, there will come a day when conscience will speak, and he will know hell on this side of the grave.

The world is full of voices crying out that he is a fool who sells real life for material things.

(iv) Finally Jesus asks: " What will a man give in exchange for his soul? " The Greek is, " What *antallagma* will a man give for his soul? " *Antallagma* is an interesting word. In the book of *Ecclesiasticus* we read: " There is no *antallagma* for a faithful friend," and, " There is no *antallagma* for a disciplined soul " (*Ecclesiasticus* 6: 15; 26: 14). It means that there is no price which will buy a faithful friend or a disciplined soul. So then this final saying of Jesus can mean two things.

(*a*) It can mean: Once a man has lost his real life, because of his desire for security and for material things, there is no price that he can pay to get it back again. He has done something to himself which cannot ever be fully obliterated.

(*b*) It can mean: A man owes himself and everything else to Jesus Christ; and there is nothing that a man can give to Christ in place of his life. It is quite possible for a man to try to give his money to Christ and to withhold his life. It is still more possible for a man to give lip-service to Christ and to withhold his life. Many a person gives his weekly freewill offering to the Church, but does not attend; obviously that does not satisfy the demands of church membership. The only possible gift to the Church is ourselves; and the only possible gift to Christ is our whole life. There is no substitute for it. Nothing less will do.

THE WARNING AND THE PROMISE

Matthew 16: 27, 28

" For the Son of Man will come with the glory of his Father, with his angels, and then he will render to each man in accordance with his way of action. This is the truth I tell you—there are some of those who are standing here who will not taste death, until they see the Son of Man coming in his Kingdom."

THERE are two quite distinct sayings here.

(i) The first is a *warning*, the warning of inevitable judgment. Life is going somewhere—and life is going to judgment. In any sphere of life there inevitably comes the day of reckoning. There is no escape from the fact that Christianity teaches that after life there comes the judgment; and when we take this passage in conjunction with the passage which goes before, we see at once what the standard of judgment is. The man who selfishly hugs life to himself, the man whose first concern is his own safety, his own security and his own comfort, is in heaven's eyes the failure, however rich and successful and prosperous he may seem to be. The man who spends himself for others, and who lives life as a gallant adventure, is the man who receives heaven's praise and God's reward.

(ii) The second is a *promise*. As Matthew records this phrase, it reads as if Jesus spoke as if he expected his own visible return in the lifetime of some of those who were listening to him. If Jesus said that he was mistaken. But we see the real meaning of what Jesus said when we turn to Mark's record of it. Mark has: And he said to them, " Truly, I say to you, there are some standing here who will not taste death before they see the Kingdom of God come with power " (*Mark* 9: 1).

It is of the mighty working of his Kingdom that Jesus is speaking; and what he said came most divinely true. There were those standing there who saw the coming of Jesus in the coming of the Spirit at the day of Pentecost. There were those who were to see Gentile and Jew swept into the Kingdom; they were to see the tide of the Christian message sweep across Asia Minor and cover Europe until it reached Rome. Well within the life-time of those who heard Jesus speak, the Kingdom came with power.

Again, this is to be taken closely with what goes before. Jesus warned his disciples that he must go to Jerusalem, and that there he must suffer many things and die. That was the shame; but the shame was not the end. After the Cross there came the Resurrection. The Cross was not to be the end; it was to be the beginning of the unleashing of that power which was to surge throughout the whole world. This is a promise to the disciples of Jesus Christ that nothing men can do can hinder the expansion of the Kingdom of God.

THE MOUNT OF TRANSFIGURATION

Matthew 17: 1–8

Six days after, Jesus took Peter, and James, and John his brother, and brought them by themselves to a high mountain, and his appearance was changed in their presence. His face shone like the sun, and his garments became as white as the light. And, look you, Moses and Elijah appeared to them, talking with him. Peter said to Jesus, " Lord, it is a fine thing for us to be here. I will make three booths, one for you, one for Moses, and one for Elijah." While he was still speaking, look you, a shining cloud overshadowed them; and, look you, there came a voice out of the cloud saying, " This is my beloved Son, in whom I am well pleased. Hear him! " When the disciples heard that, they fell on their faces and were exceedingly afraid. Jesus came and touched them and said, " Rise, and do not be afraid." They lifted up their eyes, and saw no one, except Jesus alone.

THE great moment of Caesarea Philippi was followed by the great hour on the Mount of Transfiguration. Let us first look at the scene where this time of glory came to Jesus and his three chosen disciples. There is a tradition which connects the Transfiguration with Mount Tabor, but that is unlikely. The top of Mount Tabor was an armed fortress and a great castle; it seems almost impossible that the Transfiguration could have happened on a mountain which was a fortress. Much more likely the scene of the Transfiguration was Mount Hermon. Hermon was fourteen miles from Caesarea Philippi. Hermon is 9,400 feet high, 11,000 feet above the level of the Jordan valley, so high that it can actually be seen from the Dead Sea, at the other end of Palestine, more than one hundred miles away.

It cannot have been on the very summit of the mountain that this happened. The mountain is too high for that. Canon Tristram tells how he and his party ascended it. They were able to ride practically to the top, and the ride took five hours. Activity is not easy on so high a summit. Tristram says, " We spent a great part of the day on the summit, but were before long painfully affected by the rarity of the atmosphere."

It was somewhere on the slopes of the beautiful and stately Mount Hermon that the Transfiguration happened. It must have happened in the night. Luke tells us that the disciples were weighted down with sleep (*Luke* 9: 32). It was the next day when Jesus and his disciples came back to the plain to find the father of the epileptic boy waiting for them (*Luke* 9: 37). It was some time in the sunset, or the late evening, or the night, that this amazing vision took place.

Why did Jesus go there? Why did he make this expedition to these lonely mountain slopes? Luke gives us the clue. He tells us that Jesus was praying (*Luke* 9: 29).

We must put ourselves, as far as we can, in Jesus' place. By this time he was on the way to the Cross. Of that he was quite sure; again and again he told his disciples that it was so. At Caesarea Philippi we have seen him facing one problem and dealing with one question. We have seen him seeking to find out if there was anyone who had recognized him for who and what he was.

We have seen that question triumphantly answered, for Peter had grasped the great fact that Jesus could only be described as the Son of God. But there was an even greater question than that which Jesus had to solve before he set out on the last journey.

He had to make quite sure, sure beyond all doubt, that he was doing what God wished him to do. He had to make certain that it was indeed God's will that he should go to the Cross. Jesus went up Mount Hermon to ask God: " Am I doing your will in setting my face to go to Jerusalem? " Jesus went up Mount Hermon to listen for the voice of God. He would take no step without consulting God. How then could he take the biggest step of all without consulting him? Of everything Jesus asked one question and only one question: " Is it God's will for me? " And that is the question he was asking in the loneliness of the slopes of Hermon.

It is one of the supreme differences between Jesus and us, that Jesus always asked: " What does *God* wish me to do? "; we nearly always ask: " What do *I* wish to do? " We often say that the unique characteristic of Jesus was that he was *sinless*. What do we mean by that? We mean precisely this, that Jesus had no will but the will of God. The hymn of the Christian must always be:

> " Thy way, not mine, O lord,
>   However dark it be!
> Lead me by thine own hand;
>   Choose out the path for me.
>
> I dare not choose my lot,
>   I would not if I might:
> Choose thou for me, my God,
>   So shall I walk aright.
>
> Not mine, not mine the choice
>   In things or great or small;
> Be thou my Guide, my Strength,
>   My Wisdom and my All."

When Jesus had a problem, he did not seek to solve it only by the power of his own thought; he did not take it to others for human advice; he took it to the lonely place and to God.

THE BENEDICTION OF THE PAST

Matthew 17: 1–8 *(continued)*

THERE on the mountain slopes two great figures appeared to Jesus—Moses and Elijah.

It is fascinating to see in how many respects the experience of these two great servants of God matched the experience of Jesus. When Moses came down from the mountain of Sinai, he did not know that the skin of his face shone (*Exodus* 34: 29). Both Moses and Elijah had their most intimate experiences of God on a mountain top. It was into Mount Sinai that Moses went to receive the tables of the law (*Exodus* 31: 18). It was on Mount Horeb that Elijah found God, not in the wind, and not in the earthquake, but in the still small voice (1 *Kings* 19: 9–12). It is a strange thing that there was something awesome about the deaths of both Moses and Elijah. *Deuteronomy* 34: 5, 6 tells of the lonely death of Moses on Mount Nebo. It reads as if God himself was the burier of the great leader of the people: " And he buried him in the valley in the land of Moab, opposite Beth-peor; but no man knows the place of his burial to this day." As for Elijah, as the old story has it, he took his departure from the astonished Elisha in a chariot and horses of fire (2 *Kings* 2: 11). The two great figures who appeared to Jesus as he was setting out for Jerusalem were men who seemed too great to die.

Further, as we have already seen, it was the consistent Jewish belief that Elijah was to be forerunner and herald of the Messiah, and it was also believed by at least some Jewish teachers that, when the Messiah came, he would be accompanied by Moses.

It is easy to see how appropriate this vision of Moses and Elijah was. But none of these reasons is the real reason why the vision of Moses and Elijah came to Jesus.

Once again we must turn to Luke's account of the Transfiguration. He tells us that Moses and Elijah spoke with Jesus,

as the Revised Standard Version has it, " of his departure which
he was to accomplish at Jerusalem " (*Luke* 9: 31). The word
which is used for *departure* in the Greek is very significant. It is
exodos, which is exactly the same as the English word *exodus*.

The word *exodus* has one special connection; it is the word
which is always used of the departure of the people of Israel out
of the land of Egypt, into the unknown way of the desert, which
in the end was going to lead them to the Promised Land. The
word *exodus* is the word which describes what we might well
call the most adventurous journey in human history, a journey
in which a whole people in utter trust in God went out into the
unknown. *That is precisely what Jesus was going to do.* In utter
trust in God he was going to set out on the tremendous
adventure of that journey to Jerusalem, a journey beset with
perils, a journey involving a cross, but a journey issuing in
glory.

In Jewish thought these two figures, Moses and Elijah,
always stood for certain things. Moses was the greatest of all
the *law-givers*; he was supremely and uniquely the man who
brought God's law to men. Elijah was the greatest of all the
prophets; in him the voice of God spoke to men with unique
directness. These two men were the twin peaks of Israel's
religious history and achievement. It is as if the greatest figures
in Israel's history came to Jesus, as he was setting out on the
last and greatest adventure into the unknown, and told him to
go on. In them all history rose up and pointed Jesus on his way.
In them all history recognized Jesus as its own consummation.
The greatest of the law-givers and the greatest of the prophets
recognized Jesus as the one of whom they had dreamed, as the
one whom they had foretold. Their appearance was the signal
for Jesus to go on. So, then, the greatest human figures
witnessed to Jesus that he was on the right way and bade him
go out on his adventurous *exodus* to Jerusalem and to Calvary.

But there was more than that; not only did the greatest
law-giver and the greatest prophet assure Jesus that he was
right; the very voice of God came telling him that he was on the
right way. All the gospel writers speak of the luminous cloud

which overshadowed them. That cloud was part of Israel's history. All through that history the luminous cloud stood for the *shechinah*, which was nothing less than the glory of Almighty God.

In *Exodus* we read of *the pillar of cloud* which was to lead the people on their way (*Exodus* 13: 21, 22). Again in *Exodus* we read of the building and the completing of the Tabernacle; and at the end of the story there come the words: " Then the *cloud* covered the tent of meeting, and the glory of the Lord filled the tabernacle " (*Exodus* 40: 34). It was in the *cloud* that the Lord descended to give the tables of the law to Moses (*Exodus* 34: 5). Once again we meet this mysterious, luminous cloud at the dedication of Solomon's Temple: " And when the priests came out of the holy place, a *cloud* filled the house of the Lord " (1 *Kings* 8: 10, 11; cp. 2 *Chronicles* 5: 13, 14; 7: 2). All through the Old Testament there is this picture of the cloud, in which was the mysterious glory of God.

We are able to add another vivid fact to this. Travellers tell us of a curious and characteristic phenomenon connected with Mount Hermon. Edersheim writes: " A strange peculiarity has been noticed about Hermon in ' the extreme rapidity of the formation of cloud upon the summit. In a few minutes a thick cap forms over the top of the mountain, and as quickly disperses, and entirely disappears.' " No doubt on this occasion there came a cloud on the slopes of Hermon; and no doubt at first the disciples thought little enough of it, for Hermon was notorious for the clouds which came and went. But something happened; it is not for us to guess what happened; but the cloud became luminous and mysterious, and out of it there came the voice of the divine majesty, setting God's seal of approval on Jesus his Son. And in that moment Jesus' prayer was answered; he knew beyond a doubt that he was right to go on.

The Mount of Transfiguration was for Jesus a spiritual mountain peak. His *exodus* lay before him. Was he taking the right way? Was he right to adventure out to Jerusalem and the waiting arms of the Cross? First, there came to him the verdict of history, the greatest of the law-givers and the greatest of the prophets, to tell him to go on. And then, even greater still by far, there came the voice which gave him nothing less than the approval of God. It was the experience on the Mount of Transfiguration which enabled Jesus inflexibly to walk the way to the Cross.

THE INSTRUCTION OF PETER

Matthew 17: 1–8 (*continued*)

BUT the episode of the Transfiguration did something not only for Jesus but for the disciples also.

(i) The minds of the disciples must have been still hurt and bewildered by the insistence of Jesus that he must go to Jerusalem to suffer and to die. It must have looked to them as if there was nothing but black shame ahead. But start to finish, the whole atmosphere of the Mountain of Transfiguration is *glory*. Jesus' face shone like the sun, and his garments glistened and gleamed like the light.

The Jews well knew the promise of God to the victorious righteous: " Their face shall shine as the sun " (2 *Esdras* 7: 97). No Jew could ever have seen that luminous cloud without thinking of the *shechinah*, the glory of God resting upon his people. There is one very revealing little touch in this passage. No fewer than three times in its eight brief verses there occurs the little interjection: " Behold! Look you! " It is as if Matthew could not even tell the story without a catch of the breath at the sheer staggering wonder of it.

Here surely was something which would lift up the hearts of the disciples and enable them to see the glory through the shame; the triumph through the humiliation; the crown beyond the Cross. It is obvious that even yet they did not understand; but it must surely have given them some little glimmering that the Cross was not all humiliation, that somehow it was tinged with glory, that somehow glory was the very atmosphere of the exodus to Jerusalem and to death.

(ii) Further, Peter must have learned two lessons that night. When Peter woke to what was going on, his first reaction was to build three tabernacles, one for Jesus, one for Moses and one for Elijah. He was always the man for action; always the man who must be doing something. But there is a time for stillness; there is a time for contemplation, for wonder, for adoration, for awed reverence in the presence of the supreme glory. " Be still, and know that I am God " (*Psalm* 46: 10). It may be that sometimes we are too busy trying to do something when we would be better to be silent, to be listening, to be wondering, to be adoring in the presence of God. Before a man can fight and adventure upon his feet, he must wonder and pray upon his knees.

(iii) But there is a converse of that. It is quite clear that Peter wished to wait upon the mountain slopes. He wished that great moment to be prolonged. He did not want to go down to the everyday and common things again but to remain for ever in the sheen of glory.

That is a feeling which everyone must know. There are moments of intimacy, of serenity, of peace, of nearness to God, which everyone has known and wished to prolong. As A. H. McNeile has it: " The Mountain of Transfiguration is always more enjoyable than the daily ministry or the way of the Cross."

But the Mountain of Transfiguration is given to us only to provide strength for the daily ministry and to enable us to walk the way of the Cross. Susanna Wesley had a prayer: " Help me, Lord, to remember that religion is not to be confined to the church or closet, nor exercised only in prayer and meditation, but that everywhere I am in thy presence." The moment of glory does not exist for its own sake; it exists to clothe the common things with a radiance they never had before.

TEACHING THE WAY OF THE CROSS

Matthew 17: 9–13, 22, 23

As they were coming down from the mountain, Jesus gave them strict injunctions: " Tell no man about the vision until the Son of Man has been raised from the dead." The disciples asked him, " Why then do the Scribes say that Elijah must first come? " He answered, " It is true that they say that Elijah is to come and will restore all things; but I tell you that Elijah has already come, and they did not recognize him, but they did to him what they wished. So also the Son of Man is to suffer at their hands." Then the disciples understood that he spoke to them about John the Baptizer.

. . . .

When they were gathering in Galilee, Jesus said to them, " The Son of Man is going to be delivered into the hands of men, and they will kill him, and on the third day he will be raised." And they were exceedingly distressed.

HERE again is an injunction to secrecy, and it was much needed. The great danger was that men should proclaim Jesus as Messiah without knowing who and what the Messiah was. Their whole conception both of the forerunner and of the Messiah had to be radically and fundamentally changed.

It was going to take a long time for the idea of a conquering Messiah to be unlearned; it was so ingrained into the Jewish mind that it was difficult—almost impossible—to alter it. Verses 9–13 are a very difficult passage. Behind them there is this idea. The Jews were agreed that, before the Messiah came, Elijah would return to be his herald and his forerunner. " Behold I will send you Elijah the prophet before the great and terrible day of the Lord comes." So writes Malachi, and then he goes on: " And he will turn the hearts of fathers to their children, and the hearts of children to their fathers, lest I come and smite the land with a curse " (*Malachi* 4: 5, 6). Bit by bit this idea of the coming of Elijah gathered detail, until the Jews came to believe that not only would Elijah come, but he would restore all things before the Messiah came, that he would, we might put it, make the world fit for the Messiah to enter into. The idea was that Elijah would be a great and terrible reformer, who would walk throughout the world destroying all evil and setting things to rights. The result was that both the forerunner and the Messiah were thought of in terms of *power*.

Jesus corrects this. " The Scribes," he said, " say that Elijah will come like a blast of cleansing and avenging fire. *He has come*; but his way was the way of suffering and of sacrifice, as must also be the way of the Son of Man." Jesus has laid it down that the way of God's service is never the way which blasts men out of existence, but always the way which woos them with sacrificial love.

That is what the disciples had to learn; and that is why they had to be silent until they had learned. If they had gone out preaching a conquering Messiah there could have been nothing but tragedy. It has been computed that in the century previous to the Crucifixion no fewer than 200,000 Jews lost their lives in futile rebellions. Before men could preach Christ, they must know who and what Christ was; and until Jesus had taught his followers the necessity of the Cross, they had to be silent and to learn. It is not our ideas, it is Christ's message, that we must bring to men; and no man can teach others until Jesus Christ has taught him.

THE ESSENTIAL FAITH

Matthew 17: 14–20

When they came to the crowd, a man came to him and fell at his feet and said, " Sir, have pity on my son, for he is an epileptic, and he suffers severely; for often he falls into the fire, and often into the water; and I brought him to your disciples, and they were not able to cure him." Jesus answered, " O faithless and perverse generation, how long shall I be with you? How long shall I bear with you? Bring him to me! " And Jesus spoke sternly to him, and the demon came out of him, and the boy was cured from that

hour. Then the disciples came to Jesus in private and said, " Why
were we not able to cast out the demon? " Jesus said to them,
" Because of the littleness of your faith. This is the truth I tell
you—if you have your faith as a grain of mustard seed, you will
say to this mountain, ' Be removed from here,' and it will remove.
So nothing will be impossible to you."

No sooner had Jesus come down from the heavenly glory than
he was confronted with an earthly problem and a practical
demand. A man had brought his epileptic boy to the disciples in
the absence of Jesus. Matthew describes the boy by the verb
selēniazesthai, which literally means *to be moonstruck*. As was
inevitable in that age, the father attributed the boy's condition
to the malign influence of evil spirits. So serious was his
condition that he was a danger to himself and to everyone else.
We can almost hear the sigh of relief as Jesus appeared, and at
once he took a grip of a situation which had got completely out of
hand. With one strong, stern word he bade the demon be gone
and the boy was cured. This story is full of significant things.

(i) We cannot but be moved by the faith of the boy's father.
Even though the disciples had been given power to cast out
devils (*Matthew* 10: 1), here was a case in which they had
signally and publicly failed. And yet in spite of the failure of the
disciples, the father never doubted the power of Jesus. It is as if
he said: " Only let me get at Jesus himself, and my problems
will be solved and my need will be met."

There is something very poignant about that; and there is
something which is very universal and very modern. There are
many who feel that the Church, the professed disciples of Jesus
in their own day and generation, has failed and is powerless to
deal with the ills of the human situation; and yet at the back of
their minds there is the feeling: " If we could only get beyond
his human followers, if we could only get behind the façade of
ecclesiasticism and the failure of the Church, if we could only
get at Jesus himself, we would receive the things we need." It is
at once our condemnation and our challenge that, even yet,
though men have lost their faith in the Church, they have never
lost a wistful faith in Jesus Christ.

(ii) We see here the constant demands made upon Jesus. Straight from the glory of the mountain top, he was met by human suffering. Straight from hearing the voice of God, he came to hear the clamant demand of human need. The most Christ-like person in the world is the man who never finds his fellow-man a nuisance. It is easy to feel Christian in the moment of prayer and meditation; it is easy to feel close to God when the world is shut out. But that is not religion—that is escapism. Real religion is to rise from our knees before God to meet men and the problems of the human situation. Real religion is to draw strength from God *in order to give it to others*. Real religion involves both meeting God in the secret place and men in the market place. Real religion means taking our own needs to God, not that we may have peace and quiet and undisturbed comfort, but that we may be enabled graciously, effectively and powerfully to meet the needs of others. The wings of the dove are not for the Christian who would follow his Master in going about doing good.

(iii) We see here the grief of Jesus. It is not that Jesus says that he wants to be quit of his disciples. It is that he says, " How long must I be with you before you will understand? " There is nothing more Christlike than patience. When we are like to lose our patience at the follies and the foolishness of men, let us call to mind God's infinite patience with the wanderings and the disloyalties and the unteachability of our own souls.

(iv) We see here the central need of faith, without which nothing can happen. When Jesus spoke about *removing mountains* he was using a phrase which the Jews knew well. A great teacher, who could really expound and interpret scripture and who could explain and resolve difficulties, was regularly known as an *uprooter*, or even a *pulverizer*, of mountains. To tear up, to uproot, to pulverize mountains were all regular phrases for removing difficulties. Jesus never meant this to be taken physically and literally. After all, the ordinary man seldom finds any necessity to remove a physical mountain. What he meant was: ' If you have faith enough, all difficulties can be solved, and even the hardest task can be accomplished." Faith in God is the instrument which enables men to remove the hills of difficulty which block their path.

THE TEMPLE TAX

Matthew 17: 24–27

> When they came to Capernaum, those who received the half-shekel Temple tax came to Peter and said, " Does your teacher not pay the tax? " Peter said, " He does pay it." When he had gone into the house, before he could speak, Jesus said to him, " What do you think, Simon? From whom do earthly kings take tax and tribute? From their sons or from strangers? " When he said, " From strangers," Jesus said to him, " So then the sons are free. But, so as not to set a stumbling-block in anyone's way, go to the sea, and cast a hook into it, and take the first fish which comes up; and when you have opened its mouth, you will find a shekel. Take it and give it to them for me and for you."

THE Temple at Jerusalem was a costly place to run. There were the daily morning and evening sacrifices which each involved the offering of a year-old lamb. Along with the lamb were offered wine and flour and oil. The incense which was burned every day had to be bought and prepared. The costly hangings and the robes of the priests constantly wore out; and the robe of the High Priest was itself worth a king's ransom. All this required money.

So, on the basis of *Exodus* 30: 13, it was laid down that every male Jew over twenty years of age must pay an annual Temple tax of one half-shekel. In the days of Nehemiah, when the people were poor, it was one-third of a shekel. One half-shekel was equal to two Greek *drachmae*; and the tax was commonly called the *didrachm*, as it is called in this passage. The value of the tax was about 8p; and that sum must be evaluated in the light of the fact that a working man's wage in Palestine in the time of Jesus was only $3\frac{1}{2}$p. The tax was in fact the equivalent of two days' pay. It brought into the Temple treasury no less than about £76,000 a year. Theoretically the tax was obligatory and the Temple authorities had power to distrain upon a man's goods, if he failed to pay.

The method of collection was carefully organized. On the first of the month Adar, which is March of our year, announcement was made in all the towns and villages of Palestine that the time to pay the tax had come. On the fifteenth of the month, booths were set up in each town and village, and at the booths the tax was paid. If the tax was not paid by the twenty-fifth of Adar, it could only be paid direct to the Temple in Jerusalem.

In this passage we see Jesus paying this Temple tax. The tax authorities came to Peter and asked him if his Master paid his taxes. There is little doubt that the question was asked with malicious intent and that the hope was that Jesus would refuse to pay; for, if he refused, the orthodox would have a ground of accusation against him. Peter's immediate answer was that Jesus did pay. Then he went and told Jesus of the situation, and Jesus used a kind of parable in verses 25 and 26.

The picture drawn has two possibilities but in either case the meaning is the same.

(i) In the ancient world conquering and colonizing nations had little or no idea of governing for the benefit of subject peoples. Rather, they considered that the subject peoples existed to make things easier for them. The result was that a king's own nation never paid tribute, if there were any nations subject to it. It was the subject nations who bore the burden and who paid the tax. So Jesus may be saying, " God is the King of Israel; but we are the true Israel, for we are the citizens of the Kingdom of Heaven; outsiders may have to pay; but we are free."

(ii) The picture is more likely a much simpler one than that. If any king imposed taxes on a nation, he certainly did not impose them on his own family. It was indeed for the support of his own household that the taxes were imposed. The tax in question was for the Temple, which was the house of God. Jesus was the Son of God. Did he not say when his parents sought him in Jerusalem: " Did you not know that I must be in *my Father's house*? " (*Luke* 2: 49). How could the Son be under obligation to pay the tax which was for his own Father's house?

None the less Jesus said that they must pay, not because of
the compulsion of the law, but because of a higher duty. He said
they must pay " lest we should offend them." The New Testament always uses the verb *to offend* (*skandalizein*) and the noun
offence (*skandalon*) in a special way. The verb never means to
insult or to annoy or to injure the pride of. It always means *to
put a stumbling-block in someone's way*, to cause someone to
trip up and to fall. Therefore Jesus is saying: " We must pay so
as not to set a bad example to others. We must not only do our
duty, we must go beyond duty, in order that we may show
others what they ought to do." Jesus would allow himself
nothing which might make someone else think less of the
ordinary obligation of life. In life there may sometimes be
exemptions we could claim; there may be things we could
quite safely allow ourselves to do. But we must claim nothing
and allow ourselves nothing which might possibly be a bad
example to someone else.

We may well ask why is it that this story was ever
transmitted at all? For reasons of space the gospel writers had
to select their material. Why select this story? Matthew's gospel
was written between A.D. 80 and 90. Now just a little before
that time Jews and Jewish Christians had been faced with a
very real and a very disturbing problem. We saw that every
male Jew over twenty had to pay the Temple tax; but the
Temple was totally destroyed in A.D. 70, never to be rebuilt.
After the destruction of the Temple, Vespasian, the Roman
emperor, enacted that the half-shekel Temple tax should now be
paid to the treasury of the Temple of Jupiter Capitolinus in
Rome.

Here indeed was a problem. Many of the Jews and of the
Jewish Christians were violently inclined to rebel against this
enactment. Any such widespread rebellion would have had
disastrous consequences, for it would have been utterly crushed
at once, and would have gained the Jews and the Christians the
reputation of being bad and disloyal and disaffected citizens.

This story was put into the gospels to tell the Christians,
especially the Jewish Christians, that, however unpleasant they

might be, the duties of a citizen must be shouldered. It tells us that Christianity and good citizenship go hand in hand. The Christian who exempts himself from the duties of good citizenship is not only failing in citizenship, he is also failing in Christianity.

HOW TO PAY OUR DEBTS

Matthew 17: 24–27 (*continued*)

Now we come to the story itself. If we take it with a bald and crude literalism, it means that Jesus told Peter to go and catch a fish, and that he would find a *stater* in the fish's mouth which would be sufficient to pay the tax for both of them. It is not irrelevant to note that the gospel never tells us that Peter did so. The story ends with Jesus' saying.

Before we begin to examine the story we must remember that all oriental people love to say a thing in the most dramatic and vivid way possible; and that they love to say a thing with the flash of a smile. This miracle is difficult on three grounds.

(i) God does not send a miracle to enable us to do what we can quite well do for ourselves. That would be to harm us and not to help us. However poor the disciples were, they did not need a miracle to enable them to earn two half-shekels. It was not beyond human power to earn such a sum.

(ii) This miracle transgresses the great decision of Jesus that he would never use his miraculous power for his own ends. He could have turned stones into bread to satisfy his own hunger——but he refused. He could have used his power to enhance his own prestige as a wonder-worker——but he refused. In the wilderness Jesus decided once and for all that he would not and could not selfishly use his power. If this story is taken with a crude literalism, it does show Jesus using his divine power to satisfy his own personal needs——and that is what Jesus would never do.

(iii) If this miracle is taken literally, there is a sense in which it is even immoral. Life would become chaotic if a man could pay his debts by finding coins in fishes' mouths. Life was never meant to be arranged in such a way that men could meet their obligations in such a lazy and effortless way. " The gods," said one of the great Greeks, " have ordained that sweat should be the price of all things." That is just as true for the Christian thinker as it was for the Greek.

If all this is so, what are we to say? Are we to say that this is a mere legendary story, mere imaginative fiction, with no truth behind it at all? Far from it. Beyond a doubt something happened.

Let us remember again the Jewish love of dramatic vividness. Undoubtedly what happened was this. Jesus said to Peter: " Yes, Peter. You're right. We, too, must pay our just and lawful debts. Well, you know how to do it. Back you go to the fishing for a day. You'll get plenty of money in the fishes' mouths to pay our dues! A day at the fishing will soon produce all we need."

Jesus was saying, " Back to your job, Peter; that's the way to pay your debts." So the typist will find a new coat in the keys of her typewriter. The motor mechanic will find food for himself and his wife and family in the cylinder of the motor car. The teacher will find money to pay his way in the blackboard and the chalk. The clerk will find enough to support himself and his dear ones in the ledger and in the account sheets.

When Jesus said this, he said it with that swift smile of his and with his gift for dramatic language. He was not telling Peter literally to get coins in fishes' mouths. He was telling him that in his day's work he would get what he needed to pay his way.

PERSONAL RELATIONSHIPS

Matthew 18 is a most important chapter for Christian Ethics, because it deals with those qualities which should characterize the personal relationships of the Christian. We shall be dealing in detail with these relationships as we study the chapter section by section; but before we do so, it will be well to look at the chapter as a whole. It singles out seven qualities which should mark the personal relationships of the Christian.

(i) First and foremost, there is the quality of *humility* (verses 1–4). Only the person who has the humility of the child is a citizen of the Kingdom of Heaven. Personal ambition, personal prestige, personal publicity, personal profit are motives which can find no place in the life of the Christian. The Christian is the man who forgets self in his devotion to Jesus Christ and in his service of his fellow-men.

(ii) Second, there is the quality of *responsibility* (verses 5–7). The greatest of all sins is to teach another to sin, especially if that other should be a weaker, a younger, and a less-experienced brother. God's sternest judgment is reserved for those who put a stumbling-block in the way of others. The Christian is constantly aware that he is responsible for the effect of his life, his deeds, his words, his example on other people.

(iii) There follows the quality of *self-renunciation* (verses 8–10). The Christian is like an athlete for whom no training is too hard, if by it he may win the prize; he is like the student who will sacrifice pleasure and leisure to reach the crown. The Christian is ready surgically to excise from life everything which would keep him from rendering a perfect obedience to God.

(iv) There is *individual care* (verses 11–14). The Christian realizes that God cares for him individually, and that he must reflect that individual care in his care for others. He never thinks in terms of crowds; he thinks in terms of persons. For God no man is unimportant and no one is lost in the crowd; for the Christian every man is important and is a child of God, who, if lost, must be found. The individual care of the Christian is in fact the motive and the dynamic of evangelism.

(v) There is the quality of *discipline* (verses 15–20). Christian kindness and Christian forgiveness do not mean that a man who is in error is to be allowed to do as he likes. Such a man must be guided and corrected and, if need be, disciplined back into the right way. But that discipline is always to be given in humble love and not in self-righteous condemnation. It is always to be given with the desire for reconciliation and never with the desire for vengeance.

(vi) There is the quality of *fellowship* (verses 19, 20). It might even be put that Christians are people who pray together. They are people who in fellowship seek the will of God, who in fellowship listen and worship together. Individualism is the reverse of Christianity.

(vii) There is the *spirit of forgiveness* (verses 23–35); and the Christian's forgiveness of his fellow-men is founded on the fact that he himself is a forgiven man. He forgives others even as God, for Christ's sake, has forgiven him.

THE MIND OF A CHILD

Matthew 18: 1–4

> On that day the disciples came to Jesus. " Who, then," they said, " is the greatest in the Kingdom of Heaven? " Jesus called a little child and made him stand in the middle of them, and said, " This is the truth I tell you—unless you turn and become as children, you will not enter into the Kingdom of Heaven. Whoever humbles himself as this little child, he is the greatest in the Kingdom of Heaven."

HERE is a very revealing question, followed by a very revealing answer. The disciples asked who was the greatest in the Kingdom of Heaven. Jesus took a child and said that unless they turned and became as this little child, they would not get into the Kingdom at all.

The question of the disciples was: " Who will be the greatest in the Kingdom of Heaven? " and the very fact that they asked that question showed that they had no idea at all what the Kingdom of Heaven was. Jesus said, " Unless you turn." He was warning them that they were going in completely the wrong direction, away from the Kingdom of Heaven and not towards it. In life it is all a question of what a man is aiming at; if he is aiming at the fulfilment of personal ambition, the acquisition of personal power, the enjoyment of personal prestige, the exaltation of self, he is aiming at precisely the opposite of the Kingdom of Heaven; for to be a citizen of the Kingdom means the complete forgetting of self, the obliteration of self, the spending of self in a life which aims at service and not at power. So long as a man considers his own self as the most important thing in the world, his back is turned to the Kingdom; if he wants ever to reach the Kingdom, he must turn round and face in the opposite direction.

Jesus took a child. There is a tradition that the child grew to be Ignatius of Antioch, who in later days became a great servant of the Church, a great writer, and finally a martyr for Christ. Ignatius was surnamed *Theophoros*, which means *God-carried*, and the tradition grew up that he had received that name because Jesus carried him on his knee. It may be so. Maybe it is more likely that it was Peter who asked the question, and that it was Peter's little boy whom Jesus took and set in the midst, because we know that Peter was married (*Matthew* 8: 14; 1 *Corinthians* 9: 5).

So Jesus said that in a child we see the characteristics which should mark the man of the Kingdom. There are many lovely characteristics in a child—the power to wonder, before he has become deadeningly used to the wonder of the world; the power to forgive and to forget, even when adults and parents treat him unjustly as they so often do; the innocence, which, as Richard Glover beautifully says, brings it about that the child has only to learn, not to unlearn; only to do, not to undo. No doubt Jesus was thinking of these things; but wonderful as they are they are not the main things in his mind. The child has three great qualities which make him the symbol of those who are citizens of the Kingdom.

(i) First and foremost, there is the quality which is the keynote of the whole passage, the child's *humility*. A child does not wish to push himself forward; rather, he wishes to fade into the background. He does not wish for prominence; he would rather be left in obscurity. It is only as he grows up, and begins to be initiated into a competitive world, with its fierce struggle and scramble for prizes and for first places, that his instinctive humility is left behind.

(ii) There is the child's *dependence*. To the child a state of dependence is perfectly natural. He never thinks that he can face life by himself. He is perfectly content to be utterly dependent on those who love him and care for him. If men would accept the fact of their dependence on God, a new strength and a new peace would enter their lives.

(iii) There is the child's *trust*. The child is instinctively dependent, and just as instinctively he trusts his parents that his needs will be met. When we are children, we cannot buy our own food or our own clothes, or maintain our own home; yet we never doubt that we will be clothed and fed, and that there will be shelter and warmth and comfort waiting for us when we come home. When we are children we set out on a journey with no means of paying the fare, and with no idea of how to get to our journey's end, and yet it never enters our heads to doubt that our parents will bring us safely there.

The child's humility is the pattern of the Christian's behaviour to his fellow-men, and the child's dependence and trust are the pattern of the Christian's attitude towards God, the Father of all.

CHRIST AND THE CHILD

Matthew 18: 5–7, 10

" Whoever receives one such little child in my name, receives me. But whoever puts a stumbling-block in the way of one of these little ones, who believe in me, it is better for him that a great millstone should be hanged about his neck, and that he should be drowned far out in the open sea. Alas for the world because of stumbling-blocks! Stumbling-blocks are bound to come; but alas for the man by whom the stumbling-block comes!

． ． ． ． ． ． ． ．

See that you do not despise one of these little ones; for, I tell you, their angels in heaven always look upon the face of my Father who is in heaven."

THERE is a certain difficulty of interpretation in this passage which must be borne in mind. As we have often seen, it is Matthew's consistent custom to gather together the teaching of Jesus under certain great heads; he arranges it systematically. In the early part of this chapter he is collecting Jesus's teaching about *children*; and we must remember that the Jews used the word *child* in a double sense. They used it literally of the *young child*; but regularly a teacher's disciples were called his *sons* or his *children*. Therefore a child also means a *beginner in the faith*, one who has just begun to believe, one who is not yet mature and established in the faith, one who has just begun on the right way and who may very easily be deflected from it. In this passage very often the child means both the *young child* and the *beginner on the Christian way*.

Jesus says that whoever receives one such little child in his name receives himself. The phrase *in my name* can mean one of two things. (i) It can mean *for my sake*. The care of children is something which is carried out for the sake of none other than Jesus Christ. To teach a child, to bring up a child in the way he ought to go, is something which is done not only for the sake of the child, but for the sake of Jesus himself. (ii) It can mean *with a blessing*. It can mean receiving the child, and, as it were, naming the name of Jesus over him. He who brings Jesus and the blessing of Jesus to a child is doing a Christlike work.

To receive the child is also a phrase which is capable of bearing more than one meaning. (i) It can mean, not so much to receive a child, as to receive a person who has this childlike quality of humility. In this highly competitive world it is very easy to pay most attention to the person who is pugnacious and aggressive and self-assertive and full of self-confidence. It is easy to pay most attention to the person who, in the worldly sense of the term, has made a success of life. Jesus may well be saying that the most important people are not the thrusters and those who have climbed to the top of the tree by pushing everyone else out of the way, but the quiet, humble, simple people, who have the heart of a child.

(ii) It can mean simply to welcome the child, to give him the care and the love and the teaching which he requires to make him into a good man. To help a child to live well and to know God better is to help Jesus Christ.

(iii) But this phrase can have another and very wonderful meaning. It can mean to see Christ in the child. To teach unruly, disobedient, restless little children can be a wearing job. To satisfy the physical needs of a child, to wash his clothes and bind his cuts and soothe his bruises and cook his meals may often seem a very unromantic task; the cooker and the sink and the work-basket have not much glamour; but there is no one in all this world who helps Jesus Christ more than the teacher of the little child and the harassed, hard-pressed mother in the home. All such will find a glory in the grey, if in the child they sometimes glimpse none other than Jesus himself.

THE TERRIBLE RESPONSIBILITY

Matthew 18: 5–7, 10 (*continued*)

BUT the great keynote of this passage is the terrible weight of responsibility it leaves upon every one of us.

(i) It stresses the terror of teaching another to sin. It is true to say that no man sins uninvited; and the bearer of the invitation is so often a fellow-man. A man must always be confronted with his first temptation to sin; he must always receive his first encouragement to do the wrong thing; he must always experience his first push along the way to the forbidden things. The Jews took the view that the most unforgivable of all sins is to teach another to sin; and for this reason—a man's own sins can be forgiven, for in a sense they are limited in their consequences; but if we teach another to sin, he in his turn may teach still another, and a train of sin is set in motion with no foreseeable end.

There is nothing in this world more terrible than to destroy someone's innocence. And, if a man has any conscience left, there is nothing which will haunt him more. Someone tells of an old man who was dying; he was obviously sorely troubled. At last they got him to tell why. " When we were boys at play," he said, " one day at a cross-roads we reversed a signpost so that its arms were pointing the opposite way, and I've never ceased to wonder how many people were sent in the wrong direction by what we did." The sin of all sins is to teach another to sin.

(ii) It stresses the terror of the punishment of those who teach another to sin. If a man teaches another to sin, it would be better for him that a millstone were hanged about his neck and he were drowned in the depths of the sea.

The millstone in this case is a *mulos onikos*. The Jews ground corn by crushing it between two circular stones. This was done at home; and in any cottage such a mill could be seen. The upper stone, which turned round upon the lower was equipped with a handle, and it was commonly of such a size that the housewife could easily turn it, for it was she who did the grinding of the corn for the household needs. But a *mulos onikos* was a grinding-stone of such a size that it needed an ass pulling it (*onos* is the Greek for an *ass* and *mulos* is the Greek for a millstone) to turn it round at all. The very size of the millstone shows the awfulness of the condemnation.

Further, in the Greek it is said, not so much that the man would be better to be drowned in the depths of the sea, but that it would be better if he were drowned far out in the open sea. The Jew feared the sea; for him Heaven was a place where there would be no more sea (*Revelation* 21: 1). The man who taught another to sin would be better to be drowned far out in the most lonely of all waste places. Moreover, the very picture of drowning had its terror for the Jew. Drowning was sometimes a Roman punishment, but never Jewish. To the Jew it was the symbol of utter destruction. When the Rabbis taught that heathen and Gentile objects were to be utterly destroyed they said that they must be " cast into the salt sea." Josephus (*Antiquities of the Jews* 14. 15. 10) has a terrible account of a

Galilaean revolt in which the Galilaeans took the supporters of
Herod and drowned them in the depths of the Sea of Galilee.
The very phrase would paint to the Jew a picture of utter
destruction. Jesus' words are carefully chosen to show the fate
that awaits a man who teaches another to sin.

(iii) It has a warning to silence all evasion. This is a
sin-stained world and a tempting world; no one can go out into
it without meeting seductions to sin. That is specially so if he
goes out from a protected home where no evil influence was
ever allowed to play upon him. Jesus says, " That is perfectly
true; this world is full of temptations; that is inevitable in a
world into which sin has entered; but that does not lessen the
responsibility of the man who is the cause of a stumbling-block
being placed in the way of a younger person or of a beginner in
the faith."

We know that this is a tempting world; it is therefore the
Christian's duty to remove stumbling-blocks, never to be the
cause of putting them in another's way. This means that it is
not only a sin to put a stumbling-block in another's way; it is
also a sin even to bring that person into any situation, or
circumstance, or environment where he may meet with such a
stumbling-block. No Christian can be satisfied to live com-
placently and lethargically in a civilization where there are
conditions of living and housing and life in general where a
young person has no chance of escaping the seductions of sin.

(iv) Finally it stresses the supreme importance of the child.
" Their angels," said Jesus, " always behold the face of my
Father who is in Heaven." In the time of Jesus the Jews had a
very highly-developed angelology. Every nation had its angel;
every natural force, such as the wind and the thunder and the
lightning and the rain, had its angel. They even went the length
of saying, very beautifully, that every blade of grass had its
angel. So, then, they believed that every child had his guardian
angel.

To say that these angels behold the face of God in heaven
means that they always have the right of direct access to God.
The picture is of a great royal court where only the most

favoured courtiers and ministers and officials have direct access to the king. In the sight of God the children are so important that their guardian angels always have the right of direct access to the inner presence of God.

For us the great value of a child must always lie in the possibilities which are locked up within him. Everything depends on how he is taught and trained. The possibilities may never be realized; they may be stifled and stunted; that which might be used for good may be deflected to the purposes of evil; or they may be unleashed in such a way that a new tide of power floods the earth.

Away back in the eleventh century Duke Robert of Burgundy was one of the great warrior and knightly figures. He was about to go off on a campaign. He had a baby son who was his heir; and, before he departed, he made his barons and nobles come and swear fealty to the little infant, in the event of anything happening to himself. They came with their waving plumes and their clanking armour and knelt before the child. One great baron smiled and Duke Robert asked him why. He said, " The child is so little." " Yes," said Duke Robert, " he's little—*but he'll grow*." Indeed he grew, for that baby became William the Conqueror of England.

In every child there are infinite possibilities for good or ill. It is the supreme responsibility of the parent, of the teacher, of the Christian Church, to see that his dynamic possibilities for good are realized. To stifle them, to leave them untapped, to twist them into evil powers, is sin.

THE SURGICAL EXCISION

Matthew 18: 8, 9

" If your hand or your foot proves a stumbling-block to you, cut it off and throw it away from you. It is the fine thing for you to enter into life maimed or lame, rather than to be cast into everlasting fire with two hands or two feet. And if your eye proves a stumbling-block to you, pluck it out and throw it away from you.

It is the fine thing for you to enter into life with one eye, rather than to be cast into the Gehenna of fire with two eyes."

THERE are two senses in which this passage may be taken. It may be taken purely *personally*. It may be saying that it is worth any sacrifice and any self-renunciation to escape the punishment of God.

We have to be clear what that punishment involves. It is here called *everlasting* and this word *everlasting* occurs frequently in Jewish ideas of punishment. The word is *aiōnios*. The Book of Enoch speaks about *eternal* judgment, about judgment *for ever*, about punishment and torture *for ever*, about the fire which burns *for ever*. Josephus calls hell an *everlasting* prison. The *Book of Jubilees* speaks about an *eternal* curse. *The Book of Baruch* says that " there will be no opportunity of returning, *nor a limit to the times*." There is a Rabbinic tale of Rabbi Jochanan ben Zaccai who wept bitterly at the prospect of death. On being asked why, he answered. " All the more I weep now that they are about to lead me before the King of kings, the Holy One, blessed is He, who lives and abides for ever and for ever and for ever; whose wrath, if he be wrathful, is an eternal wrath; and, if he bind me, his binding is an eternal binding; and if he kills me, his killing is an eternal killing; whom I cannot placate with words, nor bribe with wealth."

All these passages use the word *aiōnios*; but we must be careful to remember what it means. It literally means *belonging to the ages*; there is only one person to whom the word *aiōnios* can properly be applied, and that is God. There is far more in *aiōnios* than simply a description of that which has no end. Punishment which is *aiōnios* is punishment which it befits God to give and punishment which only God can give. When we think of punishment, we can only say, " Shall not the judge of all the earth do right? " Our human pictures, and our human time-scheme, fail; this is in the hands of God.

But there is one clue which we do have. This passage speaks of *the Gehenna of fire*. Gehenna was the valley of Hinnom, a valley below the mountain of Jerusalem. It was for ever

accursed, because it was the place where, in the days of the
kingdom, the renegade Jews had sacrificed their children in the
fire to the pagan god Moloch. Josiah had made it a place
accursed. In later days it became the refuse dump of Jerusalem;
a kind of vast incinerator. Always the refuse was burning there,
and a pall of smoke and a glint of smouldering fire surrounded
it.

Now, what was this Gehenna, this Valley of Hinnom? It was
the place into which everything that was useless was cast and
there destroyed. That is to say, God's punishment is for those
who are useless, for those who make no contribution to life, for
those who hold life back instead of urging life on, for those who
drag life down instead of lifting life up, for those who are the
handicaps of others and not their inspirations. It is again and
again New Testament teaching that *uselessness invites disaster*.
The man who is useless, the man who is an evil influence on
others, the man who cannot justify the simple fact of his
existence, is in danger of the punishment of God, unless he
excises from his life those things which make him the handicap
he is.

But it is just possible that this passage is not to be taken so
much personally as *in connection with the Church*. Matthew
has already used this saying of Jesus in a different context in
Matthew 5: 30. Here there may be a difference. The whole
passage is about children, and perhaps especially about children
in the faith. This passage may be saying, " If in your Church
there is someone who is an evil influence, if there is someone
who is a bad example to those who are young in the faith, if
there is someone whose life and conduct is damaging the body
of the Church, he must be rooted out and cast away." That may
well be the meaning. The Church is the Body of Christ; if that
body is to be healthy and health-giving, that which has the
seeds of cancerous and poisonous infection in it must be even
surgically removed.

One thing is certain, in any person and in any Church,
whatever is a seduction to sin must be removed, however
painful the removal may be, for if we allow it to flourish a worse

punishment will follow. In this passage there may well be stressed both the necessity of self-renunciation for the Christian individual and discipline for the Christian Church.

THE SHEPHERD AND THE LOST SHEEP

Matthew 18: 12–14

" What do you think? If a man has a hundred sheep, and one of them wanders away, will he not leave the ninety-nine, and go out to the hills, and will he not seek the wandering one? And if he finds it—this is the truth I tell you—he rejoices more over it than over the ninety-nine who never wandered away. So it is not the will of your Father that one of these little ones should perish."

THIS is surely the simplest of all the parables of Jesus, for it is the simple story of a lost sheep and a seeking shepherd. In Judaea it was tragically easy for sheep to go astray. The pasture land is on the hill country which runs like a backbone down the middle of the land. This ridge-like plateau is narrow, only a few miles across. There are no restraining walls. At its best, the pasture is sparse. And, therefore, the sheep are ever liable to wander; and, if they stray from the grass of the plateau into the gullies and the ravines at each side, they have every chance of finishing up on some ledge from which they cannot get up or down, and of being marooned there until they die.

The Palestinian shepherds were experts at tracking down their lost sheep. They could follow their track for miles; and they would brave the cliffs and the precipice to bring them back.

In the time of Jesus the flocks were often communal flocks; they belonged, not to an individual, but to a village. There were, therefore, usually two or three shepherds with them. That is why the shepherd could leave the ninety-nine. If he had left them with no guardian he would have come back to find still more of them gone; but he could leave them in the care of his fellow-shepherds, while he sought the wanderer. The shepherds

always made the most strenuous and the most sacrificial efforts
to find a lost sheep. It was the rule that, if a sheep could not be
brought back alive, then at least, if it was at all possible, its
fleece or its bones must be brought back to prove that it was
dead.

We can imagine how the other shepherds would return with
their flocks to the village fold at evening time, and how they
would tell that one shepherd was still out on the mountain-side
seeking a wanderer. We can imagine how the eyes of the people
would turn ever and again to the hillside watching for the
shepherd who had not come home; and we can imagine the
shout of joy when they saw him striding along the pathway with
the weary wanderer slung across his shoulder, safe at last; and
we can imagine how the whole village would welcome him, and
gather round with gladness to hear the story of the sheep who
was lost and found. Here we have what was Jesus's favourite
picture of God and of God's love. This parable teaches us many
things about that love.

(i) The love of God is an *individual love*. The ninety-and-nine
were not enough; one sheep was out on the hillside and the
shepherd could not rest until he had brought it home. However
large a family a parent has, he cannot spare even one; there is
not one who does not matter. God is like that; God cannot be
happy until the last wanderer is gathered in.

(ii) The love of God is a *patient love*. Sheep are proverbially
foolish creatures. The sheep has no one but itself to blame for
the danger it had got itself into. Men are apt to have so little
patience with the foolish ones. When they get into trouble, we
are apt to say, " It's their own fault; they brought it on
themselves; don't waste any sympathy on fools." God is not
like that. The sheep might be foolish but the shepherd would
still risk his life to save it. Men may be fools but God loves even
the foolish man who has no one to blame but himself for his sin
and his sorrow.

(iii) The love of God is a *seeking love*. The shepherd was not
content to wait for the sheep to come back; he went out to
search for it. That is what the Jew could not understand about

the Christian idea of God. The Jew would gladly agree that, if the sinner came crawling wretchedly home, God would forgive. But we know that God is far more wonderful than that, for in Jesus Christ, he came to seek for those who wander away. God is not content to wait until men come home; he goes out to search for them no matter what it costs him.

(iv) The love of God is a *rejoicing love*. Here there is nothing but joy. There are no recriminations; there is no receiving back with a grudge and a sense of superior contempt; it is all joy. So often we accept a man who is penitent with a moral lecture and a clear indication that he must regard himself as contemptible, and the practical statement that we have no further use for him and do not propose to trust him ever again. It is human never to forget a man's past and always to remember his sins against him. God puts our sins behind his back; and when we return to him, it is all joy.

(v) The love of God is a *protecting love*. It is the love which seeks and *saves*. There can be a love which ruins; there can be a love which softens; but the love of God is a protecting love which saves a man for the service of his fellow-men, a love which makes the wanderer wise, the weak strong, the sinner pure, the captive of sin the free man of holiness, and the vanquished by temptation its conqueror.

SEEKING THE STUBBORN

Matthew 18: 15–18

" If your brother sins against you, go, and try to convince him of his error between you and him alone. If he listens to you, you have gained your brother. If he will not listen to you, take with you one or two more, that the whole matter may be established in the mouth of two or three witnesses. If he refuses to listen to them, tell it to the Church. And if he refuses to listen to the Church, let him be to you as a Gentile and a tax-collector. This is the truth I tell you — all that you bind upon earth will remain bound in heaven; and all that you loose upon earth will remain loosed in heaven."

IN many ways this is one of the most difficult passages to interpret in the whole of Matthew's gospel. Its difficulty lies in the undoubted fact that it does not ring true; it does not sound like Jesus; it sounds much more like the regulations of an ecclesiastical committee.

We may go further. It is not possible that Jesus said this in its present form. Jesus could not have told his disciples to take things to the Church, for it did not exist; and the passage implies a fully developed and organized Church with a system of ecclesiastical discipline. What is more, it speaks of tax-collectors and Gentiles as irreclaimable outsiders. Yet Jesus was accused of being the friend of tax-gatherers and sinners; and he never spoke of them as hopeless outsiders, but always with sympathy and love, and even with praise (cp. *Matthew* 9: 10ff; 11: 19; *Luke* 18: 10ff; and especially *Matthew* 21: 31ff, where it is actually said that the tax-gatherers and harlots will go into the Kingdom before the orthodox religious people of the time). Further, the whole tone of the passage is that there is a limit to forgiveness, that there comes a time when a man may be abandoned as beyond hope, counsel which it is impossible to think of Jesus giving. And the last verse actually seems to give the Church the power to retain and to forgive sins. There are many reasons to make us think that this, *as it stands*, cannot be a correct report of the words of Jesus, but an adaptation made by the Church in later days, when Church discipline was rather a thing of rules and regulations than of love and forgiveness.

Although this passage is certainly not a correct report of what Jesus said, it is equally certain that it goes back to something he did say. Can we press behind it and come to the actual commandment of Jesus? At its widest what Jesus was saying was, " If anyone sins against you, spare no effort to make that man admit his fault, and to get things right again between you and him." Basically it means that we must never tolerate any situation in which there is a breach of personal relationships between us and another member of the Christian community.

Suppose something does go wrong, what are we to do to put

it right? This passage presents us with a whole scheme of action for the mending of broken relationships within the Christian fellowship.

(i) If we feel that someone has wronged us, we should immediately put our complaint into words. The worst thing that we can do about a wrong is to brood about it. That is fatal. It can poison the whole mind and life, until we can think of nothing else but our sense of personal injury. Any such feeling should be brought out into the open, faced, and stated, and often the very stating of it will show how unimportant and trivial the whole thing is.

(ii) If we feel that someone has wronged us, we should go to see him personally. More trouble has been caused by the writing of letters than by almost anything else. A letter may be misread and misunderstood; it may quite unconsciously convey a tone it was never meant to convey. If we have a difference with someone, there is only one way to settle it—and that is face to face. The spoken word can often settle a difference which the written word would only have exacerbated.

(iii) If a private and personal meeting fails of its purpose, we should take some wise person or persons with us. *Deuteronomy* 19: 15 has it: " A single witness shall not prevail against a man for any crime or for any wrong in connection with any offence that he has committed; only on the evidence of two witnesses or of three witnesses, shall a charge be sustained." That is the saying which Matthew has in mind. But in this case the taking of the witnesses is not meant to be a way of proving to a man that he has committed an offence. It is meant to help the process of reconciliation. A man often hates those whom he has injured most of all; and it may well be that nothing we can say can win him back. But to talk matters over with some wise and kindly and gracious people present is to create a new atmosphere in which there is at least a chance that we should see ourselves " as others see us." The Rabbis had a wise saying, " Judge not alone, for none may judge alone save One (that is God)."

(iv) If that still fails, we must take our personal troubles to the Christian fellowship. Why? Because troubles are never settled by going to law, or by Christless argument. Legalism merely produces further trouble. It is in an atmosphere of Christian prayer, Christian love and Christian fellowship that personal relationships may be righted. The clear assumption is that the Church fellowship *is* Christian, and seeks to judge everything, not in the light of a book of practice and procedure, but in the light of love.

(v) It is now we come to the difficult part. Matthew says that, if even that does not succeed, then the man who has wronged us is to be regarded as a Gentile and a tax-collector. The first impression is that the man must be abandoned as hopeless and irreclaimable, but that is precisely what Jesus cannot have meant. He never set limits to human forgiveness. What then did he mean?

We have seen that when he speaks of tax-gatherers and sinners he always does so with sympathy and gentleness and an appreciation of their good qualities. It may be that what Jesus said was something like this: " When you have done all this, when you have given the sinner every chance, and when he remains stubborn and obdurate, you may think that he is no better than a renegade tax-collector, or even a godless Gentile. Well, you may be right. But I have not found the tax-gatherers and the Gentiles hopeless. My experience of them is that they, too, have a heart to be touched; and there are many of them, like Matthew and Zacchaeus, who have become my best friends. Even if the stubborn sinner is like a tax-collector or a Gentile, you may still win him, as I have done."

This, in fact, is *not* an injunction to abandon a man; it is a challenge to win him with the love which can touch even the hardest heart. It is not a statement that some men are hopeless; it is a statement that Jesus Christ has found no man hopeless—and neither must we.

(vi) Finally, there is the saying about loosing and binding. It is a difficult saying. It cannot mean that the Church can remit or forgive sins, and so settle a man's destiny in time or in eternity. What it may well mean is that the relationships which we establish with our fellow-men last not only through time but into eternity—therefore we *must* get them right.

THE POWER OF THE PRESENCE

Matthew 18: 19, 20

" Again, I tell you, that if two of you agree upon earth upon any matter for which you are praying, you will receive it from my Father who is in Heaven. Where two or three are assembled together in my name, there am I in the midst of them."

HERE is one of these sayings of Jesus, whose meaning we need to probe or we will be left with heartbreak and great disappointment. Jesus says that, if two upon earth agree upon any matter for which they are praying, they will receive it from God. If that is to be taken literally, and without any qualification, it is manifestly untrue. Times without number two people have agreed to pray for the physical or the spiritual welfare of a loved one—and their prayer has not, in the literal sense, been answered. Times without number God's people have agreed to pray for the conversion of their own land or the conversion of the heathen and the coming of the Kingdom, and even yet that prayer is far from being fully answered. People agree to pray—and pray desperately—and do not receive that for which they pray. There is no point in refusing to face the facts of the situation, and nothing but harm can result from teaching people to expect what does not happen. But when we come to see what this saying means, there is a precious depth in it.

(i) First and foremost, it means that prayer must never be selfish and that selfish prayer cannot find an answer. We are not meant to pray only for our own needs, thinking of nothing and no one but ourselves; we are meant to pray as members of a fellowship, in agreement, remembering that life and the world are not arranged for us as individuals but for the fellowship as a whole. It would often happen that, if our prayers were answered, the prayers of someone else would be disappointed.

Often our prayers for our success would necessarily involve someone else's failure. Effective prayer must be the prayer of agreement, from which the element of selfish concentration on our own needs and desires has been quite cleansed away.

(ii) When prayer is unselfish, it is always answered. But here as everywhere we must remember the basic law of prayer; that law is that in prayer we receive, not the answer which we desire, but the answer which God in his wisdom and his love knows to be best. Simply because we are human beings, with human hearts and fears and hopes and desires, most of our prayers are prayers for escape. We pray to be saved from some trial, some sorrow, some disappointment, some hurting and difficult situation. And always God's answer is the offer not of escape, but of victory. God does not give us escape from a human situation; he enables us to accept what we cannot understand; he enables us to endure what without him would be unendurable; he enables us to face what without him would be beyond all facing. The perfect example of all this is Jesus in Gethsemane. He prayed to be released from the dread situation which confronted him, he was not released from it; but he was given power to meet it, to endure it, and to conquer it. When we pray unselfishly, God sends his answer—but the answer is always his answer and not necessarily ours.

(iii) Jesus goes on to say that where two or three are gathered in his name, he is there in the midst of them. The Jews themselves had a saying, " Where two sit and are occupied with the study of the Law, the glory of God is among them." We may take this great promise of Jesus into two spheres.

(*a*) We may take it into the sphere of the *Church*. Jesus is just as much present in the little congregation as in the great mass meeting. He is just as much present at the Prayer Meeting or the Bible Study Circle with their handful of people as in the crowded arena. He is not the slave of numbers. He is there wherever faithful hearts meet, however few they may be, for he gives all of himself to each individual person.

(*b*) We may take it into the sphere of the *home*. One of the earliest interpretations of this saying of Jesus was that *the two*

or three are *father, mother, and child,* and that it means that
Jesus is there, the unseen guest in every home.

There are those who never give of their best except on the
so-called great occasion; but for Jesus Christ every occasion
where even two or three are gathered in his name is a great
occasion.

HOW TO FORGIVE

Matthew 18: 21–35

Then Peter came and said to him, " Lord, how often will my
brother sin against me, and I forgive him? Up to seven times? "
Jesus said to him, " I tell you not up to seven times, but up to
seventy times seven. That is why the Kingdom of Heaven can be
likened to what happened when a king wished to make a
reckoning with his servants. When he began to make a reckoning
one debtor was brought to him who owed him £2,400,000. Since
he was quite unable to pay, his master ordered him to be sold,
together with his wife and children, and all his possessions, and
payment to be made. The servant fell on his face and besought
him: ' Sir, have patience with me, and I will pay you in full.' The
master of the servant was moved with compassion, and let him go,
and forgave him the debt. When that servant went out, he found
one of his fellow-servants, who owed him £5. He caught hold of
him and seized him by the throat: ' Pay what you owe,' he said.
The fellow-servant fell down and besought him, ' Have patience
with me, and I will pay you in full.' But he refused. Rather, he
went away and flung him into prison, until he should pay what
was due. So, when his fellow-servants saw what had happened,
they were very distressed; and they went and informed their
master of all that had happened. Then the master summoned him,
and said to him, ' You wicked servant! I forgave you all that debt
when you besought me to do so. Ought you not to have had pity
on your fellow-servant, as I had pity on you? ' And his master
was angry with him and handed him over to the torturers, until he
should pay all that was due.

Even so shall my heavenly Father do to you, if you do not each
one forgive his brother from your hearts."

WE owe a very great deal to the fact that Peter had a quick tongue. Again and again he rushed into speech in such a way that his impetuosity drew from Jesus teaching which is immortal. On this occasion Peter thought that he was being very generous. He asked Jesus how often he ought to forgive his brother, and then answered his own question by suggesting that he should forgive seven times.

Peter was not without warrant for this suggestion. It was Rabbinic teaching that a man must forgive his brother *three* times. Rabbi Jose ben Hanina said, " He who begs forgiveness from his neighbour must not do so more than three times." Rabbi Jose ben Jehuda said, " If a man commits an offence once, they forgive him; if he commits an offence a second time, they forgive him; if he commits an offence a third time, they forgive him; the fourth time they do not forgive." The Biblical proof that this was correct was taken from *Amos*. In the opening chapters of *Amos* there is a series of condemnations on the various nations *for three transgressions and for four* (*Amos* 1: 3, 6, 9, 11, 13; 2: 1, 4, 6). From this it was deduced that God's forgiveness extends to three offences and that he visits the sinner with punishment at the fourth. It was not to be thought that a man could be more gracious than God, so forgiveness was limited to three times.

Peter thought that he was going very far, for he takes the Rabbinic three times, multiplies it by two for good measure adds one, and suggests, with eager self-satisfaction, that it will be enough if he forgives seven times. Peter expected to be warmly commended; but Jesus's answer was that the Christian must forgive seventy times seven. In other words there is no reckonable limit to forgiveness.

Jesus then told the story of the servant forgiven a great debt who went out and dealt mercilessly with a fellow-servant who owed him a debt that was an infinitesimal fraction of what he himself had owed; and who for his mercilessness was utterly condemned. This parable teaches certain lessons which Jesus never tired of teaching.

(i) It teaches that lesson which runs through all the New

Testament—a man must forgive in order to be forgiven. He who will not forgive his fellow-men cannot hope that God will forgive him. " Blessed are the merciful," said Jesus, " for they shall obtain mercy " (*Matthew* 5: 7). No sooner had Jesus taught his men his own prayer, than he went on to expand and explain one petition in it: " For if you forgive men their trespasses, your heavenly Father also will forgive you; but if you do not forgive men their trespasses, neither will your Father forgive your trespasses " (*Matthew* 6: 14, 15). As James had it, " For judgment is without mercy to one who has shown no mercy " (*James* 2: 13). Divine and human forgiveness go hand in hand.

(ii) Why should that be so? One of the great points in this parable is the contrast between the two debts.

The first servant owed his master 10,000 talents; a talent was the equivalent of £240; therefore 10,000 talents is £2,400,000. That is an incredible debt. It was more than the total budget of the ordinary province. The total revenue of the province which contained Idumaea, Judaea and Samaria was only 600 talents; the total revenue of even a wealthy province like Galilee was only 300 talents. Here was a debt which was greater than a king's ransom. It was this that the servant was forgiven.

The debt which a fellow-servant owed him was a trifling thing; it was 100 *denarii*; a *denarius* was worth about 4p in value; and therefore the total debt was less than £5. It was approximately one five-hundred-thousandth of his own debt.

A. R. S. Kennedy drew this vivid picture to contrast the debts. Suppose they were paid in sixpences. The 100 denarii debt could be carried in one pocket. The ten tousand talent debt would take to carry it an army of about 8,600 carriers, each carrying a sack of sixpences 60 lbs. in weight; and they would form, at a distance of a yard apart, a line five miles long! The contrast between the debts is staggering. The point is that nothing men can do to us can in any way compare with what we have done to God; and if God has forgiven us the debt we owe to him, we must forgive our fellow-men the debts they owe to us. Nothing that we have to forgive can even faintly or remotely compare with what we have been forgiven.

> " Not the labours of my hands
> Can fulfil thy law's demands;
> Could my zeal no respite know,
> Could my tears for ever flow,
> *All for sin could not atone.*"

We have been forgiven a debt which is beyond all paying—for the sin of man brought about the death of God's own Son—and, if that is so, we must forgive others as God has forgiven us, or we can hope to find no mercy.

JEWISH MARRIAGE AND DIVORCE

Matthew 19: 1–9

When Jesus had finished these words, he left Galilee, and came into the districts of Judaea which are on the far side of the Jordan. Many crowds followed him, and he healed them there.

Pharisees came to him, trying to test him. " It is lawful," they said, " for a man to divorce his wife for any cause? " He answered, " Have you not read that from the beginning the Creator made them male and female, and he said, ' For this cause a man shall leave his father and his mother, and shall cleave to his wife, and the two shall become one flesh '? They are therefore no longer two, but one flesh. What, then, God has joined together, let no man separate." They said to him, " Why, then, did Moses lay it down to give her a bill of divorcement, and to divorce her? " He said to them, " It was to meet the hardness of your heart that Moses allowed you to divorce your wives; but in the beginning that was not the state of things which was intended. I tell you that whoever divorces his wife, except on the ground of fornication, and marries another, commits adultery; and he who marries her who has been divorced commits adultery."

HERE Jesus is dealing with what was in his day, as it is in our own, a vexed and burning question. Divorce was something about which there was no unanimity among the Jews; and the

Pharisees were deliberately trying to involve Jesus in controversy.

No nation has ever had a higher view of marriage than the Jews. Marriage was a sacred duty. To remain unmarried after the age of twenty, except in order to concentrate upon the study of the Law, was to break a positive commandment to " be fruitful and multiply." He who had no children " slew his own posterity," and " lessened the image of God upon earth." " When husband and wife are worthy, the glory of God is with them."

Marriage was not to be entered into carelessly or lightly. Josephus outlines the Jewish approach to marriage, based on the Mosaic teaching (*Antiquities of the Jews* 4. 8. 23). A man must marry a virgin of good parentage. He must never corrupt another man's wife; and he must not marry a woman who had been a slave or a harlot. If a man accused his wife of not being a virgin when he married her, he must bring proofs of his accusation. Her father or brother must defend her. If the girl was vindicated he must take her in marriage, and could never again put her away, except for the most flagrant sin. If the accusation was proved to have been reckless and malicious, the man who made it must be beaten with forty stripes save one, and must pay fifty shekels to the girl's father. But if the charge was proved and the girl found guilty, if she was one of the ordinary people, the law was that she must be stoned to death, and if she was the daughter of a priest, she must be burned alive.

If a man seduced a girl who was espoused to be married, and the seduction took place with her consent, both he and she must be put to death. If in a lonely place or where there was no help present, the man forced the girl into sin, the man alone was put to death. If a man seduced an unespoused girl, he must marry her, or, if her father was unwilling for him to marry her, he must pay the father fifty shekels.

The Jewish laws of marriage and of purity aimed very high. Ideally divorce was hated. God had said, " I hate divorce " (*Malachi* 2: 16). It was said that the very altar wept tears when a man divorced the wife of his youth.

But ideal and actuality did not go hand in hand. In the situation there were two dangerous and damaging elements.

First, in the eyes of Jewish law a woman was a thing. She was the possession of her father, or of her husband as the case might be; and, therefore, she had, technically, no legal rights at all. Most Jewish marriages were arranged either by the parents or by professional match-makers. A girl might be engaged to be married in childhood, and was often engaged to be married to a man whom she had never seen. There was this safeguard——when she came to the age of twelve she could repudiate her father's choice of husband. But in matters of divorce, the general law was that the initiative must lie with the husband. The law ran: " A woman may be divorced with or without her consent, but a man can be divorced only with his consent." The woman could never initiate the process of divorce; she could not divorce, she had to be divorced.

There were certain safeguards. If a man divorced his wife on any other grounds than those of flagrant immorality, he must return her dowry; and this must have been a barrier to irresponsible divorce. The courts might put pressure on a man to divorce his wife, in the case, for instance, of refusal to consummate the marriage, of impotence, or of proved inability to support her properly. A wife could force her husband to divorce her, if he contracted a loathsome disease, such as leprosy, or if he was a tanner, which involved the gathering of dog's dung, or if he proposed to make her leave the Holy Land. But, by and large, the law was that the woman had no legal rights, and the right to divorce lay entirely with the husband.

Second, the process of divorce was fatally easy. That process was founded on the passage in the Mosaic Law to which Jesus's questioners referred: " When a man takes a wife and marries her, if then she finds no favour in his eyes because he has found some indecency in her, and he writes her a bill of divorce and puts it in her hand and sends her out of his house ... " (*Deuteronomy* 24: 1). The bill of divorcement was a simple, one-sentence statement that the husband dismissed his wife. Josephus writes, " He that desires to be divorced from his wife for any cause whatsoever (and many such causes happen among men) let him, in writing, give assurance that he will never use her as his wife any more; for by this means she may be at liberty to marry another husband." The one safeguard against the dangerous ease of the divorce process was the fact that, unless the woman was a notorious sinner, her dowry must be returned.

JEWISH GROUNDS OF DIVORCE

Matthew 19: 1–9 (*continued*)

ONE of the great problems of Jewish divorce lies within the Mosaic enactment. .That enactment states that a man may divorce his wife, " if she finds no favour in his eyes, because he has found *some indecency* in her." The question is—how is the phrase *some indecency* to be interpreted?

On this point the Jewish Rabbis were violently divided, and it was here that Jesus's questioners wished to involve him. The school of Shammai were quite clear that *a matter of indecency* meant fornication, and fornication alone, and that for no other cause could a wife by put away. Let a woman be as mischievous as Jezebel, so long as she did not commit adultery she could not be put away. On the other hand, the school of Hillel interpreted this *matter of indecency* in the widest possible way. They said that it meant that a man could divorce his wife if she spoiled his dinner, if she spun, or went with unbound hair, or spoke to men in the streets, if she spoke disrespectfully of his parents in his presence, if she was a brawling woman whose voice could be heard in the next house. Rabbi Akiba even went the length of saying that the phrase *if she finds no favour in his eyes* meant that a man could divorce his wife if he found a woman whom he liked better and considered more beautiful.

The tragedy was that, as was to be expected, it was the school of Hillel whose teachings prevailed; the marriage bond was often lightly held, and divorce on the most trivial ground was sadly common.

To complete the picture certain further facts must be added. It is relevant to note that under Rabbinic law divorce was *compulsory* for two reasons. It was compulsory for adultery. " A woman who has committed adultery must be divorced." Second, divorce was compulsory for *sterility*. The object of marriage was the procreation of children; and if after ten years a couple were still childless divorce was compulsory. In this case the woman might remarry, but the same regulation governed the second marriage.

Two further interesting Jewish regulations in regard to divorce must be added. First, *desertion* was never a cause for divorce. If there was desertion, death must be proved. The only relaxation was that, whereas all other facts needed the corroboration of two witnesses in Jewish law, one witness was enough to prove the death of a partner in marriage who had vanished and not come back.

Secondly, strangely enough, *insanity* was not a ground of divorce. If the wife became insane, the husband could not divorce her, for, if she was divorced, she would have no protector in her helplessness. There is a certain poignant mercy in that regulation. If the husband became insane, divorce was impossible, for in that case he was incapable of writing a bill of divorcement, and without such a bill, initiated by him, there could be no divorce.

When Jesus was asked this question, at the back of it was a situation which was vexed and troubled. He was to answer it in a way which came as a staggering surprise to both parties in the dispute, and which suggested a radical change in the whole situation.

THE ANSWER OF JESUS

Matthew 19: 1–9 (*continued*)

IN effect, the Pharisees were asking Jesus whether he favoured the strict view of Shammai or the laxer view of Hillel; and thereby seeking to involve him in controversy.

Jesus's answer was to take things back to the very beginning, back to the ideal of creation. In the beginning, he said, God created Adam and Eve, man and woman. Inevitably, in the very circumstances of the creation story, Adam and Eve were created for each other and for no one else; their union was necessarily complete and unbreakable. Now, says Jesus, these two are the pattern and the symbol of all who were to come. As A. H. McNeile puts it, " Each married couple is a reproduction of Adam and Eve, and their union is therefore no less indissoluble."

The argument is quite clear. In the case of Adam and Eve divorce was not only inadvisable; it was not only wrong; it was completely impossible, for the very simple reason that there was no one else whom either of them could possibly marry. Therefore Jesus was laying down the principle that all divorce is wrong. Thus early we must note that it is not a *law*; it is a *principle*, which is a very different thing.

Here, at once, the Pharisees saw a point of attack. Moses (*Deuteronomy* 24: 1) had said that, if a man wished to divorce his wife because she had found no favour in his eyes, and because of some matter of indecency in her, he could give her a bill of divorce and the marriage was dissolved. Here was the very chance the Pharisees wanted. They could now say to Jesus, " Are you saying Moses was wrong? Are you seeking to abrogate the divine law which was given to Moses? Are you setting yourself above Moses as a law-giver? "

Jesus's answer was that what Moses said was not in fact a *law*, but nothing more than a *concession*. Moses did not *command* divorce; at the best he only *permitted* it in order to regulate a situation which would have become chaotically promiscuous. The Mosaic regulation was only a concession to fallen human nature. In *Genesis* 2: 23, 24, we have the ideal which God intended, the ideal that two people who marry should become so indissolubly one that they are one flesh. Jesus's answer was: " True, Moses *permitted* divorce; but that was a *concession* in view of a lost ideal. The ideal of marriage is to be found in the unbreakable, perfect union of Adam and Eve. *That* is what God meant marriage to be."

It is now that we are face to face with one of the most real and most acute difficulties in the New Testament. What did Jesus mean? There is even a prior question—what did Jesus say? The difficulty is—and there is no escaping it—that Mark and Matthew report the words of Jesus differently.
Matthew has:

> I say to you: whoever divorces his wife, except for unchastity, and marries another commits adultery (*Matthew* 19: 9).

Mark has:

> Whoever divorces his wife and marries another, commits adultery against her; and if she divorces her husband and marries another, she commits adultery (*Mark* 10: 11, 12).

Luke has still another version of this saying:

> Everyone who divorces his wife and marries another commits adultery, and he who marries a woman divorced from her husband commits adultery. (*Luke* 16: 18).

There is the comparatively small difficulty that Mark implies that a woman can divorce her husband, a process which, as we have seen, was not possible under Jewish law. But the explanation is that Jesus must have well known that under Gentile law a woman could divorce her husband and in that particular clause he was looking beyond the Jewish world. The great difficulty is that both Mark and Luke make the prohibition of divorce *absolute*; with them there are no exceptions whatsoever. But Matthew has one saving clause—divorce is permitted on the ground of adultery. In this case there is no real escape from a decision. The only possible way out would be to say that in point of fact, under Jewish law, divorce for adultery was in any event *compulsory*, as we have seen, and that therefore Mark and Luke did not think that they need mention it; but then so was divorce for sterility.

In the last analysis we must choose between Matthew's version of this saying and that of Mark and Luke. We think there is little doubt that the version of Mark and Luke is right. There are two reasons. Only the absolute prohibition of separation will satisfy the ideal of the Adam and Eve symbolic complete union. And the staggered words of the disciples imply this absolute prohibition, for, in effect, they say (verse 10) that if marriage is as binding as that, it is safer not to marry at all. There is little doubt that here we have Jesus laying down the *principle*—mark again, not, the *law*—that the ideal of marriage is a union which cannot be broken. There is much more to be said—but here the *ideal*, as God meant it, is laid down, and Matthew's saving clause is a later interpretation inserted in the light of the practice of the Church when he wrote.

THE HIGH IDEAL

Matthew 19: 1–9 (*continued*)

LET us now go on to see the high ideal of the married state which Jesus sets before those who are willing to accept his commands. We will see that the Jewish ideal gives us the basis of the Christian ideal. The Jewish term for marriage was *Kiddushin*. *Kiddushin* meant *sanctification* or *consecration*. It was used to describe something which was dedicated to God as his exclusive and peculiar possession. Anything totally surrendered to God was *kiddushin*. This meant that in marriage the husband was consecrated to the wife, and the wife to the husband. The one became the exclusive possession of the other, as much as an offering became the exclusive possession of God.

That is what Jesus meant when he said that for the sake of marriage a man would leave his father and his mother and cleave to his wife; and that is what he meant when he said that man and wife became so totally one that they could be called one flesh. That was God's ideal of marriage as the old *Genesis* story saw it (*Genesis* 2: 24), and that is the ideal which Jesus restated. Clearly that idea has certain consequences.

(i) This total unity means that marriage is not given for one act in life, however important that act may be, but for all. That is to say that, while sex is a supremely important part of marriage, it is not the whole of it. Any marriage entered into simply because an imperious physical desire can be satisfied in no other way is foredoomed to failure. Marriage is given, not that two people should do one thing together, but that they should do all things together.

(ii) Another way to put this is to say that marriage is the total union of two personalities. Two people can exist together in a variety of ways. One can be the dominant partner to such an extent that nothing matters but his wishes and his convenience and his aims in life, while the other is totally subservient and exists only to serve the desires and the needs of the other. Again, two people can exist in a kind of armed neutrality, where there is continuous tension and continuous opposition, and continuous collision between their wishes. Life can be one long argument, and the relationship is based at best on an uneasy compromise. Again, two people can base their relationship on a more or less resigned acceptance of each other. To all intents and purposes, while they live together, each goes his or her own way, and each has his or her own life. They share the same house but it would be an exaggeration to say that they share the same home.

Clearly none of these relationships is the ideal. The ideal is that in the marriage state two people find the completing of their personalities. Plato had a strange idea. He has a kind of legend that originally human beings were double what they are now. Because their size and strength made them arrogant, the gods cut them in halves; and real happiness comes when the two halves find each other again, and marry, and so complete each other.

Marriage should not narrow life; it should complete it. For both partners it must bring a new fulness, a new satisfaction, a new contentment into life. It is the union of two personalities in which the two complete each other. That does not mean that adjustments, and even sacrifices, have not to be made; but it does mean that the final relationship is fuller, more joyous, more satisfying than any life in singleness could be.

(iii) We may put this even more practically—marriage must be a sharing of all the circumstances of life. There is a certain danger in the delightful time of courtship. In such days it is almost inevitable that the two people will see each other at their best. These are days of glamour. They see each other in their best clothes; usually they are bent on some pleasure together; often money has not yet become a problem. But in marriage two people must see each other when they are not at their best; when they are tired and weary; when children bring the upset to a house and home that children must bring; when money is tight, and food and clothes and bills become a problem; when moonlight and roses become the kitchen sink and walking the floor at night with a crying baby. Unless two people are prepared to face the routine of life as well as the glamour of life together, marriage must be a failure.

(iv) From that there follows one thing, which is not universally true, but which is much more likely than not to be true. Marriage is most likely to be successful after a fairly long acquaintanceship, when the two people involved really know each other's background. Marriage means constantly living together. It is perfectly possible for ingrained habits, unconscious mannerisms, ways of upbringing to collide. The fuller the knowledge people have of each other before they decide indissolubly to link their lives together the better. This is not to deny that there can be such a thing as love at first sight, and that love can conquer all things, but the fact is that the greater mutual knowledge people have of each other the more likely they are to succeed in making their marriage what it ought to be.

(v) All this leads us to a final practical conclusion—the basis of marriage is *togetherness*, and the basis of togetherness is nothing other than *considerateness*. If marriage is to succeed, the partners must always be thinking more of each other than of themselves. Selfishness is the murderer of any personal relationship; and that is truest of all when two people are bound together in marriage.

Somerset Maughan tells of his mother. She was lovely and charming and beloved by all. His father was not by any means handsome, and had few social and surface gifts and graces. Someone once said to his mother, " When everyone is in love with you, and when you could have anyone you liked, how can you remain faithful to that ugly little man you married? " She answered simply: " He never hurts my feelings." There could be no finer tribute.

The true basis of marriage is not complicated and recondite —it is simply the love which thinks more of the happiness of others than it thinks of its own, the love which is proud to serve, which is able to understand, and therefore always able to forgive. That is to say, it is the Christlike love, which knows that in forgetting self it will find self, and that in losing itself it will complete itself.

THE REALIZATION OF THE IDEAL

Matthew 19: 10–12

His disciples said to him, " If the only reason for divorce between a man and his wife stands thus, it is not expedient to marry." He said to them, " Not all can receive this saying, but only those to whom it has been granted to do so. There are eunuchs who were born so from their mothers' womb; and there are eunuchs who have been made eunuchs by men; and there are eunuchs who have made themselves eunuchs for the sake of the Kingdom of Heaven. Let him who is able to receive this saying, receive it."

HERE we come to the necessary amplification of what has gone before. When the disciples heard the ideal of marriage which

Jesus set before them, they were daunted. Many a rabbinic saying would come into the mind of the disciples. The Rabbis had many sayings about unhappy marriages. " Among those who will never behold the face of Gehinnom is he who has had a bad wife." Such a man is saved from hell because he has expiated his sins on earth! " Among those whose life is not life is the man who is ruled by his wife." " A bad wife is like leprosy to her husband. What is the remedy? Let him divorce her and be cured of his leprosy." It was even laid down: " If a man has a bad wife, it is a religious duty to divorce her."

To men who had been brought up to listen to sayings like that the uncompromising demand of Jesus was an almost frightening thing. Their reaction was that, if marriage is so final and binding a relationship and if divorce is forbidden, it is better not to marry at all, for there is no escape route—as they understood it—from an evil situation. Jesus gives two answers.

(i) He says quite clearly that not everyone can in fact accept this situation but only those to whom it has been granted to do so. In other words, *only the Christian can accept the Christian ethic.* Only the man who has the continual help of Jesus Christ and the continual guidance of the Holy Spirit can build up the personal relationship which the ideal of marriage demands. Only by the help of Jesus Christ can he develop the sympathy, the understanding, the forgiving spirit, the considerate love, which true marriage requires. Without that help these things are impossible. The Christian ideal of marriage involves the pre-requisite that the partners are Christian.

Here is a truth which goes far beyond this particular application of it. We continually hear people say, " We accept the ethics of the Sermon on the Mount; but why bother about the divinity of Jesus, and his Resurrection, and his risen presence, and his Holy Spirit, and all that kind of thing? We accept that he was a good man, and that his teaching is the highest teaching ever given. Why not leave it at that, and get on with the living out of that teaching and never mind the theology? " The answer is quite simple. No one can live out Jesus Christ's teaching without Jesus Christ. And if Jesus was only a great and good man, even if he was the greatest and the best of men, then at most he is only a great example. His teaching becomes possible only in the conviction that he is not dead but present here to help us to carry it out. The teaching of Christ demands the presence of Christ; otherwise it is only an impossible—and a torturing—ideal. So, then, we have to face the fact that Christian marriage is possible only for Christians.

(ii) The passage finishes with a very puzzling verse about eunuchs. It is quite possible that Jesus said this on some other occasion, and that Matthew puts it here because he is collecting Jesus's teaching on marriage, for it was always Matthew's custom to gather together teaching on a particular subject.

A eunuch is a man who is unsexed. Jesus distinguishes three classes of people. There are those who, through some physical imperfection or deformity, can never be capable of sexual intercourse. There are those who have been made eunuchs by men. This represents customs which are strange to western civilization. Quite frequently in royal palaces servants, especially those who had to do with the royal harem, were deliberately castrated. Also, quite frequently priests who served in temples were castrated; this, for instance, is true of the priests who served in the Temple of Diana in Ephesus.

Then Jesus talks about those who have made themselves eunuchs for the sake of the Kingdom of God. We must be quite clear that this is not to be taken literally. One of the tragedies of the early Church was the case of Origen. When he was young he took this text quite literally and castrated himself, although he came to see that he was in error. Clement of Alexandria comes nearer it. He says, " The true eunuch is not he who cannot, but he who will not indulge in fleshly pleasures." By this phrase Jesus meant those who for the sake of the Kingdom deliberately bade farewell to marriage and to parenthood and to human physical love.

How can that be? It can happen that a man has to choose between some call to which he is challenged and human love. It has been said, " He travels the fastest who travels alone." A man may feel that he can do the work of some terrible slum parish only by living in circumstances in which marriage and a home are impossible. He may feel that he must accept some missionary call to a place where he cannot in conscience take a wife and beget children. He may even find that he is in love and then is offered an exacting task which the person he loves refuses to share. Then he must choose between human love and the task to which Christ calls him.

Thank God it is not often that such a choice comes to a man; but there are those who have taken upon themselves voluntarily vows of chastity, celibacy, purity, poverty, abstinence, continence. That will not be the way for the ordinary man, but the world would be a poorer place were it not for those who accept the challenge to travel alone for the sake of the work of Christ.

MARRIAGE AND DIVORCE

Matthew 19: 10–12 (*continued*)

IT would be wrong to leave this matter without some attempt to see what it actually means for the question of divorce at the present time.

We may at the beginning note this. *What Jesus laid down was a principle and not a law*. To turn this saying of Jesus into a law is gravely to misunderstand it. The Bible does not give us *laws*; it gives *principles* which we must prayerfully and intelligently apply to any given situation.

Of the Sabbath the Bible says, " In it you shall not do any work " (*Exodus* 20: 10). In point of fact we know that a complete cessation of work was never possible in any civilization. In an agricultural civilization cattle had still to be tended and cows had to be milked no matter what the day was. In a developed civilization certain public services must go on, or transport will stand still and water, light, and heat will not be available. In any home, especially where there are children, there has to be a certain amount of work.

A principle can never be quoted as a final law; a principle

must always be applied to the individual situation. We cannot therefore settle the question of divorce simply by quoting the words of Jesus. That would be legalism; we must take the words of Jesus as a principle to apply to the individual cases as they meet us. That being so, certain truths emerge.

(i) Beyond all doubt the *ideal* is that marriage should be an indissoluble union between two people, and that marriage should be entered into as a total union of two personalities, not designed to make one act possible, but designed to make all life a satisfying and mutually completing fellowship. That is the essential basis on which we must proceed.

(ii) But life is not, and never can be, a completely tidy and orderly business. Into life there is bound to come sometimes the element of the unpredictable. Suppose, then, that two people enter into the marriage relationship; suppose they do so with the highest hopes and the highest ideals; and then suppose that something unaccountably goes wrong, and that the relationship which should be life's greatest joy becomes hell upon earth. Suppose all available help is called in to mend this broken and terrible situation. Suppose the doctor is called in to deal with physical things; the psychiatrist to deal with psychological things; the priest or the minister to deal with spiritual things. Suppose the trouble still to be there; suppose one of the partners to the marriage to be so constituted physically, mentally or spiritually that marriage is an impossibility, and suppose that discovery could not have been made until the experiment itself had been made—are then these two people to be for ever fettered together in a situation which cannot do other than bring a lifetime of misery to both?

It is extremely difficult to see how such reasoning can be called Christian; it is extremely hard to see Jesus legalistically condemning two people to any such situation. This is not to say that divorce should be made easy, but it is to say that when all the physical and mental and spiritual resources have been brought to bear on such a situation, and the situation remains incurable and even dangerous, then the situation should be ended; and the Church, so far from regarding people who have

been involved in such a situation as being beyond the pale,
should do everything it can in strength and tenderness to help
them. There does not seem any other way than that in which to
bring the real Spirit of Christ to bear.

(iii) But in this matter we are face to face with a most tragic
situation. It often happens that the things which wreck marriage
are in fact the things which the law cannot touch. A man in a
moment of passion and failure of control commits adultery and
spends the rest of his life in shame and in sorrow for what he
did. That he should ever repeat his sin is the least likely thing in
the world. Another man is a model of rectitude in public; to
commit adultery is the last thing he would do; and yet by a
day-to-day sadistic cruelty, a day-to-day selfishness, a day-
to-day criticism and sarcasm and mental cruelty, he makes life
a hell for those who live with him; and he does it with callous
deliberation.

We may well remember that the sins which get into the
newspapers and the sins whose consequences are most glaringly
obvious need not be in the sight of God the greatest sins. Many
a man and many a woman wreck the marriage relationship and
yet present to the outer world a front of unimpeachable
rectitude.

This whole matter is one to which we might well bring more
sympathy and less condemnation, for of all things the failure of
a marriage must least be approached in legalism and most in
love. In such a case it is not a so-called law that must be
conserved; it is human heart and soul. What is wanted is that
there should be prayerful care and thought before the married
state is entered upon; that if a marriage is in danger of failure
every possible medical, psychological and spiritual resource
should be mobilized to save it; but, that if there is something
beyond the mending, the situation should be dealt with not with
rigid legalism, but with understanding love.

JESUS' WELCOME FOR THE CHILDREN

Matthew 19: 13–15

> Children were brought to him, that he might lay his hands on them, and pray for them. The disciples spoke sternly to them. Jesus said, " Let the little children come to me, and do not hinder them, for the Kingdom of Heaven belongs to such as they are." And after he had laid his hands on them, he went away from there.

IT may well be said that here we have the loveliest incident in the gospel story. The characters all stand out clear and plain, although it only takes two verses to tell it.

(i) There are those who brought the children. No doubt these would be their mothers.

No wonder they wished Jesus to lay his hands on them. They had seen what these hands could do; had seen them touch disease and pain away; had seen them bring sight to the blind eyes, and peace to the distracted mind; and they wanted hands like that to touch their children. There are few stories which show so clearly the sheer loveliness of the life of Jesus. Those who brought the children would not know who Jesus was; they would be well aware that Jesus was anything but popular with the Scribes and the Pharisees, and the Priests and the Sadducees and the leaders of orthodox religion; but there was a loveliness on him.

Premanand tells of a thing his mother once said to him. When Premanand became a Christian his family cast him off, and the doors were shut against him; but sometimes he used to slip back to see his mother. She was broken-hearted that he had become a Christian, but she did not cease to love him. She told him that when she was carrying him in her womb a missionary gave her a copy of one of the gospels. She read it; she still had it. She told her son that she had no desire to become a Christian, but that sometimes, in those days before he was born, she used to long that he might grow up to be a man like this Jesus.

There is a loveliness on Jesus Christ that anyone can see. It is easy to think of these mothers in Palestine feeling that the touch of a man like that on their children's heads would bring a blessing, even if they did not understand why.

(ii) There are the disciples. The disciples sound as if they were rough and stern; but, if they were, it was love that made them so. Their one desire was to protect Jesus.

They saw how tired he was; they saw what healing cost him. He was talking to them so often about a cross, and they must have seen on his face the tension of his heart and soul. All that they wanted was to see that Jesus was not bothered. They could only think that at such a time as this the children were a nuisance to the Master. We must not think of them as hard; we must not condemn them; they wished only to save Jesus from another of those insistent demands which were always laying their claims upon his strength.

(iii) There is Jesus himself. This story tells us much about him.

He was the kind of person children loved. George Macdonald used to say that no man could be a follower of Jesus if the children were afraid to play at his door. Jesus was certainly no grim ascetic, if the children loved him.

Further, to Jesus no one was unimportant. Some might say, " It's only a child; don't let him bother you." Jesus would never say that. No one was ever a nuisance to Jesus. He was never too tired, never too busy to give all of himself to anyone who needed it. There is a strange difference between Jesus and many a famous preacher or evangelist. It is often next door to impossible to get into the presence of one of these famous ones. They have a kind of retinue and bodyguard which keep the public away lest the great man be wearied and bothered. Jesus was the opposite of that. The way to his presence was open to the humblest person and to the youngest child.

(iv) There are the children. Jesus said of them that they were nearer God than anyone else there. The child's simplicity is, indeed, closer to God than anything else. It is life's tragedy that, as we grow older, we so often grow further from God rather than nearer to him.

THE GREAT REFUSAL

Matthew 19: 16–22

> And, look you, a man came to him and said, " Teacher, what good thing am I to do to possess eternal life? " He said to him, " Why do you ask me about the good? There is One who is good. If you wish to enter into life, keep the commandments." He said to him, " What kind of commandments? " Jesus said, " ' You must not kill; you must not commit adultery; you must not steal; honour your father and your mother.' And, ' You must love your neighbour as yourself.' " The young man said, " I have observed all these things. What am I still lacking? " Jesus said to him, " If you wish to be complete, go, sell your possessions, and give to the poor, and you will have treasure in heaven; and come, follow me! " When the young man heard that saying, he went away in sorrow, for he had many possessions.

HERE is one of the best-known and best-loved stories in the gospel history. One of the most interesting things about it is the way in which most of us, quite unconsciously, unite different details of it from the different gospels in order to get a complete picture. We usually call it the story of the Rich Young Ruler. All the gospels tell us that this man was *rich*, for therein is the point of the story. But only Matthew says that he was *young* (*Matthew* 19: 20); and only Luke says that he was a *ruler* (*Luke* 18: 18). It is interesting to see how, quite unconsciously, we have created for ourselves a composite picture composed of elements taken from all three gospels (*Matthew* 19: 16–22; *Mark* 10: 17–22; *Luke* 18: 18–23).

There is another interesting point about this story. Matthew alters the question put to Jesus by this man. Both Mark and Luke say that the question was: " Why do you call me good? No one is good but God alone " (*Mark* 10: 18; *Luke* 18: 19). Matthew says that the question was: " Why do you ask me about what is good? One there is who is good " (*Matthew* 19: 17). (The text of the Authorized Version is in error here, as reference to any of the newer and more correct translations will show.) Matthew's is the latest of the first three gospels, and his reverence for Jesus is such that he cannot bear to show Jesus asking the question: " Why do you call me good? " That almost sounds to him as if Jesus was refusing to be called good, so he alters it into: " Why do you ask me about what is good? " in order to avoid the seeming irreverence.

This story teaches one of the deepest of all lessons for it has within it the whole basis of the difference between the right and the wrong idea of what religion is.

The man who came to Jesus was seeking for what he called *eternal life*. He was seeking for happiness, for satisfaction, for peace with God. But his very way of phrasing his question betrays him. He asks, " What must I *do*? " He is thinking in terms of *actions*. He is like the Pharisees; thinking in terms of keeping rules and regulations. He is thinking of piling up a credit balance-sheet with God by keeping the works of the law. He clearly knows nothing of a religion of grace. So Jesus tries to lead him on to a correct view.

Jesus answers him in his own terms. He tells him to keep the commandments. The young man asks what kind of commandments Jesus means. Thereupon Jesus cites five of the ten commandments. Now there are two important things about the commandments which Jesus chooses to cite.

First, they are all commandments from the second half of the decalogue, the half which deals, not with our duty to God, but with our *duty to men*. They are the commandments which govern our *personal relationships*, and our *attitude to our fellow-men*.

Second, Jesus cites one commandment, as it were, out of order. He cites the command to honour parents last, when in point of fact it ought to come first. It is clear that Jesus wishes to lay special stress on that commandment. Why? May it not be that this young man had grown rich and successful in his career, and had then forgotten his parents, who may have been very poor. He may well have risen in the world, and have been half-ashamed of the folks in the old home; and then he may have justified himself perfectly legally by the law of *Korban*, which Jesus had so unsparingly condemned (*Matthew* 15: 1–6; *Mark* 7: 9–13). These passages show that he could well have done that, and still have legally claimed to have obeyed the commandments. In the very commandments which he cites Jesus is asking this young man what his attitude to his fellow-men and to his parents was, asking what his personal relationships were like.

The young man's answer was that he had kept the commandments; and yet there was still something which he knew he ought to have and which he had not got. So Jesus told him to sell all he had and give it to the poor and follow him.

It so happens that we have another account of this incident in the *Gospel according to the Hebrews*, which was one of the very early gospels which failed to be included in the New Testament. Its account gives us certain very valuable additional information. Here it is:

" The second of the rich men said to him, ' Master, what good thing can I do and live? ' He said unto him, ' O man, fulfil the law and the prophets.' He answered him, 'I have kept them.' He said unto him, ' Go, sell all that thou ownest, and distribute it unto the poor, and, come, follow me.' But the rich man began to scratch his head, and it pleased him not. And the Lord said unto him, ' How sayest thou, I have kept the law and the prophets? For it is written in the law: Thou shalt love thy neighbour as thyself; and lo, many of thy brethren, sons of Abraham, are clad in filth, dying of hunger, and thine house is full of many good things, and nought at all goeth out of it unto them.' "

Here is the key to the whole passage. The young man claimed to have kept the law. In the legal sense that might be true; but in the spiritual sense it was not true, because his attitude to his fellow-men was wrong. In the last analysis his attitude was utterly selfish. That is why Jesus confronted him with the challenge to sell all and to give to the poor. This man was so shackled to his possessions that nothing less than surgical excision of them would suffice. If a man looks on his possessions as given to him for nothing but his own comfort and convenience, they are a chain which must be broken; if he looks on his possessions as a means to helping others, they are his crown.

The great truth of this story lies in the way it illumines the meaning of eternal life. Eternal life is life such as God himself lives. The word for *eternal* is *aiōnios*, which does not mean *lasting for ever*; it means such as befits God, or such as belongs to God, or such as is characteristic of God. The great characteristic of God is that he so loved and he gave. Therefore the essence of eternal life is not a carefully calculated keeping of the commandments and the rules and the regulations; eternal life is based on an attitude of loving and sacrificial generosity to our fellow-men. If we would find eternal life, if we would find happiness, joy, satisfaction, peace of mind and serenity of heart, it shall not be by piling up a credit balance with God through keeping commandments and observing rules and regulations; it shall be through reproducing God's attitude of love and care to our fellow-men. To follow Christ and in grace and generosity to serve the men for whom Christ died are one and the same thing.

In the end the young man turned away in great distress. He refused the challenge, because he had great possessions. His tragedy was that he loved things more than he loved people; and he loved himself more than he loved others. Any man who puts things before people and self before others, must turn his back on Jesus Christ.

THE PERIL OF RICHES

Matthew 19: 23–26

> Jesus said to the disciples, " This is the truth I tell you—it is with difficulty that a rich man shall enter into the Kingdom of Heaven. Again I say unto you—it is easier for a camel to pass through the eye of a needle than for a rich man to enter into the Kingdom of Heaven." When the disciples heard this, they were exceedingly astonished. " What rich man, then," they said, " can be saved? "

Jesus looked at them, " With men," he said, " this is impossible, but with God all things are possible."

THE case of the Rich Young Ruler shed a vivid and a tragic light on the danger of riches; here was a man who had made the great refusal because he had great possessions. Jesus now goes on to underline that danger. " It is difficult," he said, " for a rich man to enter into the Kingdom of Heaven."

To illustrate how difficult that was he used a vivid simile. He said that it was as difficult for a rich man to enter the Kingdom of Heaven as it was for a camel to pass through the eye of a needle. Different interpretations have been given of the picture which Jesus was drawing.

The camel was the largest animal which the Jews knew. It is said that sometimes in walled cities there were two gates. There was the great main gate through which all trade and traffic moved. Beside it there was often a little low and narrow gate. When the great main gate was locked and guarded at night, the only way into the city was through the little gate, through which even a man could hardly pass erect. It is said that sometimes that little gate was called " The Needle's Eye." So it is suggested that Jesus was saying that it was just as difficult for a rich man to enter the Kingdom of Heaven as for a huge camel to get through the little gate through which a man can hardly pass.

There is another, and very attractive, suggestion. The Greek word for *camel* is *kamēlos*; the Greek word for a *ship's hawser* is *kamilos*. It was characteristic of later Greek that the vowel sounds tended to lose their sharp distinctions and to approximate to each other. In such Greek there would be hardly any discernible difference between the sound of *i* and *ē*; they would both be pronounced as *ee* is in English. So, then, what Jesus may have said is that it was just as difficult for a rich man to enter into the Kingdom of Heaven as it would be to thread a darning-needle with a ship's cable or hawser. That indeed is a vivid picture.

But the likelihood is that Jesus was using the picture quite literally, and that he was actually saying that it was as hard for a rich man to enter the Kingdom of Heaven as it was for a camel to go through the eye of a needle. Wherein then lies this difficulty? Riches have three main effects on a man's outlook.

(i) *Riches encourage a false independence.* If a man is well-supplied with this world's goods, he is very apt to think that he can well deal with any situation which may arise.

There is a vivid instance of this in the letter to the Church of Laodicaea in the *Revelation*. Laodicaea was the richest town in Asia Minor. She was laid waste by an earthquake in A.D. 60. The Roman government offered aid and a large grant of money to repair her shattered buildings. She refused it, saying that she was well able to handle the situation by herself. " Laodicaea," said Tacitus, the Roman historian, " rose from the ruins entirely by her own resources and with no help from us." The Risen Christ hears Laodicaea say, " I am rich, I have prospered, and I need nothing " (*Revelation* 3: 17).

It was Walpole who coined the cynical epigram that every man has his price. If a man is wealthy he is apt to think that everything has its price, that if he wants a thing enough he can buy it, that if any difficult situation descends upon him he can buy his way out of it. He can come to think that he can buy his way into happiness and buy his way out of sorrow. So he comes to think that he can well do without God and is quite able to handle life by himself. There comes a time when a man discovers that that is an illusion, that there are things which money cannot buy, and things from which money cannot save him. But always there is the danger that great possessions encourage that false independence which thinks—until it learns better—that it has eliminated the need for God.

(ii) *Riches shackle a man to this earth.* " Where your treasure is," said Jesus, " there will your heart be also " (*Matthew* 6: 21). If everything a man desires is contained within this world, if all his interests are here, he never thinks of another world and of a hereafter. If a man has too big a stake on earth, he is very apt to forget that there is a heaven. After a tour of a certain wealthy and luxurious castle and estate, Dr. Johnson grimly remarked: " These are the things which make it difficult to die." It is perfectly possible for a man to be so interested in earthly things that he forgets heavenly things, to be so involved in the things that are seen that he forgets the things that are unseen—and therein lies tragedy, for the things which are seen are temporal but the things which are unseen are eternal.

(iii) *Riches tend to make a man selfish.* However much a man has, it is human for him to want still more, for, as it has been epigrammatically said, " Enough is always a little more than a man has." Further, once a man has possessed comfort and luxury, he always tends to fear the day when he may lose them. Life becomes a strenuous and worried struggle to retain the things he has. The result is that when a man becomes wealthy, instead of having the impulse to give things away, he very often has the impulse to cling on to them. His instinct is to amass more and more for the sake of the safety and the security which he thinks they will bring. The danger of riches is that they tend to make a man forget that he loses what he keeps, and gains what he gives away.

But Jesus did not say that it was *impossible* for a rich man to enter the Kingdom of Heaven. Zacchaeus was one of the richest men in Jericho, yet, all unexpectedly, he found the way in (*Luke* 19: 9). Joseph of Arimathaea was a rich man (*Matthew* 27: 57); Nicodemus must have been very wealthy, for he brought spices to anoint the dead body of Jesus, which were worth a king's ransom (*John* 19: 39). It is not that those who have riches are shut out. It is not that riches are a sin—but they are a danger. The basis of all Christianity is an imperious sense of need; when a man has many things on earth, he is in danger of thinking that he does not need God; when a man has few things on earth, he is often driven to God because he has nowhere else to go.

A WISE ANSWER TO A MISTAKEN QUESTION

Matthew 19: 27–30

Then Peter said to him, " Look you, we have left everything and
have followed you. What then will we get? " Jesus said to him,
" When all things are reborn, and when the Son of Man shall sit
on the throne of his glory, you too, who have followed me, will
also sit on twelve thrones, judging the twelve tribes of Israel.
Anyone who has left houses, or brothers, or sisters, or father, or
mother, or children, or lands for my name, will receive them a
hundred times over, and he will enter into possession of eternal
life. But many who were first will be last, and many who were last
will be first."

IT would have been very easy for Jesus to dismiss Peter's
question with an impatient rebuke. In a sense, it was entirely the
wrong question to ask. To put it bluntly, Peter was asking,
" What do we get out of following you? " Jesus could well have
said that anyone who followed him in that kind of spirit had no
idea what following him meant at all. And yet it was a natural
question. True, it had its implicit rebuke in the parable which
followed; but Jesus did not scold Peter. He took his question,
and out of it laid down three great laws of the Christian life.

(i) It is always true that he who shares Christ's campaign will
share Christ's victory. In human warfare it has been too often
true that the common soldiers who fought the battles were
forgotten once the warfare was ended, and the victory won, and
their usefulness past. In human warfare it has been too often
true that men who fought to make a country in which heroes
might live found that that same country had become a place
where heroes might starve. It is not so with Jesus Christ. He
who shares Christ's warfare will share Christ's triumph; and he
who bears the Cross will wear the crown.

(ii) It is always true that the Christian will receive far more
than ever he has to give up; but what he receives is not new
material possessions, but a new fellowship, human and divine.

When a man becomes a Christian he enters into a new

human fellowship; so long as there is a Christian Church, a Christian should never be friendless. If his Christian decision has meant that he has had to give up friends, it ought also to mean that he has entered into a wider circle of friendship than ever he knew before. It ought to be true that there is hardly a town or village or city anywhere where the Christian can be lonely. For where there is a Church, there is a fellowship into which he has a right to enter. It may be that the Christian who is a stranger is too shy to make that entry as he ought; it may be that the Church in the place where he is a stranger has become too much of a private clique to open its arms and its doors to him. But if the Christian ideal is being realized there is no place in the world with a Christian Church where the individual Christian should be friendless or lonely. Simply to be a Christian means to have entered into a fellowship which goes out to the ends of the earth.

Further, when a man becomes a Christian, he enters into a new *divine* fellowship. He enters into possession of eternal life, the life which is the very life of God. From other things a Christian may be separated, but he can never be separated from the love of God in Christ Jesus his Lord.

(iii) Finally, Jesus lays it down that there will be surprises in the final assessment. God's standards of judgment are not men's, if for no other reason than that God sees into the hearts of men. There is a new world to redress the balance of the old; there is eternity to adjust the misjudgments of time. And it may be that those who were humble on earth will be great in heaven, and that those who were great in this world will be humbled in the world to come.

THE MASTER SEEKS HIS WORKERS

Matthew 20: 1–16

" For the situation in the Kingdom of Heaven is like what happened when a householder went out first thing in the morning to hire workers for his vineyard. When he had come to an agreement with them that they would work for 4p a day, he sent them into his vineyard. He went out again about nine o'clock in the morning, and saw others standing idle in the market-place. He said to them, ' Go you also into the vineyard, and I will pay you whatever is right.' And they went. He went out again about twelve o'clock midday, and about three o'clock in the afternoon, and did the same. About five o'clock in the evening he went out and found others standing there, and said to them, ' Why are you standing here the whole day idle? ' They said to him, ' Because no one has hired us.' He said to them, ' Go you also to the vineyard.' When evening came, the master of the vineyard said to his steward, ' Call the workers, and give them their pay, beginning from the last and going on until you come to the first.' So, when those who had been engaged about five o'clock in the afternoon, came, they received 4p each. Those who had come first thought that they would receive more; but they too received 4p each. When they received it, they grumblingly complained against the master. ' These last,' they said, ' have only worked for one hour, and you have made them equal to us, who have borne the burden and the hot wind of the day.' He answered one of them, ' Friend, I am doing you no wrong. Did you not come to an agreement with me to work for 4p? Take what is yours and go! It is my will to give to this last man the same as to you. Can I not do what I like with my own money? Or, are you grudging because I am generous? ' Even so the last shall be first, and the first shall be last."

THIS parable may sound to us as if it described a purely imaginary situation, but that is far from being the case. Apart from the method of payment, the parable describes the kind of thing that frequently happened at certain times in Palestine. The grape harvest ripened towards the end of September, and then close on its heels the rains came. If the harvest was not ingathered before the rains broke, then it was ruined; and so to get the harvest in was a frantic race against time. Any worker was welcome, even if he could give only an hour to the work.

The pay was perfectly normal; a *denarius* or a *drachma* was the normal day's wage for a working man; and, even allowing for the difference in modern standards and in purchasing power, 4p a day was not a wage which left any margin.

The men who were standing in the market-place were not street-corner idlers, lazing away their time. The market-place was the equivalent of the labour exchange. A man came there first thing in the morning, carrying his tools, and waited until someone hired him. The men who stood in the market-place were waiting for work, and the fact that some of them stood on until even five o'clock in the evening is the proof of how desperately they wanted it.

These men were hired labourers; they were the lowest class of workers, and life for them was always desperately precarious. Slaves and servants were regarded as being at least to some extent attached to the family; they were within the group; their fortunes would vary with the fortunes of the family, but they would never be in any imminent danger of starvation in normal times. It was very different with the hired day-labourers. They were not attached to any group; they were entirely at the mercy of chance employment; they were always living on the semi-starvation line. As we have seen, the pay was 4p a day; and, if they were unemployed for one day, the children would go hungry at home, for no man ever saved much out of 4p a day. With them, to be unemployed for a day was disaster.

The hours in the parable were the normal Jewish hours. The Jewish day began at sunrise, 6 a.m., and the hours were counted from then until 6 p.m., when officially the next day began. Counting from 6 a.m. therefore, the third hour is 9 a.m., the sixth hour is twelve midday, and the eleventh hour is 5 p.m.

This parable gives a vivid picture of the kind of thing which could happen in the market-place of any Jewish village or town any day, when the grape harvest was being rushed in to beat the rains.

WORK AND WAGES IN THE KINGDOM OF GOD

Matthew 20: 1–16 (*continued*)

C. G. MONTEFIORE calls this parable " one of the greatest and most glorious of all." It may indeed have had a comparatively limited application when it was spoken for the first time; but it contains truth which goes to the very heart of the Christian religion. We begin with the comparatively limited significance it originally had.

(i) It is in one sense a warning to the disciples. It is as if Jesus said to them, " You have received the great privilege of coming into the Christian Church and fellowship very early, right at the beginning. In later days others will come in. You must not claim a special honour and a special place because you were Christians before they were. All men, no matter when they come, are equally precious to God." ·

There are people who think that, because they have been members of a Church for a long time, the Church practically belongs to them and they can dictate its policy. Such people resent what seems to them the intrusion of new blood or the rise of a new generation with different plans and different ways. In the Christian Church seniority does not necessarily mean honour.

(ii) There is an equally definite warning to the Jews. They knew that they were the chosen people, nor would they ever willingly forget that choice. As a consequence they looked down on the Gentiles. Usually they hated and despised them, and hoped for nothing but their destruction. This attitude threatened to be carried forward into the Christian Church. If the Gentiles were to be allowed into the fellowship of the Church at all, they must come in as inferiors.

" In God's economy," as someone has said, " there is no such thing as a most favoured nation clause." Christianity knows nothing of the conception of a *herrenvolk*, a master race. It may well be that we who have been Christian for so long have much to learn from those younger Churches who are late-comers to the fellowship of the faith.

(iii) These are the original lessons of this parable, but it has very much more to say to us.

In it there is *the comfort of God*. It means that no matter when a man enters the Kingdom, late or soon, in the first flush of youth, in the strength of the midday, or when the shadows are lengthening, he is equally dear to God. The Rabbis had a saying, " Some enter the Kingdom in an hour; others hardly enter it in a lifetime." In the picture of the holy city in the *Revelation* there are twelve gates. There are gates on the *East* which is the direction of the dawn, and whereby a man may enter in the glad morning of his days; there are gates on the *West* which is the direction of the setting sun, and whereby a man may enter in his age. No matter when a man comes to Christ, he is equally dear to him.

May we not go even further with this thought of comfort? Sometimes a man dies full of years and full of honour, with his day's work ended and his task completed. Sometimes a young person dies almost before the door of life and achievement have opened at all. From God they will both receive the same welcome, for both Jesus Christ is waiting, and for neither, in the divine sense, has life ended too soon or too late.

(iv) Here, also, is the infinite *compassion* of God. There is an element of human tenderness in this parable.

There is nothing more tragic in this world than a man who is unemployed, a man whose talents are rusting in idleness because there is nothing for him to do. Hugh Martin reminds us that a great teacher used to say that the saddest words in all Shakespeare's plays are the words: " Othello's occupation's gone." In that market-place men stood waiting because no one had hired them; in his compassion the master gave them work to do. He could not bear to see them idle.

Further, in strict justice the fewer hours a man worked, the less pay he should have received. But the master well knew that 4p a day was no great wage; he well knew that, if a workman went home with less, there would be a worried wife and hungry children; and therefore he went beyond justice and gave them more than was their due.

As it has been put, this parable states implicitly two great truths which are the very charter of the working man—the right of every man to work and the right of every man to a living wage for his work.

(v) Here also is the *generosity* of God. These men did not all do the same work; but they did receive the same pay. There are two great lessons here. The first is, as it has been said, " All service ranks the same with God." It is not the amount of service given, but the love in which it is given which matters. A man out of his plenty may give us a gift of a hundred pounds, and in truth we are grateful; a child may give us a birthday or Christmas gift which cost only a few pence but which was laboriously and lovingly saved up for—and that gift, with little value of its own, touches our heart far more. God does not look on the amount of our service. So long as it is all we have to give, all service ranks the same with God.

The second lesson is even greater—all God gives is of grace. We cannot earn what God gives us; we cannot deserve it; what God gives us is given out of the goodness of his heart; what God gives is not pay, but a gift; not a reward, but a grace.

(vi) Surely that brings us to the supreme lesson of the parable—*the whole point of work is the spirit in which it is done*. The servants are clearly divided into two classes. The first came to an agreement with the master; they had a contract; they said, " We work, if you give us so much pay." As their conduct showed, all they were concerned with was to get as much as possible out of their work. But in the case of those who were engaged later, there is no word of contract; all they wanted was the chance to work and they willingly left the reward to the master.

A man is not a Christian if his first concern is pay. Peter asked: " What do we get out of it? " The Christian works for the joy of serving God and his fellow-men. That is why the first will be last and the last will be first. Many a man in this world, who has earned great rewards, will have a very low place in the Kingdom because rewards were his sole thought. Many a man, who, as the world counts it, is a poor man, will be great in the Kingdom, because he never thought in terms of reward but worked for the thrill of working and for the joy of serving. It is the paradox of the Christian life that he who aims at reward loses it, and he who forgets reward finds it.

TOWARDS THE CROSS

Matthew 20: 17–19

> As he was going up to Jerusalem, Jesus took the twelve disciples
> apart, and said to them, while they were on the road, " Look you,
> we are going up to Jerusalem, and the ‹Son of Man will be
> delivered to the chief priests and the Scribes, and they will
> condemn him to death, and they will hand him over to the
> Gentiles to mock, and to scourge, and to crucify; and on the third
> day he will be raised."

THIS is the third time that Jesus warned his disciples that he
was on the way to the Cross (*Matthew* 16: 21; 17: 22, 23). Both
Mark and Luke add their own touches to the story, to show that
on this occasion there was in the atmosphere of the apostolic
band a certain tenseness and a certain foreboding of tragedy to
come. Mark says that Jesus was walking ahead by himself, and
that the disciples were amazed and afraid (*Mark* 10: 32–34).
They did not understand what was happening, but they could
see in every line of Jesus's body the struggle of his soul. Luke,
too, tells how Jesus took the disciples to himself alone that he
might try to compel them to understand what lay ahead (*Luke*
18: 31–34). There is here the first decisive step to the last act of
the inescapable tragedy. Jesus deliberately and open-eyed sets
out for Jerusalem and the Cross.

There was a strange inclusiveness in the suffering to which
Jesus looked forward; it was a suffering in which no pain of
heart or mind or body was to be lacking.

He was to be *betrayed* into the hands of the chief priests and
Scribes; there we see the suffering of the *heart broken by the
disloyalty of friends.* He was to be *condemned to death*; there
we see the suffering of *injustice*, which is very hard to bear. He
was to be *mocked* by the Romans; there we see the suffering of
humiliation and of *deliberate insult.* He was to be scourged; few
tortures in the world compared with the Roman scourge, and
there we see the suffering of *physical pain.* Fina[l]ly, he was to be

crucified; there we see the ultimate suffering of *death*. It is as if Jesus was going to gather in upon himself every possible kind of physical and emotional and mental suffering that the world could inflict.

Even at such a time that was not the end of his words, for he finished with the confident assertion of the Resurrection. Beyond the curtain of suffering lay the revelation of glory; beyond the Cross was the Crown; beyond the defeat was triumph; and beyond death was life.

THE FALSE AND THE TRUE AMBITION

Matthew 20: 20–28

> At that time the mother of Zebedee's sons came to him with her sons, kneeling before him, and asking something from him. He said to her, " What do you wish? " She said to him, " Speak the word that these two sons of mine may sit, one on your right hand, and one on your left, in your Kingdom." Jesus answered, " You do not know what you are asking. Can you drink the cup which I have to drink? " They said to him, " We can." He said to them, " My cup you are to drink; but to sit on my right hand and my left is not mine to give, but that belongs to those for whom it has been prepared by my Father." When the ten heard about this, they were angry with the two brothers. Jesus called them to him and said, " You know that the rulers of the Gentiles lord it over them, and their great ones exercise authority over them. It shall not be so among you, but whoever wishes to prove himself great among you must be your servant; and whoever wishes to occupy the foremost place will be your slave, just as the Son of Man did not come to be served but to serve, and to give his life a ransom for many."

HERE we see the worldly ambition of the disciples in action. There is one very revealing little difference between Matthew's and Mark's account of this incident. In *Mark* 10: 35–45 it is James and John who come to Jesus with this request. In *Matthew* it is their mother. The reason for the change is this—Matthew was writing twenty-five years later than Mark; by that time a kind of halo of sanctity had become attached to the disciples. Matthew did not wish to show James and John guilty of worldly ambition, and so he puts the request into the mouth of their mother rather than of themselves.

There may have been a very natural reason for this request. It is probable that James and John were closely related to Jesus. Matthew, Mark and John all give lists of the women who were at the Cross when Jesus was crucified. Let us set them down.

Matthew's list is:

> Mary Magdalene, Mary the mother of James and Joseph, and the mother of the sons of Zebedee (*Matthew* 27: 56).

Mark's list is:

> Mary Magdalene, Mary the mother of James the Younger and of Joses, and Salome (*Mark* 15: 40).

John's list is:

> Jesus's mother, his mother's sister, Mary the wife of Clopas, and Mary Magdalene.

Mary Magdalene is named in all the lists; Mary the mother of James and Joses must be the same person as Mary the wife of Clopas; therefore the third woman is described in three different ways. Matthew calls her *the mother of the sons of Zebedee*; Mark calls her *Salome*; and John calls her *Jesus's mother's sister*. So, then, we learn that the mother of James and John was named Salome, and that she was the sister of Mary the mother of Jesus. That means that James and John were full cousins of Jesus; and it may well have been that they felt that this close relationship entitled them to a special place in his Kingdom.

This is one of the most revealing passages in the New Testament. It sheds light in three directions.

First, it sheds a light on the *disciples*. It tells us three things about them. It tells us of their *ambition*. They were still thinking in terms of personal reward and personal distinction; and they were thinking of personal success without personal sacrifice. They wanted Jesus with a royal command to ensure for them a princely life. Every man has to learn that true greatness lies, not in dominance, but in service; and that in every sphere the price of greatness must be paid.

That is on the debit side of the account of the disciples; but there is much on the credit side. There is no incident which so demonstrates their *invincible faith in Jesus*. Think of when this request was made. It was made after a series of announcements by Jesus that ahead of him lay an inescapable Cross; it was made at a moment when the air was heavy with the atmosphere of tragedy and the sense of foreboding. And yet in spite of that the disciples are thinking of a Kingdom. It is of immense significance to see that, even in a world in which the dark was coming down, the disciples would not abandon the conviction that the victory belonged to Jesus. In Christianity there must always be this invincible optimism in the moment when things are conspiring to drive a man to despair.

Still further, here is demonstrated the *unshakable loyalty* of the disciples. Even when they were bluntly told that there lay ahead a bitter cup, it never struck them to turn back; they were determined to drink it. If to conquer with Christ meant to suffer with Christ, they were perfectly willing to face that suffering.

It is easy to condemn the disciples, but the faith and the loyalty which lay behind the ambition must never be forgotten.

THE MIND OF JESUS

Matthew 20: 20–28 (*continued*)

SECOND, this passage sheds a light upon the *Christian life*. Jesus said that those who would share his triumph must drink his cup. What was that cup? It was to James and John that Jesus spoke. Now life treated James and John very differently. James was the first of the apostolic band to die a martyr (*Acts* 12: 2). For him the cup was martyrdom. On the other hand, by far the greater weight of tradition goes to show that John lived to a great old age in Ephesus and died a natural death when he must have been close on a hundred years old. For him the cup was the constant discipline and struggle of the Christian life throughout the years.

It is quite wrong to think that for the Christian the cup must always mean the short, sharp, bitter, agonizing struggle of martyrdom; the cup may well be the long routine of the Christian life, with all its daily sacrifice, its daily struggle, and its heart-breaks and its disappointments and its tears. A Roman coin was once found with the picture of an ox on it; the ox was facing two things—an altar and a plough; and the inscription read: " Ready for either." The ox had to be ready either for the supreme moment of sacrifice on the altar or the long labour of the plough on the farm. There is no one cup for the Christian to drink. His cup may be drunk in one great moment; his cup may be drunk throughout a lifetime of Christian living. To drink the cup simply means to follow Christ wherever he may lead, and to be like him in any situation life may bring.

Third, this passage sheds a light on *Jesus*.It shows us his *kindness*. The amazing thing about Jesus is that he never lost patience and became irritated. In spite of all he had said, here were these men and their mother still chattering about posts in an earthly government and kingdom. But Christ does not explode at their obtuseness, or blaze at their blindness, or despair at their unteachableness. In gentleness, in sympathy, and in love, with never an impatient word, he seeks to lead them to the truth.

It shows us his *honesty*. He was quite clear that there was a bitter cup to be drunk and did not hesitate to say so. No man can ever claim that he began to follow Jesus under false pretences. He never failed to tell men that, even if life ends in crown-wearing, it continues in cross-bearing.

It shows us his *trust in men*. He never doubted that James and John would maintain their loyalty. They had their mistaken ambitions; they had their blindness; they had their wrong ideas; but he never dreamed of writing them off as bad debts.

He believed that they could and would drink the cup, and that
in the end they would still be found at his side. One of the great
fundamental facts to which we must hold on, even when we hate
and loathe and despise ourselves, is that Jesus believes in us.
The Christian is a man put upon his honour by Jesus.

THE CHRISTIAN REVOLUTION

Matthew 20: 20–28 (*continued*)

THE request of James and John not unnaturally annoyed the
other disciples. They did not see why the two brothers should
steal a march on them, even if they were the cousins of Jesus.
They did .not see why they should be allowed to stake their
claims to pre-eminence. Jesus knew what was going on in their
minds; and he spoke to them words which are the very basis of
the Christian life. Out in the world, said Jesus, it is quite true
that the great man is the man who controls others; the man to
whose word of command others must leap; the man who with a
wave of his hand can have his slightest need supplied. Out in
the world there was the Roman governor with his retinue and
the eastern potentate with his slaves. The world counts them
great. But among my followers service alone is the badge of
greatness. Greatness does not consist in commanding others to
do things for you; it consists in doing things for others; and the
greater the service, the greater the honour. Jesus uses a kind of
gradation. " If you wish to be *great*," he says, " be a *servant*; if
you wish to be *first of all* be a *slave*." Here is the Christian
revolution; here is the complete reversal of all the world's
standards. A complete new set of values has been brought into
life.

The strange thing is that instinctively the world itself has
accepted these standards. The world knows quite well that a
good man is a man who serves his fellow-men. The world will
respect, and admire, and sometimes fear, the man of power; but
it will love the man of love. The doctor who will come out at

any time of the day or night to serve and save his patients; the parson who is always on the road amongst his people; the employer who takes an active interest in the lives and troubles of his employees; the person to whom we can go and never be made to feel a nuisance—these are the people whom all men love, and in whom instinctively they see Jesus Christ.

When that great saint Toyohiko Kagawa first came into contact with Christianity, he felt its fascination, until one day the cry burst from him: " O God, make me like Christ." To be like Christ he went to live in the slums, even though he himself was suffering from tuberculosis. It seemed the last place on earth to which a man in his condition should have gone.

Cecil Northcott in *Famous Life Decisions* tells of what Kagawa did. He went to live in a six foot by six hut in a Tokyo slum. " On his first night he was asked to share his bed with a man suffering from contagious itch. That was a test of his faith. Would he go back on his point of no return? No. He welcomed his bed-fellow. Then a beggar asked for his shirt and got it. Next day he was back for Kagawa's coat and trousers, and got them too. Kagawa was left standing in a ragged old kimono. The slum dwellers of Tokyo laughed at him, but they came to respect him. He stood in the driving rain to preach, coughing all the time. ' God is love,' he shouted. ' God is love. Where love is, there is God.' He often fell down exhausted, and the rough men of the slums carried him gently back to his hut."

Kagawa himself wrote: " God dwells among the lowliest of men. He sits on the dust heap among the prison convicts. He stands with the juvenile delinquents. He is there with the beggars. He is among the sick, he stands with the unemployed. Therefore let him who would meet God visit the prison cell before going to the temple. Before he goes to Church let him visit the hospital. Before he reads his Bible let him help the beggar."

Therein is greatness. The world may assess a man's greatness by the number of people whom he controls and who are at his beck and call; or by his intellectual standing and his academic eminence; or by the number of committees of which he is a member; or by the size of his bank balance and the material possessions which he has amassed; but in the assessment of Jesus Christ these things are irrelevant. His assessment is quite simply—how many people has he helped?

THE LORDSHIP OF THE CROSS

Matthew 20: 20–28 (*continued*)

WHAT Jesus calls upon his followers to do he himself did. He came not to be served, but to serve. He came to occupy not a throne, but a cross. It was just because of this that the orthodox religious people of his time could not understand him. All through their history the Jews had dreamed of the Messiah; but the Messiah of whom they had dreamed was always a conquering king, a mighty leader, one who would smash the enemies of Israel and reign in power over the kingdoms of the earth. They looked for a conqueror; they received one broken on a cross. They looked for the raging Lion of Judah; they received the gentle Lamb of God. Rudolf Bultmann writes: " In the Cross of Christ Jewish standards of judgment and human notions of the splendour of the Messiah are shattered." Here is demonstrated the new glory and the new greatness of suffering love and sacrificial service. Here is royalty and kingship restated and remade.

Jesus summed up his whole life in one poignant sentence: " The Son of Man came to give his life a ransom for many." It is worth stopping to see what the crude hands of theology have done with that lovely saying. Very early men began to say, " Jesus gave his life a ransom for many. Well, then, to whom was the ransom paid? " Origen has no doubt that the ransom was paid to the devil. " The ransom could not have been paid to God; it was therefore paid to the Evil One, who was holding us fast until the ransom should be given to him, even the life of Jesus." Gregory of Nyssa saw the glaring fault in that theory. It puts the Devil on a level with God; it means that the Devil could dictate his terms to God, before he would let men go. So Gregory of Nyssa has a strange idea. The devil was tricked by God. He was tricked by the seeming helplessness of Jesus; he took Jesus to be a mere man; he tried to retain hold of Jesus, and in trying to do so, he lost his power and was broken for ever. Gregory the Great took the picture to even more grotesque, almost revolting, lengths. The Incarnation, he said, was a divine stratagem to catch the great leviathan. The deity of Christ was the hook; his flesh was the bait; the bait was dangled before leviathan; he swallowed it and was taken. The limit was reached by Peter the Lombard. " The cross," he said, " was a mousetrap (*muscipula*) to catch the devil, baited with the blood of Christ."

All this is what happens when men take the poetry of love and try to turn it into man-made theories. Jesus came to give his life a ransom for many. What does it mean? It means quite simply this. Men were in the grip of a power of evil which they could not break; their sins dragged them down; their sins separated them from God; their sins wrecked life for themselves and for the world and for God himself. A ranson is something paid or given to liberate a man from a situation from which it is impossible for him to free himself. Therefore what this saying means is quite simply—*it cost the life and the death of Jesus Christ to bring men back to God.*

There is no question of to whom the ransom was paid. There is simply the great, tremendous truth that without Jesus Christ and his life of service and his death of love, we could never have found our way back to the love of God. Jesus gave everything to bring men back to God; and we must walk in the steps of him who loved to the uttermost.

LOVE'S ANSWER TO NEED'S APPEAL

Matthew 20: 29–34

When they were leaving Jericho, a great crowd followed him. And, look you, two blind men were sitting by the roadside, and,

when they heard that Jesus was passing by, they shouted out,
" Lord, have pity on us, you Son of David! " The crowd rebuked
them, so that they might be silent. Jesus stood and called them.
" What do you want me to do for you? " he said. " Lord," they
said, " what we want is that our eyes should be opened." Jesus
was moved with compassion to the depths of his being, and
touched their eyes; and immediately they recovered their sight
and followed him.

HERE is the story of two men who found their way to a miracle.
It is a very significant story, for it paints a picture of the spirit
and of the attitude of mind and heart to which the most
precious gifts of God are open.

(i) These two blind men were waiting, and when their chance
came they seized it with both hands. No doubt they had heard
of the wondrous power of Jesus; and no doubt they wondered if
that power might ever be exercised for them. Jesus was passing
by. If they had let him pass, their chance would have gone by
for ever; but when the chance came they seized it.

There are a great many things which have to be done at the
moment or they will never be done. There are a great many
decisions which have to be taken on the spot or they will never
be taken. The moment to act goes past; the impulse to decide
fades. After Paul had preached on Mars Hill, there were those
who said, " We will hear you again about this " (*Acts* 17: 32).
They put it off until a more convenient time, but so often the
more convenient time never comes.

(ii) These two blind men were undiscourageable. The crowd
commanded them to stop their shouting; they were making a
nuisance of themselves. It was the custom in Palestine for a
Rabbi to teach as he walked along the road; and no doubt those
around Jesus could not hear what Jesus was saying for this
clamorous uproar. But nothing would stop the two blind men;
for them it was a matter of sight or blindness, and nothing was
going to keep them back.

It often happens that we are easily discouraged from seeking
the presence of God. It is the man who will not be kept from
Christ who in the end finds him.

(iii) These two blind men had an imperfect faith but they were determined to act on the faith they had. It was as *Son of David* that they addressed Jesus. That meant that they did believe him to be the Messiah, but it also meant that they were thinking of Messiahship in terms of kingly and of earthly power. It was an imperfect faith but they acted on it; and Jesus accepted it.

However imperfect it may be, if faith is there, Jesus accepts it.

(iv) These two blind men were not afraid to bring a great request. They were beggars; but it was not money they asked for, it was nothing less than sight.

No request is too great to bring to Jesus.

(v) These two blind men were grateful. When they had received the boon for which they craved, they did not go away and forget; they followed Jesus.

So many people, both in things material and in things spiritual, get what they want, and then forget even to say thanks. Ingratitude is the ugliest of all sins. These blind men received their sight from Jesus, and then they gave to him their grateful loyalty. We can never repay God for what he has done for us but we can always be grateful to him.

THE BEGINNING OF THE LAST ACT OF THE DRAMA

Matthew 21: 1–11

When they had come near to Jerusalem, and when they had come to Bethphage, to the Mount of Olives, then Jesus sent on two disciples ahead. " Go into the village which is facing you," he said, " and immediately you will find an ass tethered, and a colt with her. Loose them, and bring them to me. And, if anyone says anything to you, say, ' The Master needs them.' Immediately he will send them on." This was done that there might be fulfilled that which was spoken through the prophet, when he said, " Say to the daughter of Sion, Look you, your king comes to you, gentle, and riding upon an ass, and a colt, the foal of a beast who bears the yoke." So the disciples went, and they carried out Jesus's orders, and they brought the ass and the colt, and put their cloaks upon them; and he took his seat on them. The very large crowd spread their cloaks on the road. Others cut down branches from the trees and strewed them on the road; and the crowds who went in front and followed behind kept shouting, " Hosanna to the Son of David! Blessed in the name of the Lord is he who comes. Hosanna in the highest! " As he entered Jerusalem, the whole city was shaken. " Who is this? " they asked; and the crowds said, " This is the prophet, Jesus, who comes from Nazareth in Galilee."

WITH this passage we embark on the last act in the drama of the life of Jesus; and here indeed is a dramatic moment.

It was the Passover time, and Jerusalem and the whole surrounding neighbourhood was crowded with pilgrims. Thirty years later a Roman governor was to take a census of the lambs slain in Jerusalem for the Passover and find that the number was not far off a quarter of a million. It was the Passover regulation that there must be a party of a minimum of ten for each lamb which means that at that Passover time more than two and a half million people had crowded their way into Jerusalem. The law was that every adult male Jew who lived within twenty miles of Jerusalem must come to the Passover; but not only the Jews of Palestine, Jews from every corner of the world made their way to the greatest of their national festivals. Jesus could not have chosen a more dramatic moment; it was into a city surging with people keyed up with religious expectations that he came.

Nor was this a sudden decision of Jesus, taken on the moment. It was something which he had prepared in advance. The whole tone of the story shows that he was carrying out plans which he had made ahead. He sent his disciples into " the village " to collect the ass and her foal. Matthew mentions Bethphage only (the pronunciation is not *Bethphage* with the *age* as in the English word *page*; the *e* at the end is pronounced as *ae*; the word is *Bethphagae*). But Mark also mentions Bethany (*Mark* 11: 1). No doubt the village was Bethany. Jesus had already arranged that the ass and her foal should be waiting for him, for he must have had many friends in Bethany; and the phrase, " The Master needs them," was a password by which their owner would know that the hour which Jesus had arranged had come.

So Jesus rode into Jerusalem. The fact that the ass had never been ridden before made it specially suitable for sacred purposes. The red heifer which was used in the ceremonies of cleansing must be a beast " upon which a yoke has never come " (*Numbers* 19: 2; *Deuteronomy* 21: 3); the cart on which the ark of the Lord was carried had to be a vehicle which had never been used for any other purpose (1 *Samuel* 6: 7). The special sacredness of the occasion was underlined by the fact that the ass had never been ridden by any man before.

The crowd received Jesus like a king. They spread their cloaks in front of him. That is what his friends had done when Jehu was proclaimed king (2 *Kings* 9: 13). They cut down and waved the palm branches. That is what they did when Simon Maccabaeus entered Jerusalem after one of his most notable victories (1 *Maccabees* 13: 51).

They greeted him as they would greet a pilgrim, for the greeting: " Blessed be he who enters in the name of the Lord " (*Psalm* 118: 26) was the greeting which was addressed to pilgrims as they came to the Feast.

They shouted " Hosanna! " We must be careful to see what this word means. *Hosanna* means *Save now*! and it was the cry for help which a people in distress addressed to their king or their god. It is really a kind of quotation from *Psalm* 118: 25: " *Save us*, we beseech Thee, O Lord." The phrase, " Hosanna in the highest! " must mean, " Let even the angels in the highest heights of heaven cry unto God, Save now! "

It may be that the word *hosanna* had lost some of its original meaning; and that it had become to some extent only a cry of welcome and of acclamation, like " Hail! "; but essentially it is a people's cry for deliverance and for help in the day of their trouble; it is an oppressed people's cry to their saviour and their king.

THE INTENTION OF JESUS

Matthew 21: 1–11 (*continued*)

WE may then take it that Jesus's actions in this incident were planned and deliberate. He was following a method of awakening men's minds which was deeply interwoven with the methods of the prophets. Again and again in the religous history of Israel, when a prophet felt that words were of no avail against a barrier of indifference or incomprehension, he put his message into a dramatic act which men could not fail to see and to understand. Out of many Old Testament instances we choose two of the most outstanding.

When it became clear that the kingdom would not stand the excesses and extravagances of Rehoboam, and that Jeroboam was marked out as the rising power, the prophet Ahijah the Shilonite chose a dramatic way of foretelling the future. He clad himself in a new garment; he went out and he met Jeroboam alone; he took the new garment and tore it into twelve pieces; then of the pieces he gave to Jeroboam ten and two of the pieces he kept; and by this dramatic action he made it clear that ten of the twelve tribes were about to revolt in support of Jeroboam, while only two would remain faithful to Rehoboam (1 *Kings* 11: 29–32). Here is the prophetic message delivered in dramatic action.

When Jeremiah was convinced that Babylon was about to conquer Palestine in spite of the easy optimism of the people, he made bonds and yokes and sent them to Edom, to Moab, to Ammon, to Tyre and to Sidon; and put a yoke upon his own neck that all might see it. By this dramatic action he made it clear that, as he saw it, nothing but slavery and servitude lay ahead (*Jeremiah* 27: 1–6); and when Hananiah, the false prophet with the mistaken optimism, wished to show that he thought Jeremiah's gloomy foreboding altogether wrong, he took the yoke from Jeremiah's neck and broke it (*Jeremiah* 28: 10, 11).

It was the custom of the prophets to express their message in dramatic action when they felt that words were not enough. And that was what Jesus was doing when he entered Jerusalem. There are two pictures behind Jesus's dramatic action.

(i) There is the picture of *Zechariah* 9: 9, in which the prophet saw the king coming to Jerusalem, humble and riding upon an ass, on a colt the foal of an ass. In the first instance, Jesus's dramatic action is a deliberate Messianic claim. He was here offering himself to the people, at a time when Jerusalem was surging with Jews from all over the country and from all over the world, as the Anointed One of God. Just what Jesus meant by that claim we shall go on to see; but that he made the claim there is no doubt.

(ii) There may have been another intention in Jesus's mind. One of the supreme disasters of Jewish history was the capture of Jerusalem by Antiochus Epiphanes about 175 B.C. Antiochus was determined to stamp out Judaism and to introduce into Palestine Greek ways of life and worship. He deliberately profaned the Temple, offering swine's flesh on the altar, making sacrifices to Olympian Zeus, and even turning the Temple chambers into public brothels. It was then that the Maccabees rose against him, and ultimately rescued their native land. In due time Jerusalem was retaken and the desecrated Temple was restored and purified and rededicated. In 2 *Maccabees* 10: 7 we read of the rejoicing of that great day: " Therefore they bare branches, and fair boughs, and palms also, and sang psalms unto Him that had given them good success in cleansing His place." On that day the people carried the palm branches and sung their psalms; it is an almost exact description of the actions of the crowd who welcomed Jesus into Jerusalem.

It is at least possible that Jesus knew this, and that he entered into Jerusalem with the deliberate intention of cleansing God's house as Judas Maccabaeus had done two hundred years before. That was in fact what Jesus did. He may well be saying in dramatic symbol, not only that he was the Anointed One of God, but also that he had come to cleanse the House of God from the abuses which defiled it and its worship. Had not

Malachi said that the Lord would suddenly come to his Temple (*Malachi* 3: 1)? And, in his vision of judgment had not Ezekiel seen the terrible judgment of God begin at the sanctuary (*Ezekiel* 9: 6)?

THE CLAIM OF THE KING

Matthew 21: 1–11 (*continued*)

To conclude our study of this incident, let us look at Jesus in its setting. It shows us three things about him.

(i) I shows us his *courage*. Jesus knew full well that he was entering a hostile city. However enthusiastic the crowd might be, the authorities hated him and had sworn to eliminate him; and with them lay the last word. Almost any man in such a case would have considered discretion the better part of valour; and, if he had come to Jerusalem at all, would have slipped in under cover of night and kept prudently to the back streets until he reached his shelter. But Jesus entered Jerusalem in a way that deliberately set himself in the centre of the stage and deliberately riveted every eye upon himself. All through his last days there is in his every action a kind of magnificent and sublime defiance; and here he begins the last act with a flinging down of the gauntlet, a deliberate challenge to the authorities to do their worst.

(ii) It shows us his *claim*. Certainly it shows us his claim to be God's Messiah, God's Anointed One; very probably it shows us his claim to be the cleanser of the Temple. If Jesus had been content to claim to be a prophet, the probability is that he need never have died. But he could be satisfied with nothing less than the topmost place. With Jesus it is all or nothing. Men must acknowledge him as king, or not receive him at all.

(iii) Equally it shows us his *appeal*. It was not the kingship of the throne which he claimed; it was the kingship of the heart. He came humbly and riding upon an ass. We must be careful to see the real meaning of that. In western lands the ass is a despised beast; but in the east the ass could be a noble animal. Often a king came riding upon an ass, but when he did, it was the sign that *he came in peace*. The horse was the mount of *war*; the ass was the mount of *peace*. So when Jesus claimed to be king, he claimed to be the king of peace. He showed that he came, not to destroy, but to love; not to condemn, but to help; not in the might of arms, but in the strength of love.

So here, at one and the same time, we see the courage of Christ, the claim of Christ, and the appeal of Christ. It was a last invitation to men to open, not their palaces but their hearts to him.

THE SCENE IN THE TEMPLE

Matthew 21: 12–14

> And Jesus entered into the precincts of the Temple of God, and cast out all who were selling and buying in the Temple precincts, and overturned the tables of the money-changers, and of those who were selling doves. " It is written," he said to them, " My house shall be called a house of prayer, but you make it ' a robbers' cave.' "
>
> And the blind and the lame came to him in the Temple and he healed them.

IF the entry into Jerusalem had been defiance, here is defiance added to defiance. To see this scene unfolding before our eyes we need to visualize the picture of the Temple.

There are in the New Testament two words which are translated *Temple*, and rightly so, but there is a clear distinction between them. The Temple itself is called the *naos*. It was a comparatively small building, and contained the Holy Place and the Holy of Holies into which only the High Priest might enter, and he only on the great Day of Atonement. But the *naos* itself was surrounded by a vast space which was occupied by successive and ascending courtyards. First there was the *Court of the Gentiles*, into which anyone might come, and beyond

which it was death for a Gentile to penetrate. Then there came
the *Court of the Women*, entered by the Beautiful Gate of the
Temple, into which any Israelite might come. Next there came
the *Court of the Israelites*, entered by the gate called Nicanor's
Gate, a great gate of Corinthian bronze which needed twenty
men to open and shut it. It was in this court that the people
assembled for the Temple services. Lastly there came the *Court
of the Priests*, into which only the priests might enter; in it there
stood the great altar of the burnt-offering, the altar of the
incense, the seven-branched lamp-stand, the table of the shewbread, and the great brazen laver; and at the back of it there
stood the *naos* itself. This whole area, including all the courts, is
also in the Revised Standard Version called the *Temple*; the
Greek is *hieron*. It is better to keep a distinction between the
two words; and to retain the word *Temple* for the Temple
proper, that is the *naos*, and to use the term the *Temple
Precincts*, for the whole area, that is the word *hieron*.

The scene of this incident was the Court of the Gentiles into
which anyone might come. It was always crowded and busy;
but at Passover, with pilgrims there from all over the world, it
was thronged to capacity. There would, even at any time, be
many Gentiles there, for the Temple at Jerusalem was famous
throughout the world, so that even the Roman writers described
it as one of the world's most amazing buildings.

In this Court of the Gentiles two kinds of trading were going
on. There was the business of *money-changing*. Every Jew had
to pay a temple tax of one half-shekel, and that tax had to be
paid near to the Passover time. A month before, booths were set
up in all the towns and villages, and the money could be paid
there, but after a certain date it could be paid only in the
Temple itself; and it would be there that the vast majority of
pilgrim Jews from other lands paid it. This tax had to be paid in
certain currency, although for general purposes all kinds of
currencies were equally valid in Palestine. It must not be paid in
ingots of silver, but in stamped currency; it must not be paid in
coins of inferior alloy or coins which had been clipped, but in
coins of high-grade silver. It could be paid in shekels of the

sanctuary, in Galilaean half-shekels, and especially in Tyrian currency which was of a very high standard.

The function of the money-changers was to change unsuitable currency into the correct currency. That seems on the face of it to be an entirely necessary function; but the trouble was that these money-changers charged the equivalent of 1p for changing the currency at all; and, if the coin was of greater value than a half-shekel, they charged another 1p for giving back the surplus change. That is to say, many a pilgrim had not only to pay his half-shekel—which was about 7p in value—but another 2p also in changing dues; and this has to be evaluated against a background where a working man's wage was about 3p a day.

This surplus charge was called the *qolbon*. It did not by any means all go into the money-changer's pockets; some of it was classed as freewill offerings; some of it went to the repair of the roads; some of it went to purchase the gold plates with which it was planned entirely to cover the Temple proper; and some of it found its way into the Temple treasury. The whole matter was not necessarily an abuse; but the trouble was that it lent itself to abuse. It lent itself to the exploitation of the pilgrims who had come to worship, and there is no doubt that the Temple money-changers made large profits out of it.

The selling of doves was worse. For most visits to the Temple some kind of offering was essential. Doves, for instance, were necessary when a woman came for purification after childbirth, or when a leper came to have his cure attested and certified (*Leviticus* 12: 8; 14: 22; 15: 14, 29). It was easy enough to buy animals for sacrifice outside the Temple; but any animal offered in sacrifice must be without blemish. There were official inspectors of the animals, and it was to all intents and purposes certain that they would reject an animal bought outside and would direct the worshipper to the Temple stalls and booths.

No great harm would have been done if the prices had been the same inside and outside the Temple, but a pair of doves could cost as little as 4p outside the Temple and as much as 75p inside the Temple. This was an old abuse. A certain Rabbi,

Simon ben Gamaliel, was remembered with gratitude because "he had caused doves to be sold for silver coins instead of gold." Clearly he had attacked this abuse. Further, these stalls where the victims were sold were called the Bazaars of Annas, and were the private property of the family of the High Priest of that name.

Here, again, there was no necessary abuse. There must have been many honest and sympathetic traders. But abuse readily and easily crept in. Burkitt can say that "the Temple had become a meeting place of scamps," the worst kind of commercial monopoly and vested interest. Sir George Adam Smith can write: "In those days every priest must have been a trader." There was every danger of shameless exploitation of poor and humble pilgrims—and it was that exploitation which raised the wrath of Jesus.

THE WRATH AND THE LOVE

Matthew 21: 12–14 (*continued*)

THERE is hardly anywhere in the gospel story where we need to make a more deliberate and more conscious effort to be fair than in this passage. It is easy to use it as a basis for a complete condemnation of the whole Temple worship. There are two things to be said.

There were many traders and hucksters in the Temple Court, but there were also many whose hearts were set on God. As Aristotle said long ago, a man and an institution must be judged at their best, and not at their worst.

The other thing to be said is simply this—let the man and the Church without sin cast the first stone. The traders were not all exploiters, and even those who seized the opportunity of making a quick profit were not all simply money-grabbers. The great Jewish scholar Israel Abrahams has a comment on the too common Christian treatment of this passage: " When Jesus

overturned the money-changers and ejected the sellers of doves
from the Temple, he did a service to Judaism. . . . But were the
money-changers and the dove-sellers the only people who
visited the Temple? And was everyone who bought or sold a
dove a mere formalist? Last Easter I was in Jerusalem, and
along the façade of the Church of the Holy Sepulchre I saw the
stalls of the vendors of sacred relics, of painted beads and
inscribed ribbons, of coloured candles, gilded crucifixes, and
bottles of Jordan water. There these Christians babbled and
swayed and bargained, a crowd of buyers and sellers in front of
the Church sacred to the memory of Jesus. Would, I thought,
that Jesus were come again to overthrow these false servants of
his, even as he overthrew his false brothers in Israel long ago."

This incident shows us certain things about Jesus.

(i) It shows us one of the fiercest manifestations of his anger
directed against those who exploited their fellow-men, and
especially against those who exploited them in the name of
religion. It was Jeremiah who had said that men made the
Temple a den of thieves (*Jeremiah* 7: 11). Jesus could not bear to
see simple people exploited for profit.

Too often the Church has been silent in such a situation; it
has a duty to protect those who in a highly competitive
economic situation cannot protect themselves.

(ii) It shows us his anger was specially directed against those
who made it impossible for simple people to worship in the
House of God. It was Isaiah who said that God's House was a
House of Prayer for all peoples (*Isaiah* 56: 7). The Court of the
Gentiles was, in fact, the only part of the Temple into which
Gentiles might come. It is not to be thought that every Gentile
came to sight-see. Some, at least, must have come with haunting
longings in their souls to worship and to pray. But in that
uproar of buying and selling and bargaining and auctioneering
prayer was impossible. Those who sought God's presence were
being debarred from it by the very people of God's House.

God will never hold guiltless those who make it impossible
for others to worship him. It can happen yet. A spirit of
bitterness, a spirit of argument, a spirit of strife can get into a

Church, which makes worship impossible. Men and office-bearers can become so concerned with their rights and their wrongs, their dignities and their prestiges, their practice and their procedure, that in the end no one can worship God in the atmosphere which is created. Even ministers of God can be more concerned with imposing their ways of doing things on a congregation than with preaching the gospel, and the end is a service with an atmosphere which makes true worship impossible. The worship of God and the disputes of men can never go together. Let us remember the wrath of Jesus at those who blocked the approach to God for their fellow-men.

(iii) There remains one thing to note. Our passage ends with Jesus healing the blind and the lame in the Temple Court. They were still there; Jesus did not clear everyone out. Only those with guilty consciences fled before the eyes of his wrath. Those who needed him stayed.

Need is never sent empty away by Jesus Christ. Jesus's anger was never merely negative; it never stopped with the attack on that which was wrong; it always went on to the positive helping of those who were in need. In the truly great man anger and love go hand in hand. There is anger at those who exploit the simple and bar the seeker; but there is love for those whose need is great. The destructive force of anger must always go hand in hand with the healing power of love.

THE KNOWLEDGE OF THE SIMPLE IN HEART

Matthew 21: 15–17

When the chief priests and Scribes saw the wonderful things that he did, and the children shouting in the Temple, " Hosanna to the Son of David! " they were angry. " Do you hear what these are saying? " they said. Jesus said to them, " Yes! Have you never read: ' Out of the mouths of babes and sucklings you have the perfect praise '? " And he left them, and went out of the city to Bethany, and lodged there.

SOME scholars have found difficulty with this passage. It is said that it is unlikely that there would be crowds of children in the Temple Court; and that, if the children were there at all, the Temple police would have dealt swiftly and efficiently with them if they had dared to cry out as this passage says they did. Now earlier in the story *Luke* has an incident where the *disciples* are depicted as shouting their glad cries to Jesus, and where the authorities are described as trying to silence them (*Luke* 19: 39, 40). Very often a Rabbi's disciples were called his *children*. We see, for instance, the phrase *my little children* occurring in the writings of John. So it is suggested that Luke and Matthew are really telling the same story and that the *children* are in fact the *disciples* of Jesus.

No such explanation is necessary. The use that Matthew makes of the quotation from *Psalm* 8: 2 makes it clear that he had real children in mind; and, in any event, things were happening that day in the Temple Court which had never happened before. It was not every day that the traders and the money-changers were sent packing; and it was not every day that the blind and the lame were healed. Maybe ordinarily it would have been impossible for the children to shout like this, but this was no ordinary day.

When we take this story just as it stands and listen again to the fresh, clear voices of the children shouting their praises, we are faced with one great fact. There are truths which only the simple in heart can see and which are hidden from the wise and the learned and the sophisticated. There are many times when heaven is nearer the child than it is to the cleverest men.

Thorwaldsen, the great sculptor, once carved a statue of Jesus. He wished to see if the statue would cause the right reaction in those who saw it. He brought a little child to look at the statue and asked him: " Who do you think that is? " The child answered: " It is a great man." Thorwaldsen knew that he had failed; so he scrapped his statue and began again. Again when he had finished, he brought the child and asked the same question: " Who do you think that is? " The child smiled and answered: " That is Jesus who said: ' Let the children come to me.' " Thorwaldsen knew that this time he had succeeded. The statue had passed the test of a child's eyes.

That is no bad test. George Macdonald once said that h placed no value on the alleged Christianity of a man at whose door, or at whose garden gate, the children were afraid to play If a child thinks a person good, the likelihood is that he is good, if a child shrinks away, a man may be great but certainly he is not Christlike. Somewhere Barrie draws a picture of a mother putting her little one to bed at night and looking down on him when he is half asleep, with an unspoken question in her eyes and in her heart: " My child, have I done well today? " The goodness which can meet the clear gaze of a child and stand the test of a child's simplicity is goodness indeed. It was but natural that the children should recognize Jesus when the scholars were blind.

THE WAY OF THE FIG TREE

Matthew 21: 18–22

> When Jesus was returning to the city early in the morning, he was hungry. When he saw a fig tree by the roadside, he went up to it, and found nothing but leaves. He said to it, " Let no fruit come from you any more for ever! " And immediately the fig tree withered away. When the disciples saw it, they were astonished. " How did the fig tree immediately wither away? " they said. Jesus answered them: " This is the truth I tell you—if you have faith, and, if you do not doubt, not only will you do what happened to the fig tree, but you will even say to this mountain: ' Be removed and be cast into the sea,' and it will happen. All that you ask in prayer, if you believe, you will receive."

FEW honest readers of the Bible would deny that this is perhaps the most uncomfortably difficult passage in the New Testament. If it be taken with complete literalism, it shows Jesus in an action which is an acute shock to our whole conception of him. It must, therefore, be approached with a real desire to find out the truth which lies behind it and with the courage to think our way through it.

Mark also tells this story (*Mark* 11: 12–14, 20, 21) but with one basic difference. In Matthew the withering of the fig tree takes place at once. (The Authorized Version has: " And *presently* the fig tree withered away." In Elizabethan English *presently* meant *immediately*, *at that present moment*. The Greek is *parachrēma*, which the Revised Standard Version translates *at once*, and which Moffatt translates *instantly*.) On the other hand, in Mark nothing happened to the tree immediately, and it is only next morning, when they are passing on the same road, that the disciples see that the tree has withered away. From the existence of these two versions of the story, it is quite clear that some development has taken place; and, since Mark's is the earliest gospel, it is equally clear that his version must be nearer to the actual historical facts.

It is necessary to understand the growing and fruit-bearing habits of fig trees. The fig tree was the favourite of all trees. The picture of the Promised Land was the picture of " a land of wheat and barley, of vines and fig trees " (*Deuteronomy* 8: 8). Pomegranates and figs were part of the treasures which the spies brought back to show the rich fertility of the land (*Numbers* 13: 23). The picture of peace and prosperity which is common to every part of the old Testament is the picture of a time when every man will sit under his own vine and his own fig tree (1 *Kings* 4: 25; *Micah* 4: 4; *Zechariah* 3: 10). The picture of the wrath of God is the picture of a day when he would smite and destroy the fig trees (*Psalm* 105: 33; *Jeremiah* 8: 13; *Hosea* 2: 12). The fig tree is the very symbol of fertility and peace and prosperity.

The tree itself is a handsome tree; it can be three feet thick in its trunk. It grows to a height of from fifteen to twenty feet; and the spread of its thick branches can be twenty-five to thirty feet. It was, therefore, much valued for its shade. In Cyprus the cottages have their fig trees at the door, and Tristram tells how often he sheltered under them and found coolness on the hottest day. Very commonly the fig tree grows overshadowing wells so

that there is shade and water in the one place. Often it was the
shade of the fig tree which was a man's private room for
meditation and prayer; and that is why Nathanael was amazed
that Jesus had marked him under the fig tree (*John* 1: 48).

But it is the fig tree's habit of fruit-bearing which is relevant
here. The fig tree is unique in that it bears two full crops in the
year. The first is borne on the old wood. Quite early in the year
little green knobs appear at the end of the branches. They are
called *Paggim* and they will one day be the figs. These fruit buds
come in April but they are quite uneatable. Bit by bit the leaves
and the flowers open out, and another unique thing about the fig
is that it is in full fruit and full leaf and full flower all at the same
time; that happens by June. No fig tree ever bore fruit in April;
that is far too early. The process is then repeated with the new
wood; and the second crop comes in September.

The strangest thing about this story is twofold. First, it tells
of a fig tree in full leaf in April. Jesus was at Jerusalem for the
Passover; the Passover fell on 15th April; and this incident
happened a week before. The second thing is that Jesus looked
for figs on a tree where no figs could possibly be; and Mark
says, " For it was not the season for figs " (*Mark* 11: 13).

The difficulty of this story is not so much a difficulty of
possibility. It is a *moral* difficulty; and it is twofold. First, we
see Jesus blasting a fig tree for not doing what it was not able to
do. The tree could not have borne fruit in the second week of
April, and yet we see Jesus destroying it for not doing that very
thing. Second, we see Jesus using his miraculous powers for his
own ends. That is precisely what in the temptations in the
wilderness he determined never to do. He would not turn stones
into bread to satisfy his own hunger. The plain truth is this—if
we had read of anyone else blasting a fig tree for not bearing
figs in April, we would have said it was the act of ill-tempered
petulance, springing from personal disappointment. In Jesus
that is inconceivable; therefore there must be some explanation.
What is it?

Some have found an explanation on the following lines. In
Luke there is the parable of the fig tree which failed to bear

fruit. Twice the gardener pleaded for mercy for it; twice mercy and delay were granted; in the end it was still fruitless and was therefore destroyed (*Luke* 13: 6–9). The curious thing is that Luke has the parable of the barren fig tree, but he has not this incident of the withering of the fig tree; Matthew and Mark have this incident of the withering of the fig tree, but they have not the parable of the barren fig tree. It looks very much as if the gospel writers felt that if they included the one they did not need to include the other. It is suggested that the parable of the barren fig tree has been misunderstood and been turned into an actual incident. Confusion has changed a *story* Jesus *told* into an *action* Jesus *did*. That is by no means impossible; but it seems to us that the real explanation must be sought elsewhere. And now we go on to seek it.

PROMISE WITHOUT PERFORMANCE

Matthew 21: 18–22 (*continued*)

WHEN we were studying the story of the entry of Jesus into Jerusalem, we saw that frequently the prophets made use of symbolic actions; that when they felt that words would not penetrate, they did something dramatic to drive a lesson home. Let us suppose that some such symbolic action is at the back of this story.

Jesus, let us suppose, was on his way to Jerusalem. By the wayside he saw a tree in full leaf. It was perfectly legitimate for him to pluck the figs from it, if there had been any. Jewish law allowed that (*Deuteronomy* 23: 24, 25); and Thomson in *The Land and the Book* tells us that even in modern times the wayside fig tree is open to all. Jesus went up to the fig tree, well knowing that there could be no fruit, and well knowing that there must be something radically wrong with it. One of two things could have happened. The fig tree could have reverted to its wild state, just as roses revert to briars. Or, it could be in some way diseased. Then Jesus said: " This tree will never bear fruit; it will certainly wither." It was the statement of a man who knew nature, because he had lived with nature. And on the next day it was clear that the diagnosis of his expert eye of Jesus was exactly right.

If this was a symbolic action, it was meant to teach something. What it was meant to teach was two things about the Jewish nation.

(i) It taught that *uselessness invites disaster*. That is the law of life. Anything which is useless is on the way to elimination; anything can justify its existence only by fulfilling the end for which it was created. The fig tree was useless; therefore it was doomed.

The nation of Israel had been brought into existence for one reason and one reason only—that from it there might come God's Anointed One. He had come; the nation had failed to recognize him; more, they were about to crucify him. The nation had failed in its function which was to welcome God's Son—therefore the nation was doomed.

Failure to realize the purpose of God brings necessary disaster. Everyone in this world is judged in terms of usefulness. Even if a person is helpless on a bed, he can be of the greatest use by patient example and by prayer. No one need be useless; and he who is useless is heading for disaster.

(ii) It taught that *profession without practice is condemned*. The tree had leaves; the leaves were a claim to have figs; the tree had no figs; its claim was false; therefore it was doomed. The Jewish nation professed faith in God; but in practice they were out for the blood of God's Son; therefore they stood condemned.

Profession without practice was not only the curse of the Jews; it has been throughout the ages the curse of the Church. During his early days in South Africa—in Pretoria—Gandhi enquired into Christianity. For several Sundays he attended a Christian Church, but, he says, " the congregation did not strike me as being particularly religious; they were not an assembly of devout souls, but appeared rather to be worldly-minded people going to Church for recreation and in conformity to custom." He, therefore, concluded that there was nothing in Christianity which he did not already possess—and so

Gandhi was lost to the Christian Church with incalculable consequences to India and to the world.

Profession without practice is something of which we are all more or less guilty. It does incalculable harm to the Christian Church; and it is doomed to disaster, for it produces a faith which cannot do anything else but wither away.

We may well believe that Jesus used the lesson of a diseased and degenerate fig tree to say to the Jews—and to us—that uselessness invites disaster, and profession without practice is doomed. That is surely what this story means, for we cannot think of Jesus as literally and physically blasting a fig tree for failing to bear fruit at a season when fruit was impossible.

THE DYNAMIC OF PRAYER

Matthew 21: 18–22 (*continued*)

THIS passage concludes with certain words of Jesus about the dynamic of prayer. If these words are misunderstood, they can bring nothing but heartbreak; but if they are correctly understood, they can bring nothing but power.

In them Jesus says two things; that prayer can remove mountains, and that, if we ask in belief, we will receive. It is abundantly clear that these promises are not to be taken physically and literally. Neither Jesus himself nor anyone else ever removed a physical, geographical mountain by prayer. Moreover, many and many a person has prayed with passionate faith that something may happen or that something may not happen, that something may be given or that someone may be spared from death, and in the literal sense of the words that prayer has not been answered. What then is Jesus promising us through prayer?

(i) He promises that prayer gives us *the ability to do*. Prayer is never the easy way out; never simply pushing things on to God for him to do them for us. *Prayer is power*. It is not asking God to do something; it is asking him to make us able to do it ourselves. Prayer is not taking the easy way; it is the way to receive power to take the hard way. It is the channel through which comes power to tackle and remove mountains of difficulty by ourselves with the help of God. If it were simply a method of getting things done for us, prayer would be very bad for us, for it would make us flabby and lazy and inefficient. Prayer is the means whereby we receive power to do things for ourselves. Therefore, no man should pray and then sit and wait; he must pray and then rise and work; but he will find that, when he does, a new dynamic enters his life, and that in truth with God all things are possible, and with God the impossible becomes that which can be done.

(ii) Prayer is *the ability to accept*, and in accepting, *to transform*. It is not meant to bring deliverance from a situation; it is meant to bring the ability to accept it and transform it. There are two great examples of that in the New Testament.

The one is the example of Paul. Desperately he prayed that he might be delivered from the thorn in his flesh. He was not delivered from that situation; he was made able to accept it; and in that very situation he discovered the strength that was made perfect in his weakness and the grace which was sufficient for all things—and in that strength and grace the situation was not only accepted, but also transformed into glory (2 *Corinthians* 12: 1–10).

The other is Jesus himself. In Gethsemane he prayed that the cup might pass from him and he be delivered from the agonizing situation in which he found himself; that request could not be granted, but in that prayer he found the ability to accept the situation; and, in being accepted, the situation was transformed, and the agony of the Cross led straight to the glory of the Resurrection. We must always remember that prayer does not bring deliverance from a situation; it brings conquest of it. Prayer is not a means of running away from a situation; it is a means whereby we may gallantly face it.

(iii) Prayer brings *the ability to bear*. It is natural and inevitable that, in our human need and with our human hearts and our human weakness, there should be things which we feel

we cannot bear. We see some situation developing; we see some
tragic happening approaching with a grim inevitability; we see
some task looming ahead which is obviously going to demand
more than we have to give to it. At such a time our inevitable
feeling is that we cannot bear this thing. Prayer does not
remove the tragedy; it does not give us escape from the
situation; it does not give us exemption from the task; but it
does make us able to bear the unbearable, to face the unface-
able, to pass the breaking point and not to break.

So long as we regard prayer as escape, nothing but bewildered disappointment can result; but when we regard it as the
way to conquest and the divine dynamic, things happen.

THE EXPEDIENT IGNORANCE

Matthew 21: 23-27

> When Jesus had come into the Temple precincts, the chief priests
> and elders of the people came to him as he was teaching and said,
> " By what authority do you do these things? And who gave you
> this authority? " Jesus answered them, " I will ask you one
> question, and if you give me an answer to it, I too will tell you by
> what authority I do these things. Whence was the baptism of
> John? Was it from heaven? Or, was it from men? " They debated
> within themselves. " If," they said, " we say ' From heaven,' he
> will say to us, ' Why then did you not believe in him? ' But, if we
> say, ' From men,' we fear the crowd, for all regard John as a
> prophet." So they answered Jesus, " We do not know." So he too
> said to them, " Neither do I tell you by what authority I do these
> things."

WHEN we think of the extraordinary things Jesus had been
doing, we cannot be surprised that the Jewish authorities asked
him what right he had to do them. At the moment Jesus was not
prepared to give them the direct answer that his authority came
from the fact that he was the Son of God. To do so would have
been to precipitate the end. There were actions still to be done

and teaching still to be given. It sometimes takes more courage to bide one's time and to await the necessary moment, than it does to throw oneself on the enemy and invite the end. For Jesus everything had to be done in God's time; and the time for the final crisis had not yet come.

So he countered the question of the Jewish authorities with a question of his own, one which placed them in a dilemma. He asked them whether John's ministry came from heaven or from men, whether it was divine or merely human in its origin. Were those who went out to be baptized at the Jordan responding to a merely human impulse or were they in fact answering a divine challenge? The dilemma of the Jewish authorities was this. If they said that the ministry of John was from God, then they had no alternative to admitting that Jesus was the Messiah, for John had borne definite and unmistakable witness to that fact. On the other hand, if they denied that John's ministry came from God, then they would have to bear the anger of the people, who were convinced that he was the messenger of God.

For a moment the Jewish chief priests and elders were silent. Then they gave the lamest of all lame answers. They said, " We do not know." If ever men stood self-condemned, they did. They ought to have known; it was part of the duty of the Sanhedrin, of which they were members, to distinguish between true and false prophets; and they were saying that they were unable to make that distinction. Their dilemma drove them into a shameful self-humiliation.

There is a grim warning here. There is such a thing as the deliberately assumed ignorance of cowardice. If a man consults *expediency* rather than *principle*, his first question will be, not, " What is the truth? " but, " What is it safe to say? " Again and again his worship of expediency will drive him to a cowardly silence. He will lamely say, " I do not know the answer," when he well knows the answer, but is afraid to give it. The true question is not: " What is it safe to say? " but, " What is it right to say? "

The deliberately assumed ignorance of fear, the cowardly silence of expediency are shameful things. If a man knows the truth, he is under obligation to tell it, though the heavens should fall.

THE BETTER OF TWO BAD SONS

Matthew 21: 28–32

> Jesus said: " What do you think? A man had two children, He went to the first and said, ' Child, go and work in my vineyard today.' He answered, ' I will not.' But afterwards he changed his mind and went. He went to the second and spoke to him in the same way. He answered, ' Certainly, sir.' And he did not go. Which of these two did the will of his father? " " The first," they answered. Jesus said to them: " This is the truth I tell you—the tax-collectors and harlots go into the Kingdom of Heaven before you. For John came to you in the way of righteousness, and you did not believe in him; but the tax-gatherers and harlots did believe in him. And when you saw this, you did not even then change your minds, and so come to believe in him."

THE meaning of this parable is crystal clear. The Jewish leaders are the people who said they would obey God and then did not. The tax-gatherers and the harlots are those who said that they would go their own way and then took God's way.

The key to the correct understanding of this parable is that it is not really praising anyone. It is setting before us a picture of two very imperfect sets of people, of whom one set were none the less better than the other. Neither son in the story was the kind of son to bring full joy to his father. Both were unsatisfactory; but the one who in the end obeyed was incalculably better than the other. The ideal son would be the son who accepted the father's orders with obedience and with respect and who unquestioningly and fully carried them out. But there are truths in this parable which go far beyond the situation in which it was first spoken.

It tells us that there are two very common classes of people in this world. First, there are the people whose profession is much better than their practice. They will promise anything; they make great protestations of piety and fidelity; but their practice lags far behind. Second, there are those whose practice is far better than their profession. They claim to be tough, hard-headed materialists, but somehow they are found out doing kindly and generous things, almost in secret, as if they were ashamed of it. They profess to have no interest in the Church and in religion, and yet, when it comes to the bit, they live more Christian lives than many professing Christians.

We have all of us met these people, those whose practice is far away from the almost sanctimonious piety of their profession, and those whose practice is far ahead of the sometimes cynical, and sometimes almost irreligious, profession which they make. The real point of the parable is that, while the second class are infinitely to be preferred to the first, neither is anything like perfect. The really good man is the man in whom profession and practice meet and match.

Further, this parable teaches us that promises can never take the place of performance, and fine words are never a substitute for fine deeds. The son who said he would go, and did not, had all the outward marks of courtesy. In his answer he called his father " Sir " with all respect. But a courtesy which never gets beyond words is a totally illusory thing. True courtesy is obedience, willingly and graciously given. On the other hand the parable teaches us that a man can easily spoil a good thing by the way he does it. He can do a fine thing with a lack of graciousness and a lack of winsomeness which spoil the whole deed. Here we learn that the Christian way is in performance and not promise, and that the mark of a Christian is obedience graciously and courteously given.

THE VINEYARD OF THE LORD

Matthew 21: 33–46

Jesus said, " Listen to another parable. There was a householder who planted a vineyard, and surrounded it with a hedge, and dug a wine press in it, and built a tower, and gave it out to cultivators

and went away. When the time of the fruits had come, he
dispatched his servants to the cultivators, to receive his fruits; and
the cultivators took his servants, and beat one of them, and killed
another of them, and stoned another of them. Again he dispatched
other servants, more than the first; and they did the same to them.
Afterwards he dispatched his son to them. ' They will respect my
son,' he said. But when the cultivators saw the son, they said to
themselves, ' This is the heir. Come, let us kill him, and let us take
the inheritance.' And they threw him out of the vineyard and
killed him. When the owner of the vineyard comes, what will he
do to these cultivators? " They said to him, " He will bring these
evil men to an evil end, and he will give out the vineyard to other
cultivators, who will pay him the fruits at their correct time."
Jesus said to them, " Have you never read in the Scriptures: ' The
stone which the builders rejected, this has become the headstone
of the corner. This is the doing of the Lord, and it is amazing in
our eyes '? That is why I tell you that the Kingdom of God will be
taken from you, and will be given to a nation which produces its
fruits. And he who falls against the stone will be broken; and it
will shatter to powder him on whom it falls."

When the chief priests and Pharisees heard his parables, they
knew that he was speaking about them. They tried to find a way to
lay hold on him, but they were afraid of the crowds, for they
regarded him as a prophet.

IN interpreting a parable it is normally a first principle that
every parable has only one point and that the details are not to
be stressed. Normally to try to find a meaning for every detail is
to make the mistake of treating the parable as an allegory. But
in this case it is different. In this parable the details do have a
meaning and the chief priests and the Pharisees well knew what
Jesus was meaning this parable to say to them.

Every detail is founded on what, for those who heard it, was
familiar fact. The Jewish nation as the vineyard of God was a
familiar prophetic picture. " The vineyard of the Lord of hosts
is the house of Israel " (*Isaiah* 5: 7). The hedge was a thick-set
thorn hedge, designed to keep out both the wild boars who
might ravage the vineyard, and the thieves who might steal the
grapes. Every vineyard had its wine press. The wine press

consisted of two troughs either hollowed out of the rock, or
built of bricks; the one was a little higher than the other, and
was connected with the lower one by a channel. The grapes
were pressed in the higher trough and the juice ran off into the
lower trough. The tower served a double purpose. It served as a
watch-tower, from which to watch for thieves when the grapes
were ripening; and it served as a lodging for those who were
working in the vineyard.

The actions of the owner of the vineyard were all quite
normal. In the time of Jesus, Palestine was a troubled place with
little luxury; it was, therefore, very familiar with absentee
landlords, who let out their estates and were interested only in
collecting the rental at the right time. The rent might be paid in
any of three ways. It might be a money rent; it might be a fixed
amount of the fruit, no matter what the crop might be; and it
might be an agreed percentage of the crop.

Even the action of the cultivators was not out of the
common. The country was seething with economic unrest; the
working people were discontented and rebellious; and the action
of the cultivators in seeking to eliminate the son was not by
any means impossible.

As we have said, it would be easy for those who heard this
parable to make the necessary identifications. Before we treat it
in detail, let us set these identifications down. The vineyard is
the nation of Israel, and its owner is God. The cultivators are
the religious leaders of Israel, who as it were had charge for God
of the welfare of the nation. The messengers who were sent
successively are the prophets sent by God and so often.rejected
and killed. The son who came last is none other than Jesus
himself. Here in a vivid story Jesus set out at one and the same
time the history and the doom of Israel.

PRIVILEGE AND RESPONSIBILITY

Matthew 21: 33–46 (*continued*)

THIS parable has much to tell us in three directions.

(i) It has much to tell us about God.

(*a*) It tells of God's *trust* in men. The owner of the vineyard entrusted it to the cultivators. He did not even stand over them to exercise a police-like supervision. He went away and left them with their task. God pays men the compliment of entrusting them with his work. Every task we receive is a task given us to do by God.

(*b*) It tells of God's *patience*. The master sent messenger after messenger. He did not come with sudden vengeance when one messenger had been abused and ill-treated. He gave the cultivators chance after chance to respond to his appeal. God bears with men in all their sinning and will not cast them off.

(*c*) It tells of God's *judgment*. In the end the master of the vineyard took the vineyard from the cultivators and gave it to others. God's sternest judgment is when he takes out of our hands the task which he meant us to do. A man has sunk to his lowest level when he has become useless to God.

(ii) It has much to tell us about men.

(*a*) It tells of human *privilege*. The vineyard was equipped with everything—the hedge, the wine press, the tower—which would make the task of the cultivators easy and enable them to discharge it well. God does not only give us a task to do; he also gives us the means whereby to do it.

(*b*) It tells of human *freedom*. The master left the cultivators to do the task as they liked. God is no tyrannical task-master; he is like a wise commander who allocates a task and then trusts a man to do it.

(*c*) It tells of human *answerability*. To all men comes a day of reckoning. We are answerable for the way in which we have carried out the task God gave us to do.

(*d*) It tells of the *deliberateness of human sin*. The cultivators carry out a deliberate policy of rebellion and disobedience towards the master. Sin is deliberate opposite to God; it is the taking of our own way when we know quite well what the way of God is.

(iii) It has much to tell us about Jesus.

(*a*) *It tells of the claim of Jesus.* It shows us quite clearly Jesus lifting himself out of the succession of the prophets. Those who come before him were the messengers of God; no one could deny them that honour; but they were *servants*; he was the *Son*. This parable contains one of the clearest claims Jesus ever made to be unique, to be different from even the greatest of those who went before.

(*b*) It tells of the *sacrifice of Jesus.* It makes it clear that Jesus knew what lay ahead. In the parable the hands of wicked men killed the son. Jesus was never in any doubt of what lay ahead. He did not die because he was compelled to die; he went willingly and open-eyed to death.

THE SYMBOL OF THE STONE

Matthew 21: 33–46 (*continued*)

THE parable concludes with the picture of the stone. There are two pictures really.

(i) The first is quite clear. It is the picture of a stone which the builders rejected but became the most important stone in the whole building. The picture is from *Psalm* 118: 22: " The stone which the builders rejected has become the head of the corner." Originally the Psalmist meant this as a picture of the nation of Israel. Israel was the nation which was despised and rejected. The Jews were hated by all men. They had been servants and slaves of many nations; but none the less the nation which all men despised was the chosen people of God.

It may be that men reject Christ, and refuse him, and seek to eliminate him, but they will yet find that the Christ whom they rejected is the most important person in the world. It was Julian, the Roman Emperor, who tried to turn the clock back, tried to banish Christianity, and to bring back the old pagan gods. He failed and failed completely; and at the end of it the dramatist makes him say, " To shoulder Christ from out the topmost niche was not for me." The man upon the Cross has become the Judge and King of all the world.

(ii) The second " stone " picture is in verse 44, although it is to be noted that some manuscripts omit this verse altogether. This is a more difficult picture—of a stone which breaks a man, if he stumbles against it, and which crushes a man to powder, if it falls upon him. It is a composite picture, put together from three Old Testament passages. The first is *Isaiah* 8: 13, 14, 15: " The Lord of hosts him you shall regard as holy; let him be your fear, and let him be your dread. And he will become a sanctuary, and a stone of offence, and a rock of stumbling to both houses of Israel a trap and a snare to the inhabitants of Jerusalem. And many shall stumble thereon; they shall fall and be broken; they shall be snared and taken." The second is *Isaiah* 28: 16: " Behold, I am laying in Zion for a foundation a stone, a tested stone, a precious cornerstone, of a sure foundation." The third is *Daniel* 2: 34, 44, 45 where there is a strange picture of a stone, cut without hands, which broke in pieces the enemies of God.

The idea behind this is that all these Old Testament pictures of a stone are summed up in Jesus Christ. Jesus is the foundation stone on which everything is built, and the corner stone which holds everything together. To refuse his way is to batter one's head against the walls of the law of God. To defy him is in the end to be crushed out of life. However strange these pictures may seem to us, they were familiar to every Jew who knew the prophets.

JOY AND JUDGMENT

Matthew 22: 1–10

Jesus again answered them in parables: ' The Kingdom of Heaven is like the situation which arose when a man who was a king arranged a wedding for his son. He sent his servants to summon those who had been invited to the wedding, and they refused to come. He again sent other servants. ' Tell those who have been invited,' he said, ' look you, I have my meal all prepared; my oxen and my specially fattened animals have been killed; and everything is ready. Come to the wedding.' But they disregarded the invitation and went away, one to his estate, and another to his business. The rest seized the servants and treated them shamefully and killed them. The king was angry, and sent his armies, and destroyed those murderers, and set fire to their city. Then he said to his servants, ' The wedding is ready. Those who have been invited did not deserve to come. Go, then, to the highways and invite to the wedding all you may find.' So the servants went out to the roads, and collected all whom they found, both bad and good; and the wedding was supplied with guests."

VERSES 1–14 of this chapter form not one parable, but two; and we will grasp their meaning far more easily and far more fully if we take them separately.

The events of the first of the two were completely in accordance with normal Jewish customs. When the invitations to a great feast, like a wedding feast, were sent out, the time was not stated; and when everything was ready the servants were sent out with a final summons to tell the guests to come. So, then, the king in this parable had long ago sent out his invitations; but it was not till everything was prepared that the final summons was issued—and insultingly refused. This parable has two meanings.

(i) It has a purely local meaning. Its local meaning was a driving home of what had already been said in the Parable of the Wicked Husbandmen; once again it was an accusation of the Jews. The invited guests who when the time came refused to come, stand for the Jews. Ages ago they had been invited by God to be his chosen people; yet when God's son came into the world, and they were invited to follow him they contemptuously refused. The result was that the invitation of God went out direct to the highways and the byways; and the people in the highways and the byways stand for the sinners and the Gentiles, who never expected an invitation into the Kingdom.

As the writer of the gospel saw it, the consequences of the refusal were terrible. There is one verse of the parable which is strangely out of place; and that because it is not part of the original parable as Jesus told it, but an interpretation by the writer of the gospel. That is verse 7, which tells how the king sent his armies against those who refused the invitation, and burned their city.

This introduction of armies and the burning of the city seems at first sight completely out of place taken in connexion with invitations to a wedding feast. But Matthew was composing his gospel some time between A.D. 80 and 90. What had happened during the period between the actual life of Jesus and now? The answer is—*the destruction of Jerusalem by the armies of Rome* in A.D. 70. The Temple was sacked and burned and the city destroyed stone from stone, so that a plough was drawn across it. Complete disaster had come to those who refused to recognize the Son of God when he came.

The writer of the gospel adds as his comment the terrible things which did in fact happen to the nation which would not take the way of Christ. And it is indeed the simple historical fact that if the Jews had accepted the way of Christ, and had walked in love, in humility and in sacrifice they would never have been the rebellious, warring people who finally provoked the avenging wrath of Rome, when Rome could stand their political machinations no longer.

(ii) Equally this parable has much to say on a much wider scale.

(*a*) It reminds us that the invitation of God is to a feast as joyous as a wedding feast. His invitation is to joy. To think of Christianity as a gloomy giving up of everything which brings laughter and sunshine and happy fellowship is to mistake its whole nature. It is to joy that the Christian is invited; and it is joy he misses, if he refuses the invitation.

(*b*) It reminds us that the things which make men deaf to the invitation of Christ are not necessarily bad in themselves. One man went to his estate; the other to his business. They did not go off on a wild carousal or an immoral adventure. They went off on the, in itself, excellent task of efficiently administering their business life. It is very easy for a man to be so busy with the things of time that he forgets the things of eternity, to be so preoccupied with the things which are seen that he forgets the things which are unseen, to hear so insistently the claims of the world that he cannot hear the soft invitation of the voice of Christ. The tragedy of life is that it is so often the second bests which shut out the bests, that it is things which are good in themselves which shut out the things that are supreme. A man can be so busy making a living that he fails to make a life; he can be so busy with the administration and the organization of life that he forgets life itself.

(c) It reminds us that the appeal of Christ is not so much to consider how we will be punished as it is to see what we will miss, if we do not take his way of things. Those who would not come were punished, but their real tragedy was that they lost the joy of the wedding feast. If we refuse the invitation of Christ, some day our greatest pain will lie, not in the things we suffer, but in the realization of the precious things we have missed.

(d) It reminds us that in the last analysis God's invitation is the invitation of grace. Those who were gathered in from the highways and the byways had no claim on the king at all; they could never by any stretch of imagination have expected an invitation to the wedding feast, still less could they ever have deserved it. It came to them from nothing other than the wide-armed, open-hearted, generous hospitality of the king. It was grace which offered the invitation and grace which gathered men in.

THE SCRUTINY OF THE KING

Matthew 22: 11–14

> The king came in to see those who were sitting at table, and he saw there a man who was not wearing a wedding garment. " Friend," he said to him, " how did you come here with no wedding garment? " The man was struck silent. Then the king

said to the attendants, " Bind him hands and feet, and throw him out into the outer darkness. There shall be weeping and gnashing of teeth there. For many are called, but few are chosen."

THIS is a second parable, but it is also a very close continuation and amplification of the previous one. It is the story of a guest who appeared at a royal wedding feast without a wedding garment.

One of the great interests of this parable is that in it we see Jesus taking a story which was already familiar to his hearers and using it in his own way. The Rabbis had two stories which involved kings and garments. The first told of a king who invited his guests to a feast, without telling them the exact date and time; but he did tell them that they must wash, and anoint, and clothe themselves that they might be ready when the summons came. The wise prepared themselves at once, and took their places waiting at the palace door, for they believed that in a palace a feast could be prepared so quickly that there would be no long warning. The foolish believed that it would take a long time to make the necessary preparations and that they would have plenty of time. So they went, the mason to his lime, the potter to his clay, the smith to his furnace, the fuller to his bleaching-ground, and went on with their work. Then, suddenly, the summons to the feast came without any warning. The wise were ready to sit down, and the king rejoiced over them, and they ate and drank. But those who had not arrayed themselves in their wedding garments had to stand outside, sad and hungry, and look on at the joy that they had lost. That rabbinic parable tells of the duty of preparedness for the summons of God, and the garments stand for the preparation that must be made.

The second rabbinic parable told how a king entrusted to his servants royal robes. Those who were wise took the robes, and carefully stored them away, and kept them in all their pristine loveliness. Those who were foolish wore the robes to their work, and soiled and stained them. The day came when the king demanded the robes back. The wise handed them back fresh and clean; so the king laid up the robes in his treasury and bade them go in peace. The foolish handed them back stained and soiled. The king commanded that the robes should be given to the fuller to cleanse, and that the foolish servants should be cast into prison. This parable teaches that a man must hand back his soul to God in all its original purity; but that the man who has nothing but a stained soul to render back stands condemned.

No doubt Jesus had these two parables in mind when he told his own story. What, then, was he seeking to teach? This parable also contains both a local and a universal lesson.

(i) The local lesson is this. Jesus has just said that the king, to supply his feast with guests, sent his messengers out into the highways and byways to gather all men in. That was the parable of the open door. It told how the Gentiles and the sinners would be gathered in. This parable strikes the necessary balance. It is true that the door is open to all men, but when they come they must bring a life which seeks to fit the love which has been given to them. Grace is not only a gift; it is a grave responsibility. A man cannot go on living the life he lived before he met Jesus Christ. He must be clothed in a new purity and a new holiness and a new goodness. The door is open, but the door is not open for the sinner to come and remain a sinner, but for the sinner to come and become a saint.

(ii) This is the permanent lesson. The way in which a man comes to anything demonstrates the spirit in which he comes. If we go to visit in a friend's house, we do not go in the clothes we wear in the shipyard or the garden. We know very well that it is not the clothes which matter to the friend. It is not that we want to put on a show. It is simply a matter of respect that we should present ourselves in our friend's house as neatly as we can. The fact that we prepare ourselves to go there is the way in which we outwardly show our affection and our esteem for our friend. So it is with God's house. This parable has nothing to do with the *clothes* in which we go to church; it has everything to do with the *spirit* in which we go to God's house. It is profoundly true that church-going must never be a fashion parade. But there are garments of the mind and of the heart and of the soul—the garment of expectation, the garment of humble penitence, the garment of faith, the garment of reverence—and these are the garments without which we ought not to approach God. Too often we go to God's house with no preparation at all; if every man and woman in our congregations came to church *prepared to worship*, after a little prayer, a little thought, and a little self-examination, then worship would be worship indeed—the worship in which and through which things happen in men's souls and in the life of the Church and in the affairs of the world.

HUMAN AND DIVINE RIGHT

Matthew 22: 15–22

> Then the Pharisees came, and tried to form a plan to ensnare him in his speech. So they sent their disciples to him, along with the Herodians. " Teacher," they said, " we know that you are true, and that you teach the way of God in truth, and that you never allow yourself to be swayed by any man, for you are no respecter of persons. Tell us, then, your opinion—is it right to pay tribute to Caesar, or not? " Jesus was well aware of their malice. " Hypocrites," he said, " why do you try to test me? Show me the tribute coin." They brought him a denarius. " Whose image is this," he said to them, " and whose inscription? " " Caesar's," they said to him. " Well then," he said to them, " render to Caesar the things which are Caesar's, and to God the things which are God's." When they heard this answer, they were amazed, and left him and went away.

Up to this point we have seen Jesus, as it were, on the attack. He had spoken three parables in which he had plainly indicted the orthodox Jewish leaders. In the parable of the two sons (*Matthew* 21: 28–32) the Jewish leaders appear under the guise of the unsatisfactory son who did not do his father's will. In the parable of the wicked husbandmen (*Matthew* 21: 33–46) they are the wicked husbandmen. In the parable of the king's feast (*Matthew* 22: 1–14) they are the condemned guests.

Now we see the Jewish leaders launching their counter-attack; and they do so by directing at Jesus carefully formulated questions. They ask these questions in public, while the crowd look on and listen, and their aim is to make Jesus discredit himself by his own words in the presence of the people. Here, then, we have the question of the Pharisees, and it was subtly framed. Palestine was an occupied country and the Jews were subject to the Roman Empire; and the question was: " Is it, or is it not, lawful to pay tribute to Rome? "

There were, in fact, three regular taxes which the Roman government exacted. There was a *ground tax*; a man must pay to the government one tenth of the grain, and one fifth of the oil and wine which he produced; this tax was paid partly in kind, and partly in a money equivalent. There was *income tax*, which was one per cent of a man's income. There was a *poll tax*; this tax had to be paid by every male person from the age of fourteen to the age of sixty-five, and by every female person from the age of twelve to sixty-five; it amounted to one *denarius*—that is what Jesus called *the tribute coin*—and was the equivalent of about 4p, a sum which is to be evaluated in the awareness that 3p was the usual day's wage for a working-man. The tax in question here is the poll tax.

The question which the Pharisees asked set Jesus a very real dilemma. If he said that it was unlawful to pay the tax, they would promptly report him to the Roman government officials as a seditious person and his arrest would certainly follow. If he said that it was lawful to pay the tax, he would stand discredited in the eyes of many of the people. Not only did the people resent the tax as everyone resents taxation; they resented it even more for religious reasons. To a Jew God was the only king; their nation was a theocracy; to pay tax to an earthly king was to admit the validity of his kingship and thereby to insult God. Therefore the more fanatical of the Jews insisted that any tax paid to a foreign king was necessarily wrong. Whichever way Jesus might answer—so his questioners thought—he would lay himself open to trouble.

The seriousness of this attack is shown by the fact that the

Pharisees and the *Herodians* combined to make it, for normally these two parties were in bitter opposition. The Pharisees were the supremely orthodox, who resented the payment of the tax to a foreign king as an infringement of the divine right of God. The Herodians were the party of Herod, king of Galilee, who owed his power to the Romans and who worked hand in glove with them. The Pharisees and the Herodians were strange bed-fellows indeed; their differences were for the moment forgotten in a common hatred of Jesus and a common desire to eliminate him. Any man who insists on his own way, no matter what it is, will hate Jesus.

This question of tax-paying was not of merely historical interest. Matthew was writing between A.D. 80 and 90. The Temple had been destroyed in A.D. 70. So long as it stood, every Jew had been bound to pay the half-shekel Temple tax. After the destruction of the Temple, the Roman government demanded that that tax should be paid to the temple of Jupiter Capitolinus in Rome. It is obvious how bitter a regulation that was for a Jew to stomach. The matter of taxes was a real problem in the actual ministry of Jesus; and it was still a real problem in the days of the early Church.

But Jesus was wise. He asked to see a denarius, which was stamped with the Emperor's head. In the ancient days coinage was the sign of kingship. As soon as a king came to the throne he struck his own coinage; even a pretender would produce a coinage to show the reality of his kingship; and that coinage was held to be the property of the king whose image it bore. Jesus asked whose image was on the coin. The answer was that Caesar's head was on it. " Well then," said Jesus, " give it back to Caesar; it is his. Give to Caesar what belongs to him; and give to God what belongs to him."

With his unique wisdom Jesus never laid down rules and regulations; that is why his teaching is timeless and never goes out of date. He always lays down principles. Here he lays down a very great and very important one.

Every Christian man has a double citizenship. He is a citizen of the country in which he happens to live. To it he owes many things. He owes the safety against lawless men which only settled government can give; he owes all public services. To take a simple example, few men are wealthy enough to have a lighting system or a cleansing system or a water system of their own. These are public services. In a welfare state the citizen owes still more to the state—education, medical services, provision for unemployment and old age. This places him under a debt of obligation. Because the Christian is a man of honour, he must be a responsible citizen; failure in good citizenship is also failure in Christian duty. Untold troubles can descend upon a country or an industry when Christians refuse to take their part in the administration and leave it to selfish, self-seeking, partisan, and unchristian men. The Christian has a duty to Caesar in return for the privileges which the rule of Caesar brings to him.

But the Christian is also a citizen of heaven. There are matters of religion and of principle in which the responsibility of the Christian is to God. It may well be that the two citizenships will never clash; they do not need to. But when the Christian is convinced that it is God's will that something should be done, it must be done; or, if he is convinced that something is against the will of God, he must resist it and take no part in it. Where the boundaries between the two duties lie, Jesus does not say. That is for a man's own conscience to test. But a real Christian—and this is the permanent truth which Jesus here lays down—is at one and the same time a good citizen of his country and a good citizen of the Kingdom of Heaven. He will fail in his duty neither to God nor to man. He will, as Peter said, " Fear God. Honour the emperor " (1 *Peter* 2: 17).

THE LIVING GOD OF LIVING MEN

Matthew 22: 23–33

On that day the Sadducees, who deny that there is any resurrection, came to him, and questioned him. " Teacher," they said,

" Moses said, ' If anyone dies without children, his brother shall marry his wife, and shall raise up a family for his brother.' Amongst us there were seven brothers. The first married and died, and, since he had no children, he left his wife to his brother. The same thing happened with the second and the third, right to the end of the seven of them. Last of all the woman died. Of which of the seven will she be the wife in the resurrection? For they all had her." Jesus answered: " You are in error, because you do not know the Scriptures or the power of God. In the resurrection they neither marry nor are married, but they are as the angels in heaven. Now, in regard to the resurrection of the dead, have you never read what God said, ' I am the God of Abraham, the God of Isaac, and the God of Jacob.' God is not the God of dead men, but of those who live." When the crowds heard this answer, they were amazed at his teaching.

WHEN the Pharisees had made their counter-attack on Jesus and been routed, the Sadducees took up the battle.

The Sadducees were not many in number; but they were the wealthy, the aristocratic, and the governing class. The chief priests, for instance, were Sadducees. In politics they were collaborationist; quite ready to co-operate with the Roman government, if co-operation was the price of the retention of their own privileges. In thought they were quite ready to open their minds to Greek ideas. In their Jewish belief they were traditionalists. They refused to accept the oral and scribal law, which to the Pharisees was of such paramount importance. They went even further; the only part of scripture which they regarded as binding was the Pentateuch, the Law *par excellence*, the first five books of the Old Testament. They did not accept the prophets or the poetical books as scripture at all. In particular they were at variance with the Pharisees in that they completely denied any life after death, a belief on which the Pharisees insisted. The Pharisees indeed laid it down that any man who denied the resurrection of the dead was shut out from God.

The Sadducees insisted that the doctrine of life after death could not be proved from the Pentateuch. The Pharisees said

that it could and it is interesting to look at the proofs which
they adduced. They cited *Numbers* 18: 28 which says, " You
shall give the Lord's offering to Aaron the priest." That is
permanent regulation; the verb is in the present tense; therefore
Aaron is still alive! They cited *Deuteronomy* 31: 16: " This
people will rise," a peculiarly unconvincing citation, for the
second half of the verse goes on, " and play the harlot after the
strange gods of the land "! They cited *Deuteronomy* 32: 39: " I
kill and I make alive." Outside the Pentateuch they cited *Isaiah*
26: 19: " Thy dead shall live." It cannot be said that any of the
citations of the Pharisees were really convincing; and no real
argument for the resurrection of the dead had ever been
produced from the Pentateuch.

The Pharisees were very definite about the resurrection of *the
body*. They discussed recondite points—Would a man rise
clothed or unclothed? If clothed, would he rise with the clothes
in which he died, or other clothes? They used 1 *Samuel* 28: 14
(the witch of Endor's raising of the spirit of Samuel at the
request of Saul) to prove that after death men retain the
appearance they had in this world. They even argued that men
rose with the physical defects with which, and from which they
died—otherwise they would not be the same persons! All Jews
would be resurrected in the Holy Land, so they said that under
the earth there were cavities and, when a Jew was buried in a
foreign land, his body rolled through these cavities until it
reached the homeland. The Pharisees held as a primary
doctrine the bodily resurrection of the dead; the Sadducees
completely denied it.

The Sadducees produced a question which, they believed,
reduced the doctrine of the resurrection of the body to an
absurdity. There was a Jewish custom called Levirate Marriage.
How far it was ever carried out in practice is very doubtful.
If a man died childless, his brother was under obligation to
marry the widow, and to beget children for his brother; such
children were legally regarded as the brother's children. If the
man refused to marry the widow, they must both go to the
elders. The woman must loosen the man's shoe, spit in his face,

and curse him; and the man was thereafter under a stigma of refusal (*Deuteronomy* 25: 5–10). The Sadducees cited a case of Levirate Marriage in which seven brothers, each dying childless, one after another married the same woman; and then asked, " When the resurrection takes place, whose wife will this much-married woman be? " Here indeed was a catch question.

Jesus began by laying down one principle—the whole question starts from a basic error, the error of thinking of heaven in terms of earth, and of thinking of eternity in terms of time. Jesus's answer was that anyone who reads scripture must see that the question is irrelevant, for heaven is not going to be simply a continuation or an extension of this world. There will be new and greater relationships which will far transcend the physical relationships of time.

Then Jesus went on to demolish the whole Sadducean position. They had always held that there was no text in the Pentateuch which could be used to prove the resurrection of the dead. Now, what was one of the commonest titles of God in the Pentateuch? " The God of Abraham, and of Isaac, and of Jacob." God cannot be the God of dead men and of mouldering corpses. The living God must be the God of living men. The Sadducean case was shattered. Jesus had done what the wisest Rabbis had never been able to do. Out of Scripture itself he had confuted the Sadducees, and had shown them that there is a life after death which must not be thought of in earthly terms. The crowds were amazed at a man who was a master of argument like this, and even the Pharisees can hardly have forborne to cheer.

DUTY TO GOD AND DUTY TO MAN

Matthew 22: 34–40

When the Pharisees heard that he had silenced the Sadducees, they gathered together. One of them, who was an expert in the Law, asked him a question as a test: " What commandment in the Law is greatest? " He said to him, " ' You must love the Lord your God with your whole heart, and your whole soul, and your whole mind.' This is the great and the chief commandment; and the second is like it, ' You must love your neighbour as yourself.' On these two commandments the whole Law and the prophets depend."

IN *Matthew* this question looks like a return to the attack on the part of the Pharisees; but in *Mark* the atmosphere is different. As Mark tells the story (*Mark* 12: 28–34) the scribe did not ask Jesus this question to trip him up. He asked it in gratitude that Jesus had confuted the Sadducees and to enable Jesus to demonstrate how well he could answer; and the passage ends with the scribe and Jesus very close to each other.

We may well say that here Jesus laid down the complete definition of religion.

(i) Religion consists in loving God. The verse which Jesus quotes is *Deuteronomy* 6: 5. That verse was part of the *Shema*, the basic and essential creed of Judaism, the sentence with which every Jewish service still opens, and the first text which every Jewish child commits to memory. It means that to God we must give a total love, a love which dominates our emotions, a love which directs our thoughts, and a love which is the dynamic of our actions. All religion starts with the love which is total commitment of life to God.

(ii) The second commandment which Jesus quotes comes from *Leviticus* 19: 18. Our love for God must issue in love for men. But it is to be noted in which order the commandments come; it is love of God first, and love of man second. It is only when we love God that man becomes lovable. The Biblical teaching about man is not that man is a collection of chemical elements, not that man is part of the brute creation, but that man is made in the image of God (*Genesis* 1: 26, 27). It is for that reason that man is lovable. The true basis of all democracy is in fact the love of God. Take away the love of God and we can become angry at man the unteachable; we can become pessimistic about man the unimprovable; we can become callous to man the machine-minder. The love of man is firmly grounded in the love of God.

To be truly religious is to love God and to love the men whom God made in his own image; and to love God and man, not with a nebulous sentimentality, but with that total commitment which issues in devotion to God and practical service of men.

NEW HORIZONS

Matthew 22: 41–46

> When the Pharisees had come together, Jesus asked them a question: " What is your opinion about The Anointed One? Whose son is he? " " David's son," they said. He said to them, " How, then, does David in the Spirit call Him *Lord*, when he says, ' The Lord said to my Lord, Sit on my right hand till I put your enemies beneath your feet.' If David calls Him *Lord*, how is he his son? " And no one was able to give him any answer. And from that day no one any longer dared to ask him a question.

To us this may seem one of the most obscure things which Jesus ever said. This may be so, but none the less it is a most important statement. Even if, at first sight, we do not fully grasp its meaning, we can still feel the air of awe and astonishment and mystery which it has about it.

We have seen again and again that Jesus refused to allow his followers to proclaim him as the Messiah until he had taught them what Messiahship meant. Their ideas of Messiahship needed the most radical change.

The commonest title of the Messiah was *Son of David*. Behind it lay the expectation that there would one day come a great prince of the line of David who would shatter Israel's enemies and lead the people to the conquest of all nations. The Messiah was most commonly thought of in nationalistic, political, military terms of power and glory. This is another attempt by Jesus to alter that conception.

He asked the Pharisees whose son they understood the Messiah to be: they answered, as he knew they would, " David's son." Jesus then quotes *Psalm* 110: 1: " The Lord says to my Lord; Sit at my right hand." All accepted that as a Messianic text. In it the first *Lord* is God; the second *Lord* is the Messiah. That is to say David calls the Messiah *Lord*. But, if the Messiah is David's son, how could David call his own son *Lord*?

The clear result of the argument is that *it is not adequate to call the Messiah Son of David*. He is not David's son; he is David's Lord. When Jesus healed the blind men, they called him Son of David (*Matthew* 20: 30). When he entered Jerusalem the crowds hailed him as Son of David (*Matthew* 21: 9). Jesus is here saying, " It is not enough to call the Messiah Son of David. It is not enough to think of him as a Prince of David's line and an earthly conqueror. You must go beyond that, for the Messiah is David's *Lord*."

What did Jesus mean? He can have meant only one thing—that the true description of him is *Son of God*. *Son of David* is not an adequate title; only *Son of God* will do. And, if that be so, Messiahship is not to be thought of in terms of Davidic conquest, but in terms of divine and sacrificial love. Here, then, Jesus makes his greatest claim. In him there came, not the earthly conqueror who would repeat the military triumphs of David, but the Son of God who would demonstrate the love of God upon his Cross.

There would be few that day who caught anything like all that Jesus meant; but when Jesus spoke these words, even the densest of them felt a shiver in the presence of the eternal mystery. They had the awed and the uncomfortable feeling that they had heard the voice of God, and for a moment, in this man Jesus, they glimpsed God's very face.

SCRIBES AND PHARISEES

IF a man is characteristically and temperamentally an irritable, ill-tempered and irascible creature, notoriously given to uncontrolled outbursts of passionate anger, his anger is neither effective nor impressive. Nobody pays any attention to the anger of a bad-tempered man. But when a person who is characteristically meek and lowly, gentle and loving, suddenly erupts into blazing wrath, even the most thoughtless person is shocked into taking thought. That is why the anger of Jesus is so awe-inspiring a sight. It is seldom in literature that we find so unsparing and sustained an indictment as we find in this chapter when the wrath of Jesus is directed against the Scribes and Pharisees. Before we begin to study the chapter in detail, it will be well to see briefly what the Scribes and Pharisees stood for.

The Jews had a deep and lasting sense of the continuity of their religion; and we can see best what the Pharisees and Scribes stood for by seeing where they came into the scheme of Jewish religion. The Jews had a saying, " Moses received the Law and delivered it to Joshua; and Joshua to the elders; and the elders to the prophets; and the prophets to the men of the Great Synagogue." All Jewish religion is based first on the Ten Commandments and then on the Pentateuch, the Law.

The history of the Jews was designed to make them a people of the Law. As every nation has, they had their dream of greatness. But the experiences of history had made that dream take a special direction. They had been conquered by the Assyrians, the Babylonians, the Persians, and Jerusalem had been left desolate. It was clear that they could not be pre-eminent in political power. But although political power was an obvious impossibility, they none the less possessed the Law, and to them the Law was the very word of God, the greatest and most precious possession in the world.

There came a day in their history when that pre-eminence of the Law was, as it were, publicly admitted; there came what one can only call a deliberate act of decision, whereby the people of Israel became in the most unique sense the people of the Law. Under Ezra and Nehemiah the people were allowed to come back to Jerusalem, and to rebuild their shattered city, and to take up their national life again. When that happened, there came a day when Ezra, the Scribe, took the book of the Law, and read it to them, and there happened something that was

nothing less than a national dedication of a people to the
keeping of the Law (*Nehemiah* 8: 1–8).

From that day the study of the Law became the greatest of
all professions; and that study of the Law was committed to the
men of the Great Synagogue, the *Scribes.*

We have already seen how the great principles of the Law
were broken up into thousands upon thousands of little rules
and regulations (see section on *Matthew* 5: 17–20). We have
seen, for instance, how the Law said that a man must not work
on the Sabbath day, and how the Scribes laboured to define
work, how they laid it down how many paces a man might walk
on the Sabbath, how heavy a burden he might carry, the things
he might and might not do. By the time this scribal interpretation
of the Law was finished, it took more than fifty volumes to hold
the mass of regulations which resulted.

The return of the people to Jerusalem and the first dedication
of the Law took place about 450 B.C. But it is not till long after
that that the Pharisees emerge. About 175 B.C. Antiochus
Epiphanes of Syria made a deliberate attempt to stamp out the
Jewish religion and to introduce Greek religion and Greek
customs and practices. It was then that the Pharisees arose as a
separate sect. The name means *The Separated Ones*; and they
were the men who dedicated their whole life to the careful and
meticulous observance of every rule and regulation which the
Scribes had worked out. In face of the threat directed against it,
they determined to spend their whole lives in one long observance of Judaism in its most elaborate and ceremonial and legal
form. They were men who accepted the ever-increasing number
of religious rules and regulations extracted from the Law.

There were never very many of them; at most there were not
more than six thousand of them; for the plain fact was that, if a
man was going to accept and carry out every little regulation of
the Law, he would have time for nothing else; he had to
withdraw himself, to separate himself, from ordinary life in
order to keep the Law.

The Pharisees then were two things. First, they were dedicated legalists; religion to them was the observance of every

detail of the Law. But second—and this is never to be forgotten—they were men in desperate earnest about their religion, for no one would have accepted the impossibly demanding task of living a life like that unless he had been in the most deadly earnest. They could, therefore, develop at one and the same time all the faults of legalism and all the virtues of complete self-dedication. A Pharisee might either be a desiccated or arrogant legalist, or a man of burning devotion to God.

To say this is not to pass a particularly Christian verdict on the Pharisees, for the Jews themselves passed that very verdict. The *Talmud* distinguishes seven different kinds of Pharisee.

(i) There was the *Shoulder Pharisee*. He was meticulous in his observance of the Law; but he wore his good deeds upon his shoulder. He was out for a reputation for purity and goodness. True, he obeyed the Law, but he did so in order to be seen of men.

(ii) There was the *Wait-a-little Pharisee*. He was the Pharisee who could always produce an entirely valid excuse for putting off a good deed. He professed the creed of the strictest Pharisees but he could always find an excuse for allowing practice to lag behind. He spoke, but he did not do.

(iii) There was the *Bruised* or *Bleeding Pharisee*. The Talmud speaks of the plague of *self-afflicting Pharisees*. These Pharisees received their name for this reason. Women had a very low status in Palestine. No really strict orthodox teacher would be seen talking to a woman in public, even if that woman was his own wife or sister. These Pharisees went even further; they would not even allow themselves to look at a woman on the street. In order to avoid doing so they would shut their eyes, and so bump into walls and buildings and obstructions. They thus bruised and wounded themselves, and their wounds and bruises gained them a special reputation for exceeding piety.

(iv) There was the Pharisee who was variously described as the *Pestle and Mortar Pharisee*, or the *Hump-backed Pharisee*, or the *Tumbling Pharisee*. Such men walked in such ostentatious humility that they were bent like a pestle in a mortar or like a hunch-back. They were so humble that they would not

even lift their feet from the ground and so tripped over every
obstruction they met. Their humility was a self-advertising
ostentation.

(v) There was the *Ever-reckoning* or *Compounding Pharisee.*
This kind of Pharisee was for ever reckoning up his good deeds;
he was for ever striking a balance sheet between himself and
God, and he believed that every good deed he did put God a
little further in his debt. To him religion was always to be
reckoned in terms of a profit and loss account.

(vi) There was the *Timid* or *Fearing Pharisee.* He was always
in dread of divine punishment. He was, therefore, always
cleansing the outside of the cup and the platter, so that he might
seem to be good. He saw religion in terms of judgment and life
in terms of a terror-stricken evasion of this judgment.

(vii) Finally, there was the *God-fearing Pharisee;* he was the
Pharisee who really and truly loved God and who found his
delight in obedience to the Law of God, however difficult that it
might be.

That was the Jew's own classification of the Pharisees; and it
is to be noted that there were six bad types to one good one.
There would be not a few listening to Jesus's denunciation of
the Pharisees who agreed with every word of it.

MAKING RELIGION A BURDEN

Matthew 23: 1–4

> Then Jesus said to the crowds and to his disciples, " The Scribes
> and Pharisees sit on Moses's seat. Therefore do and observe
> everything they tell you; but do not act as they act; for they speak,
> but they do not do. They bind burdens that are heavy and hard to
> bear, and place them on men's shoulders; but they themselves
> refuse to lift a finger to remove them."

HERE we see the lineaments of the Pharisees already beginning
to appear. Here we see the Jewish conviction of the continuity
of the faith. God gave the Law to Moses; Moses handed it to

Joshua; Joshua transmitted it to the elders; the elders passed it down to the prophets; and the prophets gave it to the Scribes and Pharisees.

It must not for a moment be thought that Jesus is commending the Scribes and Pharisees with all their rules and regulations. What he is saying is this, " In so far as these Scribes and Pharisees have taught you the great principles of the Law which Moses received from God, you must obey them." When we were studying *Matthew* 5: 17–20 we saw what these principles were. The whole of the Ten Commandments are based on two great principles. They are based on *reverence*,reverence for God, for God's name, for God's day, for the parents God has given to us. They are based on *respect*, respect for a man's life, for his possessions, for his personality, for his good name, for oneself. These principles are eternal; and, in so far as the Scribes and Pharisees teach reverence for God and respect for men, their teaching is eternally binding and eternally valid.

But their whole outlook on religion had one fundamental effect. It made it a thing of thousands upon thousands of rules and regulations; and therefore *it made it an intolerable burden*. Here is the test of any presentation of religion. Does it make it wings to lift a man up, or a deadweight to drag him down? Does it make it a joy or a depression? Is a man helped by his religion or is he haunted by it? Does it carry him, or has he to carry it? Whenever religion becomes a depressing affair of burdens and prohibitions, it ceases to be true religion.

Nor would the Pharisees allow the slightest relaxation. Their whole self-confessed purpose was to " build a fence around the Law." Not one regulation would they relax or remove. Whenever religion becomes a burden, it ceases to be true religion.

THE RELIGION OF OSTENTATION

Matthew 23: 5–12

" They perform all their actions to be seen by men. They broaden their phylacteries; they wear outsize tassels. They love the highest

places at meals, and the front seats in the synagogues, and
greetings in the market-place, and to be called Rabbi by men. You
must not be called Rabbi; for you have only one teacher, and you
are all brothers. Call no one upon earth father; you have one
Father—your Father in Heaven. Nor must you be called leaders;
you have one leader—Christ. He who is greatest among you will
be your servant. Anyone who will exalt himself will be humbled;
and whoever will humble himself will be exalted."

THE religion of the Pharisees became almost inevitably a
religion of ostentation. If religion consists in obeying countless
rules and regulations, it becomes easy for a man to see to it that
everyone is aware how well he fulfils the regulations, and how
perfect is his piety. Jesus selects certain actions and customs in
which the Pharisees showed their ostentation.

They made broad their *phylacteries*. It is said of the commandments of God in *Exodus* 13: 9: " It shall be to you as a
sign on your hand, and a memorial between your eyes." The
same saying is repeated, " It shall be as a mark on your hand,
or frontlets between your eyes " (*Exodus* 13: 16; cp. *Deuteronomy* 6: 8; 11: 18). In order to fulfil these commandments the
Jew wore at prayer, and still wears, what are called *tephillin* or
phylacteries. They are worn on every day except the Sabbath
and special holy days. They are like little leather boxes,
strapped one on the wrist and one on the forehead. The one on
the wrist is a little leather box of one compartment, and inside it
there is a parchment roll with the following four passages of
scripture written on it—*Exodus* 13: 1–10; 13: 11–16; *Deuteronomy* 6: 4–9; 11: 13–21. The one worn on the forehead is the
same except that in it there are four little compartments, and in
each compartment there is a little scroll inscribed with one of
these four passages. The Pharisees, in order to draw attention to
himself, not only wore phylacteries, but wore specially big ones,
so that he might demonstrate his exemplary obedience to the
Law and his exemplary piety.

They wear outsize *tassels*; the tassels are in Greek *kraspeda*
and in Hebrew *zizith*. In *Numbers* 15: 37–41 and in *Deuteronomy* 22: 12 we read that God commanded his people to make

fringes on the borders of their garments, so that when they looked on them they might remember the commandments of God. These fringes were like tassels worn on the four corners of the outer garment. Later they were worn on the inner garment, and today they are perpetuated in the tassels of the prayer-shawl which the devout Jew wears at prayer. It was easy to make these tassels of specially large size so that they became an ostentatious display of piety, worn, not to remind a man of the commandments, but to draw attention to himself.

Further, the Pharisees liked to be given the principal places at meals, on the left and on the right of the host. They liked the front seats in the synagogues In Palestine the back seats were occupied by the children and the most unimportant people; the further forward the seat, the greater the honour. The most honoured seats of all were the seats of the elders, which *faced* the congregation. If a man was seated there, everyone would see that he was present and he could conduct himself throughout the service with a pose of piety which the congregation could not fail to notice. Still further, the Pharisee liked to be addressed as Rabbi and to be treated with the greatest respect. They claimed, in point of fact, greater respect than that which was given to parents, for, they said, a man's parents give him ordinary, physical life, but a man's teacher gives him eternal life. They even liked to be called *father* as Elisha called Elijah (2 *Kings* 2: 12) and as the fathers of the faith were known.

Jesus insists that the Christian should remember that he has one teacher only—and that teacher is Christ; and only one Father in the faith—and that Father is God.

The whole design of the Pharisees was to dress and act in such a way as to draw attention to themselves; the whole design of the Christian should be to obliterate himself, so that if men see his good deeds, they may glorify not him, but his Father in Heaven. Any religion which produces ostentation in action and pride in the heart is a false religion.

SHUTTING THE DOOR

Matthew 23: 13

> " Alas for you, Scribes and Pharisees, hypocrites, for you shut the door to the Kingdom of Heaven in the face of men! You yourselves are not going into it; nor do you allow those who are trying to get into it to enter it."

VERSES 13–26 of this chapter form the most terrible and the most sustained denunciation in the New Testament. Here we hear what A. T. Robertson called " the rolling thunder of Christ's wrath." As Plummer has written, these *woes* are " like thunder in their unanswerable severity, and like lightning in their unsparing exposure.... They illuminate while they strike.

Here Jesus directs a series of seven *woes* against the Scribes and Pharisees. The Revised Standard Version begins every one of them: " Woe to you! " The Greek word for *woe* is *ouai*; it is hard to translate for it includes not only *wrath*, but also *sorrow*. There is righteous anger here, but it is the anger of the heart of love, broken by the stubborn blindness of men. There is not only an air of savage denunciation; there is also an atmosphere of poignant tragedy.

The word *hypocrite* occurs here again and again. Originally the Greek word *hupokritēs* meant *one who answers*; it then came to be specially connected with the statement and answer, the dialogue, of the stage; and it is the regular Greek word for an *actor*. It then came to mean an actor in the worse sense of the term, a *pretender*, one who acts a part, one who wears a mask to cover his true feelings, one who puts on an external show while inwardly his thoughts and feelings are very different.

To Jesus the Scribes and Pharisees were men who were acting a part. What he meant was this. Their whole idea of religion consisted in outward observances, the wearing of elaborate phylacteries and tassels, the meticulous observance of the rules and regulations of the Law. But in their hearts there was bitterness and envy and pride and arrogance. To Jesus these Scribes and Pharisees were men who, under a mask of elaborate godliness, concealed hearts in which the most godless feelings and emotions held sway. And that accusation holds good in greater or lesser degree of any man who lives life on the assumption that religion consists in external observances and external acts.

There is an unwritten saying of Jesus which says, " The key of the Kingdom they hid." His condemnation of these Scribes and Pharisees is that they are not only failing to enter the Kingdom themselves, they shut the door on the faces of those who seek to enter. What did he mean by this accusation?

We have already seen (*Matthew* 6: 10) that the best way to think of the Kingdom is to think of it as a society on earth where God's will is as perfectly done as it is in heaven. To be a citizen of the Kingdom, and to do God's will, are one and the same thing. The Pharisees believed that to do God's will was to observe their thousands of petty rules and regulations; and nothing could be further from that Kingdom whose basic idea is love. When people tried to find entry into the Kingdom the Pharisees presented them with these rules and regulations, which was as good as shutting the door in their faces.

The Pharisees preferred their ideas of religion to God's idea of religion. They had forgotten the basic truth that, if a man would teach others, he must himself first listen to God. The gravest danger which any teacher or preacher encounters is that he should erect his own prejudices into universal principles and substitute his own ideas for the truth of God. When he does that he is not a guide, but a barrier, to the Kingdom, for, misled himself, he misleads others.

MISSIONARIES OF EVIL

Matthew 23: 15

" Alas for you, Scribes and Pharisees, for you range over the sea and the dry land to make one proselyte, and, when that happens, you make him twice as much a son of hell as yourselves! "

A STRANGE feature of the ancient world was the repulsion and attraction which Judaism exercised over men at one and the same time. There was no more hated people than the Jews. Their separatism and their isolation and their contempt of other nations gained them hostility. It was, in fact, believed that a basic part of their religion was an oath that they would never under any circumstances give help to a Gentile, even to the extent of giving him directions if he asked the way. Their observance of the Sabbath gained them a reputation for laziness; their refusal of swine's flesh gained them mockery, even to the extent of the rumour that they worshipped the pig as their god. Anti-semitism was a real and universal force in the ancient world.

And yet there was an attraction. The idea of one God came as a wonderful thing to a world which believed in a multitude of gods. Jewish ethical purity and standards of morality had a fascination in a world steeped in immorality, especially for women. The result was that many were attracted to Judaism.

Their attraction was on two levels. There were those who were called the *god-fearers*. These accepted the conception of one God; they accepted the Jewish moral law; but they took no part in the ceremonial law and did not become circumcised. Such people existed in large numbers, and were to be found listening and worshipping in every synagogue, and indeed provided Paul with his most fruitful field for evangelization. They are, for instance, the *devout Greeks* of Thessalonica (*Acts* 17: 4).

It was the aim of the Pharisees to turn these *god-fearers* into *proselytes*; the word *proselyte* is an English transliteration of a Greek word *prosēlutos*, which means *one who has approached* or *drawn near*. The *proselyte* was the full convert who had accepted the ceremonial law and circumcision and who had become in the fullest sense a Jew. As so often happens, " the most converted were the most perverted." A convert often becomes the most fanatical devotee of his new religion; and many of these proselytes were more fanatically devoted to the Jewish Law than even the Jews themselves.

Jesus accused these Pharisees of being missionaries of evil. It was true that very few became proselytes, but those who did went the whole way. The sin of the Pharisees was that they were not really seeking to lead men to God, they were seeking to lead them to Pharisaism. One of the gravest dangers which any missionary runs is that he should try to convert people to a sect rather than to a religion, and that he should be more concerned in bringing people to a Church than to Jesus Christ.

Premanand has certain things to say about this sectarianism which so often disfigures so-called Christianity: " I speak as a Christian, God is my Father, the Church is my Mother. Christian is my name; Catholic is my surname. Catholic, because we belong to nothing less than the Church Universal. So do we need any other names? Why go on to add Anglican, Episcopalian, Protestant, Presbyterian, Methodist, Congregational, Baptist, and so on, and so on? These terms are divisive, sectarian, narrow. They shrivel up one's soul."

It was not to God the Pharisees sought to lead men; it was to their own sect of Pharisaism. That in fact was their sin. And is that sin even yet gone from the world, when it would still be insisted in certain quarters that a man must leave one Church and become a member of another before he can be allowed a place at the Table of the Lord? The greatest of all heresies is the sinful conviction that any Church has a monopoly of God or of his truth, or that any Church is the only gateway to God's Kingdom.

THE SCIENCE OF EVASION

Matthew 23: 16–22

" Alas for you, Scribes and Pharisees! Blind guides! You who say,
  ' If any one swears by the Temple, it is nothing; but whoever
  swears by the gold of the Temple is bound by his oath.' Foolish
  ones and blind! Which is the greater? The gold? Or the Temple
  which hallows the gold? You say, ' If anyone swears by the altar,
  it is nothing; but if anyone swears by the gift that is on it, he is

bound by his oath.' Blind ones! Which is greater? The gift? Or the altar which hallows the gift? He who swears by the altar, swears by it and all that is on it. He who swears by the Temple, swears by it, and by him who inhabits it. And he who swears by heaven, swears by the throne of God, and by him who sits upon it."

WE have already seen that in matters of oaths the Jewish legalists were masters of evasion (*Matthew* 5: 33–37). The general principle of evasion was this. To the Jew an oath was absolutely binding, *so long as it was a binding oath*. Broadly speaking, a binding oath was an oath which definitely and without equivocation employed the name of God; such an oath must be kept, no matter what the cost. Any other oath might be legitimately broken. The idea was that, if God's name was actually used, then God was introduced as a partner into the transaction, and to break the oath was not only to break faith with men but to insult God.

The science of evasion had been brought to a high degree. It is most probable that in this passage Jesus is presenting a caricature of Jewish legalistic methods. He is saying, " You have brought evasion to such a fine art that it is possible to regard an oath by the Temple as not binding, while an oath by the gold of the Temple is binding; and an oath by the altar as not binding, while an oath by the gift on the altar is binding." This is rather to be regarded as a *reductio ad absurdum* of Jewish methods than as a literal description.

The idea behind the passage is just this. The whole idea of treating oaths in this way, the whole conception of a kind of technique of evasion, is born of a fundamental deceitfulness. The truly religious man will never make a promise with the deliberate intention of evading it; he will never, as he makes it, provide himself with a series of escape routes, which he may use if he finds his promise hard to keep.

We need not with conscious superiority condemn the Pharisaic science of evasion. The time is not yet ended when a man seeks to evade some duty on a technicality or calls in the strict letter of the law to avoid doing what the spirit of the law clearly means he ought to do.

For Jesus the binding principle was twofold. God hears every word we speak and God sees every intention of our hearts. In view of that the fine art of evasion is one to which a Christian should be foreign. The technique of evasion may suit the sharp practice of the world; but never the open honesty of the Christian mind.

THE LOST SENSE OF PROPORTION

Matthew 23: 23, 24

" Alas for you, Scribes and Pharisees, hypocrites! for you tithe mint, and dill, and cummin, and let go the weightier matters of the Law—justice and mercy and fidelity. These you ought to have done without neglecting the others. Blind guides who strain out a gnat and swallow a camel! "

THE tithe was an essential part of Jewish religious regulations. " You shall tithe all the yield of your seed, which comes forth from the field year by year " (*Deuteronomy* 14: 22). " All the tithe of the land, whether of the seed of the land, or of the fruit of the trees is the Lord's; it is holy to the Lord " (*Leviticus* 27: 30). This tithe was specially for the support of the Levites, whose task it was to do the material work of the Temple. The things which had to be tithed were further defined by the Law—" Everything which is eatable, and is preserved, and has its nourishment from the soil, is liable to be tithed." It is laid down: " Of dill one must tithe the seeds, the leaves and the stalks." So, then, it was laid down that every man must lay aside one-tenth of his produce for God.

The point of Jesus's saying is this. It was universally accepted that tithes of the main crops must be given. But mint and dill and cummin are herbs of the kitchen garden and would not be grown in any quantity; a man would have only a little patch of them. All three were used in cooking, and dill and cummin had medicinal uses. To tithe them was to tithe an infinitesimally small crop, maybe not much more than the produce of one plant. Only those who were superlatively meticulous would tithe the single plants of the kitchen garden.

That is precisely what the Pharisees were like. They were so absolutely meticulous about tithes that they would tithe even one clump of mint; and yet these same men could be guilty of injustice; could be hard and arrogant and cruel, forgetting the claims of mercy; could take oaths and pledges and promises with the deliberate intention of evading them, forgetting fidelity. In other words, many of them kept the trifles of the Law and forgot the things which really matter.

That spirit is not dead; it never will be until Christ rules in the hearts of men. There is many a man who wears the right clothes to church, carefully hands in his offering to the Church, adopts the right attitude at prayer, is never absent from the celebration of the sacrament, and who is not doing an honest day's work and is irritable and bad-tempered and mean with his money. There are women who are full of good works and who serve on all kinds of committees, and whose children are lonely for them at night. There is nothing easier than to observe all the outward actions of religion and yet be completely irreligious.

There is nothing more necessary than a sense of proportion to save us from confusing religious observances with real devotion.

Jesus uses a vivid illustration. In verse 24 a curious thing has happened in the Authorized Version. It should not be to strain *at* a gnat, but to strain *out* a gnat as in the Revised Standard Version. Originally that mistake was simply a misprint but it has been perpetuated for centuries. In point of fact the older versions—Tyndale, Coverdale, and the Geneva Bible—all correctly have to strain *out* a gnat. The picture is this. A gnat was an insect and therefore unclean; and so was a camel. In order to avoid the risk of drinking anything unclean, wine was strained through muslin gauze so that any possible impurity might be strained *out* of it. This is a humorous picture which must have raised a laugh, of a man carefully straining his wine through gauze to avoid swallowing a microscopic insect and yet cheerfully swallowing a camel. It is the picture of a man who has completely lost his sense of proportion.

THE REAL CLEANNESS

Matthew 23 : 25, 26

> " Alas for you, Scribes and Pharisees, hypocrites! for you cleanse
> the outside of the cup and the plate, but inside they are full of
> rapacity and lust. Blind Pharisee! cleanse the inside of the cup and
> the plate first, that the outside of it also may be clean."

THE idea of uncleanness is continually arising in the Jewish
Law. It must be remembered that this uncleanness was not
physical uncleanness. An unclean vessel was not in our sense of
the term a dirty vessel. For a person to be ceremonially unclean
meant that he could not enter the Temple or the synagogue; he
was debarred from the worship of God. A man was unclean if,
for instance, he touched a dead body, or came into contact with
a Gentile. A woman was unclean if she had a haemorrhage,
even if that haemorrhage was perfectly normal and healthy. If a
person who was himself unclean touched any vessel, that vessel
became unclean; and, thereafter, any other person who touched
or handled the vessel became in turn unclean. It was, therefore,
of paramount importance to have vessels cleansed; and the law
for cleansing them is fantastically complicated. We can quote
only certain basic examples of it.

An *earthen* vessel which is *hollow* becomes unclean only on
the inside and not on the outside; and it can be cleansed only by
being broken. The following cannot become unclean at all—a
flat plate without a rim, an open coal-shovel, a grid-iron with
holes in it for parching grains of wheat. On the other hand, a
plate with a rim, or an earthen spice-box, or a writing-case
can become unclean. Of vessels made of leather, bone, wood
and glass, flat ones do not become unclean; deep ones do. If
they are broken, they become clean. Any metal vessel which
is at once smooth and hollow can become unclean; but a door,
a bolt, a lock, a hinge, a knocker cannot become unclean. If a
thing is made of wood *and* metal, then the wood can become
unclean, but the metal cannot. These regulations seem to us

fantastic, and yet these are the regulations the Pharisees meticulously kept.

The food or drink inside a vessel might have been obtained by cheating or extortion or theft; it might be luxurious and gluttonous; that did not matter, so long as the vessel itself was ceremonially clean. Here is another example of fussing about trifles and letting the weightier matters go.

Grotesque as the whole thing may seem, it can happen yet. A church can be torn in two about the colour of a carpet, or a pulpit-fall, or about the shape or metal of the cups to be used in the Sacrament. The last thing that men and women seem to learn in matters of religion is a relative sense of values; and the tragedy is that it is so often magnification of matters of no importance which wreck the peace.

DISGUISED DECAY

Matthew 23:27, 28

" Alas for you, Scribes and Pharisees! for you are like white-washed tombs, which look beautiful on the outside, but inside are full of the bones of dead men, and of all corruption. So you, too, outwardly look righteous to men, but inwardly you are full of hypocrisy and lawlessness."

HERE again is a picture which any Jew would understand. One of the commonest places for tombs was by the wayside. We have already seen that anyone who touched a dead body became unclean (*Numbers* 19: 16). Therefore, anyone who came into contact with a tomb automatically became unclean. At one time in particular the roads of Palestine were crowded with pilgrims—at the time of the Passover Feast. For a man to become unclean on his way to the Passover Feast would be a disaster, for that meant he would be debarred from sharing in it. It was then Jewish practice in the month of Adar to whitewash all wayside tombs, so that no pilgrims might accidentally come into contact with one of them and be rendered unclean.

So, as a man journeyed the roads of Palestine on a spring day, these tombs would glint white, and almost lovely, in the sunshine; but within they were full of bones and bodies whose touch would defile. That, said Jesus, was a precise picture of what the Pharisees were. Their outward actions were the actions of intensely religious men; their inward hearts were foul and putrid with sin.

It can still happen. As Shakespeare had it, a man may smile and smile and be a villain. A man may walk with bowed head and reverent steps and folded hands in the posture of humility, and all the time be looking down with cold contempt on those whom he regards as sinners. His very humility may be the pose of pride; and, as he walks so humbly, he may be thinking with relish of the picture of piety which he presents to those who are watching him. There is nothing harder than for a good man not to know that he is good; and once he knows he is good, his goodness is gone, however he may appear to men from the outside.

THE TAINT OF MURDER

Matthew 23: 29–36

" Alas for you, Scribes and Pharisees, hypocrites! for you erect the tombs of the prophets, and adorn the memorials of the righteous, and say, ' If we had lived in the days of our fathers, we would not have been partners with them in the murder of the prophets.' Thus you witness against yourselves that you are the sons of those who slew the prophets. Fill up the measure of your fathers. Serpents, brood of vipers, how are you to escape being condemned to hell fire? For this reason, look you, I send you the prophets and the wise men and the scribes. Some of them you will kill and crucify; and some of them you will scourge in your synagogues, and pursue them with persecution from city to city, that on you there may fall the responsibility for all the righteous blood shed upon the earth from the blood of Abel, the righteous, to the blood of Zacharias, the son of Barachios, whom you murdered between the

Temple and the altar. This is the truth I tell you—the responsibility for all these crimes shall fall on this generation."

JESUS is charging the Jews that the taint of murder is in their
history and that that taint has not even yet worked itself out.
The Scribes and Pharisees tend the tombs of the martyrs and
beautify their memorials, and claim that, if they had lived in the
old days, they would not have slain the prophets and the men of
God. But that is precisely what they would have done, and
precisely what they are going to do.

Jesus's charge is that the history of Israel is the history of the
murder of the men of God. He says that the righteous men from
Abel to Zacharias were murdered. Why are these two chosen?
The murder of Abel by Cain everyone knows; but the murder of
Zacharias is not nearly so well known. The story is told in a
grim little cameo in 2 *Chronicles* 24: 20–22. It happened in the
days of Joash. Zacharias rebuked the nation for their sin, and
Joash stirred up the people to stone him to death in the very
Temple court; and Zacharias died saying, " May the Lord see
and avenge! " (Zacharias is called the son of Barachios,
whereas, in fact, he was the son of Jehoiada, no doubt a slip of
the gospel writer in retelling the story.)

Why should Zacharias be chosen? In the Hebrew Bible
Genesis is the first book, as it is in ours; but, unlike our order of
the books, 2 *Chronicles* is the last in the Hebrew Bible. We
could say that the murder of Abel is the first in the Bible story,
and the murder of Zacharias the last. From beginning to end,
the history of Israel is the rejection, and often the slaughter, of
the men of God.

Jesus is quite clear that the murder taint is still there. He
knows that now he must die, and that in the days to come his messengers will be persecuted and ill-treated and rejected and slain.

Here indeed is tragedy; the nation which God chose and
loved had turned their hands against him; and the day of
reckoning was to come.

It makes us think. When history judges us, will its verdict be
that we were the hinderers or the helpers of God? That is a

question which every individual, and every nation, must answer.

THE REJECTION OF LOVE'S APPEAL

Matthew 23: 37–39

' Jerusalem, Jerusalem, killer of the prophets, stoner of those sent to you, how often have I wished to gather your children together, as a bird gathers her nestlings under her wings—and you refused. Look you, your house is left to you desolate, for I tell you from now you will not see me until you will say, ' Blessed in the name of the Lord is he that comes.' "

HERE is all the poignant tragedy of rejected love. Here Jesus speaks, not so much as the stern judge of all the earth, as the lover of the souls of men.

There is one curious light this passage throws on the life of Jesus which we may note in the passing. According to the Synoptic Gospels Jesus was never in Jerusalem after his public ministry began, until he came to this last Passover Feast. We can see here how much the gospel story leaves out, for Jesus could not have said what he says here unless he had paid repeated visits to Jerusalem and issued to the people repeated appeals. A passage like this shows us that in the gospels we have the merest sketch and outline of the life of Jesus.

This passage shows us four great truths.

(i) It shows us *the patience of God*. Jerusalem had killed the prophets and stoned the messengers of God; yet God did not cast her off; and in the end he sent his Son. There is a limitless patience in the love of God which bears with men's sinning and will not cast them off.

(ii) It shows us *the appeal of Jesus*. Jesus speaks as the lover. He will not force an entry; the only weapon he can use is the appeal of love. He stands with outstretched hands of appeal, an appeal which men have the awful responsibility of being able to accept or to refuse.

(iii) It shows us *the deliberation of the sin of man*. Men looked on Christ in all the splendour of his appeal—and refused him. There is no handle on the outside of the door of the human heart; it must be opened from the inside; and sin is the open-eyed deliberate refusal of the appeal of God in Jesus Christ.

(iv) It shows us *the consequences of rejecting Christ*. Only forty years were to pass and in A.D. 70 Jerusalem would be a heap of ruins. That disaster was the direct consequence of the rejection of Jesus Christ. Had the Jews accepted the Christian way of love and abandoned the way of power politics, Rome would never have descended on them with its avenging might. It is the fact of history—even in time—that the nation which rejects God is doomed to disaster.

THE VISION OF THINGS TO COME

WE have already seen that it is one of the great characteristics of Matthew that he gathers together in large blocks the teaching of Jesus about different subjects. In chapter 24 he gathers together things that Jesus said about the future and gives us the vision of things to come. In so doing Matthew weaves together sayings of Jesus about different aspects of the future; and it will make this difficult chapter very much easier to understand if we can disentangle the various strands and look at them one by one.

Matthew's interweaving of the sayings of Jesus lasts throughout the first 31 verses of the chapter. It will be best if, first of all, we set down these verses as a whole; if, next, we set down the various aspects of the future with which they deal; and if, last, we try to assign each section to its place in the pattern. We cannot claim certainty or finality for the pattern which we obtain; but, the general picture will become clear.

First then, we set down the verses, and we shall number them to make easier their assignment to their place in the pattern.

THE VISION OF THE FUTURE

Matthew 24: 1–31

1. When Jesus had left the precincts of the Temple, he was going away; and his disciples came to him to point out to him the
2. buildings of the Temple area. He said to them, " Do you not see all these things? This is the truth I tell you—one stone will not be left here upon another that will not be thrown down."
3. His disciples came to him privately when he was sitting on the Mount of Olives. " Tell us," they said, " when these things shall be. And tell us what will be the sign of your coming, and of the
4. consummation of the age." Jesus answered, " Be on the look-out
5. lest anyone lead you astray, for many will come in my name saying, ' I am God's Anointed One,' and they will lead many
6. astray. You will hear of wars and reports of wars. See that you are not disturbed; for these things must happen; but the end is not
7. yet. For nation shall rise against nation, and kingdom against kingdom, and there will be famines and earthquakes in various
8. places. All these things are the beginning of the agonies. Then
9. they will deliver you to affliction, and they will kill you, and you
10. will be hated by all nations because of my name. And then many will stumble, and will betray each other, and will hate each other.
11. And many false prophets will arise, and they will lead many
12. astray. And the love of many will grow cold, because lawlessness
13. will be multiplied. But it is he who endures to the end who will be
14. saved. And the gospel will be proclaimed to the whole inhabited world, for a testimony to all nations—and then the end will come.
15. When you see the desolating abomination, which was spoken of by the prophet Daniel, standing in the Holy Place (let him who
16. reads understand), then let him who is in Judaea flee to the
17. mountains. Let him who is on the housetop not come down to
18. remove his goods from his house; and let him who is in the field
19. not come back to remove his cloak. Alas for those who in those days are carrying children in the womb, and who are suckling
20. children. Pray that your flight may not be in the winter time, nor
21. on a Sabbath. For at that time there will be great affliction, such as has never happened from the beginning of the world until now,
22. and such as never will happen. And, if the days had not been shortened, no human being would have survived. But the days

23. will be shortened for the sake of the elect. At that time, if anyone says to you, ' Look you, here, or here, is the Anointed One of
24. God,' do not believe him. For false Messiahs and false prophets will arise, and they will produce great signs and wonders, the consequences of which will be, if possible, to lead astray the elect.
25. Look you, I have told you about these things before they happen.
26. If anyone says to you, ' Look you, he is in the wilderness,' do not go out. ' Look you, he is in the inner chambers,' do not believe him. For as the lightning comes from the east and shines as far as
28. the west, so shall be the coming of the Son of Man. Where the
29. body is, there the vultures will be gathered. Immediately after the affliction of these days the sun will be darkened, and the moon will not give her light, and the stars will fall from heaven, and the
30. powers of heaven will be shaken. Then there will appear the sign of the Son of Man in heaven. And then all the tribes of the earth will lament, and they will see the Son of Man coming on the
31. clouds of heaven with power and much glory. And he will send his angels with a great trumpet call, and they will gather the elect from the four winds, from one boundary of heaven to the other."

THE INTERWEAVING OF THE STRANDS

THERE then is the composite vision of the future which Matthew collects for us; we must now try to disentangle the various strands in it. At this stage we only indicate the strands and leave fuller explanation for the detailed commentary.

(i) Some verses which foretell the terrible days of *the siege of Jerusalem* by Titus, the Roman general, a siege which was one of the most terrible in all history. These are verses 15–22.

(ii) Some verses tell of the ultimate complete *destruction of Jerusalem* and its reduction to a heap of ruins. These are verses 1 and 2.

(iii) Some verses paint pictures taken from the Jewish conception of the *Day of the Lord*. We have spoken about that conception before but we must briefly outline it again. The Jews divided all time into two ages—this present age, and the age to come. The present age is wholly bad and beyond all hope of human reformation. It can be mended only by the direct intervention of God. When God does intervene the golden age, the age to come, will arrive. But in between the two ages there will come the *Day of the Lord*, which will be a time of terrible and fearful upheaval, like the birth-pangs of a new age.

In the Old Testament itself there is many a picture of the Day of the Lord; and in the Jewish books written between the Old and the New Testaments these pictures are further developed and made still more vivid and still more terrible.

It will be a time of *terror*. " A day of wrath is that day, a day of distress and anguish, a day of ruin and devastation, a day of darkness and gloom, a day of clouds and thick darkness " (*Zephaniah* 1: 14–18). The pictures of that terror became ever more lurid.

It will come *suddenly*. " The Day of the Lord will come like a thief in the night " (1 *Thessalonians* 5: 2). " Three things," said the Rabbis, " are sudden—the coming of the Messiah, a discovery, and a scorpion."

The universe will be *shattered to pieces*. The sun will be turned into darkness and the moon into blood (*Joel* 2: 30, 31; *Isaiah* 13: 10, 13).

It will be a time of *moral chaos*, when moral standards will be turned upside down, and when even nature will act contrary to herself, and when wars and violence and hatred will be the common atmosphere of life.

Schürer (*The Jewish People in the Time of Christ* ii, 154) sums up the Jewish ideas of the day of the Lord, ideas with which Jewish literature was full and which everyone knew in the time of Jesus. " The sun and moon will be darkened, swords appear in heaven, trains of horses and foot march through the clouds. Everything in nature falls into commotion and confusion. The sun appears by night, the moon by day. Blood trickles from wood, the stone gives forth a voice, and salt is found in fresh water. Places that have been sown will appear as unsown, full barns be found empty, and the springs of wells be stopped. Among men all restraints of order will be dissolved, sin and ungodliness rule upon earth. And men will fight against each other as if stricken with madness, the friend against the friend, the son against the father, the daughter against the mother. Nation will rise against nation, and to war shall be added earthquake, fire and famine, whereby men shall be carried off."

Such were the terrible pictures of the day of the Lord.. The verses are 6–8 and 29–31.

(iv) Some verses deal with the *persecution* which the followers of Christ will have to endure. These are verses 9 and 10.

(v) Some verses deal with the *threats* which will develop against the life and purity of the Church. These are verses 4 and 5, 11–13, 23–26.

(vi) Some verses speak directly of the *Second Coming* of Christ. These are verses 3, 14, 27 and 28.

So, in this amazing and difficult chapter of *Matthew*, we have in the first 31 verses a kind of sixfold vision of the future. We now go on to look at this vision, not taking the verses of the chapter consecutively, but taking together in turn those which deal with each strand.

THE DOOM OF THE HOLY CITY

Matthew 24: 1, 2

When Jesus had left the precincts of the Temple, he was going away; and his disciples came to him to point out to him the buildings of the Temple area. He said to them, " Do you not see all these things? This is the truth I tell you—one stone will not be left here upon another that will not be thrown down."

IT may well be that at least some of the disciples had not been very often to Jerusalem. They were Galilaeans, men of the highlands and of the country, fishermen who knew the lakeside far better than they knew the city. Some of them at least would be like country folk come up to London for a visit, staggered by what they saw; and well they might be, for there was nothing quite like the Temple in the ancient world.

The summit of Mount Sion had been dug away to leave a plateau of 1,000 feet square. At the far end of it was the Temple itself (the *naos*). It was built of white marble plated with gold, and it shone in the sun so that a man could scarcely bear to look at it. Between the lower city and the Temple mount lay the valley of the Tyropoeon, and across this valley stretched a colossal bridge. Its arches had a span of $41\frac{1}{2}$ feet, and its spring stones were 24 feet long by 6 inches thick. The Temple area was surrounded by great porches, Solomon's Porch and the Royal Porch. These porches were upheld by pillars, cut out of solid blocks of marble in one piece. They were $37\frac{1}{2}$ feet high, and of such a thickness that three men linked together could scarcely put their arms round them. At the corners of the Temple angle stones have been found which measure from 20 to 40 feet in length, and which weigh more than 100 tons. How they were ever cut and placed in position is one of the mysteries of ancient engineering. Little wonder that the Galilaean fishermen looked and called Jesus's attention to them.

Jesus answered that the day would come when not one of these stones would be left standing upon the other—and Jesus was right. In A.D. 70 the Romans, finally exasperated by the rebellious intransigence of the Jews, gave up all attempt at pacification and turned to destruction, and Jerusalem and the Temple were laid waste so that Jesus's prophecy literally came true.

Here speaks Jesus the prophet. Jesus knew that the way of power politics can end only in doom. The man and the nation which will not take the way of God are heading for disaster —even in material things. The man and the nation which refuse the dream of God will find their own dreams shattered also.

THE GRIM TERROR OF THE SIEGE

Matthew 24: 15–22

" When you see the desolating abomination, which was spoken of by the prophet Daniel, standing in the Holy Place (let him who reads understand), then let him who is in Judaea flee to the mountains. Let him who is on the housetop not come down to remove his goods from his house; and let him who is in the field not come back to remove his cloak. Alas for those who in those days are carrying children in the womb, and who are suckling children. Pray that your flight may not be in the winter time, nor on a Sabbath. For at that time there will be great affliction, such as has never happened from the beginning of the world until now, and such as never will happen. And, if the days had not been shortened, no human being would have survived. But the days will be shortened for the sake of the elect."

THE siege of Jerusalem was one of the most terrible sieges in all history. Jerusalem was obviously a difficult city to take, being a city set upon a hill and defended by religious fanatics; so Titus determined to starve it out.

No one quite knows what the *desolating abomination* is. The phrase itself comes from *Daniel* 12: 11. There it is said that the *abomination that makes desolate* is set up in the Temple. The *Daniel* reference is quite clear. About 170 B.C. Antiochus Epiphanes, the king of Syria, determined to stamp out Judaism and to introduce into Judaea Greek religion and Greek practices. He captured Jerusalem, and desecrated the Temple by erecting an altar to Olympian Zeus in the Temple Court and by sacrificing swines' flesh upon it, and by turning the priests' rooms and the Temple chambers into public brothels. It was a deliberate attempt to stamp out Jewish religion.

It was the prophecy of Jesus that the same thing would happen again, and that once again the Holy Place would be desecrated, as indeed it was. Jesus saw coming upon Jerusalem a repetition of the terrible things which had happened 200 years ago; only this time there would arise no Judas Maccabaeus; this time there would be no deliverance and no purification; there would be nothing but ultimate destruction.

Jesus foretold of that siege that unless its days had been shortened, no human being could have survived it. It is strange to see how Jesus gave practical advice which was not taken, the disregarding of which multiplied the disaster. Jesus's advice was that when that day came men ought to flee to the mountains. They did not; they crammed themselves into the city and into the walls of Jerusalem from all over the country, and that very folly multiplied the grim horror of the famine of the siege a hundredfold.

When we go to the history of Josephus we see how right Jesus was about that terrible future. Josephus writes of these fearful days of siege and famine: " Then did the famine widen its progress, and devoured the people by whole houses and families; the upper rooms were full of women and children that were dying of famine; and the lanes of the city were full of the dead bodies of the aged; the children also and the young men wandered about the market-places like shadows, all swelled with famine, and fell down dead wheresoever their misery seized them. As for burying them, those that were sick themselves were not able to do it; and those that were hearty and well were deterred from doing it by the great multitude of those dead bodies, and by the uncertainty there was how soon they should die themselves, for many died as they were burying others, and many went to their coffins before the fatal hour was come. Nor was there any lamentation made under these calamities, nor were heard any mournful complaints; but the famine confounded all natural passions; for those who were just going to die looked upon those who were gone to their rest before them with dry eyes and open mouths. A deep silence, also, and a kind of deadly night had seized upon the city. . . . And every one of them died with their eyes fixed upon the Temple " (Josephus, *Wars of the Jews*, 5. 12. 3).

Josephus tells a dreadful story of a woman who in those days actually killed and roasted and ate her suckling child (6. 3. 4). He tells us that even the Romans, when they had taken the city and were going through it to plunder, were so stricken with horror at the sights they saw that they could not but stay their hands. " When the Romans were come to the houses to plunder them, they found in them entire families of dead men, and the upper rooms full of dead corpses. . . . They then stood on a horror of this sight, and went out without touching anything "

(6. 8. 5). Josephus himself shared in the horrors of this siege, and he tells us that 97,000 were taken captive and enslaved, and 1,100,000 died.

That is what Jesus foresaw; these are the things he fore-warned. We must never forget that not only men but nations need the wisdom of Christ. Unless the leaders of the nations are themselves led by Christ, they cannot do other than lead men not only to spiritual but also to physical disaster. Jesus was no impractical dreamer; he laid down the laws by which alone a nation can prosper, and by disregard of which it can do no other than miserably perish.

THE DAY OF THE LORD

Matthew 24: 6–8, 29–31

" You will hear of wars and reports of wars. See that you are not disturbed; for these things must happen; for the end is not yet. For nation shall rise against nation, and kingdom against kingdom, and there will be famines and earthquakes in various places.

. . . .

Immediately after the affliction of these days the sun will be darkened, and the moon will not give her light, and the stars will fall from heaven, and the powers of heaven will be shaken. Then there will appear the sign of the Son of Man in heaven. And then all the tribes of the earth will lament, and they will see the Son of Man coming in the clouds of heaven with power and much glory. And he will send his angels with a great trumpet call, and they will gather the elect from the four winds, from one boundary of heaven to the other."

WE have already seen that an essential part of the Jewish thought of the future was the *Day of the Lord*, that day when God was going to intervene directly in history, and when the present age, with all its incurable evil, would begin to be transformed into the age to come.

Very naturally the New Testament writers to a very great extent identified the Second Coming of Jesus and the Day of the

Lord; and they took over all the imagery which had to do with the Day of the Lord and applied them to the Second Coming. None of these pictures is to be taken literally; they *are* pictures, and they *are* visions; they are attempts to put the indescribable into human words and to find some kind of picture for happenings for which human language has no picture.

But from all these pictures there emerge certain great truths.

(i) They tell us that God has not abandoned the world; for all its wickedness, the world is still the scene in which God's purpose is being worked out. It is not abandonment that God contemplates; it is intervention.

(ii) They tell us that even a very crescendo of evil must not discourage us. An essential part of the Jewish picture of the Day of the Lord is that a complete breakdown of all moral standards and an apparent complete disintegration of the world must precede it. But, for all that, this is not the prelude to destruction; it is the prelude to recreation.

(iii) They tell us that both judgment and a new creation are certain. They tell us that God contemplates the world both in justice and in mercy; and that God's plan is not the obliteration of the world, but the creation of a world which is nearer to his heart's desire.

The value of these pictures is not in their details, which at best are only symbolic and which use the only pictures which the minds of men could conceive, but in the eternal truth which they conserve; and the basic truth in them is that, whatever the world is like, God has not abandoned it.

THE PERSECUTION TO COME

Matthew 24: 9, 10

" Then they will deliver you to affliction, and they will kill you, and you will be hated by all nations because of my name. And then many will stumble and will betray each other, and will hate each other."

THIS passage shows the uncompromising honesty of Jesus. He never promised his disciples an easy way; he promised them death and suffering and persecution. There is a sense in which a real Church will always be a persecuted Church, so long as it exists in a world which is not a Christian world. Whence comes that persecution?

(i) Christ offers a *new loyalty*; and again and again he declared that this new loyalty must surpass all earthly ties. The greatest ground of hatred in the days of the early Church was the fact that Christianity split homes and families, when one member decided for Christ and the others did not. The Christian is one who is pledged to give Jesus Christ the first place in his life—and many a human clash is liable to result from that.

(ii) Christ offers a *new standard*. There are customs and practices and ways of life which may be all right for the world, but which are far from being all right for the Christian. For many people the difficulty about Christianity is that it is a judgment upon themselves and upon their way of life in their business or in their personal relationships. The awkward thing about Christianity is that anyone who does not wish to be changed is bound to hate it and resent it.

(iii) The Christian, if he is a true Christian, introduces into the world a *new example*. There is a daily beauty in his life which makes the life of others ugly. The Christian is the light of the world, not in the sense that he criticizes and condemns others, but in the sense that he demonstrates in himself the beauty of the Christ-filled life and therefore the ugliness of the Christless life.

(iv) This is all to say that Christianity brings a *new conscience* into life. Neither the individual Christian nor the Christian Church can ever know anything of a cowardly concealment or a cowardly silence. The Church and the individual Christian must at all times constitute the conscience of Christianity—and it is characteristic of men that there are many times when they would wish to silence conscience.

THREATS TO THE FAITH

Matthew 24: 4, 5, 11–13, 23–26

Jesus answered, " Be on the look-out lest anyone lead you astray, for many will come in my name saying, ' I am God's Anointed One,' and they will lead many astray.

.   .   .   .

And many false prophets will arise, and they will lead many astray. And the love of many will grow cold, because lawlessness will be multiplied. But it is he who endures to the end who will be saved.

.   .   .   .

At that time, if anyone says to you, ' Look you, here, or here, is the Anointed One of God,' do not believe him. For false Messiahs and false prophets will arise, and they will produce great signs and wonders, the consequence of which will be, if possible, to lead astray the elect. Look you, I have told you about these things before they happen. If anyone says to you, ' Look you, he is in the wilderness,' do not go out. ' Look you, he is in the inner chambers,' do not believe him."

IN the days to come Jesus saw that two dangers would threaten the Church.

(i) There would be the danger of *false leaders*. A false leader is a man who seeks to propagate his own version of the truth rather than the truth as it is in Jesus Christ; and a man who tries to attach other men to himself rather than to Jesus Christ. The inevitable result is that a false leader spreads division instead of building up unity. The test of any leader is likeness to Christ.

(ii) The second danger is that of *discouragement*. There are those whose love will grow cold because of the increasing lawlessness of the world. The true Christian is the man who holds to his belief, when belief is at its most difficult; and who, in the most discouraging circumstances, refuses to believe that God's arm is shortened or his power grown less.

THE COMING OF THE KING

Matthew 24: 3, 14, 27, 28

His disciples came to him privately, when he was sitting on the Mount of Olives. " Tell us," they said, " when these things shall be. And tell us what will be the sign of your coming, and of the consummation of the age."

. . . .

The gospel will be proclaimed to the whole inhabited world, for a testimony to all nations—and then the end will come.

. . . .

For as the lightning comes from the east and shines as far as the west, so shall be the coming of the Son of Man. Where the body is, there the vultures will be gathered together."

HERE Jesus speaks of his Second Coming directly. The New Testament does not ever use the phrase *the Second Coming*. The word which it uses to describe the return of Christ in glory is interesting. It is *Parousia*; this word has come into English as a description of the Second Coming; it is quite common in the rest of the New Testament, but in the gospels this is the only chapter in which it occurs (verses 3, 27, 37, 39). The interesting thing is that it is the regular word for the arrival of a governor into his province or for the coming of a king to his subjects. It regularly describes a coming in authority and in power.

The remainder of this chapter will have much to tell us about it, but at the moment we note that, whatever else is true about the doctrine of the Second Coming, it certainly conserves two great facts.

(i) It conserves the fact of the ultimate triumph of Christ. He whom men crucified on a cross will one day be the Lord of all men. For Jesus Christ the end is sure—and that end is his universal kingship.

(ii) It conserves the fact that history is going somewhere. Sometimes men have felt that history was plunging to an ever wilder and wilder chaos, that it is nothing more than " the record of the sins and follies of men." Sometimes men have felt that history was cyclic and that the same weary round of things would happen over and over again. The Stoics believed that there are certain fixed periods, that at the end of each the world is destroyed in a great conflagration; and that then the same story in every littlest detail takes place all over again.

As Chrysippus had it: " Then again the world is restored anew in a precisely similar arrangement as before. The stars again move in their orbits, each performing its revolution in the former period, without any variation. Socrates and Plato and each individual man will live again, with the same friends and fellow-citizens. They will go through the same experiences and the same activities. Every city and village and field will be restored, just as it was. And this restoration of the universe takes place, not once, but over and over again—indeed to all eternity, without end." This is a grim thought that men are bound to an eternal tread-mill in which there is no progress and from which there is no escape.

But the Second Coming has in it this essential truth—that there is " one divine far-off event, to which the whole creation moves," and that event is not dissolution but the universal and eternal rule of God.

THE COMING OF THE KING

Matthew 24: 32–41

" Learn the lesson which comes from the fig tree. Whenever the branch has become tender, and puts forth its leaves, you know that summer is near. Even so, when you too see these things, know that he is near at the doors. This is the truth I tell you—this generation shall not pass away, until these things have happened. Heaven and earth will pass away, but my words will not pass away.

No one knows about that day and hour, not even the angels of heaven, not even the Son, but only the Father. As were the days of

Noah, so will be the coming of the Son of Man. For, as in those days before the flood they spent their time eating and drinking, marrying and giving in marriage, until the day that Noah entered into the ark, and were quite unaware of what was to happen until the flood came and swept them all away, so will be the coming of the Son of Man. At that time there will be two men in the field; one is taken, and the other is left. There will be two women grinding with the mill; one is taken, and the other is left."

FEW passages confront us with greater difficulties than this. It is in two sections and they seem to contradict each other. The first (verses 32–35) seems to indicate that, as a man can tell by the signs of nature when summer is on the way, so he can tell by the signs of the world when the Second Coming is on the way. Then it seems to go on to say that the Second Coming will happen within the lifetime of the generation listening to Jesus at that moment.

The second section (verses 36–41) says quite definitely that no one knows the time of the Second Coming, not the angels, not even Jesus himself, but only God; and that it will come upon men with the suddenness of a rainstorm out of a blue sky.

There is a very real difficulty here which, even if we cannot completely solve it, we must nevertheless boldly face.

Let us take as our starting-point verse 34: " This is the truth I tell you—this generation shall not pass away, until these things have happened." When we consider that saying, three possibilities emerge.

(*a*) If Jesus said it in reference to the Second Coming, he was mistaken for he did not return within the lifetime of the generation listening to his words. Many accept that point of view, believing that Jesus in his humanity had limitations of knowledge and did believe that within that generation he would return. We can readily accept that in his humanity Jesus had limitations of knowledge; but it is difficult to believe that he was in error regarding so great a spiritual truth as this.

b) It is possible that Jesus said something like this which was changed in the transmitting. In *Mark* 9: 1 Jesus is reported as saying, " Truly I say to you, there are some standing here who will not taste death before they see the Kingdom of God come with power." That was gloriously and triumphantly true. Within that generation the Kingdom of God did spread mightily until there were Christians throughout the known world.

Now the early Christians did look for the Second Coming immediately. In their situation of suffering and persecution they looked and longed for the release that the coming of their Lord would bring, and sometimes they took sayings which were intended to speak of the *Kingdom* and attached them to the *Second Coming* which is a very different thing. Something like that may have happened here. What Jesus may have said was that his *kingdom* would come mightily before that generation had passed away.

(c) But there is a third possibility. What if the phrase *until these things have happened* has no reference to the Second Coming? What if their reference is, in fact, to the prophecy with which the chapter began, the siege and fall of Jerusalem? If we accept that, there is no difficulty. What Jesus is saying is that these grim warnings of his regarding the doom of Jerusalem will be fulfilled within that very generation—and they were, in fact, fulfilled forty years later. It seems by far the best course to take verses 32–35 as referring, not to the Second Coming, but to the doom of Jerusalem, for then all the difficulties in them are removed.

Verses 36–41 do refer to the Second Coming; and they tell us certain most important truths.

(i) They tell us that the hour of that event is known to God and to God alone. It is, therefore, clear that speculation regarding the time of the Second Coming is nothing less than blasphemy, for the man who so speculates is seeking to wrest from God secrets which belong to God alone. It is not any man's duty to speculate; it is his duty to prepare himself, and to watch.

(ii) They tell us that that time will come with shattering suddenness on those who are immersed in material things. In the old story Noah prepared himself in the calm weather for the flood which was to come, and when it came he was ready. But the rest of mankind were lost in their eating and drinking and marrying and giving in marriage, and were caught completely unawares, and were therefore swept away. These verses are a warning never to become so immersed in time that we forgot eternity, never to let our concern with worldly affairs, however necessary, completely distract us from remembering that there is a God, that the issues of life and death are in his hands, and that whenever his call comes, at morning, at midday, or at evening, it must find us ready.

(iii) They tell us that the coming of Christ will be a time of separation and of judgment, when he will gather to himself those who are his own.

Beyond these things we cannot go—for God has kept the ultimate knowledge to himself and his wisdom.

READY FOR THE COMING OF THE KING

Matthew 24: 42–51

" Watch, therefore, for you do not know on what day your Lord comes. Understand this—that if the householder had known at what watch of the night the thief was coming, he would have been awake, and he would not have allowed him to break into his house. That is why you, too, must show yourselves ready; for the Son of Man is coming at an hour you do not expect.

Who, then, is the dependable and wise servant whom his master put in charge over his household staff, to give them their food at the right time? Happy is the servant whom his master, when he has come, will find acting thus. This is the truth I tell you—he will put him in charge of all his belongings. But if that bad servant says to himself, ' My master will not be back for a long time yet,' and if he begins to beat his fellow-servants, and if he eats and drinks with drunkards, then the master of that servant will come on a day when he is not expecting him, and at an hour which he does not know, and will cut him in pieces, and assign him a place with the hypocrites. There will be weeping and gnashing of teeth there."

HERE is the practical outcome of all that has gone before. If the day and the hour of the coming of Christ are known to none save God, then all life must be a constant preparation for that coming. And, if that is so, there are certain basic sins.

(i) To live without watchfulness invites disaster. A thief does not send a letter saying when he is going to burgle a house; his principal weapon in his nefarious undertakings is surprise; therefore a householder who has valuables in his house must maintain a constant guard. But to get this picture right, we must remember that the watching of the Christian for the coming of Christ is not that of terror-stricken fear and shivering apprehension; it is the watching of eager expectation for the coming of glory and joy.

(ii) The spirit which leads to disaster is the spirit which says there is plenty of time. It is the comfortable delusion of the servant that he will have plenty of time to put things to rights before his master returns.

There is a fable which tells of three apprentice devils who were coming to this earth to finish their apprenticeship. They were talking to Satan, the chief of the devils, about their plans to tempt and ruin men. The first said, " I will tell them there is no God." Satan said, " That will not delude many, for they know that there is a God." The second said, " I will tell men there is no hell." Satan answered, " You will deceive no one that way; men know even now that there is a hell for sin." The third said, " I will tell men there is no hurry." " Go," said Satan, " and you will ruin them by the thousand." The most dangerous of all delusions is that there is plenty of time. The most dangerous day in a man's life is when he learns that there is such a word as *tomorrow*. There are things which must not be put off, for no man knows if for him tomorrow will ever come.

(iii) Rejection is based on failure in duty, and reward is based on fidelity. The servant who fulfilled his duty faithfully was given a still greater place; and the servant who failed was dealt with in severity. The inevitable conclusion is that, when he comes, Jesus Christ can find us employed in no better and greater task than in doing our duty.

A negro poet writes:

" There's a king and a captain high,
 And he's coming by and by,
 And he'll find me hoeing cotton when he comes.
 You can hear his legions charging in the regions of the sky,
 And he'll find me hoeing cotton when he comes.
 There's a man they thrust aside,
 Who was tortured till he died,
 And he'll find me hoeing cotton when he comes.
 He was hated and rejected,
 He was scorned and crucified,
 And he'll find me hoeing cotton when he comes.
 When he comes! When he comes!
 He'll be crowned by saints and angels when he comes.
 They'll be shouting out Hosanna! to the man that men denied,
 And I'll kneel among my cotton when he comes."

If a man is doing his duty, however simple that duty may be, on
the day Christ comes there will be joy for him.

THE FATE OF THE UNPREPARED

Matthew 25: 1–13

" What will happen in the Kingdom of Heaven is like the situation
which arose when ten virgins took their lamps and went out to
meet the bridegroom. Five of them were foolish and five were
wise. The foolish took their lamps, but did not take oil with them;
but the wise took oil in their vessels together with their lamps.
When the bridegroom was long in coming, all of them settled
down to rest and slept. In the middle of the night the cry went up,
' Look you, the bridegroom! Go out to meet him! ' Then all these
virgins awoke, and they prepared their lamps. The foolish ones
said to the wise ones. ' Give us some of your oil, for our lamps
have gone out.' But the wise answered, ' No; we cannot do that in
case there is not enough for us and for you. Go rather to those
who sell oil, and buy it for yourselves.' While they went away to
buy oil, the bridegroom came; and those who were ready entered
with him into the marriage celebrations, and the door was shut.

Later the rest of the virgins came too. ' Sir, sir,' they said, ' open the door to us.' But he answered, ' This is the truth I tell you—I do not know you.' Be on the watch then, for you do not know the day and the hour."

IF we look at this parable with western eyes, it may seem an unnatural and a " made-up " story. But, in point of fact, it tells a story which could have happened at any time in a Palestinian village and which could still happen today.

A wedding was a great occasion. The whole village turned out to accompany the couple to their new home, and they went by the longest possible road, in order that they might receive the glad good wishes of as many as possible. " Everyone," runs the Jewish saying, " from six to sixty will follow the marriage drum." The Rabbis agreed that a man might even abandon the study of the law to share in the joy of a wedding feast.

The point of this story lies in a Jewish custom which is very different from anything we know. When a couple married, they did not go away for a honeymoon; they stayed at home; for a week they kept open house; they were treated, and even addressed, as prince and princess; it was the gladdest week in all their lives. To the festivities of that week their chosen friends were admitted; and it was not only the marriage ceremony, it was also that joyous week that the foolish virgins missed, because they were unprepared.

The story of how they missed it all is perfectly true to life. Dr. J. Alexander Findlay tells of what he himself saw in Palestine. " When we were approaching the gates of a Galilaean town," he writes, " I caught a sight of ten maidens gaily clad and playing some kind of musical instrument, as they danced along the road in front of our car; when I asked what they were doing, the dragoman told me that they were going to keep the bride company till her bridegroom arrived. I asked him if there was any chance of seeing the wedding, but he shook his head, saying in effect: ' It might be tonight, or tomorrow night, or in a fortnight's time; nobody ever knows for certain.' Then he went on to explain that one of the great things to do, if you could, at a middle-class wedding in Palestine was to catch the bridal party napping. So the bridegroom comes unexpectedly, and sometimes in the middle of the night; it is true that he is required by public opinion to send a man along the street to shout: ' Behold! the bridegroom is coming! ' but that may happen at any time; so the bridal party have to be ready to go out into the street at any time to meet him, whenever he chooses to come. . . . Other important points are that no one is allowed on the streets after dark without a lighted lamp, and also that, when the bridegroom has once arrived, and the door has been shut, late-comers to the ceremony are not admitted." There the whole drama of Jesus's parable is re-enacted in the twentieth century. Here is no synthetic story but a slice of life from a village in Palestine.

Like so many of Jesus's parables, this one has an immediate and local meaning, and also a wider and universal meaning.

In its immediate significance it was directed against the Jews. They were the chosen people; their whole history should have been a preparation for the coming of the Son of God; they ought to have been prepared for him when he came. Instead they were quite unprepared and therefore were shut out. Here in dramatic form is the tragedy of the unpreparedness of the Jews.

But the parable has at least two universal warnings.

(i) It warns us that there are certain things which cannot be obtained at the last minute. It is far too late for a student to be preparing when the day of the examination has come. It is too late for a man to acquire a skill, or a character, if he does not already possess it, when some task offers itself to him. Similarly, it is easy to leave things so late that we can no longer prepare ourselves to meet with God. When Mary of Orange was dying, her chaplain sought to tell her of the way of salvation. Her answer was: " I have not left this matter to this hour." To be too late is always tragedy.

(ii) It warns us that there are certain things which cannot be borrowed. The foolish virgins found it impossible to borrow oil, when they discovered they needed it. A man cannot borrow a relationship with God; he must possess it for himself. A man cannot borrow a character; he must be clothed with it. We cannot always be living on the spiritual capital which others have amassed. There are certain things we must win or acquire for ourselves, for we cannot borrow them from others.

Tennyson took this parable and turned it into verse in the song the little novice sang to Guinevere the queen, when Guinevere had too late discovered the cost of sin:

> " Late, late so late! and dark the night and chill!
> Late, late so late! but we can enter still.
> Too late, too late! ye cannot enter now.
>
> No light had we; for that we do repent;
> And learning this, the bridegroom will relent.
> Too late, too late! ye cannot enter now.
>
> No light: so late! and dark and chill the night!
> O let us in, that we may find the light!
> Too late, too late: ye cannot enter now.
>
> Have we not heard the bridegroom is so sweet?
> O let us in, tho' late, to kiss his feet!
> No, no, too late! ye cannot enter now."

There is no knell so laden with regret as the sound of the words *too late*.

THE CONDEMNATION OF THE BURIED TALENT

Matthew 25: 14–30

" Even so, a man who was going abroad called his servants, and handed over his belongings to them. To one he gave a thousand pounds; to another five hundred pounds; to another two hundred and fifty pounds; to each according to his individual ability. So he went away. Straightway the man who had received the thousand pounds went and worked with them, and made another thousand pounds. In the same way the man who had received the five hundred pounds made another five hundred pounds of profit. But the man who had received the two hundred and fifty pounds went away and dug up the earth, and hid his master's money. After a long time the master of those servants came, and struck a reckoning with them. The one who had received the thousand pounds came and brought another thousand pounds. ' Sir,' he said, ' you gave me a thousand pounds. Look! I have made a profit of another thousand pounds.' His master said to him, ' Well done! good and faithful servant. You have been faithful in a few things; I will put you in charge over many things; enter into the joy of your master.' The one who had received the five hundred pounds came and said, ' Sir, you handed over to me five hundred pounds. Look! I have made a profit of another five hundred pounds.' His master said to him, ' Well done! good and faithful servant. You have been faithful in a few things. I will put you in charge over many things.' The one who had received the two hundred and fifty pounds came also. ' Sir,' he said, ' I knew that you are a harsh man, reaping where you did not sow, and gathering where you do not winnow. So I was afraid, and I went away and hid your two hundred and fifty pounds in the earth. Look! you have what is yours.' The master answered him, ' Evil and timid servant! You were well aware that I reap where I have not sowed, and that I gather where I have not winnowed. You ought to have put my money out to the bankers, and when I came I would have received back what is my own with interest. Take, then, the two hundred and fifty pounds from him, and give it to him who has the two thousand pounds. For to everyone who has, it will be given, and he will have abundance; but from him who has not, even what he has will be taken away from him. And cast the useless servant into the outer darkness. There shall be weeping and gnashing of teeth there.' "

LIKE the preceding one this parable had an immediate lesson for those who heard it for the first time, and a whole series of permanent lessons for us today. It is always known as the Parable of the Talents; in our translation we have changed the talents into modern currency. The *talent* was not a *coin*, it was a *weight*; and therefore its value obviously depended on whether the coinage involved was copper, gold or silver. The commonest metal involved was silver; and the value of a talent of silver was about £240. It is on that basis that we have made the translations of the various sums.

There can be no doubt that originally in this parable the whole attention is riveted on the useless servant. There can be little doubt that he stands for the Scribes and the Pharisees, and for their attitude to the Law and the truth of God. The useless servant buried his talent in the ground, in order that he might hand it back to his master exactly as it was. The whole aim of the Scribes and Pharisees was to keep the Law exactly as it was. In their own phrase, they sought " to build a fence around the Law." Any change, any development, any alteration, anything new was to them anathema. Their method involved the paralysis of religious truth.

Like the man with the talent, they desired to keep things exactly as they were—and it is for that that they are condemned. In this parable Jesus tells us that there can be no religion without adventure, and that God can find no use for the shut mind. But there is much more in this parable than that.

(i) It tells us that God gives men differing gifts. One man received five talents, another two, and another one. It is not a man's talent, which matters; what matters is how he uses it. God never demands from a man abilities which he has not got; but he does demand that a man should use to the full the abilities which he does possess. Men are not equal in talent; but men can be equal in effort. The parable tells us that whatever talent we have, little or great, we must lay it at the service of God.

(ii) It tells us that the reward of work well done is still more work to do. The two servants who had done well are not told to lean back and rest on their oars because they have done well. They are given greater tasks and greater responsibilities in the work of the master.

(iii) It tells us that the man who is punished is the man who will not try. The man with the one talent did not lose his talent; he simply did nothing with it. Even if he had adventured with it and lost it, it would have been better than to do nothing at all. It is always a temptation for the one talent man to say, " I have so small a talent and I can do so little with it. It is not worth while to try, for all the contribution I can make." The condemnation is for the man who, having even one talent, will not try to use it, and will not risk it for the common good.

(iv) It lays down a rule of life which is universally true. It tells us that to him who has more will be given, and he who has not will lose even what he has. The meaning is this. If a man has a talent and exercises it, he is progressively able to do more with it. But, if he has a talent and fails to exercise it, he will inevitably lose it. If we have some proficiency at a game or an art, if we have some gift for doing something, the more we exercise that proficiency and that gift, the harder the work and the bigger the task we will be able to tackle. Whereas, if we fail to use it, we lose it. That is equally true of playing golf or playing the piano, or singing songs or writing sermons, of carving wood or thinking out ideas. It is the lesson of life that the only way to keep a gift is to use it in the service of God and in the service of our fellow-men.

GOD'S STANDARD OF JUDGMENT

Matthew 25: 31–46

" When the Son of Man shall come in his glory, and all the angels with him, then he will take his seat upon the throne of his glory, and all nations will be assembled before him, and he will separate them from each other, as a shepherd separates the sheep from the goats, and he will place the sheep on his right hand and the goats on his left. Then the King will say to those on his right hand, ' Come, you who are blessed by my Father, enter into possession of the Kingdom which has been prepared for you since the creation of the world. For I was hungry, and you gave me to eat; I was thirsty, and you gave me to drink; I was a stranger, and you gathered me in; naked, and you clothed me; I was sick, and you came to visit me; in prison, and you came to me.' Then the righteous will answer him, ' Lord, when did we see you hungry, and nourish you? Or thirsty, and gave you to drink? When did we see you a stranger, and gather you to us? Or naked, and clothed you? When did we see you sick, or in prison, and come to you?' And the King will answer them, ' This is the truth I tell you— insomuch as you did it to one of the least of these my brothers, you did it to me.' then he will say to those on the left, ' Go from

me, you cursed ones, to the eternal fire prepared for the devil and
his angels. For I was hungry, and you did not give me to eat; I
was thirsty, and you did not give me to drink; I was a stranger,
and you did not gather me to you; naked, and you did not clothe
me; sick and in prison, and you did not come to visit me.' Then
these too will answer, ' Lord, when did we see you hungry, or
thirsty, or a stranger, or naked, or sick, or in prison, and did not
render service to you? ' Then he will answer them, ' This is the
truth I tell you—in so far as you did not do it to one of the least of
these, you did not do it to me.' And these will go away to eternal
punishment, but the righteous will go away to eternal life."

THIS is one of the most vivid parables Jesus ever spoke, and the
lesson is crystal clear—that God will judge us in accordance
with our reaction to human need. His judgment does not depend on the knowledge we have amassed, or the fame that we
have acquired, or the fortune that we have gained, but on the
help that we have given. And there are certain things which this
parable teaches us about the help which we must give.

(i) It must be help in simple things. The things which Jesus
picks out—giving a hungry man a meal, or a thirsty man a
drink, welcoming a stranger, cheering the sick, visiting the
prisoner—are things which anyone can do. It is not a question
of giving away thousands of pounds, or of writing our names in
the annals of history; it is a case of giving simple help to the
people we meet every day. There never was a parable which so
opened the way to glory to the simplest people.

(ii) It must be help which is uncalculating. Those who helped
did not think that they were helping Christ and thus piling up
eternal merit; they helped because they could not stop themselves. It was the natural, instinctive, quite uncalculating reaction of the loving heart. Whereas, on the other hand, the
attitude of those who failed to help was; ' If we had known it
was *you* we would gladly have helped; but we thought it was
only some common man who was not worth helping." It is still
true that there are those who will help if they are given praise
and thanks and publicity; but to help like that is not to help, it is
to pander to self-esteem. Such help is not generosity; it is

disguised selfishness. The help which wins the approval of God is that which is given for nothing but the sake of helping.

(iii) Jesus confronts us with the wonderful truth that all such help given is given to himself, and all such help withheld is withheld from himself. How can that be? If we really wish to delight a parent's heart, if we really wish to move him to gratitude the best way to do it is to help his child. God is the great Father; and the way to delight the heart of God is to help his children, our fellow-men.

There were two men who found this parable blessedly true. The one was Francis of Asissi; he was wealthy and high-born and high-spirited. But he was not happy. He felt that life was incomplete. Then one day he was out riding and met a leper, loathsome and repulsive in the ugliness of his disease. Something moved Francis to dismount and fling his arms around this wretched sufferer; and in his arms the face of the leper changed to the face of Christ.

The other was Martin of Tours. He was a Roman soldier and a Christian. One cold winter day, as he was entering a city, a beggar stopped him and asked for alms. Martin had no money; but the beggar was blue and shivering with cold, and Martin gave what he had. He took off his soldier's coat, worn and frayed as it was; he cut it in two and gave half of it to the beggar man. That night he had a dream. In it he saw the heavenly places and all the angels and Jesus in the midst of them; and Jesus was wearing half of a Roman soldier's cloak. One of the angels said to him, " Master, why are you wearing that battered old cloak? Who gave it to you? " And Jesus answered softly, " My servant Martin gave it to me."

When we learn the generosity which without calculation helps men in the simplest things, we too will know the joy of helping Jesus Christ himself.

THE BEGINNING OF THE LAST ACT
OF THE TRAGEDY

Matthew 26: 1–5

> When Jesus had completed all these sayings, he said to his
> disciples. " You know that in two days time it is the Passover
> Feast, and the Son of Man is going to be delivered to be
> crucified." At that time the chief priests and the elders of the
> people gathered in the courtyard of the High Priest, who was
> called Caiaphas, and took counsel together to seize Jesus by guile
> and to kill him. They said, " Not at the time of the Feast, lest a
> tumult arise among the people."

HERE then is the definite beginning of the last act of the divine
tragedy. Once again Jesus warned his disciples of what was to
come. For the last few days he had been acting with such
magnificent defiance that they might have thought he proposed
to defy the Jewish authorities; but here once again he makes it
clear that his aim is the Cross.

At the same time the Jewish authorities were laying their
plots and stratagems. Joseph Caiaphas, to give him his full
name, was High Priest. We know very little about him but we
do know one most suggestive fact. In the old days the office of
High Priest had been hereditary and had been for life; but when
the Romans took over in Palestine, High Priests came and went
in rapid series, for the Romans erected and deposed High
Priests to suit their own purposes. Between 37 B.C. and A.D. 67,
when the last was appointed before the destruction of the
Temple, there were no fewer than twenty-eight High Priests.
The suggestive thing is that Caiaphas was High Priest from
A.D. 18 to A.D. 36. This was an extraordinarily long time for a
High Priest to last, and Caiaphas must have brought the
technique of co-operating with the Romans to a fine art. And
therein precisely there lay his problem.

The one thing the Romans would not stand was civil
disorder. Let there be any rioting and certainly Caiaphas would

lose his position. At the Passover time the atmosphere in Jerusalem was always explosive. The city was packed tight with people. Josephus tells us of an occasion when an actual census of the people was taken (Josephus, *Wars of the Jews*, 6. 9. 3). It happened in this way.

The governor at the time was Cestius; Cestius felt that Nero did not understand the number of the Jews and the problems which they posed to any governor. So he asked the High Priests to take a census of the lambs slain for sacrifice at a certain Passover time. Josephus goes on to say, " A company of not less than ten must belong to every sacrifice (for it is not lawful for them to feast singly by themselves), and many of us are twenty in a company." It was found that on this occasion the number of lambs slain was 256,500. It is Josephus's estimate that there were in the city for that Passover some two and three-quarter million people.

It is little wonder that Caiaphas sought some stratagem to take Jesus secretly and quietly, for many of the pilgrims were Galilaeans and to them Jesus was a prophet. It was in fact his plan to leave the whole thing over until after the Passover Feast had ended, and the city was quieter; but Judas was to provide him with a solution to his problem.

LOVE'S EXTRAVAGANCE

Matthew 26: 6–13

> When Jesus was in Bethany, in the house of Simon the leper, a woman came to him with an alabaster phial of very costly perfume, and poured it over his head as he reclined at table. When the disciples saw it, they were vexed. " What is the good of this waste? " they said. " For this could have been sold for much money, and the proceeds given to the poor." When Jesus knew what they were saying, he said to them, " Why do you distress the woman? It is a lovely thing that she has done to me. For you always have the poor with you, but you have not me always. When she poured this perfume on my body, she did it to prepare

me beforehand for burial. This is the truth I tell you—wherever the gospel is preached throughout the whole world, this too that she has done shall be spoken of so that all will remember her."

THIS story of the anointing at Bethany is told also by Mark and by John. Mark's story is almost exactly the same; but John adds the information that the woman who anointed Jesus was none other than Mary, the sister of Martha and of Lazarus. Luke does not tell this story; he does tell the story of an anointing in the house of Simon the Pharisee (*Luke* 7: 36–50), but in Luke's story the woman who anointed Jesus's feet and wiped them with the hair of her head was a notorious sinner.

It must always remain a most interesting question whether the story Luke tells is, in fact, the same story as is told by Matthew and Mark and John. In both cases the name of the host is Simon, although in *Luke* he is Simon the Pharisee, and in *Matthew* and *Mark* he is Simon the leper; in *John* the host is not named at all, although the narrative reads as if it took place in the house of Martha and Mary and Lazarus. Simon was a very common name; there are at least ten Simons in the New Testament, and more than twenty in the history of Josephus. The greatest difficulty in identifying the stories of Luke and of the other three gospel writers is that in Luke's story the woman was a notorious sinner; and there is no indication that that was true of Mary of Bethany. And yet the very intensity with which Mary loved Jesus may well have been the result of the depths from which he had rescued her.

Whatever the answer to the question of identification, the story is indeed what Jesus called it—the story of a lovely thing; and in it are enshrined certain very precious truths.

(i) It shows us love's *extravagance*. The woman took the most precious thing she had and poured it out on Jesus. Jewish women were very fond of perfume; and often they carried a little alabaster phial of it round their necks. Such perfume was very valuable. Both Mark and John make the disciples say that this perfume could have been sold for three hundred *denarii* (*Mark* 14: 5; *John* 12: 5); which means that this phial of perfume represented very nearly a whole year's wages for a working man. Or we may think of it this way. When Jesus and his disciples were discussing how the multitude were to be fed, Philip's answer was that two hundred *denarii* would scarcely be enough to feed them. This phial of perfume, therefore, cost as much as it would take to feed a crowd of five thousand people.

It was something as precious as that which this woman gave to Jesus, and she gave it because it was the most precious thing she had. Love never calculates; love never thinks how little it can decently give; love's one desire is to give to the uttermost limits; and, when it has given all it has to give, it still thinks the gift too little. We have not even begun to be Christian if we think of giving to Christ and to his Church in terms of as little as we respectably can.

(ii) It shows us that there are times when the commonsense view of things fails. On this occasion the voice of common sense said, " What waste! " and no doubt it was right. But there is a world of difference between the economics of common sense and the economics of love. Common sense obeys the dictates of prudence; but love obeys the dictates of the heart. There is in life a large place for common sense; but there are times when only love's extravagance can meet love's demands. A gift is never really a gift when we can easily afford it; a gift truly becomes a gift only when there is sacrifice behind it, and when we give far more than we can afford.

(iii) It shows us that certain things must be done when the opportunity arises, or they can never be done at all. The disciples were anxious to help the poor, but the Rabbis themselves said, " God allows the poor to be with us always, that the opportunities for doing good may never fail." There are some things which we can do at any time; there are some things which can be done only once; and to miss the opportunity to do them then is to miss the opportunity for ever. Often we are moved by some generous impulse, and do not act upon it; and all the chances are that the circumstances, the person, the time, and the impulse, will never return. For so many of us the tragedy is that life is the history of the lost opportunities to do the lovely thing.

(iv) It tells us that the fragrance of a lovely deed lasts for ever. There are so few lovely things that one shines like a light in a dark world. At the end of Jesus's life there was so much bitterness, so much treachery, so much intrigue, so much tragedy that this story shines like an oasis of light in a darkening world. In this world there are few greater things that a man may do than leave the memory of a lovely deed.

THE LAST HOURS IN THE LIFE OF THE TRAITOR

INSTEAD of taking the story of Judas piece-meal as it occurs in the gospel record, we shall take it as a whole, reading one after another the last incidents and the final suicide of the traitor.

THE TRAITOR'S BARGAIN

Matthew 26: 14–16

> Then one of the Twelve, called Judas Iscariot, went to the chief priests and said, " What are you willing to give me, if I hand him over to you? " They settled with him for a sum of thirty shekels; and from that time he sought for an opportunity to betray him.

WE have seen that the Jewish authorities wished to find a way in which to arrest Jesus without provoking riotous disturbances, and now that way was presented to them by the approach of Judas. There can be only three real reasons why Judas betrayed Jesus. All other suggestions are variations of these three.

(i) It may have been because of avarice. According to Matthew and Mark it was immediately after the anointing at Bethany that Judas struck his dreadful bargain; and when John tells his story of that event, he says that Judas made his protest against the anointing because he was a thief and pilfered from the money that was in the box (*John* 12: 6). If that is so, Judas struck one of the most dreadful bargains in history. The sum for which he agreed to betray Jesus was thirty *arguria*. An *argurion* was a *shekel*, and was worth about three shillings. Judas, therefore, sold Jesus for less than five pounds. If avarice was the cause of his act of treachery, it is the most terrible example in history of the depths which love of money can reach.

(ii) It may have been because of bitter hatred, based on complete disillusionment. The Jews always had their dream of power; therefore they had their extreme nationalists who were prepared to go to any lengths of murder and violence to drive the Romans from Palestine. These nationalists were called the *sicarii*, the dagger-bearers, because they followed a deliberate policy of assassination. It may be that Judas was such, and that he had looked on Jesus as the divinely sent leader, who, with his miraculous powers, could lead the great rebellion. He may have seen that Jesus had deliberately taken another way, the way that led to a cross. And in his bitter disappointment, Judas's devotion may have turned, first to disillusionment, and then to a hatred which drove him to seek the death of the man from whom he had expected so much. Judas may have hated Jesus because he was not the Christ he wished him to be.

(iii) It may be that Judas never intended Jesus to die. It may be that, as we have seen, he saw in Jesus the divine leader. He may have thought that Jesus was proceeding far too slowly; and he may have wished for nothing else than to force his hand. He may have betrayed Jesus with the intention of compelling him to act. That is in fact the view which best suits all the facts. And that would explain why Judas was shattered into suicide when his plan went wrong.

However we look at it, the tragedy of Judas is that he refused to accept Jesus as he was and tried to make him what he wanted him to be. It is not Jesus who can be changed by us, but we who must be changed by Jesus. We can never use him for our purposes; we must submit to be used for his. The tragedy of Judas is that of a man who thought he knew better than God.

LOVE'S LAST APPEAL

Matthew 26: 20–25

> When evening had come, Jesus was reclining at able with the twelve disciples. While they were eating he said, " This is the truth I tell you—one of you will betray me." They were greatly distressed and began one by one to say to him, " Lord, can it be I? " He answered, " He who dips his hand with me in the dish, it is he who will betray me. The Son of Man is going to go away, as it stands written concerning him, but alas for that man through whom the Son of Man is betrayed! It had been good for that man if he had not been born." Judas, who betrayed him, said, " Master, can it be I? " He said to him, " It is you who have said it."

THERE are times in these last scenes of the gospel story when Jesus and Judas seem to be in a world where there is none other present except themselves. One thing is certain—Judas must have gone about his grim business with complete secrecy. He must have kept his comings and goings completely hidden, for, if the rest of the disciples had known what Judas was doing, he would never have escaped with his life.

He had concealed his plans from his fellow-disciples—but he could not conceal them from Christ. It is always the same; a man can hide his sins from his fellow-men, but he can never hide them from the eyes of Christ who sees the secrets of the heart. Jesus knew, although no other knew, what Judas was about.

And now we can see Jesus's methods with the sinner. He could have used his power to blast Judas, to paralyse him, to render him helpless, even to kill him. But the only weapon that Jesus will ever use is the weapon of love's appeal. One of the great mysteries of life is the respect that God has for the free will of man. God does not coerce; God only appeals.

When Jesus seeks to stop a man from sinning, he does two things.

First, he confronts him with his sin. He tries to make him stop and think what he is doing. He, as it were, says to him,

" Look at what you are contemplating doing—can you really do a thing like that? " It has been said that our greatest security against sin lies in our being shocked by it. And again and again Jesus bids a man pause and look and realize so that he may be shocked into sanity.

Second, he confronts him with himself. He bids a man look at him, as if to say, " Can you look at me, can you meet my eyes, and go out to do the thing you purpose doing? " Jesus seeks to make a man become aware of the horror of the thing he is about to do, and of the love which yearns to stop him doing it.

It is just here that we see the real awfulness of sin in its terrible deliberation. In spite of love's last appeal Judas went on. Even when he was confronted with his sin and confronted with the face of Christ, he would not turn back. There is sin and sin. There is the sin of the passionate heart, of the man who, on the impulse of the moment, is swept into wrong doing. Let no man belittle such sin; its consequences can be very terrible. But far worse is the calculated, callous sin of deliberation, which in cold blood knows what it is doing, which is confronted with the bleak awfulness of the deed and with the love in the eyes of Jesus, and still takes its own way. Our hearts revolt against the son or daughter who cold-bloodedly breaks a parent's heart— which is what Judas did to Jesus—and the tragedy is that this is what we ourselves so often do.

THE TRAITOR'S KISS

Matthew 26: 47–50

> While Jesus was still speaking, there came Judas, one of the Twelve, and a great crowd with swords and cudgels, from the chief priests and the elders of the people. The traitor had given them a sign. " Whom I shall kiss," he said, " that is the man. Lay hold on him! " Immediately he went up to Jesus and said, ' Greetings, Master! " and kissed him lovingly. Jesus said to him, ' Comrade, get on with the deed for which you have come! " Then they came forward, and laid hands on Jesus, and held him.

As we have already seen, the actions of Judas may spring from one of two motives. He may really, either from avarice or from disillusionment, have wished to see Jesus killed; or he may have been trying to force his hand, and may have wished not to see him killed but to compel him to act.

There is, therefore, a double way of interpreting this incident. If in Judas's heart there was nothing but black hatred and a kind of maniacal avarice, this is simply the most terrible kiss in history and a sign of betrayal. If that is so, there is nothing too terrible to be said about Judas.

But there are signs that there is more to it than that. When Judas told the armed mob that he would indicate the man whom they had come to arrest by a kiss, the word he uses is the Greek word *philein*, which is the normal word for a kiss; but when it is said that Judas actually did kiss Jesus, the word used is *kataphilein*, which is the word for a lover's kiss, and means to kiss repeatedly and fervently. Why should Judas do that?

Further, why should any identification of Jesus have been necessary? It was not identification of Jesus the authorities required; it was a convenient opportunity to arrest him. The people who came to arrest him were from the chief priests and the elders of the people; they must have been the Temple police, the only force the chief priests had at their disposal. It is incredible that the Temple police did not already know only too well the man who just days before had cleansed the Temple and driven the money-changers and the sellers of doves from the Temple court. It is incredible that they should not have known the man who had taught daily in the Temple cloisters. Having been led to the garden, they well knew the man whom they had come to arrest.

It is much more likely that Judas kissed Jesus as a disciple kissed a master and meant it; and that then he stood back with expectant pride waiting on Jesus at last to act. The curious thing is that from the moment of the kiss Judas vanishes from the scene in the garden, not to reappear until he is bent on suicide. He does not even appear as a witness at the trial of Jesus. It is far more likely that in one stunning, blinding staggering, searing moment Judas saw how he had mis-calculated and staggered away into the night a for ever broken and for ever haunted man. If this be true, at that moment Judas entered the hell which he had created for himself, for the worst kind of hell is the full realization of the terrible consequences ot sin.

THE TRAITOR'S END

Matthew 27: 3–10

> When Judas the traitor saw that Jesus had been condemned, he repented, and he brought the thirty shekels back to the chief priests and the elders. " I have sinned," he said, " for I have betrayed an innocent man." " What has that got to do with us? " they said. " It is you who must see to that." He threw the money into the Temple and went away. And when he had gone away, he hanged himself. The chief priests took the money. " We cannot," they said, " put these into the treasury, for they are the price of blood." They took counsel, and bought with them the potter's field, to be a burying place for strangers. That is why to this day that field is called The Field of Blood. Then there was fulfilled that which was spoken through Jeremiah the prophet, when he said: " And they took the thirty shekels, the price of him on whom a price had been set by the sons of Israel, and they gave them for the field of the potter, as the Lord instructed me."

HERE in all its stark grimness is the last act of the tragedy of Judas. However we interpret his mind, one thing is clear— Judas now saw the horror of the thing that he had done. Matthew tells us that Judas took the money and flung it into the Temple, and the interesting thing is that the word he uses is not the word for the Temple precincts in general (*hieron*), it is the word for the actual Temple itself (*naos*). It will be remembered that the Temple consisted of a series of courts each opening off the other. Judas in his blind despair came into the Court of the Gentiles; passed through it into the Court of the Women; passed through that into the Court of the Israelites; beyond

that he could not go; he had come to the barrier which shut off
the Court of the Priests with the Temple itself at the far end of
it. He called on them to take the money; but they would not;
and he flung it at them and went away and hanged himself. And
the priests took the money, so tainted that it could not be put
into the Temple treasury, and with it bought a field to bury the
unclean bodies of Gentiles who died within the city.

The suicide of Judas is surely the final indication that his
plan had gone wrong. He had meant to make Jesus blaze forth as
a conqueror; instead he had driven him to the Cross and life for
Judas was shattered There are two great truths about sin here.

(i) The terrible thing about sin is that we cannot put the clock
back. We cannot undo what we have done. Once a thing is done
nothing can alter it or bring it back.

> " The Moving Finger writes; and having writ?
> Moves on: nor all thy Piety nor Wit
>   Shall lure it back to cancel half a Line,
>   Nor all thy Tears wash out a Word of it."

No one needs to be very old to have that haunting longing for
some hour to be lived over again. When we remember that no
action can ever be recalled, it should make us doubly careful
how we act.

(ii) The strange thing about sin is that a man can come to
hate the very thing he gained by it. The very prize he won by
sinning can come to digust and to revolt and to repel him, until
his one desire is to fling it from him. Most people sin because
they think that if they can only possess the forbidden thing it
will make them happy. But the thing which sin desired can
become the thing that a man above all would rid himself
of—and so often he cannot.

As we have seen, Matthew finds forecasts of the events of the
life of Jesus in the most unlikely places. Here there is, in fact, an
actual mistake. Matthew is quoting from memory; and the
quotation which he makes is, in fact, not from *Jeremiah* but
from *Zechariah*. It is from a strange passage (*Zechariah* 11:
10–14) in which the prophet tells us how he received an

unworthy reward and flung it to the potter. In that old picture Matthew saw a symbolic resemblance to the thing that Judas did.

It might have been that, if Judas had remained true to Jesus, he would have died a martyr's death; but, because he wanted his own way too much, he died by his own hand. He missed the glory of the martyr's crown to find life intolerable because he had sinned.

THE LAST SUPPER

As we took together the passages which tell the story of Judas so now we take the passages which tell the story of the Last Supper.

THE ANCESTRAL FEAST

Matthew 26: 17–19

> On the first day of the Feast of Unleavened Bread the disciples came to Jesus. " Where," they said, " do you wish that we should make the necessary preparations for you to eat the Passover? " He said, " Go into the city to such and such a man, and say to him, ' The Teacher says, my time is near. I will keep the Passover with my disciples at your house.' " And the disciples did as Jesus instructed them, and made the preparations for the Passover.

It was for the Passover Feast that Jesus had come to Jerusalem. We have seen how crowded the city was at such a time. During the Passover Feast all Jews were supposed to stay within the boundaries of the city, but the numbers made that impossible; and for official purposes villages like Bethany, where Jesus was staying, ranked as the city.

But the Feast itself had to be celebrated within the city. The disciples wished to know what preparation they must make Clearly Jesus had not left the matter to the last moment; he had already made his arrangements with a friend in Jerusalem, and he had already arranged a password—" The Teacher says, my time is near." So the disciples were sent on to give the password and to make all the necessary preparations.

The whole week of which the Passover Feast occupied the first evening was called The Feast of Unleavened Bread. In following the events we must remember that for the Jew the next day began at 6 o'clock in the evening. In this case the Feast of Unleavened Bread began on Thursday morning. On the Thursday morning every particle of leaven was destroyed, after a ceremonial search throughout the house.

There was a double reason for that. The Feast commemorated the greatest event in the history of Israel, the deliverance from slavery in Egypt. And when the Israelites had fled from Egypt, they had to flee in such haste that they had not time to bake their bread leavened (*Exodus* 12: 34). Dough without leaven (that is, a little piece of fermented dough) cooks very quickly, but produces a substance more like a water biscuit than a loaf; and that is what unleavened bread is like. So the leaven was banished and the bread unleavened to repeat the acts of the night on which they left Egypt and its slavery behind them.

Second, in Jewish thought leaven is the symbol of corruption. As we have said, leaven is fermented dough and the Jews identified fermentation and putrefaction; so leaven stood for all that was rotten and corrupt, and was, therefore, as a sign of purification, cleansed away.

When, then, were the preparations which the disciples would make?

On the Thursday morning, they would prepare the unleavened bread and rid the house of every scrap of leaven. The other staple ingredient of the Feast was the Passover Lamb. It was indeed from the lamb that the Feast took its name. The last terrible plague which fell on the Egyptians and which compelled them to let the people go, was that the Angel of Death walked throughout the land of Egypt and slew the firstborn son in every house. To identify their houses, the Israelites had to kill a lamb and smear the lintel and the side posts of their doors with its blood, so that the avenging angel seeing that sign would *pass over* that house (*Exodus* 12: 21–23). On the Thursday afternoon the lamb had to be taken to the Temple and slain, and its blood—which was the life—had to be offered to God in sacrifice.

There were four other items necessary for the Feast.

(i) A bowl of *salt water* had to be set upon the table, to remind them of the tears they had shed while they were slaves in Egypt and of the salt waters of the Red Sea through which God's hand had wondrously brought them.

(ii) A collection of *bitter herbs* had to be prepared, composed of horse-radish, chicory, endive, lettuce, hore-hound and the like. This was again to remind them of the bitterness of slavery, and of the bunch of hyssop with which the blood of the lamb had been smeared on the lintel and the door-posts.

(iii) There was a paste called the *Charosheth*. It was a mixture of apples, dates, pomegranates and nuts. It was to remind them of the clay with which they had been compelled to make bricks in Egypt, and through it there were sticks of cinnamon to remind them of the straw with which the bricks had been made.

(iv) Lastly, there were *four cups of wine*. These were to remind them of the four promises of *Exodus* 6: 6, 7: " I will bring you out from under the burdens of the Egyptians; I will deliver you from their bondage, and I will redeem you with an outstretched arm and with great acts of judgment; I will take you for my people, and I will be your God."

Such then were the preparations of the Thursday morning and afternoon. These were the things that the disciples prepared; and at any time after 6 p.m., that is when Friday, the 15th Nisan, had began, the guests might gather at the table.

HIS BODY AND HIS BLOOD

Matthew 26: 26–30

> While they were eating, Jesus took bread and blessed it and broke it, and gave it to his disciples and said, " Take, eat; this is my body." Then he took a cup, and when he had given thanks, he gave it to them. " Drink all of you from it," he said, " for this is my blood, the blood of the covenant, which is poured out for many, that their sins may be forgiven. I tell you that from now on I will not drink of this fruit of the vine until that day when I drink it new with you in the Kingdom of my Father." And when they had sung a hymn, they went out to the Mount of Olives.

WE have already seen how the prophets, when they wished to say something in a way that people could not fail to understand, made use of symbolic actions. We have already seen Jesus using that method both in his Triumphal Entry and in the incident of the fig tree. That is what Jesus is doing here. All the symbolism and all the ritual action of the Passover Feast was a picture of what he wished to say to men, for it was a picture of what he was to do for men. What then was the picture which Jesus was using, and what is the truth which lies behind it?

(i) The Passover Feast was a *commemoration of deliverance*; its whole intention was to remind the people of Israel of how God had liberated them from slavery in Egypt. First and foremost then, Jesus claimed to be *the great liberator*. He came to liberate men from fear and from sin. He liberates men from the fears which haunt them and from the sins which will not let them go.

(ii) In particular the Passover Lamb was *the symbol of safety*. On that night of destruction it was the blood of the Passover Lamb which kept Israel safe. So, then, *Jesus was claiming to be Saviour*. He had come to save men from their sins and from their consequences. He had come to give men safety on earth and safety in heaven, safety in time and safety in eternity.

There is a word here which is a key word and enshrines the

whole of Jesus's work and intention. It is the word *covenant*. Jesus spoke of his blood being the blood of the covenant. What did he mean by that? A covenant is a relationship between two people; but the covenant of which Jesus spoke was not between man and man; it was between God and man. That is to say, it was a new relationship between God and man. What Jesus was saying at the Last Supper was this: " Because of my life, and above all because of my death, a new relationship has become possible between you and God." It is as if he said, " You have seen me; and in me you have seen God; I have told you, I have shown you, how much God loves you; he loves you even enough to suffer this that I am going through; that is what God is like." Because of what Jesus did, the way for men is open to all the loveliness of this new relationship with God.

This passage concludes by saying that, when the company of Jesus and the disciples had sung a hymn, they went out to the Mount of Olives. An essential part of the Passover ritual was the singing of the *Hallel*. *Hallel* means *Praise God*! And the *Hallel* consisted of Psalms 113–118, which are all praising psalms. At different points of the Passover Feast these psalms were sung in sections; and at the very end there was sung *The Great Hallel*, which is Psalm 136. That was the hymn they sang before they went out to the Mount of Olives.

Here is another thing to note. There was one basic difference between the Last Supper and the Sacrament which we observe. The Last Supper was a real meal; it was, in fact, the law that the whole lamb and everything else must be eaten and nothing left. This was no eating of a cube of bread and drinking of a sip of wine. It was a meal for hungry men. We might well say that what Jesus is teaching men is not only to assemble in church and eat a ritual and symbolic Feast; he is telling them that every time they sit down to eat a meal, that meal is in memory of him. Jesus is not only Lord of the Communion Table; he must be Lord of the dinner table, too.

There remains one final thing. Jesus says that he will not feast with his disciples again until he does so in his Father's Kingdom. Here, indeed, is divine faith and divine optimism.

Jesus was going out to Gethsemane, out to trial before the Sanhedrin, out to the Cross—and yet *he is still thinking in terms of a Kingdom.* To Jesus the Cross was never defeat; it was the way to glory. He was on his way to Calvary, but he was also on his way to a throne.

THE COLLAPSE OF PETER

WE now gather together the passages which tell the story of Peter.

THE MASTER'S WARNING

Matthew 26: 31–35

> Then Jesus said to them, " Every one of you will be made to stumble because of me during this night; for it stands written, ' I will smite the shepherd, and the sheep of the flock shall be scattered abroad.' But after I have been raised, I will go before you into Galilee." Peter answered him, " If all are made to stumble because of you, I will never be made to stumble." Jesus said to him, " This is the truth I tell you—during this night, before the cock crows, you will deny me three times." Peter said to him, " Even if I have to die with you, I will not deny you." So also spoke all the disciples.

IN this passage certain characteristics of Jesus are clear.

(i) We see the *realism* of Jesus. He knew what lay ahead. Matthew actually sees the flight of the disciples foretold in the Old Testament in *Zechariah* 13: 7. Jesus was no easy optimist, who could comfortably shut his eyes to the facts. He foresaw what would inevitably happen and yet he went on.

(ii) We see the *confidence* of Jesus. " After I have been raised," he says, " I will go before you into Galilee." Always Jesus saw beyond the Cross. He was every bit as certain of the glory as he was of the suffering.

(iii) We see the *sympathy* of Jesus. He knew that his men were going to flee for their lives and abandon him in the moment of his deepest need; but he does not upbraid them, he does not condemn them, he does not heap reproaches on them, or call them useless creatures and broken reeds. So far from that, he tells them that when that terrible time is past, he will meet them again. It is the greatness of Jesus that he knew men at their worst and still loved them. He knows our human weakness; he knows how certain we are to make mistakes and to fail in loyalty; but that knowledge does not turn his love to bitterness or contempt. Jesus has nothing but sympathy for the man who in his weakness is driven to sin.

Further, this passage shows us something about Peter. Surely his fault is clear; *over-confidence in himself*. He knew that he loved Jesus—that was never in doubt—and he thought that all by himself he could face any situation which might arise. He thought that he was stronger than Jesus knew him to be. We shall be safe only when we replace the confidence which boasts by the humility which knows its weakness and which depends not on itself but the help of Christ.

The Romans and the Jews divided the night into four watches—6 p.m. to 9 p.m.; 9 p.m. to midnight; midnight to 3 a.m.; 3 a.m. to 6 a.m. It was between the third and the fourth watch that the cock was supposed to crow. What Jesus is saying is that before the dawn comes Peter will deny him three times.

THE FAILURE OF COURAGE

Matthew 26: 57, 58, 69—75

Those who had laid hold of Jesus led him away to the house of Caiaphas the High Priest, where the Scribes and the elders were assembled. Peter followed him at a distance, right into the courtyard of the High Priest's house, and he went inside and sat down with the servants to see the end.

· · · · · · ·

Peter was sitting outside in the courtyard. A maid-servant came up to him and said, " You, too, were with Jesus the Galilaean." He denied it in the presence of them all. " I do not know," he said, " what you are saying." When he went out to the porch, another maid-servant saw him, and said to those who were there, " This man too was with Jesus of Nazareth." And again he denied it with an oath: " I do not know the man." A little later those who were standing there said to Peter, " Truly you too were one of them; for your accent gives you away." Then he began to curse and to swear: " I do not know the man." And immediately the cock crew. And Peter remembered the saying of Jesus, when he said, " Before the cock crows, you will deny me three times." And he went out and wept bitterly.

No one can read this passage without being struck with the staggering honesty of the New Testament. If ever there was an incident which one might have expected to be hushed up, this was it—and yet here it is told in all its stark shame. We know that Matthew very closely followed the narrative of Mark; and in Mark's gospel this story is told in even more vivid detail (*Mark* 14: 66–72). We also know, as Papias tells us, that Mark's gospel is nothing other than the preaching material of Peter written down. And so we arrive at the amazing fact that we possess the story of Peter's denial because Peter himself told it to others.

So far from suppressing this story, Peter made it an essential part of his gospel; and did so for the very best of reasons. Every time he told the story, he could say, " That is the way that this Jesus can forgive. He forgave me when I failed him in his bitterest hour of need. That is what Jesus can do. He took me, Peter the coward, and used even me." We must never read this story without remembering that it is Peter himself who is telling of the shame of his own sin that all men may know the glory of the forgiving love and cleansing power of Jesus Christ.

And yet it is quite wrong to regard Peter with nothing but unsympathetic condemnation. The blazing fact is that the disaster which happened to Peter is one which could have happened only to a man of the most heroic courage. All the other disciples ran away: Peter alone did not. In Palestine the houses of the well-to-do were built in a hollow square around an open courtyard, off which the various rooms opened. For Peter to enter that courtyard in the centre of the High Priest's house was to walk into the lion's den—and yet he did it. However this story ends, it begins with Peter the one brave man.

The first denial happened in the courtyard; no doubt the maid-servant had marked Peter as one of the most prominent followers of Jesus and had recognized him. After that recognition anyone would have thought that Peter would have fled for his life; a coward would certainly have been gone into the night as quickly as he could. But not Peter; although he did retire as far as the porch.

He was torn between two feelings. In his heart there was a fear that made him want to run away; but in his heart, too, there was a love which kept him there. Again, in the porch he was recognized; and this time he swore he did not know Jesus. And still he did not go. Here is the most dogged courage.

But Peter's second denial had given him away. From his speech it was clear that he was a Galilaean. The Galilaeans spoke with a burr; so ugly was their accent that no Galilaean was allowed to pronounce the benediction at a synagogue service. Once again Peter was accused of being a follower of Jesus. Peter went further this time; not only did he swear that he did not know Jesus; he actually cursed his Master's name. But still it is clear that Peter had no intention of leaving that courtyard. And then the cock crew.

There is a distinct possibility here which would provide us with a vivid picture. It may well be that the cock-crow was not the voice of a bird; and that from the beginning it was not meant to mean that. After all, the house of the High Priest was right in the centre of Jerusalem, and there was not likely to be poultry in the centre of the city. There was, in fact, a regulation in the Jewish law that it was illegal to keep cocks and hens in the Holy City, because they defiled the holy things. But the hour of 3 a.m. was called cock-crow, and for this reason. At that hour the Roman guard was changed in the Castle of Antonia;

and the sign of the changing of the guard was a *trumpet call* The Latin for that trumpet call was *gallicinium*, which means *cock-crow*. It is at least possible that just as Peter made his third denial the trumpet from the castle battlements rang out over the sleeping city—the *gallicinium*, the cock-crow—and Peter remembered; and thereupon he went and wept his heart out.

What happened to Peter after that we do not know, for the gospel story draws a kindly veil over the agony of his shame. But before we condemn him, we must remember very clearly that few of us would ever have had the courage to be in that courtyard at all. And there is one last thing to be said—it was love which gave Peter that courage; it was love which riveted him there in spite of the fact that he had been recognized three times; it was love which made him remember the words of Jesus; it was love which sent him out into the night to weep—and it is love which covers a multitude of sins. The lasting impression of this whole story is not of Peter's cowardice, but of Peter's love.

THE SOUL'S BATTLE IN THE GARDEN

Matthew 26: 36–46

Then Jesus went with them to a place called Gethsemane, and he said to his disciples, " Sit here, while I go away and pray in this place." So he took Peter and the two sons of Zebedee, and began to be distressed and in sore trouble. Then he said to them, " My soul is much distressed with a distress like death. Stay here, and watch with me." He went a little way forward and fell on his face in prayer. " My Father," He said, " if it is possible, let this cup pass from me. But let it be not as I will, but as you will." He came to his disciples, and he found them sleeping, and he said to Peter, " Could you not stay awake with me for this—for one hour? Watch and pray lest you enter into testing. The spirit is eager, but the flesh is weak." He went away a second time and prayed. " My Father," He said, " if it is not possible for this to pass from me

unless I drink it, your will be done." He came again and found
them sleeping, for their eyes were weighted down. He left them,
and went away again, and prayed the third time, saying the same
words over again. Then he came to his disciples and said to them,
" Sleep on now and take your rest. Look you, the hour is near,
and the Son of Man is being delivered into the hands of sinners.
Rise; let us go; look you, he who betrays me is near."

SURELY this is a passage which we must approach upon our
knees. Here study should pass into wondering adoration.

In Jerusalem itself there were no gardens of any size, for a
city set on the top of an hill has no room for open spaces; every
inch is of value for building. So, then, it came about that
wealthy citizens had their private gardens on the slopes of the
Mount of Olives. The word *Gethsemane* very probably means
an *olive-vat*, or an *olive-press*; and no doubt it was a garden of
olives to which Jesus had the right of entry. It is a strange and a
lovely thing to think of the nameless friends who rallied round
Jesus in the last days. There was the man who gave him the ass
on which he rode into Jerusalem; there was the man who gave
him the Upper Room wherein the Last Supper was eaten; and
now there is the man who gave him the right of entry to the
garden on the Mount of Olives. In a desert of hatred, there were
still oases of love.

Into the garden he took the three who had been with him on
the Mount of Transfiguration; and there he prayed; more, he
wrestled in prayer. As we look with awed reverence on the
battle of Jesus's soul in the garden we see certain things.

(i) We see the *agony* of Jesus. He was now quite sure that
death lay ahead. Its very breath was on him. No one wants to
die at thirty-three; and least of all does any man want to die in
the agony of a cross. Here Jesus had his supreme struggle to
submit his will to the will of God. No one can read this story
without seeing the intense reality of that struggle. This was no
play-acting; it was a struggle in which the outcome swayed in
the balance. The salvation of the world was at risk in the
Garden of Gethsemane, for even then Jesus might have turned
back, and God's purpose would have been frustrated.

At this moment all that Jesus knew was that he must go on, and ahead there lay a cross. In all reverence we may say that here we see Jesus learning the lesson that everyone must some day learn—how to accept what he could not understand. All he knew was that the will of God imperiously summoned him on. Things happen to every one of us in this world that we cannot understand; it is then that faith is tried to its utmost limits; and at such a time it is sweetness to the soul that in Gethsemane Jesus went through that too. Tertullian (*De Bapt.* 20) tells us of a saying of Jesus, which is not in any of the gospels: " No one who has not been tempted can enter the Kingdom of Heaven." That is, every man has his private Gethsemane, and every man has to learn to say, " Thy will be done."

(ii) We see the *loneliness* of Jesus. He took with him his three chosen disciples; but they were so exhausted with the drama of these last days and hours that they could not stay awake. And Jesus had to fight his battle all alone. That also is true of every man. There are certain things a man must face and certain decisions a man must make in the awful loneliness of his own soul; there are times when other helpers fail and comforts flee; but in that loneliness there is for us the presence of One who, in Gethsemane, experienced it and came through it.

(iii) Here we see the *trust* of Jesus. We see that trust even better in Mark's account, where Jesus begins his prayer: " *Abba*, Father " (*Mark* 14: 36). There is a world of loveliness in this word *Abba*, which to our western ears is altogether hidden, unless we know the facts about it. Joachim Jeremias, in his book *The Parables of Jesus*, writes thus: " Jesus's use of the word *Abba* in addressing God is unparalleled in the whole of Jewish literature. The explanation of this fact is to be found in the statement of the fathers Chrysostom, Theodore, and Theodoret that *Abba* (as *jaba* is still used today in Arabic) was the word used by a young child to its father; it was an everyday family word, which no one had ventured to use in addressing God. Jesus did. He spoke to his heavenly Father in as childlike, trustful, and intimate a way as a little child to its father."

We know how our children speak to us and what they call us

who are fathers. That is the way in which Jesus spoke to God. Even when he did not fully understand, even when his one conviction was that God was urging him to a cross, he called *Abba*, as might a little child. Here indeed is trust, a trust which we must also have in that God whom Jesus taught us to know as Father.

(iv) We see the *courage* of Jesus. " Rise," said Jesus, " let us be going. He who betrays me is near." Celsus, the pagan philosopher who attacked Christianity, used that sentence as an argument that Jesus tried to run away. It is the very opposite. " Rise," he said. " The time for prayer, and the time for the garden is past, Now is the time for action. Let us face life at its grimmest and men at their worst." Jesus rose from his knees to go out to the battle of life. That is what prayer is for. In prayer a man kneels before God that he may stand erect before men. In prayer a man enters heaven that he may face the battles of earth.

THE ARREST IN THE GARDEN

Matthew 26: 50–56

Then they came forward and laid hands on Jesus and held him. And, look you, one of these who was with Jesus stretched out his hand, and drew his sword, and struck the servant of the High Priest, and cut off his ear. Then Jesus said to him, " Put back your sword in its place; for all who take the sword shall perish by the sword. Or, do you not think that I am able to call on my Father, and he will on the spot send to my aid more than twelve regiments of angels? How then are the Scriptures to be fulfilled that it must happen so? " At that hour Jesus said to the crowds, " Have you come out with swords and cudgels to arrest me, as against a brigand? Daily I sat teaching in the Temple, and you did not lay hold on me. All this has happened that the writings of the prophets might be fulfilled." Then all his disciples forsook him and fled.

IT was Judas who had given the authorities the information which enabled them to find Jesus in the privacy of the Garden of Gethsemane. The forces at the disposal of the Jewish authorities were the Temple police, under the command of the Sagan, or Captain of the Temple. But the mob which surged after Judas to the Garden was more like a mob for a lynching than a detachment for an orderly arrest.

Jesus would allow no resistance. Matthew simply tells us that one of the disciples drew a knife and, prepared to resist to the death and to sell his life dearly, wounded a servant of the High Priest. When John tells the same story (*John* 18: 10), he tells us that the disciple was Peter, and the servant was Malchus. The reason why John names Peter, and Matthew does not, may simply be that John was writing much later, and that when Matthew was writing it was still not safe to name the disciple who had sprung so quickly to his Master's defence. Here we have still another instance of the almost fantastic courage of Peter. He was willing to take on the mob alone; and let us always remember that it was after that, when he was a marked man, that Peter followed Jesus right into the courtyard of the High Priest's house. But in all these incidents of the last hours it is on Jesus that our attention is fastened; and here we learn two things about him.

(i) His death was *by his own choice*. He need never have come to Jerusalem for the Passover Feast. Having come, he need never have followed his deliberate policy of magnificent defiance. Even in the Garden he could have slipped away and saved himself, for it was night, and there were many who would have smuggled him out of the city. Even here he could have called down the might of God and blasted his enemies. Every step of these last days makes it clearer and clearer that Jesus laid down his life and that his life was not taken from him. Jesus died, not because men killed him, but because he chose to die.

(ii) He chose to die because he knew that his death was *the purpose of God*. He took this way because it was the very thing that had been foretold by the prophets. He took it because love is the only way. " He who takes the sword will perish by the sword." Violence can beget nothing but violence; one drawn sword can produce only another drawn sword to meet it. Jesus knew that war and might settle nothing, but produce only a train of evil, and beget a grim horde of children worse than themselves. He knew that God's purpose can be worked out only by sacrificial love. And history proved him right; for the Jews who took him with violence, and who gloried in violence, and who would gladly have dipped their swords in Roman blood, saw forty years later their city destroyed for ever, while the man who would not fight is enthroned for ever in the hearts of men.

THE TRIAL BEFORE THE JEWS

Matthew 26: 57, 59–68

Those who had laid hold of Jesus led him away to the house of Caiaphas the High Priest, where the Scribes and the elders were assembled.

. . . .

The chief priests and the whole Sanhedrin tried to find false witness against him, in order to put him to death; but they could not find it, although many false witnesses came forward. Later two came forward and said, " This fellow said, ' I can destroy the Temple of God, and in three days I can build it again.' " The High Priest rose and said, " Do you make no answer? What is it that these witness against you? " But Jesus kept silent. So the High Priest said to him, " I adjure you by the living God, that you tell us, whether you are the Anointed One of God, the Son of God." Jesus said to him, " It is you who have said it. But I tell you that from now on you will see the Son of Man seated on the right hand of the Power and coming on the clouds of Heaven." Then the High Priest rent his garments, saying, " He has blasphemed. What further need have we of witnesses? Look you, you have now heard his blasphemy. What is your opinion?" They answered, "He has made himself liable to the death penalty." Then they spat upon his face, and buffeted him. And some struck him on the cheek saying, " Prophesy to us, you Anointed One of God! Who is he who struck you? "

THE process of the trial of Jesus is not altogether easy to follow. It seems to have fallen into three parts. The first part took place after the arrest in the Garden, during the night and in the High Priest's house, and is described in this section. The second part took place first thing in the morning, and is briefly described in *Matthew* 27: 1, 2. The third part took place before Pilate and is described in *Matthew* 27: 11–26. The salient question is this—was the meeting during the night an official meeting of the Sanhedrin, hastily summoned, or was it merely a preliminary examination, in order to formulate a charge, and was the meeting in the morning the official meeting of the Sanhedrin? However that question is answered, the Jews violated their own laws in the trial of Jesus; but if the meeting in the night was a meeting of the Sanhedrin, the violation was even more extreme. On the whole, it seems that Matthew took the night meeting to be a meeting of the Sanhedrin, for in verse 59 he says that the whole Sanhedrin sought for false witness to put Jesus to death. Let us then first look at this process from the Jewish legal point of view.

The Sanhedrin was the supreme court of the Jews. It was composed of Scribes, Pharisees, Sadducees and elders of the people; it numbered seventy-one members; and it was presided over by the High Priest. For a trial such as this a quorum was twenty-three. It had certain regulations. All criminal cases must be tried during the daytime and must be completed during the daytime. Criminal cases could not be transacted during the Passover season at all. Only if the verdict was Not Guilty could a case be finished on the day it was begun; otherwise a night must elapse before the pronouncement of the verdict, so that feelings of mercy might have time to arise. Further, no decision of the Sanhedrin was valid unless it met in its own meeting place, the Hall of Hewn Stone in the Temple precincts. All evidence had to be guaranteed by two witnesses separately examined and having not contact with each other. And false witness was punishable by death. The seriousness of the occasion was impressed upon any witness in a case where life was at stake: " Forget not, O witness, that it is one thing to give evidence in a trial for money, and another in a trial for life. In a money suit, if thy witness-bearing shall do wrong, money may repair that wrong; but in this trial for life, if thou sinnest, the blood of the accused and the blood of his seed unto the end of time shall be imputed untó thee." Still further, in any trial the process began by the laying before the court of all the evidence for the *innocence* of the accused, before the evidence for his guilt was adduced.

These were the Sanhedrin's own rules, and it is abundantly clear that, in their eagerness to get rid of Jesus, they broke their own rules. The Jews had reached such a peak of hatred that any means were justified to put an end to Jesus.

THE CRIME OF CHRIST

Matthew 26: 57, 59–68 (*continued*)

THE main business of the night meeting of the Jewish authorities was to formulate a charge against Jesus. As we have seen, all evidence had to be guaranteed by two witnesses, separately examined. For long not even two false witnesses could be found to agree. And then a charge was found, the charge that Jesus had said that he would destroy the Temple and rebuild it in three days.

It is clear that this charge is a twisting of certain things he did actually say. We have already seen that he foretold—and rightly—the destruction of the Temple. This had been twisted into a charge that he had said that he himself would destroy the Temple. We have seen that he foretold that he himself would be killed and would rise on the third day. This had been twisted into a charge that he had said that he would rebuild the Temple in three days.

This charge was formulated by deliberately and maliciously misrepeating and misinterpreting certain things which Jesus had said. To that charge Jesus utterly refused to reply. Therein the law was on his side, for no person on trial could either be asked, or compelled to answer, any question which would incriminate him.

It was then that the High Priest launched his vital question. We have seen that repeatedly Jesus warned his disciples to tell no man that he was the Messiah. How then did the High Priest know to ask the question the answer to which Jesus could not escape? It may well be that when Judas laid information against him, he also told the Jewish authorities about Jesus's revelation of his own Messiahship. It may well be that Judas had deliberately broken the bond of secrecy which Jesus had laid upon his disciples.

In any event, the High Priest asked the question, and asked it upon oath: " Are you the Messiah? " he demanded. " Do you claim to be the Son of God? " Here was the crucial moment in the trial. We might well say that all the universe held its breath as it waited for Jesus's answer. If Jesus said, " No," the bottom fell out of the trial; there was no possible charge against him. He had only to say, " No," and walk out a free man, and escape before the Sanhedrin could think out another way of entrapping him. On the other hand, if he said, " Yes," he signed his own death warrant. Nothing more than a simple " Yes " was needed to make the Cross a complete and inescapable certainty

It may be that Jesus paused for a moment once again to count the cost before he made the great decision; and then he said, " Yes." He went further. He quoted *Daniel* 7: 13 with its vivid account of the ultimate triumph and kingship of God's chosen one. He well knew what he was doing. Immediately there went up the cry of blasphemy. Garments were rent in a kind of synthetic and hysterical horror; and Jesus was condemned to death.

Then followed the spitting on him, the buffeting, the slapping of his face, the mockery. Even the externals of justice were forgotten, and the venomous hostility of the Jewish authorities broke through. That meeting in the night began as a court of justice and ended in a frenzied display of hatred, in which there was no attempt to maintain even the superficialities of impartial justice.

To this day when a man is brought face to face with Jesus Christ, he must either hate him or love him; he must either submit to him, or desire to destroy him. No man who realizes what Jesus Christ demands can possibly be neutral. He must either be his liege-man or his foe.

THE MAN WHO SENTENCED JESUS TO DEATH

Matthew 27: 1, 2, 11–26

When the morning came, all the chief priests and elders of the people took counsel against Jesus, to put him to death; so they bound him, and led him away, and handed him over to Pilate the governor.

. . . .

Jesus stood before the governor, and the governor put the question to him, " Are you the King of the Jews? " Jesus said to him, " You say so." While he was being accused by the chief priests and the elders, he returned no answer. Then Pilate said to him, " Do you not hear the evidence which they are stating against you? " Jesus answered not a single word, so that the governor was much amazed. At the time of the Feast the governor was in the habit of releasing one prisoner to the crowd, a prisoner whom they wished. At that time he was holding a very well-known prisoner called Barabbas. So, when they were assembled, Pilate said to them. " Whom do you wish me to release to you? Barabbas? Or, Jesus who is called Christ? " For he was well aware that they had delivered Jesus to him because of malice. While he was sitting on his judgment seat, his wife sent a message to him. " Have nothing to do with this just man," she said, " for today I have had an extraordinary experience in a dream because of him." The chief priests and the elders persuaded the crowds to ask for the release of Barabbas, and the destruction of Jesus. " Which of the two," said the governor, " am I to release to you? " " Barabbas," they said. " What then," said Pilate to them, " am I to do with Jesus who is called Christ." " Let him be crucified," they all said. " What evil has he done? " he said. They kept shouting all the

more: " Let him be crucified." When Pilate saw that it was
hopeless to do anything, and that rather a disturbance was liable
to arise, he took water, and washed his hands in presence of the
crowd. " I am innocent of the blood of this just man," he said.
" You must see to it." All the people answered, " Let the
responsibility for his blood be on us and on our children." Then he
released Barabbas to them; but he had Jesus scourged, and
handed him over to be crucified.

THE first two verses of this passage describe what must have
been a very brief meeting of the Sanhedrin, held early in the
morning, with a view to formulating finally an official charge
against Jesus. The necessity for this lay in the fact that, while
the Jews could themselves deal with an ordinary charge, they
could not inflict the death penalty. That was a sentence which
could be pronounced only by the Roman governor, and carried
out by the Roman authorities. The Sanhedrin had therefore to
formulate a charge with which they could go to Pilate and
demand the death of Jesus

Matthew does not tell us what that charge was; but Luke
does. In the Sanhedrin the charge which was levelled against
Jesus was a charge of blasphemy (*Matthew* 26: 65, 66). But no
one knew better than the Jewish authorities that that was a
charge to which Pilate would not listen. He would tell them to
go away and settle their own religious quarrels. So, as Luke tells
us, they appeared before Pilate with a threefold charge, every
item in which was a lie, and a deliberate lie. They charged Jesus
first with being a revolutionary, second, with inciting the people
not to pay their taxes, and third, with claiming to be a king
(*Luke* 23: 2). They fabricated three *political* charges, all of them
conscious lies, because they knew that only on such charges
would Pilate act.

So, then, everything hung on the attitude of Pilate. What
kind of man was this Roman governor?

Pilate was officially *procurator* of the province; and he was
directly responsible, not to the Roman senate, but to the Roman
Emperor. He must have been at least twenty-seven years of age,
for that was the minimum age for entering on the office of

procurator. He must have been a man of considerable experience, for there was a ladder of offices, including military command, up which a man must climb until he qualified to become a governor. Pilate must have been a tried and tested soldier and administrator. He became procurator of Judaea in A.D. 26 and held office for ten years, when he was recalled from his post.

When Pilate came to Judaea, he found trouble in plenty, and much of it was of his own making. His great handicap was that he was completely out of sympathy with the Jews. More, he was contemptuous of what he would have called their irrational and fanatical prejudices, and what they would have called their principles. The Romans knew the intensity of Jewish religion and the unbreakable character of Jewish belief, and very wisely had always dealt with the Jews with kid gloves. Pilate arrogantly proposed to use the mailed fist.

He began with trouble. The Roman headquarters were in Caesarea. The Roman standards were not flags; they were poles with the Roman eagle, or the image of the reigning emperor, on top. In deference to the Jewish hatred of graven images, every previous governor had removed the eagles and the images from the standards before he marched into Jerusalem on his state visits. Pilate refused to do so. The result was such bitter opposition and such intransigence that Pilate in the end was forced to yield, for it is not possible either to arrest or to slaughter a whole nation.

Later, Pilate decided that Jeruslaem needed a better water supply—a wise decision. To that end he constructed a new aqueduct—but he took money from the Temple treasury to pay for it.

Philo, the great Jewish Alexandrian scholar, has a character study of Pilate—and Philo, remember, was not a Christian, but was speaking from the Jewish point of view. The Jews, Philo tells us, had threatened to exercise their right to report Pilate to the Emperor for his misdeeds. This threat " exasperated Pilate to the greatest possible degree, as he feared lest they might go on an embassy to the emperor, and might impeach him with respect to other particulars of his government—his corruption, his acts of insolence, his rapine, his habit of insulting people, his cruelty, his continual murders of people untried and uncondemned, and his never-ending gratuitous and most grievous inhumanity." Pilate's reputation with the Jews stank; and the fact that they could report him made his position entirely insecure.

We follow the career of Pilate to the end. In the end he was recalled to Rome on account of his savagery in an incident in Samaria. A certain impostor had summoned the people to Mount Gerizim with the claim that he would show them the sacred vessels which Moses had hidden there. Unfortunately many of the crowd came armed, and assembled in a village called Tirabatha. Pilate fell on them and slaughtered them with quite unnecessary savagery, for it was a harmless enough movement. The Samaritans lodged a complaint with Vitellius, the legate of Syria, who was Pilate's immediate superior, and Vitellius ordered him to return to Rome to answer for his conduct.

When Pilate was on his way to Rome, Tiberius the Emperor died; and it appears that Pilate never came to trial. Legend has it that in the end he committed suicide; his body was flung into the Tiber, but the evil spirits so troubled the river that the Romans took the body to Gaul and threw it into the Rhône. Pilate's so-called tomb is still shown in Vienne. The same thing happened there; and the body was finally taken to a place near Lausanne and buried in a pit in the mountains. Opposite Lucerne there is a hill called Mount Pilatus. Originally the mountain was called *Pileatus*, which means *wearing a cap of clouds*, but because it was connected with Pilate the name was changed to *Pilatus*.

Later Christian legend was sympathetic to Pilate and tended to place all the blame for the death of Jesus on the Jews. Not unnaturally, legend came to hold that Pilate's wife, who it is said was a Jewish proselyte, and was called Claudia Procula, became a Christian. It was even held that Pilate himself became a Christian; and to this day the Coptic Church ranks both Pilate and his wife as saints.

We conclude this study of Pilate with a very interesting document. Pilate must have sent a report of the trial and death of Jesus to Rome; that would happen in the normal course of administration. An apocryphal book called *The Acts of Peter and Paul* contains an alleged copy of that report. This report is actually referred to by Tertullian and Justin Martyr and Eusebius. The report as we have it can hardly be genuine, but it is interesting to read it:

Pontius Pilate unto Claudius greeting.

There befell of late a matter of which I myself made trial; for the Jews through envy have punished themselves and their posterity with fearful judgments of their own fault; for whereas their fathers had promises that their God would send them out of heaven his Holy One, who should of right be called king, and did promise he would send him on earth by a virgin; he then came when I was governor of Judaea, and they beheld him enlightening the blind, cleansing lepers, healing the palsied, driving devils out of men, raising the dead, rebuking the winds, walking on the waves of the sea dry-shod, and doing many other wonders, and all the people of the Jews calling him the Son of God; the chief priests therefore moved with envy against him, took him and delivered him unto me and brought against him one false accusation after another, saying that he was a sorcerer and that he did things contrary to the law..

But I, believing that these things were so, having scourged him, delivered him to their will; and they crucified him, and, when he was buried, they set their guards upon him. But while my soldiers watched him, he rose again on the third day; yet so much was the malice of the Jews kindled, that they gave money to the soldiers saying: Say ye that his disciples stole away his body. But they, though they took the money, were not able to keep silence concerning that which had come to pass, for they also have testified that they saw him arisen, and that they received money from the Jews. And these things have I reported unto thy mightiness for this cause, lest some other should lie unto thee, and thou shouldest deem right to believe the false tales of the Jews.

Although that report is no doubt mere legend, Pilate certainly knew that Jesus was innocent; but his past misdeeds gave the

Jews a lever with which to compel him to do their will against
his wishes and his sense of justice.

PILATE'S LOSING STRUGGLE

Matthew 27: 1, 2, 11–26 (*continued*)

THIS whole passage gives the impression of a man fighting a
losing battle. It is clear that Pilate did not wish to condemn
Jesus. Certain things emerge.

(i) Pilate was clearly impressed with Jesus. Plainly he did not
take the King of the Jews claim seriously. He knew a revolutionary when he saw one, and Jesus was no revolutionary. His
dignified silence made Pilate feel that it was not Jesus but he
himself who was on trial. Pilate was a man who felt the power
of Jesus—and was afraid to submit to it. There are still those
who are afraid to be as Christian as they know they ought to be.

(ii) Pilate sought some way of escape. It appears to have been
the custom at the time of the Feast for a prisoner to be released.
In gaol there was a certain Barabbas. He was no sneak-thief; he
was most probably either a brigand or a political revolutionary.

There are two interesting speculations about him. His name
Barabbas means *Son of the Father*; *father* was a title by which
the greatest Rabbis were known; it may well be that Barabbas
was the son of an ancient and distinguished family who had
kicked over the traces and embarked on a career of magnificent
crime. Such a man would make crime glamorous and would
appeal to the people.

Still more interesting is the near certainty that Barabbas was
also called Jesus. Some of the very oldest versions of the New
Testament, for example the ancient Syriac and Armenian
versions, call him *Jesus Barabbas*; and both Origen and Jerome
knew of that reading, and felt it might be correct. It is a curious
thing that twice Pilate refers to *Jesus who is called Christ*
(verses 17 and 22), as if to distinguish him from some other
Jesus. Jesus was a common name; it is the same name as

Joshua. And the dramatic shout of the crowd most likely was:
" Not Jesus Christ, but Jesus Barabbas."

Pilate sought an escape, but the crowd chose the violent
criminal and rejected the gentle Christ. They preferred the man
of violence to the man of love.

(iii) Pilate sought to unshoulder the responsibility for condemning Jesus. There is that strange and tragic picture of him
washing his hands. That was a Jewish custom. There is a
strange regulation in *Deuteronomy* 21: 1–9. If a dead body was
found, and it was not known who the killer was, measurements
were to be taken to find what was the nearest town or village.
The elders of that town or village had to sacrifice a heifer and to
wash their hands to rid them of the guilt.

Pilate was warned by his sense of justice, he was warned by
his conscience, he was warned by the dream of his troubled
wife; but Pilate could not stand against the mob; and Pilate
made the futile gesture of washing his hands. Legend has it that
to this day there are times when Pilate's shade emerges from its
tomb and goes through the action of the hand-washing once
again.

There is one thing of which a man can never rid himself—
and that is responsibility. It is never possible for Pilate or
anyone else to say, " I wash my hands of all responsibility," for
that is something that no one and nothing can take away.

This picture of Pilate provokes in our minds pity rather than
loathing; for here was a man so enmeshed in his past, and so
rendered helpless by it, that he was unable to take the stand he
ought to take. Pilate is a figure of tragedy rather than of
villainy.

THE SOLDIERS' MOCKERY

Matthew 27: 27–31

Then the governor's soldiers took Jesus to the military headquarters, and collected to him the whole of the detachment. They
stripped him of his clothes and put a soldier's purple cloak upon

him; and they wove a crown of thorns and put it on his head, and they put a reed in his right hand; and they knelt in front of him, and mocked him by saying, " Hail! King of the Jews! " And they spat on him, and took the reed and hit him on his head. And when they had mocked him, they took off the cloak, and clothed him in his own clothes, and led him away to crucify him.

THE dreadful routine of crucifixion had now begun. The last section ended by telling us that Pilate had Jesus scourged. Roman scourging was a terrible torture. The victim was stripped; his hands were tied behind him, and he was tied to a post with his back bent double and conveniently exposed to the lash. The lash itself was a long leather thong, studded at intervals with sharpened pieces of bone and pellets of lead. Such scourging always preceded crucifixion and " it reduced the naked body to strips of raw flesh, and inflamed and bleeding weals." Men died under it, and men lost their reason under it, and few remained conscious to the end of it.

After that Jesus was handed over to the soldiers, while the last details of crucifixion were arranged, and while the cross itself was prepared. They took him to their barracks in the governor's headquarters; and they called the rest of the detachment. The detachment is called a *speira*; in a full *speira* there were six hundred men. It is not likely that there were as many as that in Jerusalem. These soldiers were Pilate's bodyguard who had accompanied him from Caesarea, where his permanent headquarters were.

We may shudder at what the soldiers did; but of all the parties involved in the crucifixion they were least to be blamed. They were not even stationed in Jerusalem; they had no idea who Jesus was; they certainly were not Jews, for the Jews were the only nation in the Roman Empire who were exempt from military service; they were conscripts who may well have come from the ends of the earth. They indulged in their rough horse-play; but, unlike the Jews and unlike Pilate, they acted in ignorance.

Maybe for Jesus of all things this was the easiest to bear, for, although they made a sham king of him, there was no hatred in their eyes. To them he was nothing more than a deluded Galilaean going to a cross. It is not without significance that Philo tells us that in Alexandria a Jewish mob did exactly the same to an imbecile boy: " They spread a strip of linen and placed it on his head instead of a diadem ... and for a sceptre they handed up to him a small piece of native papyrus bulrush which they found thrown on the roadside. And because he was adorned as a king ... some came up as though to greet him, others as though to plead a cause." So they mocked a half-idiot lad; and that is what the soldiers took Jesus to be.

Then they prepared to lead him away to crucifixion. We are sometimes told that we should not dwell on the physical aspect of the Cross; but we cannot possibly have too vivid a picture of what Jesus did and suffered for us. Klausner, the Jewish writer, says, " Crucifixion is the most terrible and cruel death which man has ever devised for taking vengeance on his fellow-men." Cicero called it " the most cruel and the most horrible torture." Tacitus called it " a torture only fit for slaves."

It originated in Persia; and its origin came from the fact that the earth was considered to be sacred to Ormuzd the god, and the criminal was lifted up from it that he might not defile the earth, which was the god's property. From Persia crucifixion passed to Carthage in North Africa; and it was from Carthage that Rome learned it, although the Romans kept it exclusively for rebels, runaway slaves, and the lowest type of criminal. It was indeed a punishment which it was illegal to inflict on a Roman citizen.

Klausner goes on to describe crucifixion. The criminal was fastened to his cross, already a bleeding mass from the scourging. There he hung to die of hunger and thirst and exposure, unable even to defend himself from the torture of the gnats and flies which settled on his naked body and on his bleeding wounds. It is not a pretty picture but that is what Jesus Christ suffered—willingly—for us.

THE CROSS AND THE SHAME

Matthew 27: 32–44

As they were going out, they found a Cyrenian man, Simon by name, and they impressed him into their service, to bear Jesus's Cross. When they had come to the place which is called Golgotha (which means the Place of a Skull), they offered him wine mingled with gall to drink, and, when he had tasted it, he refused to drink it. When they had crucified him, they divided his garments among them by casting lots for them; and as they sat there, they watched him. Above his head they placed a written copy of the charge on which he was being executed: " This is Jesus, the King of the Jews." Then they crucified along with him two brigands, one on the right hand and one on the left. Those who were passing by kept flinging their insults at him. They kept shaking their heads and saying, " Destroyer of the Temple, and builder of it in three days, save yourself. If you are really the Son of God, come down from the Cross." In the same way the chief priests also with the Scribes and the elders jeered at him, " He saved others," they kept saying, " He cannot save himself. He is King of Israel. Let him come down from the Cross now, and we will believe on him. He trusted in God. Let God rescue him now, if he wants him; for he said, ' I am the Son of God.' " The brigands too who were crucified with him hurled the same reproaches at him.

THE Story of the Crucifixion does not need commentary; its power resides simply in the telling. All we can do is to paint in the background in order that the picture may be as clear as possible.

When a criminal had been condemned, he was led away to crucifixion. He was placed in the centre of a hollow square of four Roman soldiers. It was the custom that he should carry the cross beam of his own cross; the upright was already waiting at the scene of execution. The charge on which he was being executed was written on a board; it was then either hung round his own neck, or carried by an officer in front of the procession; and it was later affixed to the cross itself. The criminal was led to the scene of crucifixion by as long a route as possible, so that as many as possible might see him and take warning from the grim sight.

Jesus had undergone the terrible scourging; after that he had undergone the mockery of the soldiers; before all that he had been under examination for most of the night; and he was, therefore, physically exhausted, and staggering under his Cross. The Roman soldiers well knew what to do under such circumstances. Palestine was an occupied country; all that a Roman officer had to do was to tap a Jew on the shoulder with the flat of his spear, and the man had to carry out any task, however menial and distasteful, that was laid upon him. Into the city, from one of the surrounding villages, there had come a man from far off Cyrene in North Africa, called Simon. It may be that for years he had scraped and saved to attend this one Passover—and now this terrible indignity and shame fell upon him; for he was compelled to carry the Cross of Jesus. When Mark tells the story, he identifies Simon as " the father of Alexander and Rufus " (*Mark* 15: 21). Such an identification can only mean that Alexander and Rufus were well known in the Church. And it must be that on that terrible day Jesus laid hold on Simon's heart. That which to Simon had seemed his day of shame became his day of glory.

The place of crucifixion was a hill called Golgotha, so called because it was shaped like a skull. When the place was reached the criminal had to be impaled upon his cross. The nails had to be driven through his hands, but commonly the feet were only loosely bound to the cross. At that moment, in order to deaden the pain, the criminal was given a drink of drugged wine, prepared by a group of wealthy women of Jerusalem as an act of mercy. A Jewish writing says, " When a man is going out to be killed, they allow him to drink a grain of frankincense in a cup of wine to deaden his senses. . . . Wealthy women of Jerusalem used to contribute these things and bring them." The drugged cup was offered to Jesus, but he would not drink it, for he was determined to accept death at its bitterest and at its grimmest, and to avoid no particle of pain.

We have already seen that the criminal was led to execution

in the middle of a square of four Roman soldiers; criminals were crucified naked, except for a loin cloth; and the criminal's clothes became the property of the soldiers as their perquisite. Every Jew wore five articles of clothing—his shoes, his turban, his girdle, his inner garment, and his outer cloak. There were thus five articles of clothing and four soldiers. The first four articles were all of equal value; but the outer cloak was more valuable than all the others. It was for Jesus's outer cloak that the soldiers drew lots, as John tells us (*John* 19: 23, 24). When the soldiers had divided the clothes, they sat down, on guard until the end should come. So there was on Golgotha a group of three crosses, in the middle the Son of God, and on either side a brigand. Truly, he was with sinners in his death.

The final verses describe the taunts flung at Jesus by the passers-by, by the Jewish authorities, and by the brigands who were crucified with him. They all centred round one thing—the claims that Jesus had made and his apparent helplessness on the Cross. It was precisely there that the Jews were so wrong. They were using the glory of Christ as a means of mocking him. " Come down," they said, " and we will believe on you." But as General Booth once said, " It is precisely because he would not come down that we believe in him." The Jews could see God only in power; but Jesus showed that God is sacrificial love.

THE TRIUMPH OF THE END

Matthew 27: 45–50

From twelve o'clock midday darkness came over the earth until three o'clock in the afternoon. About three o'clock in the afternoon Jesus cried with a loud voice, " Eli, Eli, lama sabachthani? " (that is, " My God, my God, why have you forsaken me? ") Some of those who were standing there heard this, and said, " This man is calling for Elias." And immediately one of them ran and took a sponge and filled it with vinegar and put it on a reed, and gave him to drink. The rest said, " Let be! Let us see if Elias will come to save him." When Jesus had again shouted with a great voice, he gave up his spirit.

As we have been reading the story of the Crucifixion, everything seems to have been happening very quickly; but in reality the hours were slipping past. It is Mark who is most precise in his note of time. He tells us that Jesus was crucified at the third hour, that is at nine o'clock in the morning (*Mark* 15: 25), and that he died at the ninth hour, that is at three o'clock in the afternoon (*Mark* 15: 34). That is to say, Jesus hung on the Cross for six hours. For him the agony was mercifully brief, for it often happened that criminals hung upon their crosses for days before death came to them.

In verse 46 we have what must be the most staggering sentence in the gospel record, the cry of Jesus: " My God, my God, why hast thou forsaken me? " That is a saying before which we must bow in reverence, and yet at the same time we must try to understand. There have been many attempts to penetrate behind its mystery; we can look only at three.

(i) It is strange how *Psalm* 22 runs through the whole Crucifixion narrative; and this saying is actually the first verse of that Psalm. Later on it says, " All who seek me mock at me, they make mouths at me, they wag their heads; ' He committed his cause to the Lord; let him deliver him, let him rescue him, for he delights in him!' " (*Psalm* 22: 7, 8). Still further on we read: " They divide my garments among them, and for my raiment they cast lots " (*Psalm* 22: 18). Psalm 22 is interwoven with the whole Crucifixion story.

It has been suggested that Jesus was, in fact, repeating that Psalm to himself; and, though it begins in complete dejection, it ends in soaring triumph—" From thee comes my praise in the great congregation. . . . For dominion belongs to the Lord, and he rules over the nations " (*Psalm* 22: 25–31). So it is suggested that Jesus was repeating Psalm 22 on the Cross, as a picture of his own situation, and as a song of his trust and confidence, well knowing that it began in the depths, but that it finished on the heights.

It is an attractive suggestion; but on a cross a man does not repeat poetry to himself, even the poetry of a psalm; and besides that, the whole atmosphere is one of unrelieved tragedy.

(ii) It is suggested that in that moment the weight of the

world's sin fell upon the heart and the being of Jesus; that that
was the moment when he who knew no sin was made sin for us
(2 *Corinthians* 5: 21); and that the penalty which he bore for us
was the inevitable separation from God which sin brings. No
man may say that that is not true; but, if it is, it is a mystery
which we can only state and at which we can only wonder.

(iii) It may be that there is something—if we may put it
so—more human here. It seems to me that Jesus would not be
Jesus unless he had plumbed the uttermost depths of human
experience. In human experience, as life goes on and as bitter
tragedy enters into it, there come times when we feel that God
has forgotten us; when we are immersed in a situation beyond
our understanding and feel bereft even of God. It seems to me
that that is what happened to Jesus here. We have seen in the
garden that Jesus knew only that he had to go on, because to go
on was God's will, and he must accept what even he could not
fully understand. Here we see Jesus plumbing the uttermost
depths of the human situation, so that there might be no place
that we might go where he has not been before.

Those who listened did not understand. Some thought he was
calling on Elijah; they must have been Jews. One of the great
gods of the pagans was the sun—Helios. A cry to the sun god
would have begun " Helie! " and it has been suggested that the
soldiers may have thought that Jesus was crying to the greatest
of the pagan gods. In any event, his cry was to the watchers a
mystery.

But here is the point. It would have been a terrible thing if
Jesus had died with a cry like that upon his lips—but he did
not. The narrative goes on to tell us that, when he shouted with
a great shout, he gave up his spirit. That great shout left its
mark upon men's minds. It is in every one of the gospels
(*Matthew* 27: 50; *Mark* 15: 37; *Luke* 23: 46). But there is one
gospel which goes further. John tells us that Jesus died with a
shout: " It is finished " (*John* 19: 30). *It is finished* is in English
three words; but in Greek it is one—*Tetelestai*—as it would
also be in Aramaic. And *tetelestai* is the victor's shout; it is the
cry of the man who has completed his task; it is the cry of the

man who has won through the struggle; it is the cry of the man who has come out of the dark into the glory of the light, and who has grasped the crown. So, then, Jesus died a victor with a shout of triumph on his lips.

Here is the precious thing. Jesus passed through the uttermost abyss, and then the light broke. If we too cling to God, even when there seems to be no God, desperately and invincibly clutching the remnants of our faith, quite certainly the dawn will break and we will win through. The victor is the man who refuses to believe that God has forgotten him, even when every fibre of his being feels that he is forsaken. The victor is the man who will never let go his faith, even when he feels that its last grounds are gone. The victor is the man who has been beaten to the depths and still holds on to God, for that is what Jesus did.

THE BLAZING REVELATION

Matthew 27: 51–56

> And, look you, the veil of the Temple was rent in two from top to bottom, and the earth was shaken, and the rocks were split, and the tombs were opened, and the bodies of many of God's dedicated ones were raised, and they came out of the tombs after his resurrection and came into the holy city and appeared to many. The centurion and those who were watching Jesus with him saw the earthquake and the things that had happened, and they were exceedingly afraid. " Truly," they said, " this man was the Son of God."
>
> Many women were there watching from a distance. They were the women who had followed Jesus from Galilee, giving their service to him. Among them were Mary from Magdala, and Mary the mother of James and Joses, and the mother of the sons of Zebedee.

This passage falls into three sections.

(i) There is the story of the amazing things which happened as Jesus died. Whether or not we are meant to take these things literally, they teach us two great truths.

(*a*) The Temple veil was rent from top to bottom. That was the veil which covered the Holy of Holies; that was the veil beyond which no man could penetrate, save only the High Priest on the Day of Atonement; that was the veil behind which the Spirit of God dwelt. There is symbolism here. Up to this time God had been hidden and remote, and no man knew what he was like. But in the death of Jesus we see the hidden love of God, and the way to the presence of God once barred to all men is now opened to all men. The life and the death of Jesus show us what God is like and remove for ever the veil which hid him from men.

(*b*) The tombs were opened. The symbolism of this is that Jesus conquered death. In dying and in rising again he destroyed the power of the grave. Because of his life, his death and his resurrection, the tomb has lost its power, and the grave has lost its terror, and death has lost its tragedy. For we are certain that because he lives we shall live also.

(ii) There is the story of the adoration of the centurion. There is only one thing to be said about this. Jesus had said, " I, when I am lifted up from the earth, will draw all men to myself " (*John* 12: 32). He foretold the magnetic power of the Cross; and the centurion was its first fruit. The Cross had moved him to see the majesty of Jesus as nothing else had been able to do.

(iii) There is the simple statement concerning the women who saw the end. All the disciples forsook him and fled, but the women remained. It has been said that, unlike the men, the women had nothing to fear, for so low was the public position of women that no one would take any notice of women disciples. There is more to it than that. They were there because they loved Jesus, and for them, as for so many, perfect love had cast out all fear.

THE GIFT OF A TOMB

Matthew 27: 57–61

Late in the day there came a rich man from Arimathaea, Joseph by name, who was himself a disciple of Jesus. He went to Pilate and requested the body of Jesus. Then Pilate ordered it to be given to him. So Joseph took the body and wrapped it in clean linen, and laid it in a new tomb, which he had hewn out in the rock. And he rolled a great stone across the door of the tomb and went away. And Mary from Magdala was there, and the other Mary, sitting opposite the tomb.

ACCORDING to Jewish law, even a criminal's body might not be left hanging all night, but had to be buried that day. " His body shall not remain all night upon the tree, but you shall bury him the same day " (*Deuteronomy* 21: 22, 23). This was doubly binding when, as in the case of Jesus, the next day was the Sabbath. According to Roman law, the relatives of a criminal might claim his body for burial, but if it was not claimed it was simply left to rot until the scavenger dogs dealt with it.

Now none of Jesus's relatives were in a position to claim his body, for they were all Galilaeans and none of them possessed a tomb in Jerusalem. So the wealthy Joseph from Arimathaea stepped in. He went to Pilate and asked that the body of Jesus should be given to him; and he cared for it, and put it into the rock tomb where no man had ever been laid. Joseph must be forever famous as the man who gave Jesus a tomb.

Legends have gathered around the name of Joseph and legends which are of particular interest to those who live in England. The best known is that in A.D. 61 Philip sent Joseph from Gaul to preach the gospel in England. He came bearing with him the chalice which was used at the Last Supper, and which now held the blood of Jesus shed upon the Cross. That chalice was to become the Holy Grail which is so famous in the stories of the Knights of King Arthur. When Joseph and his band of missionaries had climbed Weary-all Hill and come to the other side, they came to Glastonbury; there Joseph struck his staff into the earth and from it grew the Glastonbury Thorn. It is certainly true that for years Glastonbury was the holiest place in England; and it is still a place of pilgrimage. The story is that the original thorn was hacked down by a Puritan, but that the thorn which grows there to this day came from a shoot of it; and to this day slips of it are sent all over the world. So, then, legend connects Joseph of Arimathaea with Glastonbury and England.

But there is a lesser-known legend, commemorated in one of the most famous hymns and poems in the English language. It is a legend which is still current in Somerset. Joseph, so the legend runs, was a tin merchant, and came, long before he was sent by Philip, on quite frequent visits to the tin mines of Cornwall. The town of Marazion in Cornwall has another name. It is sometimes called Market Jew, and is said to have been the centre of a colony of Jews who traded in tin. The legend goes still further. Joseph of Arimathaea, it says, was the uncle of Mary, the mother of Jesus. (Can it possibly be that he did actually exercise a relative's right to claim the body of Jesus under Roman law?) And, it is said, he brought the young boy Jesus with him on one of his voyages to Cornwall.. That is what William Blake was thinking of when he wrote his famous poem:

> " And did those feet in ancient time
>   Walk upon England's mountains green?
> And was the Holy Lamb of God
>   In England's pleasant pastures seen?
> And did the Countenance Divine
>   Shine forth upon our clouded hills?
> And was Jerusalem builded here,
>   Among those dark Satanic mills? "

The dark Satanic mills were the tin mines of Cornwall. It is a lovely legend which we would like to be true, for there would be a thrill in the thought that the feet of the boy Jesus once touched English earth.

It is often said that Joseph gave to Jesus a tomb after he was dead, but did not support him during his life. Joseph was a member of the Sanhedrin (*Luke* 23: 50); and Luke tells us that " he had not consented to the (council's) purpose and deed " (*Luke* 23: 51). It is possible that the meeting of the Sanhedrin called in the house of Caiaphas in the middle of the night was selectively called? It hardly seems likely that the whole Sanhedrin could have been there. It may well be that Caiaphas

summoned those whom he wished to be present and packed the
meeting with his supporters, and that Joseph never even got a
chance to be there.

It is certainly true that in the end Joseph displayed the
greatest courage. He came out on the side of a crucified
criminal; he braved the possible resentment of Pilate; and he
faced the certain hatred of the Jews. It may well be that Joseph
of Arimathea did everything that it was possible for him to do.

One obscure point remains. The woman who is called *the
other Mary* is identified as Mary, the mother of Joses by *Mark*
15:47. We have already seen that these women were present at the
Cross; their love made them follow Jesus in life and in death.

AN IMPOSSIBLE ASSIGNMENT

Matthew 27:62–66

> On the next day, which is the day after the Preparation, the chief
> priests and Pharisees came to Pilate in a body. " Sir," they said,
> " we remember that, while he was still alive, that deceiver said,
> ' After three days I will rise again.' Give orders therefore that the
> tomb should be kept secure until the three days are ended, in case
> his disciples come and steal him, and say to the people, ' He has
> been raised from among the dead.' If that happens, the final
> deception will be worse than the first." Pilate said, " You have a
> guard. Go, and make it as secure as you can." They went and
> secured the tomb by setting a seal upon it as well as by placing a
> guard.

THIS passage begins in the most curious way. It says that the
chief priests and Pharisees went to Pilate on the next day, which
is the day after the Preparation. Now Jesus was crucified on the
Friday. Saturday is the Jewish Sabbath. The hours from 3 p.m.
to 6 p.m. on Friday were called The Eve, or The Preparation.
We have seen that, according to Jewish reckoning, the new day
began at 6 p.m. Therefore, the Sabbath began at 6 p.m. on
Friday; and the last hours of Friday were The Preparation. If
this is accurate, it can only mean one thing—it must mean that

the chief priests and Pharisees actually approached Pilate *on the Sabbath* with their request. If they did that, it is clear to see how radically they broke the Sabbath Law. If this is accurate, no other incident in the gospel story more plainly shows how desperately eager the Jewish authorities were totally to eliminate Jesus. In order to make certain that he was finally out of the way they were willing to break even their own most sacred laws.

There is a grim irony here. These Jews came to Pilate saying that Jesus had said that he would rise after three days. They did not admit that they envisaged the possibility that that might be true, but they thought the disciples might seek to steal away the body and say that a resurrection had happened. They, therefore, wished to take special steps to guard the tomb. Back comes Pilate's answer: " Make it as safe as you can." It is as if Pilate all unconsciously said, " Keep Christ in the tomb—if you can:" They took their steps. The door of these rock tombs was closed by a great round stone like a cartwheel, which ran in a groove. They sealed it and they set a special guard—and they made it as safe as they could.

They had not realized one thing—that there was not a tomb in the world which could imprison the Risen Christ. Not all men's plans could bind the Risen Lord. The man who seeks to put bonds on Jesus Christ is on a hopeless assignment.

THE GREAT DISCOVERY

Matthew 28: 1–10

Late on the Sabbath, when the first day of the week was beginning to dawn, Mary from Magdala and the other Mary came to see the tomb. And, look you, there was a great earthquake; for the angel of the Lord descended from heaven and came and rolled away the stone, and sat upon it. His appearance was like lightning, and his garment was as white as snow. Those who were watching were shaken with fear, and became as dead men. The angel said to the women, " Do not be afraid; for I know that you are looking for

Jesus who was crucified. He is not here; for he is risen, as he said he would. Come, see the place where the Lord lay. Go quickly and tell his disciples: ' He is risen from among the dead. And, look you, he goes before you into Galilee; there you will see him.' Look you, I have told you." So they quickly went away from the tomb with fear and with great joy, and they ran to tell the news to his disciples. And, look you, Jesus met them. " Greetings! " he said. And they came and held him by the feet, and worshipped him. Then Jesus said to them, " Fear not! Go tell my brothers to go away into Galilee, and there they will see me."

HERE we have Matthew's story of the empty tomb. And there is something peculiarly fitting in that Mary Magdalene and the other Mary should be the first to receive the news of the Risen Lord and to encounter him. They had been there at the Cross; they had been there when he was laid in the tomb; and now they were receiving love's reward; they were the first to know the joy of the Resurrection.

As we read this story of the first two people in the world to be confronted with the fact of the empty tomb and the Risen Christ, three imperatives seem to spring out of it.

(i) They are urged to *believe*. The thing is so staggering that it might seem beyond belief, too good to be true. The angel reminds them of the promise of Jesus, and confronts them with the empty tomb; his every word is a summons to believe. It is still a fact that there are many who feel that the promises of Christ are too good to be true. That hesitation can be dispelled only by taking him as his word.

(ii) They are urged to *share*. When they themselves have discovered the fact of the Risen Christ, their first duty is to proclaim it to and to share it with others. " Go, tell! " is the first command which comes to the man who has himself discovered the wonder of Jesus Christ.

(iii) They are urged to *rejoice*. The word with which the Risen Christ meets them is *Chairete*; that is the normal word of greeting; but its literal meaning is " Rejoice! " The man who has met the Risen Lord must live for ever in the joy of his presence from which nothing can part him any more.

THE LAST RESORT

Matthew 28: 11–15

> While they were on their way, certain of the guard came to the
> city and told the chief priests all that had happened. When they
> had met with the elders, they formed a plan. They gave a
> considerable amount of money to the soldiers. " Say," they said,
> " ' His disciples came by night, and stole him away while we
> slept.' And if this comes to the governor's ears, we will use our
> influence, and we will see to it that you have nothing to worry
> about." They took the money and followed their instructions. And
> this is the story which is repeated amongst the Jews to this day.

WHEN some of the guard came to the chief priests and told
them the story of the empty tomb, the Jewish authorities were
desperately worried men. Was it possible that all their planning
had come to nothing? So they formed a simple plan; they
bribed the members of the guard to say that Jesus's disciples
had come while they slept and had stolen his body.

It is interesting to note the means that the Jewish authorities
used in their desperate attempts to eliminate Jesus. They used
treachery to lay hold on him. They used illegality to try him.
They used slander to charge him to Pilate. And now they were
using bribery to silence the truth about him. *And they failed.*
Magna est veritas et praevalebit, ran the Roman proverb; great
is the truth and it will prevail. It is the fact of history that not all
men's evil machinations can in the end stop the truth. The
gospel of goodness is greater than the plots of wickedness.

THE GLORY OF THE FINAL PROMISE

Matthew 28: 16–20

> So the eleven disciples went into Galilee, to the mountain where
> Jesus had instructed them to go. And they saw him and wor-
> shipped him; but some were not sure. Jesus came and spoke to

them. " All power," he said, " is given to me in heaven and upon earth. Go, therefore, and make all nations my disciples, baptizing them in the name of the Father and of the Son and of the Holy Spirit, and teaching them to keep all the commandments I have given you. And, look you, I am with you throughout all days until the end of the world."

HERE we come to the end of the gospel story; here we listen to the last words of Jesus to his men; and in this last meeting Jesus did three things.

(i) *He assured them of his power.* Surely nothing was outside the power of him who had died and conquered death. Now they were the servants of a Master whose authority upon earth and in heaven was beyond all question.

(ii) *He gave them a commission.* He sent them out to make all the world his disciples. It may well be that the instruction to baptize is something which is a development of the actual words of Jesus. That may be argued about; the salient fact remains that the commission of Jesus is to win all men for himself.

(iii) *He promised them a presence.* It must have been a staggering thing for eleven humble Galilaeans to be sent forth to the conquest of the world. Even as they heard it, their hearts must have failed them. But, no sooner was the command given, than the promise followed. They were sent out—as we are—on the greatest task in history, but with them there was the greatest presence in the world.

> " Though few and small and weak your bands,
>   Strong in your Captain's strength,
>   Go to the conquest of all lands;
>   All must be his at length."

FURTHER READING

W. C. Allen, *St Matthew* (ICC; *G*)

J. C. Fenton, *The Gospel of St Matthew* (PC; *E*)

F. V. Filson, *The Gospel According to St Matthew* (ACB; *E*)

A. H. McNeile, *St Matthew* (MmC; *G*)

A. Plummer, *An Exegetical Commentary on the Gospel According to St Matthew* (*E*)

T. H. Robinson, *The Gospel of Matthew* (MC; *E*)

R. V. G. Tasker, *The Gospel According to St Matthew* (TC; *E*)

Abbreviations

ACB : A. and C. Black New Testament Commentary

ICC : International Critical Commentary

MC : Moffatt Commentary

MmC: Macmillan Commentary

PC : Pelican New Testament Commentary

TC : Tyndale Commentary

E : English Text

G : Greek Text

THE DAILY STUDY BIBLE

Published in 17 Volumes